PEACE PROCESSES IN NORTHERN IRELAND AND TURKEY

Edinburgh Studies on Modern Turkey

Series General Editors: **Alpaslan Özerdem**, Dean of the School for Conflict Analysis and Resolution and Professor of Peace and Conflict Studies at George Mason University, and **Ahmet Erdi Öztürk**, Lecturer in International Relations and Politics at London Metropolitan University and a visiting scholar at the Department of Political Science and International Relations, University of Birmingham.

Series Advisory Board: Ayşe Kadıoğlu (Sabancı University), Hakan Yavuz (University of Utah), Samim Akgonul (University of Strasbourg), Rebecca Bryant (Utrecht University), Nukhet Ahu Sandal (Ohio University), Mehmet Gurses (Florida Atlantic University), Paul Kubicek (Oakland University), Sinem Akgul Acıkmeşe (Kadir Has University), Gareth Jenkins (Institute for Security and Development Policy), Stephen Karam (World Bank), Peter Mandaville (George Mason University).

Edinburgh Studies on Modern Turkey is an outlet for academic works that examine the domestic and international issues of the Turkish republic from its establishment in the 1920s until the present. This broadly defined frame allows the series to adopt both interdisciplinary and trans-disciplinary approaches, covering research on the country's history and culture as well as political, religious and socio-economic developments. The titles provide wide-ranging discussions of Turkey within its local and global context, utilising an eclectic range of methodological and theoretical approaches that include non-Western political and critical theory. The series is marked by openness and invites both detailed, area-specific case studies as well as broadly construed, interdisciplinary surveys of topics that are appropriately framed by the theme of the series.

Published and forthcoming titles

Islamic Theology in the Turkish Republic
Philip Dorroll

The Kurds in Erdoğan's Turkey: Balancing Identity, Resistance and Citizenship
William Gourlay

Peace Processes in Northern Ireland and Turkey: Rethinking Conflict Resolution
İ. Aytaç Kadıoğlu

Religion, Identity and Power: Turkey and the Balkans in the Twenty-first Century
Ahmet Erdi Öztürk

The Decline of the Ottoman Empire and the Rise of the Turkish Republic: Observations of an American Diplomat, 1919–1927
Hakan Özoğlu

Electoral Integrity in Turkey
Emre Toros

edinburghuniversitypress.com/series/esmt

PEACE PROCESSES IN NORTHERN IRELAND AND TURKEY

Rethinking Conflict Resolution

İ. Aytaç Kadıoğlu

EDINBURGH
University Press

Edinburgh University Press is one of the leading university presses in the UK. We publish academic books and journals in our selected subject areas across the humanities and social sciences, combining cutting-edge scholarship with high editorial and production values to produce academic works of lasting importance. For more information visit our website: edinburghuniversitypress.com

© İ. Aytaç Kadıoğlu, 2020, 2022

Edinburgh University Press Ltd
The Tun – Holyrood Road
12(2f) Jackson's Entry
Edinburgh EH8 8PJ

First published in hardback by Edinburgh University Press 2020

Typeset in 11/15 Adobe Garamond by
IDSUK (DataConnection) Ltd

A CIP record for this book is available from the British Library

ISBN 978 1 4744 7932 5 (hardback)
ISBN 978 1 4744 7933 2 (paperback)
ISBN 978 1 4744 7935 6 (webready PDF)
ISBN 978 1 4744 7934 9 (epub)

The right of İ. Aytaç Kadıoğlu to be identified as the author of this work has been asserted in accordance with the Copyright, Designs and Patents Act 1988, and the Copyright and Related Rights Regulations 2003 (SI No. 2498).

CONTENTS

List of Figures and Tables   vi
List of Abbreviations   vii
Acknowledgements   x

1   Introduction   1
2   Understanding and Rethinking 'Conflict Resolution': A Conceptual and Theoretical Framework   24
3   Conflict and Peace: History of the Northern Irish and Turkey's Kurdish Peace Processes   72
4   Backchannel Communications: Talking to the Enemy Behind the Scenes   110
5   Peace and Conflict Resolution Organisations: Catalysts for Peace?   149
6   Official Negotiations: The Long, Narrow Road to Peace   183
7   Conclusion   221

Appendix: Index of Interviews   241
Bibliography   244
Index   283

FIGURES AND TABLES

Figures

2.1	The hourglass model	27
2.2	Actors and approaches to peacebuilding	31
2.3	Conflict resolution processes	33
3.1	The casualties in Northern Ireland (1969–98)	84
3.2	The casualties in Turkey (1984–2012)	99

Tables

2.1	Conflict resolution approaches from top to bottom	36
2.2	Conflict resolution processes for peacemaking	40
4.1	Characteristics of intermediaries in Northern Ireland and Turkey	137
4.2	Characteristics and outcomes of direct talks in Northern Ireland and Turkey	139
5.1	Consequences of incidents between 1973 and 1978	158
5.2	Methods and results of the initiatives of the P/CROs in Northern Ireland and Turkey	172
6.1	Westminster by-election results in 1986	187
6.2	The 1998 Good Friday Agreement referendums	195
6.3	Overview of the influence of official negotiations on Northern Ireland and Turkey	210

ABBREVIATIONS

AIA	Anglo-Irish Agreement
AIIC	Anglo-Irish Intergovernmental Council
AKP	Justice and Development Party
ANC	African National Congress
APNI	Alliance Party of Northern Ireland
BDP	Peace and Democracy Party
BIA	British–Irish Association
CHP	Republican People's Party
CRC	Community Relations Commission
DEP	Democracy Party
DSD	Downing Street Declaration
DTP	Democratic Society Party
DUP	Democratic Unionist Party
ETA	Basque Country and Freedom
EU	European Union
FAP	Popular Self-Defence Forces
FARC	Revolutionary Armed Forces of Colombia
FCO	Foreign and Commonwealth Office
FP	Virtue Party
FSA	Free Syrian Army
GFA	Good Friday Agreement
GOC	General Officer Commanding

HADEP	People's Democratic Party
HAK-PAR	Rights and Freedoms Party
HDP	Peoples' Democratic Party
HEP	People's Labour Party
HPG	People's Defence Forces
IICD	Independent International Commission on Decommissioning
INLA	Irish National Liberation Army
IRA	Irish Republican Army
ISIS	Islamic State of Iraq and Syria
JIC	Joint Intelligence Committee
KADEK	Kurdish Freedom and Democracy Congress
KCK	Kurdistan Communities Union
KDGM	Undersecretariat of Public Order and Security
KONGRA-GEL	Kurdistan People's Congress
LPP	Look at Peace Platform
LTTE	Liberation Tigers of Tamil Eelam
MGK	National Security Council
MHP	Nationalist Movement Party
MI6	Military Intelligence, Section 6 (Secret Intelligence Service)
MILF	Moro Islamic Liberation Front
MIT	National Intelligence Organisation
NATO	North Atlantic Treaty Organisation
NGO	Non-Governmental Organisation
NIF	New Ireland Forum
NIO	Northern Ireland Office
NIWC	Northern Ireland Women's Coalition
NUI	National University of Ireland
OHAL	State of Emergency
ÖZDEP	Freedom and Democracy Party
P/CROs	Peace and Conflict Resolution Organisations
PIRA	Provisional Irish Republican Army
PJAK	Party of Free Life of Kurdistan
PKK	Kurdistan Workers' Party
PLO	Palestinian Liberation Organisation

PM	Prime Minister
PP	Peace People
PTO	Peace Train Organisation
PUK	Patriotic Union of Kurdistan
PUP	Progressive Unionist Party
PYD	Democratic Union Party
RAF	Red Army Faction
RP	Welfare Party
RUC	Royal Ulster Constabulary
SDLP	Social Democratic and Labour Party
SF	Sinn Féin
SHP	Social Democratic People's Party
SIS	Secret Intelligence Service
START	Study of Terrorism and Response to Terrorism
TBMM	Turkish Grand National Assembly
TNA	The National Archive of London
TSK	Turkish Armed Forces
TSKA	Turkish Armed Forces Archive
UCAN	Ulster Community Action Network
UDA	Ulster Defence Association
UDP	Ulster Democratic Party
UK	United Kingdom
UKREP	UK Representative
UKUP	United Kingdom Unionist Party
UN	United Nations
US	United States
UUC	Ulster Unionist Council
UUP	Ulster Unionist Party
UWC	Ulster Workers' Council
WMD	Weapons of Mass Destruction
WPC	Wise People Committee
WWI	First World War
WWII	Second World War
YDG-H	Patriotic Revolutionary Youth Movement
YPG	People's Protection Units

ACKNOWLEDGEMENTS

This book began its journey as a PhD research project at the University of Nottingham. The writing of this book was possible only because of the generous help and encouragement of a number of people to whom I am indebted. I am very grateful, first and foremost, to Associate Professor Andrew Mumford and Professor Wyn Rees for their invaluable guidance, comments, patience and fantastic support during this journey. I feel truly privileged for being supervised by Andrew, as he has been not only a great mentor, but also a good friend. Without his guidance and invaluable input, this research would not have been possible. I am also grateful to Dr Vanessa Pupavac who supervised me for the first two and a half years of my research and helped build the theoretical and conceptual framework of this book with her insightful comments. I am also thankful to Neville Wylie for helping me to sharpen the argument of my book. Thanks are also owed to the two anonymous reviewers for their constructive and insightful comments. I also thank the members of the editorial board of the Edinburgh University Press for managing the process very carefully and efficiently. The comments and suggestions I received were very constructive, kind, insightful and helpful. I owe a special debt of gratitude to series editors of Edinburgh Studies on Modern Turkey, Professor Alpaslan Ozerdem and Dr Ahmet Erdi Ozturk for their guidance through the review process.

This research was funded by the Ministry of National Education of the Republic of Turkey. Without this financial support, this book project would not have been possible. The University of Nottingham's PGR Funding and the Centre for Conflict, Security and Terrorism's (CST) fund were very helpful with their fieldwork funding. The CST has been a great academic environment and a challenging scholarly engagement. I would like to thank the staff of the School of Politics and International Relations, University of Nottingham and Hallward Library. Jon Mansell and Dimitris Anagnostakis provided great feedback for various chapters of this book. Thank you very much for your help and comments. The friends, colleagues and contacts with whom I had a chance to brainstorm sections of my book are too many to cite. I am deeply appreciative to all of them for their time, comments and opinions. This book, a child of my mind, was a product of those as much as of me, who supported me for seven years to mature the ideas, concepts and insights of this book.

To undertake research for this project, I am indebted to the people who agreed to be interviewed by me. They were all very generous to share their experience, information and expertise on the Northern Irish and Turkey's Kurdish peace processes. I owe a debt of gratitude to all interviewees as they were all open to discuss the insights of the two conflicts. I am also grateful to the staff of the National Archives of Kew in London and the Turkish Military Forces (TSK) Archive in Ankara.

A big thank you is directed to my extended family, but especially to my mum and dad for their endless support, love, care and encouragement which made it possible to complete this book.

To my family

1

INTRODUCTION

There are two things that democratic people will always find very difficult, to begin a war and to end it.[1]

For most of the history of conflicts between states and sub-state armed groups in the twentieth century, the initial response to the violent campaigns of such groups has been through counter-terrorism tactics, namely the use of force against terrorism. Investigations into the causes of these conflicts and of the goals of these groups by decision makers have resulted in the application of non-violent, political resolution efforts between the main armed protagonists. As ethno-nationalist groups have predominantly political aims, and tend to organise violent attacks as a tactic, it is important to assess peace efforts towards ending these conflicts.[2] While states respond to the violence conducted by sub-state armed groups through counter-terrorism and counter-insurgency strategies as a first resort, their failure is most likely to result in the application of political attempts at conflict resolution. This book argues that an armed struggle between the security forces of states and sub-state armed groups is not an effective method of bringing ethno-nationalist conflicts to an end. It also argues that such conflicts are too complex to be resolved through official negotiations that only involve the main armed protagonists. Ethno-nationalist groups' ethnic identity, desire for self-determination and territorial concerns are related to a specific context, which reveals a dilemma related to the choice of whether a state pursues armed struggle or a non-military solution. There has been a marked increase in efforts to find non-violent resolutions to these intra-state conflicts, particularly in the post-Cold War era, in arenas such as the Cyprus, Israeli–Palestinian and South African conflicts.[3] However, the existing literature has paid relatively little attention to political attempts towards ending violence in ethno-nationalist conflicts. In addition, the existing conflict resolution literature primarily focuses on negotiations and largely overlooks the importance of other peace initiatives for making peace. This book aims to fill this gap in two ways: firstly, it suggests a more comprehensive framework for resolving ethno-nationalist conflicts, which begins at the pre-negotiation stage through backchannel communications and the initiatives of peace organisations. Subsequently, the momentum of a peace process is maintained through official negotiations between the major stakeholders and independent third parties at the negotiation stage. Secondly, this research applies this conflict resolution framework to the Northern Irish and Turkey's Kurdish conflicts deployed by the Irish Republican Army (IRA) and the Kurdistan Workers' Party (*Partiya Karkerên Kurdistan*, henceforth PKK) respectively.

This book analyses two comprehensive cases, the Northern Irish and Turkey's Kurdish conflicts, which have witnessed similar conflict resolution processes with different outcomes. Ethno-nationalist conflicts have taken place in Northern Ireland since the early 1920s and in Turkey since the late 1920s.[4] However, the book has a specific time frame that involves the emergence of the Provisional IRA[5] and PKK groups and it investigates the relevant conflict resolution efforts made during that time frame. This time frame covers the period between the beginning of peace efforts and the signing of a peace agreement (or the failure of a peace process). Hence, the conflict in Northern Ireland is assessed between 1969 and 1998 as peace efforts began as soon as 'the Troubles' broke out in 1969 and a final agreement, referred to as the Good Friday Agreement (GFA), was signed in 1998. The conflict in Turkey is examined from 1984 to 2015 as conflict resolution efforts collapsed and violence returned in July 2015.

This is an intensely researched book that predominantly aims to explore the impact of conflict resolution initiatives on ethno-nationalist conflicts. So, the central research question of this book is: What has been the impact of conflict resolution processes towards ending ethno-nationalist conflicts in Northern Ireland and Turkey? This question focuses on a comparison between the political resolution efforts for ending the IRA and PKK's armed campaigns and establishing a peace agreement. It assesses peace initiatives as an ongoing process containing not only formal peace initiatives, but also informal and secret peace efforts. It differs from the existing scholarly literature that tends to overemphasise the role of political actors only for peacemaking. However, I argue that other groups and actors also play a key role in establishing a political settlement. My research indicates that formal and informal initiatives together embody conflict resolution processes through three major aspects: backchannel communications as the unofficial aspect, peace organisations as the informal and semi-official aspect, and negotiations as the official aspect of conflict resolution efforts, which operate at the elite level of conflict resolution.

The central question identified above has three sub-questions which correspond to the three major aspects of a conflict resolution process. The first sub-question is: How did backchannel initiatives play a role in de-escalating the violent acts carried out by the IRA and PKK during the pre-negotiation stage? This question examines secret communication channels between the main armed protagonists and independent intermediaries and aims at ascertaining whether these channels helped reduce the level of violence. Although secret talks can create a flexible environment for states and terrorist groups to discuss their demands, there has been little exploration of the influence of backchannel initiatives in the conflict resolution processes in the existing literature. The second sub-question is: To what extent have peace and conflict resolution organisations facilitated peacemaking efforts during existing violence in Northern Ireland and Turkey? It analyses the contribution of peace and conflict resolution organisations (P/CROs) towards reaching an agreement between conflicting parties during the period of violence. The third sub-question is: What has been the impact of the official negotiations towards ending violence and reaching peace agreements in the Northern Irish and Kurdish conflicts? This question concentrates on the negotiation stage of a conflict resolution process which is mostly led by governments and the political wings of sub-state armed groups. This research includes 'mediators' in this stage and identifies them as independent third parties who assist conflicting parties to negotiate or facilitate a negotiation process.

To answer these questions, I focus on the key actors in the Northern Irish and Turkey's Kurdish peace processes. The British government and republican movement in Northern Ireland, and the Turkish government and pro-Kurdish government in Turkey are the major actors in the two peace processes. My research also utilises the role of other political parties and actors in the two cases, peace groups, and independent third parties and agents who affected the nature of these peace processes. The term 'pro-Kurdish movement' is used to refer to the population consisting of the PKK, pro-Kurdish political parties and their supporters. Although there are different classifications for this population, such as the pro-minority movement,[6] this community is mostly called the pro-Kurdish movement, even by the movement itself.[7] However, even though the Peoples' Democratic Party (HDP) and its predecessors describe themselves as part of the pro-Kurdish movement, there are some differences between the PKK and Kurdish political parties in Turkey. They have complex relationships as both sides aim to affect each other. While the PKK aims to use the Kurdish parties in Turkey as its spokespersons, the Kurdish parties aim to defend the rights of Kurdish citizens in the political arena. As both the PKK and Kurdish parties allege that they are the representatives of the Kurdish movement, they name themselves as the pro-Kurdish movement altogether. However, this claim also results in a competition within this movement with regard to which side would lead the Kurdish population. These differences are discussed and assessed in the present book.

The Irish republican movement consists of the IRA and its political wing Sinn Féin (SF). While the IRA split into two groups, comprised of the Provisional IRA and Official IRA, the book assesses the Provisional IRA (PIRA or Provos) because the PIRA (henceforth IRA) dominated the violent conflict in the 1970s as opposed to the Official IRA.[8] As regards other political parties and agents who played roles in these peace processes, the book analyses peace groups which acted in Northern Ireland and Turkey as P/CROs, key intermediaries who acted as both messengers and facilitators between the British and Turkish governments, as well as the IRA and PKK, respectively. For example, Brendan Duddy in Northern Ireland and İlhami Işık in Turkey played critical roles in making peace.[9] The book is complemented by the analysis of the role of other political parties in Northern Ireland (the unionist parties) and Turkey (the nationalist and republican parties) where necessary. Although these parties did not play a key role in the peace processes, their role in preventing or facilitating peace attempts are significant for the success of the conflict resolution processes.

The above questions are investigated through a range of source material including semi-structured interviews, archival research material, official documents, the memoirs of major actors, newspaper articles, reports and other secondary sources. The primary data are thirty-six semi-structured interviews with representatives of the conflicting parties (the British and Turkish governments on the one hand, and the republican and pro-Kurdish movements on the other), other political parties from the conflict-affected societies, peace groups, key intermediaries, and other groups and actors who played a role in the two peace processes. Fieldwork was undertaken in 2015. As the purpose was to assess peacemaking initiatives, the parties and groups that played a role in aiding, facilitating or obstructing peace initiatives were the topic of this project. Therefore, purposive sampling was adopted in order to explore the conflict resolution processes of the two cases through elite interviewing. As political resolution attempts have been dominated from the outset of conflict by disputing parties – namely, governments and the political wings of sub-state armed groups – and independent third parties, they were the sample of the research. The objectives of the IRA and PKK were examined through their political wings.

The other main research mechanism is the archival research at the UK National Archives (TNA) in London, the National University of Ireland (NUI) in the Republic of Ireland, and the Turkish Military Forces (TSK) Archive in Ankara. Each case unfolded over different timescales, which the archival research had to take into account. In the Northern Ireland case, the core events took place between 1969 and 1998; in Turkey, the relevant historical period covers 1984 through to 2015. Therefore, this analysis has investigated a wide range of information to understand the policies, intentions and efforts of political parties concerning resolution efforts of the Northern Irish and Turkey's Kurdish conflicts. This time frame covered hundreds of archival folders in the NUI and TNA archives. The NUI archive was used to access backchannel communication notes between the British government and the republican movement. These texts were not typically long, but often provided very rich information about the various forms of communication – both direct and indirect – that evolved between the mid-1970s and early 1990s. TNA provided hundreds of archival files and folders between 1969 and 1986. The archival files were not declassified after 1986, when the data were collected, until 2015 because of the thirty-year rule.[10]

In addition to the archival research, secondary sources proved essential as they offered different interpretations of this topic. A broad range of secondary sources were used, namely, academic literature, official reports published by governmental bodies, and reports of NGOs and peace groups. The academic literature mainly concentrates on peacebuilding measures regarding community relations, and on peacemaking initiatives that predominantly focus on official resolution attempts. In order to investigate unofficial and informal conflict resolution efforts, policy reports from NGOs and peace groups, and human rights reports from national and international organisations provided useful data.

By analysing these sources, the book aims to understand whether conflict resolution processes in Northern Ireland and Turkey were influential in ending violence. Considering this objective, I suggest expanding the framework of peacemaking efforts from a focus only on the conflicting sides to a wider group consisting of political parties, sub-state armed groups and their political wings, other political elites, and national and international third parties. I will argue that conflict resolution processes should be analysed in a wider context, which requires an investigation of not only official efforts but also unofficial (secret) efforts. Therefore, this book prioritises the importance of backchannel communications between the main armed protagonists, namely the representatives of the British and Turkish governments on the one hand, and the IRA and PKK, respectively, on the other. Both direct and indirect communications have played an important role in reducing the intensity of both conflicts. It is crucial to reveal the correlation between the secret talks and the outcomes of peace efforts since many ethno-nationalist conflicts use secret communication channels.

This book aims to deepen the understanding of the impact of P/CROs as a component of conflict resolution processes. The role of these organisations has been analysed with regard to community relations and reconciliation attempts in the existing literature. However, their impact on the elite level of conflict resolution has been neglected, particularly in situations where they may push political elites towards political reforms and a non-violent resolution, as well as forward the demands of conflicting communities to decision makers. The book reveals the P/CROs' contribution to a peace process in a broader context by comparing the relevant groups in Northern Ireland and Turkey. By so doing, the book advances a unique understanding through the assessment of P/CROs as both top-down and bottom-up initiatives.

The existing literature covering peace and conflict studies has focused on how a peace agreement aimed at ending a violent conflict can be reached. However, this approach has involved largely overlooking the fact that conflict resolution is an ongoing process aimed at disclosing the underlying reasons for unresolved issues between the disputing parties, such as the reaction of opposition parties and veto players who are able to affect political decisions. This book aims to close this gap in our understanding by analysing official negotiations via a tripartite approach consisting of representatives of governments, opposition groups and mediators. In this context, the role of international mediators in determining, facilitating or obstructing the two identified peace processes will be investigated by comparing the US mediation in the Northern Irish case and the British mediation in the Turkish case. This book, therefore, seeks to reveal whether the inclusion of international mediators in intra-state conflicts helps establish peace agreements. In addition, it will examine the influence of official negotiations not only in ending violence (negative peace), but also in transforming the root causes of a conflict (positive peace).[11] Although a 'positive peace' includes conflict transformation in both the conflict resolution and post-agreement processes, this research focuses only on the transformation that occurs during the conflict resolution process.

The book intends to contribute to the understanding of the Northern Irish and Turkish cases (1) through its comprehensive framework which contains the pre-negotiation and negotiation stages of conflict resolution processes, and (2) by examining and comparing backchannel communications, P/CROs and official negotiations. Regarding the Northern Irish case, I aim to reveal the influence of different attempts to achieve peace in order to represent a framework for resolving similar ethno-nationalist conflicts elsewhere. Regarding the Turkish case, I aim to explore Turkey's collapsed peace process in 2015 and the underlying reasons for its failure. In addition, comparing a successfully resolved case with an unsuccessful case can demonstrate a better understanding of conflict resolution processes as it explores the two very different consequences of similar efforts at bringing an ethno-nationalist conflict to an end.

The Northern Ireland and Turkey cases are highly popular and timely given that Brexit impacts the problem by re-igniting the border of Northern Ireland, and the Kurdish conflict has become a milestone after the Syrian civil war. In terms of the Northern Ireland case, while the majority of the nationalist community voted to remain, most unionists voted to leave the EU in the Brexit referendum. As nationalists view themselves Irish, they want to maintain their status.[12] Martin McGuinness, then former Deputy First Minister of Northern Ireland, declared after the outcome of the Brexit referendum that the British government does not represent Northern Ireland's view in any meetings and negotiations with the EU in regard to the exit of the UK from the Union, and 'there is a democratic imperative for a "border poll" to be held'.[13] Further, after the due date of the UK's withdrawal was decided, the republican movement began to fiercely criticise this decision. After meeting with Prime Minister Boris Johnson in July 2019, Mary Lou McDonald, the leader of SF, announced that 'it would be "unthinkable" if a no-deal Brexit was not followed by a poll on Irish reunification'.[14] In line with the reactions of the republican movement, the unionist community and loyalists began to be defensive to maintain the union with the UK. Loyalists in particular have a more uncompromising approach compared to the unionists. As Murphy suggests, the identity of unionists and loyalists is of crucial importance for themselves, and thus if it is attacked by others, it is sufficient to mobilise loyalist action.[15] These developments illustrate that both the republican and unionist communities threaten each other about the future of Northern Ireland.

Undoubtedly, the political environment is dissimilar between the 1990s and 2020s. While the Labour Party, which was broadly pro-European, was in power in the late 1990s, the Conservative Party of 2020 aims for the UK's withdrawal from the EU. In addition, in contrast to the US's peacemaking efforts during the Clinton administration, the Trump administration seems to support pro-Brexit UK nationalism. Hence, it is less likely that the US would act as a neutral mediator if a violent conflict re-emerges. However, it is not certain whether the post-Brexit environment will move the IRA and the loyalist groups to return to violence.[16] The Irish border is also seen as a problem: if the Brexit process is completed, the border between the Republic of Ireland and Northern Ireland will become a physical divide.[17] Therefore, as Hayward and Murphy note, the referendum in Northern Ireland emphasised the post-Brexit conditions for the border between the two sides, namely free trade and movement of people, and the potential threat to peace.[18] Although the implications of Brexit undoubtedly are not clear, as identified above, there is the potential that the peace environment might be ended in Northern Ireland. This book, therefore, provides a unique analysis of the foundations of peacemaking and reveals the insights of the conflict resolution process.

The Syrian civil war has also deeply affected the route of the peace process in Turkey. Therefore, it is crucial to understand changing dynamics in the Middle East. When the Arab uprisings spread in Syria in March 2011, the level of violence rapidly increased through the conflict between the Assad regime and opposition forces, which was then transformed into a proxy warfare through the use of sub-state armed groups by regional and global powers.[19] When the rise of Islamic State of Iraq and Syria (ISIS)[20] caused a spillover effect as neighbouring countries became involved in the war, the first resort of the regional and global powers was to use proxy groups to destroy ISIS. In this context, while the Western coalition of the US and European countries have supported the Democratic Union Party (*Partiya Yekîtiya Demokrat*, henceforth PYD) and its armed wing the People's Protection Unit (*Yekîneyên Parastine Gel*, henceforth YPG), Turkey has supported the Free Syrian Army (FSA), which is a non-Kurdish faction of defected Syrian army personnel.[21] Turkey's official view has been that there is no difference between the PKK and PYD/YPG, and thus the foundation of a Kurdish state on Turkey's border is seen as a direct security threat to the Republic of Turkey.[22] The PYD/YPG dreamed about a Kurdish state in northern Syria by taking advantage of the authority gap in the region.[23] This threat led Turkey to intervene in Syria to prevent the establishment of a Kurdish state which could trigger its Kurdish population to riot for independence.

The nature of the Kurdish conflict therefore became more complicated as PYD/YPG has been seen as the legitimate actor by Western countries which facilitated the spillover effect.[24] When the PYD/YPG began to gain territories in northern Syria, the peace process in Turkey lost its momentum. The strong ethnic and cultural ties between the Kurds in Turkey and in Syria, strong organic ties between the PKK and PYD/YPG pursuing the same ideology, with the same goal of aiming to establish an autonomous Kurdish region, caused the Kurdish conflict in Turkey to deteriorate.[25] Undoubtedly, the Turkish government's manoeuvre from a peace-oriented to war-oriented approach has also affected the success of the peace process in the mid-2010s. As Romano and Gurses note, the Kurdish conflict is a democracy problem which can only be resolved through political reforms.[26]

Background and Case Selection

There has been an increasing interest in peacekeeping, peacebuilding and peacemaking approaches relating to ethno-nationalist conflicts in the existing peace and conflict studies literature.[27] Ethno-nationalist conflicts address separatist, ethnic and territorial issues, but are not individual-level disputes. Instead, they tend to emerge as a consequence of the polarisation between ethnic identities in war-torn societies.[28] These conflicts are group movements and cannot be mitigated through the dominance of the largest ethnic group.[29] Cederman, Buhaug and Rod suggest that these are political conflicts over a modern state's control, which involve state elites on one side and ethno-nationalist groups on the other.[30]

Ethno-national understandings of national labelling and competitive nationalism (symbolic and aggressive affiliations of being British or Irish) constitute one of the major problems in Northern Ireland.[31] The strong ethno-national identities of British and Irish nationalists have been a problem because exhibiting the loyalty of militants to their nation is put first and foremost, at the cost of a mutual Northern Irish identity.[32] This ethno-nationally separated community in Northern Ireland is fundamental for resolution efforts in this type of conflict.[33] Turkey's struggle with the PKK is another significant example of ethnic and national identity issues. The pro-Kurdish paramilitary group asserts that it represents Kurdish identity and it is at war with the Turkish state.[34] As ethnic and national identity issues and the resolution efforts towards these conflicts address the political agenda, conflict resolution approaches as ongoing peace initiatives are significant for the analysis.

Ethno-nationalist conflicts are neither individual-level processes nor reducing factors for polarisation.[35] These conflicts are group movements and do not decrease differences in society. As Collier and Hoeffler suggest, these conflicts cannot be reduced to the dominance of the largest ethnic group.[36] Ethno-nationalist conflicts are displayed as a result of specific means of nation-state formation. They may emerge when the elites of national states fail to contain the majority of citizens into the imaginary society of the nation.[37] This turns into ethno-nationalist conflict between states and sub-state armed groups. The failure of counter-terrorism tactics results in the utilisation of conflict resolution efforts. Similarly, the Northern Irish and Turkey's Kurdish conflicts contain many political resolution attempts. In Ireland, for example, a hunger strike was organised by members of the IRA and the Irish National Liberation Army (INLA) to influence the public to recognise Irish self-determination in 1981. During this period, the British government urged hunger strikers to cease their strike. Nevertheless, this communication channel did not lead to official negotiations as the British government was reluctant to negotiate with the IRA.[38] Similarly, the Turkish government, namely the leading members of the AKP,[39] made some efforts to make contact with the PKK. High-level secret talks in Oslo between the PKK and the Turkish government ended as thirteen Turkish soldiers were killed by PKK militants in June 2011.[40] Conflict resolution attempts in both conflicts will be assessed through successful and unsuccessful non-violent efforts in the subsequent chapters.

There are several reasons for investigating ethno-nationalist conflicts. In the first instance, even though not all ethno-nationalist groups are violent or target civilians, many violent groups with ethno-nationalist claims utilise violence as a tactical tool and organise violent attacks in order to achieve their political aims. Furthermore, these ethno-nationalist groups attack not only the security forces of states, but also civilians, which makes it crucial to seek non-violent solutions. Finally, these groups often have political wings which sit at the negotiating table with governments and act on behalf of the movement and ethnic community that leads to a political resolution.[41] Ethno-nationalist groups are politically motivated and usually have a variety of goals ranging from independence and federation to the recognition of the ethnic identities they claim to represent. Non-military resolution attempts towards ending the violent conflicts in Northern Ireland and Turkey have been paid relatively little attention.[42] In particular, the studies on peacemaking approaches address concepts and issues related to ending conflicts, but do not sufficiently focus on the transformation of the underlying reasons of ethno-nationalist conflict.[43]

There have been many ethno-nationalist conflicts since the end of the Second World War (WWII). The Israeli–Palestinian tension is an important territorial issue which incorporates official and unofficial conflict resolution efforts for sustainable peace. Although the conflicts in this region have some political resolution attempts, they are not appropriate for this analysis due to the existence of two divided territories (Israel and West Bank); the focus of this research is ethno-nationalist conflicts 'within a state'. Similarly, many of the African conflicts have ethnic and nationalist claims. Some of them are located within states and illustrate some assumptions of conflict resolution. For example, while the Popular Self-Defence Forces (FAP) and Polisario Front had negotiations with the governments under the leadership of the UN, the negotiations with the FAP were organised for returning hostages rather than resolving this conflict. The negotiations and mediation attempts for ending the armed campaign of Polisario Front are important, but as this group disbanded itself apart from the conditions of peace talks, it is not a suitable case.[44]

The Asian mainland has several ethnic, nationalist and separatist terrorist groups. While sub-state groups in Southeast Asia are largely dominated by religious rather than ethno-nationalist claims, groups in Southwest Asia mostly have ethnic and nationalist purposes to reach their political aims. Although there are a few conflicts which are similar in structure (motivation, aims and targets) and different in outcome in Southwest Asia, such as those of the Karbi Langri in India and Liberation Tigers of Tamil Eelam (also known as the Tamil Tigers) in Sri Lanka, these conflicts are not included in the analysis as conflict resolution instruments were not applied completely. For example, the Tamil Tigers were defeated by the Sri Lankan security forces. Thus, there was no peace settlement or peace process.[45] The counterinsurgency campaign of Sri Lanka's Rajapaksa government liberated the country from the Tamil Eelam as of 2009.[46] The conflict in Kashmir is also a significant ethnic and territorial conflict, and embodies both identity issues and peace initiatives such as track-two efforts. While these informal talks reduced the concerns on trust, they did not create a measurable policy influence on both governments.[47] More importantly, this is not a suitable case for consideration here because this conflict is between two state actors. It is not an internal dispute but a regional conflict between India and Pakistan.[48] Another long-standing conflict in Southeast Asia is that in the Mindanao region of the Philippines, between the Philippines government and Moro Islamic Liberation Front (MILF). Despite the ethnic and regional motives, this is a predominantly religious conflict since the MILF seeks to rule the south-eastern Philippines along sharia guidelines and to have an Islamic education system.[49] Therefore, this conflict is not included in this project.

The mainlands of Europe and America embody various ethno-nationalist conflicts, with violent groups claiming to represent an ethnic community within a state and using violence as a tactical tool. Although armed groups in France, Corsica and Spain exhibit these conditions and illustrate similarities, their political aims could not be achieved due to the lack of political representatives, such as in the conflicts deployed by Irrintzi and the Corsican Revolutionary Armed Forces.[50] The peace process between the Colombian government and the Revolutionary Armed Forces of Colombia (FARC) does not include the three major components of peacemaking efforts during existing violence. The process was conducted by official negotiations and partially unofficial talks,[51] but despite the long-standing peace efforts with the FARC, the peace process did not bring the violent conflict in Colombia to an end.[52] Conversely, the Basque Country and Freedom (*Euskadi Ta Askatasuna*, henceforth ETA) in Spain are a distinctive example for both characteristics of the group and conflict resolution endeavours. However, this group is not suitable for study here due to one condition: despite intensive armed and political struggle until 1979, the regime change in Spain altered the status of ETA and the Basque region without a negotiated settlement.[53] This condition hinders examining the influence of political efforts and hence, it was excluded from the research. In addition, Cyprus and Serbia conflicts were not included in the analysis for several reasons. The conflict in Cyprus is not an internal conflict between the Greek and Turkish Cypriots, but an international conflict where Turkey and Greece intervened, and the three states (Greece, Turkey and the UK) became guarantors under the Treaty of Guarantee of 1960.[54] The Serbian conflict is a useful example of the initiatives of peace and conflict resolution organisations, such as the events organised by the Women in Black.[55] Nevertheless, it was part of an international conflict which emerged after the breakup of Yugoslavia as a result of intensive conflicts in the 1990s between Bosnia and Herzegovina, Serbia, Slovenia, Croatia, Macedonia and Montenegro.[56]

In contrast, the intractable conflicts in Turkey and Northern Ireland embody not only ethnic claims, territorial issues, armed campaigns and political resolution attempts, but also peace processes with regard to the elite level of conflict resolution. Although the structure and evolution of the UK's Northern Irish and Turkey's Kurdish conflicts are not identical, these two cases bear similarities in terms of the actors involved in the conflicts and peace processes, the settlement strategies, the involvement of national and international third parties, the approaches of the two governments, and the intentions of the respective republican and pro-Kurdish movements regarding the use of violence. These factors together constitute an extensive comparative analysis for several reasons. First of all, both groups primarily aimed to change the political systems of their states and organised attacks against both armed forces and civilians in order to achieve their goals.[57] While the primary objective of the IRA was the reunification of Ireland, the PKK's goal is to establish an independent Kurdish state in the southeast of Turkey.[58] The PKK's aim, however, shifted from independence to autonomy and democratic confederalism.[59] These shifting goals affected the nature of negotiations between the Turkish government and pro-Kurdish movement. Although the IRA's ultimate goal remains the same, the republican movement's position change from rejecting any political initiatives to participating in elections through SF demonstrated its shifting approach towards peacemaking.[60]

Furthermore, although the Northern Ireland conflict involved religious issues between the Catholic and Protestant communities, this conflict was dominated by political, national, ethnic and territorial concerns. The major dispute was on the constitutional status of Northern Ireland and was between two polarised groups: unionists/loyalists, the majority of whom were Protestants and who considered themselves British, and nationalists/republicans, the majority of whom were Catholics and who considered themselves Irish. While the nationalist/republican side demanded to leave the United Kingdom (UK) and join Ireland, the unionists wanted to remain part of the UK.[61] In terms of the Turkish case, the PKK has a Marxist-Leninist ideology believing that violence is necessary to achieve a radical revolution against the oppressive states (Iraq, Iran, Turkey and Syria).[62] The political project of the PKK evolved from a perceived discrimination against the Kurdish population in constitutional, economic and social areas, which led commentators to describe the movement as a class struggle.[63] Despite this ideology, the objective of the PKK has been to establish an independent state and so it is driven by ethnic and separatist concerns.[64] These political and ethnic concerns form the basis for the major focus of this research. However, the similarity between these two conflicts in terms of their structures and peace processes did not lead to the same outcomes, which demonstrates a more comprehensive analysis compared to a single case study. Although the IRA's armed campaign ended successfully in a peace agreement, there has been no success in ending the PKK's armed campaign in Turkey.

An investigation of the role of the political wings of the republican movement (SF) and the pro-Kurdish movement (the HDP[65] and its predecessors) is crucial in terms of their relationships with the IRA and PKK respectively, their respective influences on the Catholic and Kurdish communities and in the transformation of the nature of both conflicts from violence towards a peaceful resolution.[66] The relationships between the two groups and their political fronts are also important, as they may not hold parallel perspectives under all conditions. Hence, SF in Northern Ireland and the HDP and its predecessors in Turkey provide important cases for analysing the role of political elites. For example, SF had no links with parliamentary politics in Northern Ireland and the Republic of Ireland for most of its history.[67] It had only a specific policy which argued the invalidity of the partition of Ireland in 1921 and, as a result, refused to serve in any government which recognised that partition.[68] However, this view changed during the republican hunger strikes of 1981 as SF began to participate in national elections in Northern Ireland and the Republic of Ireland.[69] Indeed, the balance of power between the groups defending the armed struggle on the one hand, and others promoting the political struggle for the reunification of Ireland on the other, shifted from one to the other invariably after those strikes.[70] Similarly, despite the dominance of the PKK, the struggle within the pro-Kurdish movement between the PKK and pro-Kurdish parties for leadership of the movement continued until the peace process collapsed in July 2015.[71] Hence, an investigation into the influence of SF and the HDP on their paramilitary counterparts will help establish an understanding of the impact of conflict resolution processes on peacemaking actions.

Conflict Resolution: Theory and its Modification

This book explores non-violent resolution attempts towards ending violence and establishing political settlements in the two ethno-nationalist conflicts identified above. Here, settlement means an agreement between the main protagonists that includes both the termination of violence and the transformation of the root causes of a conflict.

A conflict resolution process is concerned with political, non-violent peace efforts by conflicting parties and national and international third parties, to address the requirements and demands of disputing parties in order to reach agreeable circumstances for ending violence.[72] Conflict resolution in the traditional sense focused on conflicts between states and addressed international negotiations between two states under the mediation of a third.[73] Since the end of WWII, the character of warfare has gradually changed with the rise of non-state actors in conflicts, which has resulted in 'asymmetric' warfare between states and sub-state actors. Such forms of warfare include terrorism, ethnic and religious conflicts and civil wars.[74] This change has led to a modification in conflict resolution theory that considers the transformation of actors in conflicts, issues, demands and resolution methods. The differences include conflict resolution processes that produce solutions accommodating some mutual gains for the opposing parties.[75] This book focuses on intra-state conflicts (rather than international conflicts) which are driven by identity, ethnicity and territorial concerns, such as independence, federation or autonomy of a region, through a new form of conflict resolution theory. This modified theory does not consider the power or authority of any of the disputing parties. Rather, it indicates a need for equality between conflicting parties in order to achieve a settlement.[76] Therefore, this theory provides a suitable framework for the analysis of ethno-nationalist conflicts, which involve a state authority, and a sub-state armed group and its political wing.[77] The Northern Irish and Kurdish conflicts relate to armed conflicts between the state security forces and sub-state armed groups, and therefore, a balance between the powerful and weak parties in the conflicts would be necessary in order to achieve the demands of both sides to avoid a zero-sum game. This describes a more complicated relationship than that involving only conflicting parties as it also contains other parties involved in a conflict resolution process.[78] This book identifies the role of the third parties as the key factor in determining the nature of the Northern Irish and Turkey's Kurdish peace processes.

Based on the existing conflict resolution literature, this book establishes the common requirements of both sides in a violent conflict, such as security, recognition and autonomy. By emphasising these requirements, conflict resolution theory concentrates on the common interests of the conflicting sides and focuses on creating trust between disputing parties. Lederach's classification of conflict resolution exhibits a comprehensive understanding of conflict resolution theory and defines an approach to this field via three levels: top (elite), middle-range and grassroots levels.[79] Whilst the grassroots level avoids the national and extra-national politics of a conflict and concentrates on local and indigenous stages of a peace process, the middle-range level covers the attempts of unofficial representatives to bring opposition parties together.[80] In contrast, the elite level addresses peace efforts which are mainly managed by negotiations among political leaders and main protagonists, and then expands it to society.[81] As this book investigates how the destructive campaigns of the IRA and PKK could be brought to an end in a political way, political parties and actors at the elite level and other non-political actors are examined, namely peace groups and both national and international intermediaries who played a role in the decisions of political elites and contributed to these peace processes.

I examine these theoretical assumptions by considering ethnic and nationalist differences in the Northern Irish and Turkish societies and to what extent the republican and pro-Kurdish movements respectively have driven these intractable conflicts. I analyse political resolution efforts by defining a conflict resolution process as a comprehensive approach containing both the pre-negotiation and negotiation stages. I, therefore, focus on the backchannel initiatives as a pre-negotiation activity between the main armed protagonists, P/CROs as national third parties involved in the two peace processes, and official negotiations between the conflicting parties and international third parties, which together identify conflict resolution processes.

Overview

The argument of this book is developed through seven chapters. Following a brief overview of the book in the first chapter, Chapter 2 examines the theoretical and conceptual framework of this book. This framework addresses conflict resolution approaches for understanding non-violent resolution efforts towards ending ethno-nationalist conflicts. The chapter divides conflict resolution approaches into three levels: the elite, middle-range and grassroots level approaches. As the book focuses on peacemaking efforts between states, opposition groups and third parties, the relevance of elite-level approaches, as well as other groups and the initiatives of other actors towards peace, is clarified by conceptualising three major parts which have a role in peacemaking efforts: backchannel communications, P/CROs and official negotiations.

Chapter 3 provides an overview of the background of the Northern Irish and Turkey's Kurdish peace processes and aims to demonstrate the relationship between the violent conflicts and non-violent, political resolution efforts. This overview demonstrates the dilemmas faced by authorities in deciding whether to adopt traditional terrorism and counter-terrorism tactics versus 'conflict resolution' measures. This historical account explores the transition in the perception of the British and Turkish governments on the one hand, and the leadership of the IRA and PKK on the other. It explores the strength of this transition in both conflicts historically and provides an understanding of how the attitudes and actions of the conflicting parties influenced the outcome of both peace processes. It reveals that peace efforts and violent campaigns were used together from the beginning of the Troubles in Northern Ireland, and since 1984 in Turkey. It provides an understanding of how the attitudes and actions of the conflicting parties influenced the outcome of both peace processes.

Chapter 4 focuses on the influence of secret communication channels between the principle armed protagonists in reducing the level of violence and facilitating a political settlement. The nature of political, non-violent peace efforts resulted in over-motivation for official negotiations between conflicting parties and so caused an intention to limit peace processes with these negotiations only. This chapter includes secret communication channels into conflict resolution processes as the pre-negotiation stage and so draws a broader framework for peacemaking. In particular, the influence of these track one-and-a-half efforts between the principle armed protagonists, namely the British and Turkish governments on the one hand, the IRA and PKK on the other, are the focus of the research in regard to reducing the level of violence and facilitating a political settlement. The chapter establishes the importance of backchannels by emphasising the characteristics of national and international intermediaries, the demands of the two governments and sub-state armed groups, and the contents of secret discussions and their influence on the achievement of a peaceful solution, through interview data and archival materials. It reveals that while the pre-negotiation stage began during the early 1970s and lasted until the early 1990s when the Northern Irish parties and British government commenced official negotiations, it was between the late 1980s and early 2010s in the Turkish case.

Chapter 5 investigates unofficial peace initiatives that were undertaken from the early stages of both conflicts by P/CROs. The existing literature has long recognised the influence of these groups at the community level, especially in the area of reconciliation. However, the impact of these track-two initiatives on the elite level of conflict resolution has been neglected, particularly in situations where they may push political elites towards political reforms and a non-violent resolution, as well as forwarding the demands of conflicting communities to decision makers. This book intends to reveal the P/CROs' contribution to peace processes in this broader sense by comparing the relevant groups in Northern Ireland and Turkey. Regarding middle-range efforts, P/CROs aim to close the gap between the elite and grassroots levels through public events, conferences and marches, which help include a war-affected society's demands for political decisions and the promotion of political resolution attempts. Regarding elite-level efforts, they play a role in political decisions thanks to their personal contacts with political elites. It assesses whether these groups have reduced the tension in the society and have encouraged political efforts in Northern Ireland and Turkey.

Chapter 6 explores official negotiations as the key factor in conflict resolution processes in both conflicts. The cross-case comparison allows for the generation of comprehensive insights into the conflict environment – which is a decisive factor for the nature of political resolution attempts – by providing an analysis of the root causes of the conflicts in both cases. This analysis broadens the process from a 'negative' to 'positive peace' that includes transformation of the underlying reasons for conflicts and restoration of relationships. It provides clear evidence from both track-one experiences and their comparison which will help to establish an extensive analysis in establishing peace. The book reaches a deeper analysis by also considering other actors and factors, namely 'spoilers' who aim to distract a peace process and mediators who facilitate or hinder progress.

Chapter 7 concludes the book by appraising its outcomes and summarising the findings that can be applied to other ethno-nationalist conflicts involving similar peace processes. It discusses the implications of conflict resolution theory and the policies applied in the two specified conflicts which demonstrate a suitable framework for further research. This book represents a challenge to the existing peace and conflict literature which primarily focuses on negotiations for making peace. Instead, this book examines conflict resolution as a process which begins with indirect communications and results in a political settlement.

Notes

1. De Tocqueville, *Democracy in America*.
2. Cordell and Wolff, *Ethnic Conflict*.
3. Bar-Siman-Tov, 'The Arab-Israeli Conflict'; Darby and MacGinty, *Contemporary Peacemaking*; Richmond, 'Ethno-nationalism, Sovereignty and Negotiating Positions in the Cyprus Conflict'.
4. Bell, 'The Escalation of Insurgency', p. 398; Ergil, 'The Kurdish Question in Turkey', pp. 122–35.
5. This book uses the term IRA to refer to the Provisional IRA (Provos, PIRA) for the sake of consistency.
6. Akbulut, 'A Critical Analysis of Current Legal Developments on the Political Participation of Minorities in Turkey'.
7. Barkey and Fuller, *Turkey's Kurdish Question*; HDP, 'History of Kurdish Political Parties in Turkey'; HRW, '"Turkey". World Report 2016'; Watts, 'Allies and Enemies'.
8. Little, *Peacemakers in Action*.
9. Craig, 'From Backdoors and Back Lanes to Backchannels'; HaberTürk, 'Barış ve Çözüm Sürecinde Geri Dönmek Mümkün Değil'.
10. All cabinet papers, memoranda and other files in TNA of London are confidential documents and are only released to the public after thirty years of creation, which is called the thirty-year rule. Please see TNA, *The National Archive of London: Meetings and Papers*.
11. Galtung, *Peace by Peaceful Means*.
12. European Parliament, *The Impact and Consequences of Brexit for Northern Ireland*, pp. 1–2.
13. McGuinness, quoted in Halpin, 'Sinn Fein Calls for Irish Unity Poll as Brexit Fallout Begins'.

14. McDonald, quoted in Walker and Elgot, 'Sinn Féin'.
15. Murphy, cited in Haverty, 'With Parliament Voting for Brexit, is Irish Unification Inevitable?'.
16. Stevenson, 'Does Brexit Threaten Peace in Northern Ireland?', pp. 123–5.
17. Gormley-Heenan and Aughey, 'Northern Ireland and Brexit'.
18. Hayward and Murphy, 'The EU's Influence on the Peace Process', p. 283.
19. Kadıoğlu, 'Challenges of International Negotiations in the Syrian Civil War'.
20. The group first used the name Jama'at al-Tawhid wal-Jihad and al-Qaeda in Iraq. Afterwards it used the name Islamic State in Iraq in 2006, and added 'al-Sham' to make ISIS in 2013. There are many abbreviations used to define the group. The most frequently used abbreviations are IS, ISIS, ISIL (the Islamic State and the Levant) and Dawlat al-Islamiyah f'al-Iraq wa al-Sham (DAESH) which is mostly used by Arabic-speaking countries (see Dearden, 'Isis vs Islamic State vs Isil vs Daesh').
21. Kadıoğlu, 'The Proxy Warfare in Syria', pp. 11–12.
22. *Guardian*, 'Turkey will not Cooperate in US Support for Kurds in Syria, Says Erdogan'.
23. Kadıoğlu, 'Yaşamın Sınırını Geçmek'; Parlar-Dal, 'Impact of the Transnationalization of the Syrian Civil War on Turkey'.
24. Parlar-Dal, 'Impact of the Transnationalization', p. 1415.
25. Ibid. p. 1403.
26. Romano and Gurses, 'Introduction', p. 9.
27. Brown, *Ethnic Conflict and International Security*; Cordell and Wolff, *Ethnic Conflict*; McGarry and O'Leary, *The Politics of Ethnic Conflict Regulation*; Stavenhagen, *Ethnic Conflicts and the Nation-State*; Welsh, 'Domestic Politics and Ethnic Conflict'.
28. Montalvo and Reynal-Qerol, 'Ethnic Polarization, Potential Conflict, and Civil Wars'.
29. Collier and Hoeffler, 'Greed and Grievance in Civil Wars'.
30. Cederman *et al.*, 'Ethno-nationalist Dyads and Civil War', p. 499.
31. McGarry and O'Leary, *Explaining Northern Ireland*.
32. Dixon, 'British Policy towards Northern Ireland 1969–2000'; Evans and Tonge, 'Catholic, Irish and Nationalist', p. 360.
33. Nagle and Clancy, 'Constructing a Shared Public Identity in Ethno-Nationally Divided Societies', p. 79.
34. Art and Richardson, 'Introduction', p. 5; Welsh, 'Domestic Politics and Ethnic Conflict', p. 44.
35. Montalvo and Reynal-Qerol, 'Ethnic Polarization, Potential Conflict, and Civil Wars'.

36. Collier and Hoeffler, 'Greed and Grievance in Civil Wars'.
37. Cederman *et al.*, 'Ethno-nationalist Dyads and Civil War', p. 499.
38. Tannam, 'Explaining the Good Friday Agreement', p. 502.
39. AKP: Justice and Development Party (*Adalet ve Kalkınma Partisi*). Although the party staff use the term 'AK Parti' (the term 'ak' means 'white or clean' in Turkish) and the English abbreviated version is the JDP, the Turkish initial AKP is widely used in the literature and so the initials AKP are adopted in this research.
40. ICC, 'Turkey', pp. 3–4.
41. Field, 'The "New Terrorism"', pp. 197–8; Simon and Benjamin, 'The Terror', p. 5.
42. There are a couple of exceptions: please see Aydınlı and Özcan, 'The Conflict Resolution and Counterterrorism Dilemma'; Çelik, 'Etnik Çatışmaların Çözümünde Siyaset Bilimi ve Uyuşmazlık Çözümü Yaklaşımları'; Cochrane, *Northern Ireland*; Dixon, *Northern Ireland*; McGarry and O'Leary, *Explaining Northern Ireland*; Ozcelik, 'Theories, Practices, and Research in Conflict Resolution and Low-Intensity Conflicts'; Yeğen, 'The Kurdish Peace Process in Turkey'. Although these studies examine political resolution methods, they do not suggest conflict resolution theory as a framework for resolution of these conflicts regarding the role of political initiatives.
43. Bloomfield, *Peacemaking Strategies in Northern Ireland*; Brewer *et al.*, *Peacemaking among Protestants and Catholics in Northern Ireland*; Curle, 'New Challenges for Citizen Peacemaking'; Walton, *Interpersonal Peacemaking*.
44. START, *Global Terrorism Database*.
45. Ibid; van de Voorde, 'Sri Lankan Terrorism'.
46. Hashim, *When Counterinsurgency Wins*.
47. Waslekar, *Track-two Diplomacy in South Asia*.
48. Wirsing, *India, Pakistan, and the Kashmir Dispute*.
49. Herbolzheimer and Leslie, '*Innovation in Mediation Support*'.
50. Forest, 'Kidnapping by Terrorist Groups, 1970–2010'; START, *Global Terrorism Database*.
51. Neumann, 'Negotiating with Terrorists'.
52. Özkan, 'Shaping Peace Processes', p. 93.
53. Barros, 'An Intervention Analysis of Terrorism'; Ekici, 'Ethnic Terrorism and the Case of the PKK'.
54. Fisher, 'Cyprus'.
55. Stephenson and Zanotti, *Peacebuilding through Community-based NGOs*.
56. Gagnon, 'Ethnic Nationalism and International Conflict'.
57. Crenshaw, *Explaining Terrorism*; Guelke, *The Age of Terrorism and International Political System*.

58. Sanchez-Cuenca, 'The Dynamics of Nationalist Terrorism'; Stavenhagen, *Ethnic Conflicts and the Nation-State*.
59. Kadıoğlu, 'The End of Turkey's Kurdish "Peace Process"?'.
60. Little, *Peacemakers in Action*.
61. Stavenhagen, *Ethnic Conflicts and the Nation-State*.
62. Aydınlı and Özcan, 'The Conflict Resolution and Counterterrorism Dilemma'; Kadıoğlu, 'Not Our War: Iraq, Iran and Syria's Approaches towards the PKK'.
63. Bell, *The IRA, 1968–2000*; Post, *The Mind of the Terrorist*.
64. Somer and Liaras, 'Turkey's New Kurdish Opening'.
65. HDP: The Peoples' Democratic Party (*Halkların Demokratik Partisi*).
66. Despite the PKK's claim of being the representative of Kurdish identity, there is no homogenous Kurdish bloc in a cultural or political sense as the term 'Kurdishness' refers to a great range of identities and dialects that are not mutually exclusive, such as the speakers of Zaza, Gorani, Kurmanji and Sorani. Please see Jacoby and Özerdem, *Peace in Turkey 2023*; McDowall, *Modern History of the Kurds*.
67. Murray and Tonge, *Sinn Fein and the SDLP*.
68. Ibid. p. 14.
69. Dixon, *Northern Ireland*, p. 12.
70. Hancock, 'The Northern Irish Peace Process', p. 206.
71. Coşkun, 'HDP Torn Between Violence and Politics'; Karayılan, 'Son Kararımız . . .'
72. Ramsbotham *et al.*, *Contemporary Conflict Resolution*.
73. Kremenyuk, *International Negotiation*.
74. Crenshaw, *Explaining Terrorism*.
75. Kriesberg, 'The Evolution of Conflict Resolution', p. 16.
76. Kelman, 'Reconciliation as Identity Change', pp. 112–19; Rouhana, 'Key Issues in Reconciliation', pp. 294–5.
77. Galtung, 'Institutionalized Conflict Resolution'.
78. Fisher, 'Third Party Consultation as a Method of Intergroup Conflict Resolution'.
79. Lederach, *Building Peace*.
80. Carayannis *et al.*, *Practice Without Evidence*; Kelman, 'Interactive Problem Solving: An Approach', pp. 190–8.
81. Hancock, 'The Northern Irish Peace Process'.

2

UNDERSTANDING AND RETHINKING 'CONFLICT RESOLUTION': A CONCEPTUAL AND THEORETICAL FRAMEWORK

> By peace, we mean the capacity to transform conflict with empathy and creativity, without violence; this is a never-ending process ... By without violence, we mean that this process should avoid any threat or use of direct violence that hurts and harms.[1]

Conflict resolution is a 'vibrant, interdisciplinary field where theory and practice pace real-world events'.[2] Conflict resolution theory seeks to understand and support practical interventions. Conflict resolution is a multilateral process which addresses both state-level and group-level aspirations behind political violence.[3] Hence, this process is relevant to explore solutions to ethno-nationalist violence between states and sub-state armed groups. In this context, conflict resolution theory differs from realism because of the realist approach's overemphasis on conflicts between states.

In this chapter, I focus on two interrelated arguments. Firstly, that conflict resolution efforts of states, sub-state groups and third parties provide a framework for ending ethno-nationalist violence. Secondly, that conflict resolution as a process develops an understanding of non-violent resolution efforts during the pre-negotiation and negotiation stages. This chapter aims to justify the theoretical foundations of the book. It outlines how the characteristics of conflict resolution approaches adapted in this book produce a convenient framework for analysing non-violent resolution attempts. These two arguments provide a comprehensive theoretical background for analysing the Northern Irish and Turkey's Kurdish conflicts. Within a specific context, the ethno-nationalist conflicts in Northern Ireland and Turkey, as well as the claims of the British and Turkish governments on the one hand, and the republican and pro-Kurdish movements on the other, can be emphasised in relation to efforts to reach a peace settlement. It underlines the importance of two directions for understanding this influence: a particular time period in which states and armed groups can be directed from an armed struggle to political or non-violent disputes, and a particular level of approaches which uncover the relationships between conflicting parties and an independent third party in terms of peace attempts. Both directions emphasise how certain approaches affect the cessation of sub-state ethno-nationalist violence. Considering that the only way for non-violent resolution of intra-state armed conflicts is not conflict resolution, I focus on a specific period for this type of tension, and thus examine a specific term of conflict resolution approaches. Hence, the research does not aim to discover post-violence process. Instead, I aim to explore the influence of peacemaking efforts during the period of violence.

The chapter, firstly, outlines the non-violent settlement theories and helps distinguish conflict resolution theory from other similar approaches. Then, it has a general overview of classifications of conflict resolution approaches. Afterwards, three major levels of conflict resolution are examined to understand the relationships between them and to highlight the relevance of the elite level of conflict resolution for assessing peace efforts towards ending ethno-nationalist conflicts. Lastly, the elite level of conflict resolution and its main dimensions are explored to analyse the Northern Irish and Turkey's Kurdish conflicts in detail.

Non-violent Settlement Theories and Conflict Resolution Theory

There are various peacemaking theories and models within the existing literature. However, different theories and models exhibit similar features and common characteristics. The impact of conflict resolution theory among these different theories and models is that it differs from other theories regarding the consideration of both conflicting sides and an independent third party, and the pre-negotiation and negotiation stages. Although it is not possible to examine all theories in the existing literature, the key differences between these approaches must be examined in order to explore the impact of conflict resolution theory.

Ramsbotham, Woodhouse and Miall developed an inclusive model called the hourglass model of conflict resolution (Figure 2.1).[4] According to their model, conflict resolution covers the whole conflict-affected environment, from conflict containment and conflict settlement to conflict transformation. The model explores the space for political resolution for constructive solution attempts. Initially, conflict containment provides limitation and peacekeeping together. In this sense, war limitation contains 'geographical constraint, mitigation and alleviation of intensity, and termination at the earliest opportunity'.[5] Next, conflict settlement addresses peacemaking and aims to overcome polarisation, which is one of the most visible threats of conflict. Finally, conflict transformation is the deepest level of the model that addresses structural and cultural peacebuilding. While structural peacebuilding examines the structural problems of violence, for example poverty, cultural peacebuilding explores the differences of group behaviours, interests and beliefs. Conflict transformation is aimed at managing reconciliation by considering cultural and structural differences in a society.[6] Each theory focuses on a specific phase of non-violent peace efforts, whereas conflict resolution is accepted as an approach which encompasses all of these theories. This model provides a comprehensive approach by focusing on major theories within the field. However, it does not describe the specific role and route of conflict resolution.

The conflict transformation theory is also analysed by other scholars in the existing literature. It involves changing relationships, discourses and crucial formations which exacerbate violent political conflict. It aims to transform negative approaches in dealing with conflicts into positive ways in the long term.[7] It also aims to decrease the influence of the negative factors of conflicts. Undoubtedly, it might require long-term effort as the conflict might deeply affect society. While positive approaches explain successful attempts at conflict resolution, negative approaches refer to unsuccessful conflict resolution efforts. The theory emphasises the value of thoughts and actions inclusively for initiating and sustaining transformation.[8] Despite this model's significance, it does not mention how to use conflict resolution and transformation together. This research aims to close this gap by identifying the role of

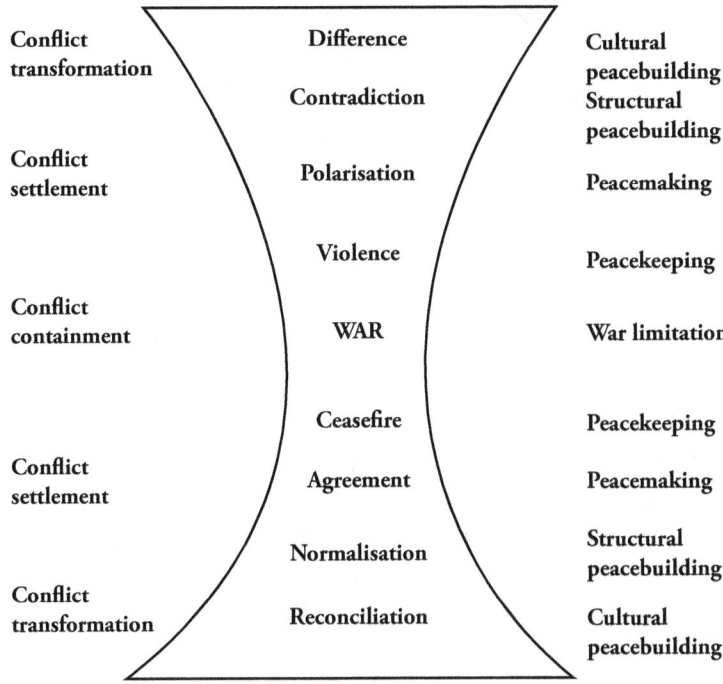

Figure 2.1 The hourglass model. Source: Ramsbotham *et al.*, *Contemporary Conflict Resolution*, p. 14.

conflict transformation during the negotiation stage of a conflict, which will be discussed in the next chapter. Such resolution attempts are described by different scholars who address different aspects of peace efforts. For example, Bendana focuses on the link between conflict management and conflict resolution.[9] He evaluates these theories in the same way:

> Conflict resolution and management are, in effect, social accords which constitute the containment of societal contradictions within a framework upholding neoliberal dogmas with regard to the role of the state, the central place of the market, fiscal responsibility, and the primacy of the private sector.[10]

However, Bendana has been criticised by a number of scholars who argue that conflict management and conflict resolution have different characteristics. On the one hand, the reconciliation or destruction of disagreements and problems implies the need for conflict resolution. This emerges when the tension between conflicting parties vanishes or the reason for the conflict disappears.[11] On the other hand, conflict management explains the control and limitation. Hence, in neither situation does conflict management remove the reasons for the conflict. However, the reasons can still be removed, as conflict management resolves the tension. If it is impossible to solve conflict, conflict management can make the situation bearable.[12] Therefore, while conflict resolution solves the problem, conflict management describes the boundaries of the problem and makes a solution achievable.

Gartner and Bercovitch describe conflict settlement in detail, suggesting it has been divided along a continuum into three types: ceasefire, partial settlement and full settlement.[13] While ceasefire refers to stopping violence, partial settlement describes not only the stopping of violence but also the initiation of engagement between parties with the resolution of certain conflict issues. For instance, the conflict between Egypt and Libya was mediated by Palestinian leader Yasser Arafat and some of the issues were agreed to have been resolved in 1977. Lastly, full settlement describes an end to violence that solves many of the parties' basic problems first hand. This condition can be illustrated by the Rhodesia–Zimbabwe conflict, which was settled by Lord Carrington in 1979.[14] However, conflict settlement is not appropriate for considering in this research as it contains only negotiation attempts and does not include other initiatives for assisting peace attempts during the pre-negotiation and negotiation stages.

Taking all these initiatives together, as I focus on a specific period of a conflict when violence existed, conflict prevention is not a suitable theory. Similarly, as the book contains the analysis of destructive campaigns of terrorist groups and how these campaigns have attempted resolution, conflict transformation will only be considered as part of conflict resolution initiatives to understand whether the root causes of the two conflicts under discussion were transformed during the negotiation and mediation efforts. Conflict transformation focuses on both ending destructive conflicts and building constructive conflicts that address a wider use of persuasion and positive incentives.[15]

Conversely, conflict resolution theory seeks to reach circumstances that are agreeable for ending tensions in a form that meets the requirements of conflicting parties. The theory does not consider the power or authority of disputing parties. It accepts both conflicting parties as equal for negotiating with each other.

Therefore, it provides a suitable ground for the analysis of ethno-nationalist conflicts, which involve a state authority and an armed group within the conflict. Besides this, conflict resolution also investigates the reasons behind conflicts by seeking out the background information and evolution of these conflicts. It also underlines the common requirements of both conflicting sides, such as security, recognition and autonomy. Conflict resolution theory encourages the identification of the common interests of opposing sides and focuses on creating trust between them. It suggests that an agreement can be reached through equality and mutuality.[16] Considering these two factors, conflict resolution involves a non-violent process and avoids dominance and oppression by one party over another through its voluntary and consensus-based structure.[17]

Moreover, this theory addresses political, non-violent resolution attempts that are relevant for answering the questions identified in this research. Lederach's classification of conflict resolution exhibits a comprehensive understanding of the theory by incorporating the whole conflict resolution theory into three levels of approaches: top (elite), middle-range and grassroots levels.[18] Whilst the grassroots level avoids the national and extra-national politics of the conflict and concentrates on local and indigenous stages of a peace process, the middle-range level contains attempts by unofficial representatives that bring opposing parties together.[19] In contrast, the elite-level approaches address peace efforts which are mainly managed by negotiations among political leaders and other institutional approaches, and then expand them to wider society.[20]

The foundations of conflict resolution theory were developed by several scholars. The foundation of the *Journal of Conflict Resolution* in 1957 by Kenneth Boulding was one of the first efforts to shape the environment of conflict resolution. Boulding argues that conflict resolution is determined by two factors: a reduction of the conflict's intensity and the growth of overruling organisations that contain both conflicting sides.[21] Based on these factors, the outcome of a successful conflict resolution process is sustainable peace, which itself requires a peaceful social system. The fault of peacemakers is that they still try to solve tension as if it was a physical problem, but in reality, tension is part of a physical system.[22] Johan Galtung explains major challenges and responses to peace efforts and puts forward not only requirements to prevent wars, but also approaches for peaceful solutions between conflicting parties.[23] He describes the necessity to transform the root causes of a conflict to terminate the conflict and establish peace.[24] John Burton was the third scholar to build the theory of conflict resolution and he examined conflict resolution as the problem of transforming the situation from power bargaining or a zero-sum result to a problem-solving one, where both sides can acquire at least their minimum aims and practical cooperation.[25] Hence, the insufficiency of traditional negotiations led him to produce the 'human needs approach', which suggests that there are negotiable and non-negotiable issues during a peace process.[26]

After Boulding, Galtung and Burton, the analysis of conflict resolution was expanded by a number of scholars. Burton's practical endeavours of conflict resolution were improved by Fisher and Kelman. Fisher established the 'third party consultation' approach to stress the scientists or practitioners' fundamental roles.[27] He aimed to differentiate his method from traditional third party interventions and mediations by including the degree of coercion applied to the parties, nature of different goals and flexibility of communication.[28] His approach involves problem-solving methods between unofficial representatives of parties engaged in violent conflict.[29] Kelman used the term 'interactive problem-solving' to assess unofficial conflict resolution attempts, which contains structural and attitudinal changes and promotes reconciliation between conflicting parties and the transformation of their relationship.[30] He applied interactive problem-solving methods to the Israeli–Palestinian conflict.[31] Holsti identified some major elements of the new international environment with respect to the use of war, systems of governance for the commonality of countries, conflict-resolving mechanisms and procedures, the solution of warfare-producing affairs and specific concepts of arrangement which will preclude wars of revenge.[32] Wallensteen applied the theory to the practice in international conflicts including the conflicts between the Israelis and Palestinians, and between Greek and Turkish Cypriots.[33]

Conflict Resolution Approaches for Understanding Non-violent Resolution Efforts

The conceptual growth of the conflict resolution field helps to identify the multilateral approaches of the theory. Boulding, Galtung and Burton established the bases of the theory as state-centric and resting on mutual agreement.[34] However, the procedures of the theory have diversified in recent decades. Some scholars emphasise the importance of an independent third party in a peace process.[35]

Others assess conflict resolution efforts as official negotiations (track-one) between conflicting parties and an independent third party.[36] Other scholars make a distinction within conflict resolution theory. For example, Babbitt and Hampson analyse conflict resolution as a constructivist theory that is divided into two approaches: conflict settlement and transformation.[37] As with conflict resolution, constructivism investigates the perceptions, beliefs and attitudes of the parties in a conflict, the communicative-discursive strategies used by intermediaries, the formation of regimes, the role of language and the events that groups and actors can take to shape the conflict-affected environment to resolve conflicts.[38]

However, none of these debates offer a comprehensive account of conflict resolution theory when examining the relationships between states and sub-state armed groups in the pre-negotiation and negotiation stages of a conflict. This book investigates political, non-violent resolution attempts to stop ethnonationalist violence and the influence of conflict resolution theory through the conflicts in Northern Ireland and Turkey. In order to do so, it divides up the approaches of conflict resolution to analyse the variables of the research. Lederach's classification of conflict resolution is useful here as it provides a comprehensive conflict resolution theory.[39] Lederach divides conflict resolution theory into three levels of approach: top, middle-range and grassroots.[40]

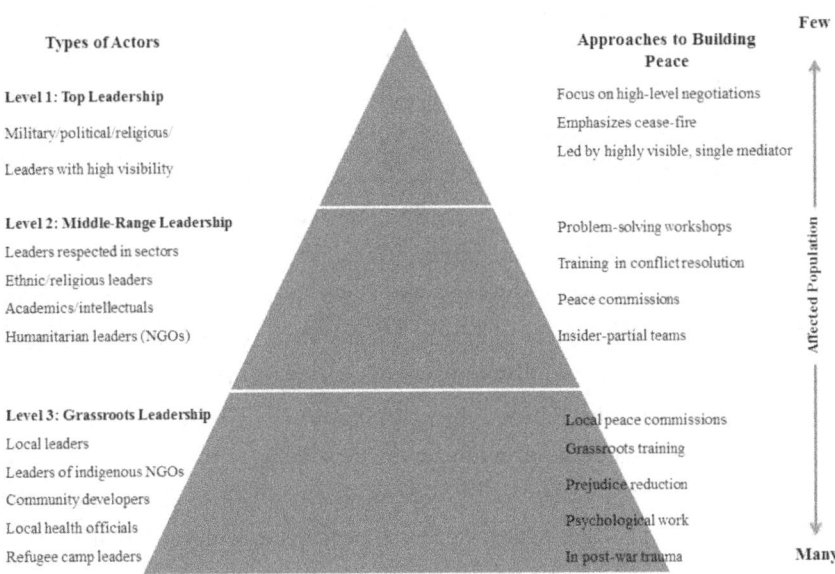

Figure 2.2 Actors and approaches to peacebuilding. Source: Lederach, *Building Peace*, p. 39.

As shown in Figure 2.2, conflict resolution approaches can be examined at three levels. On the one hand, each level has different approaches which identify horizontal effects within each phase. On the other hand, relationships between the levels demonstrate a vertical connection between actors and goals of these approaches. Thus, Lederach's classification of conflict resolution approaches allows a clear understanding of the relationships between the levels and purposes of each level.[41]

Coleman supports Lederach's classification and develops a relational design between conflict resolution approaches. Coleman argues that there are three different levels of conflict resolution, which demonstrate power relations in peace attempts: top-down, middle-out and bottom-up.[42] These approaches flow from the peak to the bottom or in the opposite direction. The top-down (the elite level) approaches apply command and control strategies that have a strong influence on organisations deployed by elite leaders and decision makers who are political parties and actors. Conversely, the bottom-up (the grassroots level) approaches address changes at the local stage, such as changes in personal attitudes or behaviours that tend to have considerable influence on democratic systems. However, these influences are more likely to take a long time to emerge. Finally, the middle-out (the middle-range level) approaches consist of the mid-level leaders and associations of social order, for example, community-based and non-governmental institutions.[43] This conflict resolution classification is supported by various scholars.[44] Yet, the subject of my book is peacemaking efforts during existing violence, which addresses the attempts of conflicting parties and independent third parties (mediators, intermediaries and other third parties) towards ending ethno-nationalist violence. The peacemaking efforts for ending a conflict between a sub-state armed group and the security forces of a state require investigating conflict resolution processes which identify a term between the beginning of non-violent, political resolution efforts and the sign of a political agreement between conflicting parties. More specifically, a conflict resolution process has two major stages: the pre-negotiation and negotiation stages (see Figure 2.3). While the negotiation stage consists of official negotiations and mediations by two conflicting parties and an independent actor as the elite level of conflict resolution processes, the pre-negotiation stage addresses secret and/or informal communications between the warring parties and intermediaries.[45] In addition, peace organisations as informal or semi-official peace efforts operate at the middle-range level

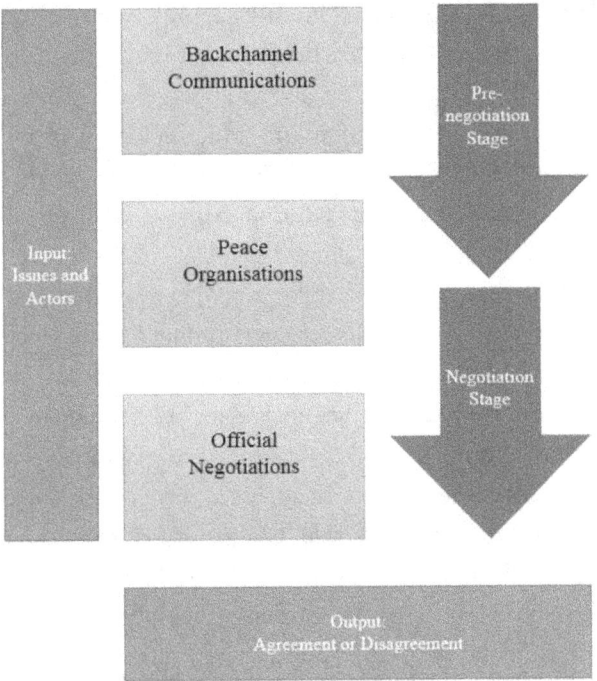

Figure 2.3   Conflict resolution processes.

of conflict resolution and affect decision-making mechanisms at the elite level by contributing to the negotiation stage, thus embodying a conflict resolution process together with official and unofficial communications. This book suggests a framework that divides conflict resolution processes into three: track-one (official efforts), track one-and-a-half (unofficial, secret conflict resolution initiatives) and track-two (informal or semi-official attempts by peace organisations) diplomacy.[46] Before explaining the relevance and dimensions of conflict resolution processes towards ending ethno-nationalist conflicts, it is necessary to provide an overview of the bottom, grassroots level of conflict resolution.

The Bottom-level (Grassroots) Approaches

The bottom-level approaches tend to avoid the national and extra-national politics of ethno-nationalist conflicts and concentrate on local and indigenous stages of a peace process.[47] The representatives of the grassroots level are local communities and members of national NGOs who are experts in local politics and have face-to-face experience with local actors in the government.[48]

Hancock classifies the bottom level into two approaches: structural and institutional.[49] While structural approaches focus on the existence of distinctive national identities and communities, and adopt large-scale political, social and economic reforms, behavioural approaches address cultural, psychological and relational forms of conflict resolution.[50] These approaches together aim to deal with the traumas which are revealed during the post-conflict process.[51]

The post-conflict stage exhibits interdependent relationships at the societal level. Although the meetings of local leaders with representatives of a society seem to include the demands of the society regarding a peace process, it mainly helps reach a resolution if an agreement exists. As this book investigates the peace settlement process, and whether the IRA and PKK groups tended to reach a peace agreement, armed struggles, ceasefires and negotiations are the main subjects of interest for the research. In addition, there is little evidence to illustrate that grassroots initiatives are able to bring armed conflicts to a halt and to play a critical role in peacemaking action. For example, as Byrne and Güller argue, the peace processes in Northern Ireland and Turkey have been conducted by the governments and are thus the product of political resolution attempts.[52] Undoubtedly, the societal level facilitates conflict resolution processes during existing violence. The outcomes of peacemaking efforts are utilised in the post-conflict stage. Particularly, disarmament, demobilisation and reintegration (DDR) come into effect at this stage through post-conflict reconstruction.[53] After the disarmament of sub-state armed groups, their members are demobilised and integrated into society, which is an integral part of peace.

The book does not ignore the role of the grassroots level in conflict resolution. Instead, as the grassroots level aids an understanding of the relationships between political elites and the war-affected communities, and within these communities, the strong relationships between these two levels help us comprehend the influence of political elites at the other levels. Hence, the interplay within the republican movement during the term of violence in Northern Ireland is assessed to understand their influence on peacemaking. Similarly, the interaction within the pro-Kurdish movement is also examined in the subsequent chapters. Although grassroots efforts address the importance of establishing a common culture of peace, the elite level leads to the grassroots level.[54] It is argued that the capability of powerful transformational politics and effective conflict resolution lead to grassroots citizen authorisation and participatory democracy.[55] Therefore, taking the elite level as the starting point of conflict resolution is the relevant approach to assess strategies towards ending terrorist violence.

The Relevance of the Elite Level of Conflict Resolution

The spectrum of activity in a peace process can be classified from violence to reconciliation. According to Kelman, resolution of a conflict begins with the pre-negotiation stage, which explores the right conditions for moving conflicting parties to the negotiating table.[56] It continues with the negotiation stage, which describes building momentum, defining options and re-evaluating the underlying reasons for a conflict. If a negotiation breaks down, trust and the sense of feasibility between conflicting parties are investigated in order to rebuild an effective negotiation environment. After an agreement is reached through negotiations, decisions are applied for contribution into a system; peacebuilding and reconciliation are performed in the post-negotiation stage.[57] However, this research focuses on the pre-negotiation and negotiation stages as it investigates the question of how ethno-nationalist conflicts can be brought to an end in a non-violent way.

The elite-level approaches address peace efforts that are mainly managed by negotiations between political leaders, and then expanded to society. This is also called the elite-oriented model of peacemaking, as the elite level is directed by political elites. The elite-oriented school of thought aims to reach an agreement first, and then to sell the idea to the members of society who would otherwise uphold the conflict environment.[58] While many scholars in the existing literature discuss the grassroots effects in conflict transformation,[59] other scholars favour official negotiations in order to reach a political settlement.[60] However, there is little interest in offering a comprehensive framework during a violent conflict to reach a political agreement.[61] Similarly, there is little attention on how elites and independent third parties can deal not only with negotiations, but also the desires of society.[62] Although the grassroots level is the responsibility of unofficial actors and international organisations, political elites are still responsible for leading peace processes. In this context, the role of unofficial actors in promoting or undermining conflict resolution towards peace is another question this book investigates, in addition to the role of political agents.

The book criticises the argument that peacemaking initiatives are only composed of negotiations. Although negotiations are one of the vital parts of conflict resolution approaches, there are some other approaches essential for making peace. This view is highlighted by some conflict resolution scholars who raise the importance of backchannel communications and P/CROs.[63] The elite level of conflict resolution is a key factor for both the top-level (horizontal) and inter-level (vertical) relations.

I must stress that not only the elite level, but also the middle-range and grassroots approaches are necessary for a peace process. However, the focal point of the book is the elite level and middle-range approaches, due to the particular focus on the pre-negotiation and negotiation stages towards a political agreement, but these do not ignore the influence of the civil-society approaches.

The elite-level (instrumental) and grassroots (identity) strategies are compared to develop an understanding of these levels. Table 2.1 indicates that while the instrumental strategies are driven by the political leaders of the society, the identity-related strategies are driven by citizens or the local leaders usually organising the society. However, the identity-based perspectives lack the power to promote large-scale reforms as they do not have long-term

Table 2.1 Conflict resolution approaches from top to bottom.

	Elite-level Approaches	Middle-range Approaches	Grassroots-level Approaches
Approaches	– Backchannel communications – Peace organisations – Official negotiations	– Problem-solving workshops – Training programmes – Semi-official peace commissions	– Structural approaches – Behavioural approaches
Stages	– Pre-negotiation – Negotiation	– Pre-negotiation – Negotiation	– Post-conflict – Post-negotiation
Actors	Officials – Political parties and actors – Independent third parties – Military and religious leaders	Unofficial – Ethnic/religious leaders – Academics/intellectuals – Humanitarian leaders (NGOs)	Civil-Society Leaders – Local leaders – Leaders of indigenous NGOs – Community developers
Perspective	– Interest-based – Resource-based	– Identity-based – Resource-based	– Identity-based – Resource-based

organisational support and sustainable citizen leadership.[64] The influence of grassroots initiatives is also controversial. Although they may include the desires of the society and represent them, there is little evidence to show that the grassroots level of conflict resolution can mitigate the level of a conflict by raising attention to local aspects and actors.[65] Similarly, even though elite-level approaches predominantly focus on making a peace agreement, they consider the requirement to transform identity issues for a peaceful resolution and focus on ethnic identity concerns through P/CROs.

There is a necessity to strengthen links between the elite and grassroots approaches to achieve peace by non-violent means.[66] Political elites close this gap through the power of a decision-making mechanism that considers the desires of the society. Van der Merwe supports this argument by underlining the requirement of cooperation between civil society (the grassroots level) and governments to achieve conflict resolution.[67] These two approaches should consider inter-generational memory, that is, the memories of the people who were exposed to violence and the next generation which will feel the effect of this trouble.[68] Yet, as this book focuses on a particular time frame, which is the pre-negotiation and negotiation stages, peacemaking initiatives are investigated by addressing conflict resolution efforts. The relationships between the elite level and other levels are looked at in terms of this specific time frame. For example, the Northern Irish peace process was initiated by political actors and reached intergovernmental agreements such as the Anglo-Irish Agreement (AIA) of 1985. These initiatives encouraged power-sharing agreements by declining the power of the central authority, transferring authority to the local level and encouraging local parties to join negotiations. The process also had exogenous motives through the US administration's involvement, originating at the elite level and later expanding to the local level.[69] Similarly, the Turkish government applied official conflict resolution methods to stop the violent campaign of the PKK through the 'democratic opening project'.[70]

Conflict resolution efforts initiated by political actors at the elite level, have received little attention as a transformative approach for resolving conflicts with sub-state armed groups. This book reveals the impact of the elite level on this transformation, such as the influence of traditional negotiations on peace between state officials and representatives of armed groups. However, this does not mean that the book focuses only on traditional modes of conflict resolution. Instead, it investigates transformational conflict resolution, which involves not only traditional resolution efforts but also political parties and actors' initiatives for transforming the root causes of conflicts for sustainable peace, and middle-range groups' initiatives at the elite level to contribute to peacemaking efforts.

To sum up, I argue that the elite level of conflict resolution does not consist only of negotiations between sub-state groups and government officials. Official negotiations (track-one) are one of the most crucial elements of the elite level of conflict resolution. However, they should be supported by back-channels (track one-and-a-half diplomacy) and peace organisations (track-two diplomacy), as they have influence over resolving disputes successfully.

Operationalising the Elite-level Approaches

The elite-level approaches describe resolution attempts of political leaders. As Lederach argues, these approaches to peacemaking focus on high-level negotiations, ceasefires and disarming under the leadership of a highly visible, single mediator.[71] This argument addresses the traditional meaning of a negotiation process. Conversely, the goals of the elite level in conflict resolution cannot only be limited to ceasefires. Political parties and actors who consolidate negotiations between conflicting parties, aim for not only a temporary solution, but also a permanent one, to reach sustainable peace in coordination with the other levels of conflict resolution.

Elite-level leaders are the highest representatives of governments and opposition parties. These leaders remain at the peak of all conflict resolution initiatives and the spokespersons for their constituencies.[72] Thus, in many cases, elite initiatives take the lead in conflict resolution efforts. For example, the long-standing Colombian peace process was dominated by the Colombian government and the FARC leadership.[73] Similarly, non-violent resolution attempts in the Northern Irish and Kurdish conflicts have been conducted by political leaders. However, the influence of the elite level in a peace settlement with the IRA and PKK groups is not precise. The influence will be explored in light of the sub-dimensions of this level. Although conflict resolution initiatives have been conducted in these cases, whether these approaches have been successful, have helped to solve these ethno-nationalist conflicts, or have had a negative effect on resolution attempts will be explored in the following chapters. As the elite level reflects the efforts of the political actors, sub-state armed groups, and independent endogenous and exogenous third parties, exploring the characteristics of this level can help to formulate this approach. First, as political parties and actors are generally visible, their behaviours and statements are easily followed by society; they get plenty of press coverage and air time.[74] It results in public pressure on them that affects conflict resolution methods in different ways. For example, while 'mediators' organised secret negotiations to prevent public reaction in the Turkish case, they arranged official meetings in the Northern Irish case, whose outcomes will be compared in the empirical chapters. Second, mediators are given significant and exclusive power by decision makers who represent conflicting parties.[75] For example, Senator George Mitchell's mediation in Northern Ireland and the British Secret Intelligence Service's (SIS) mediation in Turkey are remarkable attempts that will be investigated in the chapter on backchannel communications. Third, the elite-level approaches may produce a calendar which demonstrates a time frame and order of the peace process. The initial step of this order addresses the efforts for declaring a ceasefire between military and official leaders. The next step is a national transition which includes political leadership for establishing a new structure that provides democratic elections or decisions. It is a step-by-step process which involves an issue-oriented accomplishment dominated by top-level actors.[76] Although this feature seems systematic and puts a peace process in order, it can have an adverse effect, especially if the calendar puts pressure on conflicting sides.

Moreover, the accomplishments at the top level move through to the lower levels. Lederach argues that the highest possibility for achieving peace lies with the representative leaders of the disputing sides.[77] According to Lederach, 'If these leaders can agree, that sets the stage, the framework, and the environment for delivering the rest of society in the implementation of the agreement that will end the war.'[78] In fact, the aim of the elite level of conflict resolution is not only to make peace between political actors, but also to expand the agreements to the broader society. Political actors and independent third parties also ensure the success of a peace agreement by supporting its context in the post-conflict environment. This research does not ignore the functions which refer to post-violence processes, but focuses on the pre-negotiation and negotiation stages.

I argue that the elite-oriented school of thought has three approaches, which can be classified according to their motivations as focusing on secret talks, peace organisations and official negotiations.[79] Hence, I divide peacemaking efforts of conflict resolution processes into three approaches: backchannel communications, peace and conflict resolution organisations' initiatives, and official negotiations. As Wanis-St John argues, backchannels and official negotiations, when paired in sets, can form feedback effects that might be seen as a positive, deliberate consequence, since the product of backchannel initiatives leads to official negotiations.[80] Peace and conflict resolution organisations support these two approaches to reaching a political agreement. Each approach examines different aspects of top-leadership efforts and complements the other (Table 2.2). Together with this tripartite framework and its sub-components, conflict resolution efforts can produce a detailed understanding of violent conflicts.

Table 2.2 Conflict resolution processes for peacemaking.

Actors / Issues	Backchannel communications	Peace organisations	Official negotiations
Actors	Main armed protagonists, intermediaries	Unofficial groups, NGOs, disputing parties	Disputing parties, mediators
Process	Unofficial, secret	Informal, semi-official	Official
Stages	Pre-negotiation	Pre-negotiation, negotiation	Negotiation
Issues	Indirect, direct	From above, from below	Bilateral, multilateral
Tracks	Track 1.5	Track 2	Track 1

Backchannel Communications

The first aspect of conflict resolution processes for resolving intra-state conflicts is backchannel communication between the main armed protagonists, who are state officials and the leaders of sub-state armed groups. This research addresses the secret negotiations of these armed protagonists in an unofficial way through direct and indirect contact. It is vital to understand the relationships between these actors as they initiate a conflict resolution process and can lead to official negotiations. Although secret talks have been examined in the context of talking to terrorists, the existing literature has paid little attention to the role of backchannels as a part of conflict resolution processes.[81] The aims of this section are to close this gap by assessing their role as a pre-negotiation initiative and to produce a framework of theoretical assumptions for analysing the Northern Irish and Turkey's Kurdish peace processes. Before describing the major components and characteristics of backchannel communications, the chapter discusses them as the early stage of conflict resolution processes, describing them as high-level secret efforts and track one-and-a-half diplomatic initiatives.

Backchannel communications form the pre-negotiation stage, which embodies conflict resolution approaches prior to official negotiations.[82] This definition addresses a specific phase when there is a strong reaction against talking to terrorists; it is possible for conflicting parties to move gradually towards official negotiations through backchannel communications.[83] Therefore, even though it is possible to apply these secret initiatives in both the pre-negotiation and negotiation stages, they are mostly applied when it is difficult to achieve official negotiations between disputing parties.[84] As Kriesberg notes, secret meetings are a pre-negotiation activity which can later lead to official negotiations.[85]

Backchannel negotiations can be used together with other lower-level channels. Backchannel initiatives may operate 'in parallel with or replace acknowledged "front channels"[86] of negotiations and can be described as the "black markets" of negotiations, providing separate negotiation spaces where bargaining takes place in the shadows'.[87] These separate spaces enable third parties to make use of covert negotiations to prevent any other states or groups spoiling these initiatives, unlike in the negotiation stage.[88] Although other lower-level front channels are part of the pre-negotiation stage, these channels are not a focus of this book as they do not play a critical role in peacemaking efforts. For example, the low-level diplomats Israeli Joel Singer and Palestinian Saeb Eraqat carried out a front-channel talk in Cairo in 1994, discussing an agenda for the next round of Israeli withdrawal from occupied territories and Palestinian elections, but this did not bring about any outcome.[89] These talks do not involve any decision makers and are limited to specific discussion topics instead of negotiating an agreement. Similarly, the Northern Irish and Turkey's Kurdish conflicts do not contain any effective front channel. In contrast, backchannel talks are described as secret meetings between high-ranking leaders of states (or conflicting parties) seeking to negotiate a settlement.[90] Backchannel communications between the US diplomat Henry Kissinger and North Vietnamese officials for negotiating a ceasefire in Vietnam in 1970 are a significant example of high-level secret talks.[91] As Pruitt indicates, there would be very few negotiations and thus very few agreements without backchannel talks.[92]

Track one-and-a-half diplomacy (track 1.5), coined by Nan, describes the nature of backchannel communications as unofficial interactions between official representatives of parties in a conflict that are facilitated by unofficial bodies.[93] These parties are governments and the leadership of terrorist groups in ethno-nationalist conflicts.[94] Track 1.5 diplomacy has key differences from track-one and track-two diplomacies. The major difference between track-one and track 1.5 diplomacy is that while track one diplomacy includes official third parties, track 1.5 initiatives have unofficial groups or actors as third parties. The major difference between track 1.5 and track-two diplomacies is the parties involved in the process. The parties in track-two diplomacy are not official representatives of the conflicting parties, but those who have the capability to influence both the elite and grassroots levels. Whereas, in track 1.5 diplomacy, the parties are official representatives of the conflicting parties in the conflict resolution process.[95] Hence, as Mapendere puts it, track 1.5 is a 'hybrid diplomacy' as it is a cross-fertilisation of track-one and track-two.[96] Track 1.5 diplomacy bridges the gap between tracks one and two by providing both official actors from the conflicting parties and the strength of track-two actors to bring them together in an unofficial way.[97] Similar to the other tracks, track 1.5 diplomacy prioritises building trust between conflicting parties and intermediaries who build the communication channel or facilitate the talks between the warring parties during the pre-negotiation stage. It is argued that track 1.5 diplomacy enables the direct transfer of the outcome of these discussions to official negotiations.[98] When these discussions are successful, they are expected to be moved towards official negotiations. Thus, backchannel talks are significant for resolving violent conflicts.

Backchannel communications have two major forms, which are classified by their nature: direct or indirect talks.[99] Direct talks bring representatives of disputing parties together in a secret place.[100] For example, the British government and IRA, the Turkish government and PKK, the Israeli and Palestinian officials, and the South African government and Mandela's African National Congress (ANC) all achieved several meetings confidentially to discuss possible ways to resolve these conflicts.[101] While the Israeli–Palestinian peace process witnessed intensive secret talks in the early 1980s, the South African Minister of Justice, Jacobus Coetsee, built a secret channel to imprisoned Nelson Mandela and then the leaders of the ANC in 1985.[102] Indirect talks can be achieved through communication chains that involve one or more intermediaries.[103] For example, the indirect communication channel between the Israeli and Palestinian officials was set up by two university professors in the early 1990s.[104]

Both direct and indirect talks provide a suitable environment for the parties in a conflict to discuss their needs, aims, fears and demands without any pressure, as it is easy to keep them secret. They aim to reduce the uncertainty which prevents a move towards a political settlement.[105] However, compared to direct talks, indirect communications are easier to keep secret since it is more difficult to follow the communication chain. For instance, the indirect communication between American and Vietnamese officials in 1964 was not revealed, as American officials talked to British officials, which was followed by British officials' contacting an Eastern European country, which finally led to this country's talk with North Vietnamese authorities.[106] In this context, two conditions are essential to point out regarding the role of intermediaries in a backchannel negotiation which determines the success of secret initiatives. The first condition is about whether communication is through a single intermediary or more than one. Although it is common to have more than one intermediary in complicated issues, they might create 'messy, difficult and even chaotic' results if they are not well-organised.[107] For example, the Oslo negotiations between Israeli and Palestinian officials had more than one intermediary who acted with great leverage capacity.[108] However, having only a single intermediary can also create problems in a backchannel initiative as it is hard for a single intermediary to be sure about whether he is talking to the right people in a terrorist group when he builds the channel.[109]

The other condition is related to the role of third parties: whether they are weak or powerful third parties. While weak intermediaries transmit messages between disputing parties and coordinate concession making, powerful intermediaries help parties in a conflict to plan the process and recommend attainable solutions or put pressure on these parties to make an agreement on disputes.[110] The role of third parties determines the success of backchannel communications as they initiate the dialogue between warring parties, define the strength or looseness of the channel, dominate or facilitate the two groups' discussions and help to move gradually towards official negotiations. Chapter 4 will assess the consequences of weak and powerful intermediary efforts to understand whether they are useful for closing the gaps between states and sub-state armed groups in the Northern Irish and Turkey's Kurdish conflicts. The assumptions about the characteristics of backchannel initiatives help provide a framework for analysing their reflection in both conflicts.

The characteristics of backchannel communications are determined by the structure of terrorist groups and whether states are willing to negotiate a non-violent settlement. Pruitt defines two forces which push parties to negotiate with their opponents: 'a sense that the conflict is counterproductive or pressure from third parties, coupled with a belief that the other party is ready to make concessions' and 'contact with and dependence upon moderates'.[111] Here, the term 'moderate' refers to contingent groups who are willing to negotiate their intentions, contrary to absolute terrorists who are against any non-violent resolution.[112] Moloney argues that SF acted under real constraints and so the British and Irish governments might have had to make concessions to support their position within the republican movement.[113] These concessions and their outcomes will be examined in both peace processes. In addition, the IRA and PKK have been willing to discuss their goals with government officials, which illustrates them as moderate groups. These two important aspects need to be assessed in both conflicts together with features which determine the route of these initiatives.

As they are not formal, it is assumed that there is no cost of entry into these meetings.[114] The costs of entry into talks may result in conflicting parties being reluctant to attend official negotiations. Since official negotiations with an armed group can be seen as a governments' de facto granting of legitimacy for this group, backchannel negotiations are conducted secretly, which enables parties to maintain their opposition in public while they are seeking ways to de-escalate conflicts secretly.[115] It also helps governments to use the argument of 'we do not talk to terrorists'. It is argued that backchannels do not mean recognition of the other side of the conflict, which is one of the major concerns of states in negotiating with terrorists.[116] Chapter 4 will examine how the costs of entry to backchannels are determined for both conflicting parties. It also raises the question of whether there were any preconditions for achieving these events. As Wanis-St John argues, backchannel talks are suitable for conflicting parties to come together without facing each other's preconditions for official negotiations.[117] Despite this claim, the IRA Army Council and British government had one precondition each (the IRA's ceasefire and the government's release of political prisoners) to come together in the Whitelaw talks in 1972.[118] Similarly, both Prime Minister (PM) Süleyman Demirel and President Turgut Özal thought that a ceasefire was the precondition for initiating dialogue in 1993.[119] However, whether other backchannel initiatives had a prerequisite is an important question that will be investigated in Chapter 4.

The other feature of backchannels is that they can easily be concealed; it is difficult for outsiders to reveal these talks and also easier for both states and terrorist groups to deny that the communication chain exists.[120] In Northern Ireland, communications between the British government and republican movement were kept secret not only from the public and opposition parties but also from the security forces in the early 1970s.[121] Therefore, they excluded both internal and external spoilers from a peace process by keeping them in the dark.[122] Similarly, the secret talks in the Colombian peace process between the Santos administration and FARC successfully excluded opposition parties and groups who were against peace talks, and hence these talks were able to be maintained until they were made public in 2012.[123] However, if adversaries and spoilers reveal these communications, it can undermine the reliability of governments. This issue will be assessed in the Northern Ireland and Turkey cases to understand how adversaries might affect the success of backchannels. As they are disavowable, they have to rule out various audiences including the media and the wider public. This exclusion is a prerequisite for backchannel initiatives as the attention and reaction of the public can make it difficult to focus on the achievement of a negotiated settlement.[124] For example, when the Oslo talks were leaked to the Turkish media, it triggered a strong reaction and criticism against these talks.

Backchannel initiatives also provide flexibility by encouraging informality and frank discussions about the aims, fears and proposals of both sides for resolution, in contrast to public discussions.[125] The backchannels create an environment for conflicting parties to agree on their prerequisites, to discover common ground and to identify the root causes of conflicts through brainstorming.[126] The existing literature defines a few major features of backchannels, which provide this flexibility.[127] As mentioned before, these include a reduction in audience involvement by excluding scrutiny from society and the media. Public scrutiny may negatively affect talks; backchannels reduce the number of people who are involved in these talks.[128] This creates greater flexibility for conflicting parties to discuss their major demands and helps them focus on the root causes of the conflict. Without public involvement, it is not essential for backchannels to adhere to what the front-channels decide or discuss.[129] This point is significant as it illustrates that the outcome of these talks can lead directly to official negotiations. For example, the outcome of the secret Oslo talks between the National Intelligence Organisation (*Milli İstihbarat Teşkilatı*, henceforth MIT) of Turkey and the leadership of the PKK was reflected in the formal negotiations and regulations (namely, the Democratic Opening of 2013), which will be discussed in Chapters 4 and 6. Finally, increased informality is a result of the involvement of fewer people in backchannel negotiations, which produces a more interpersonal and less intergroup situation. It is important because people in secret talks begin to see each other as human beings, not simply as part of a rival group.[130] This is more likely to reduce issues related to trust, stereotyping and negative feelings about their opponents.[131]

Backchannel communications may not work as intended in all circumstances. Although the nature of these talks provides flexibility, lack of entry costs and deniability, these assumptions might not be achieved. Hence, they may not result in official negotiations due to a number of limitations. The credibility of backchannels is one of these limitations that affect their success. The credibility of actors who attend the secret talks is an important factor as it might create a problem in reaching a settlement due to the exclusion of major stakeholders. Therefore, whether these talks represent the main protagonists of the conflict is an important issue of this book. Even though the secrecy of these talks provides a suitable environment for negotiations, it can also create mistrust and prevent public support for political reforms.[132] When the secret talks between the Çiller administration and PKK were revealed, it created mistrust in the wider Turkish society, which caused the government to focus on hard-line policies.[133] Chapter 4 will assess the result of these initiatives to understand their role in bringing the Kurdish conflict to an end.

There are some other concerns related to the limitations of backchannels. If there is no unity among terrorist groups concerning who will represent the group, it might create a problem regarding the applicability of any decisions reached. However, this concern can be eliminated if government officials or intermediaries insist that the groups appoint a valid representative.[134] Whether such situations occurred in the backchannel communications in the Northern Irish and Kurdish conflicts is an important question to be discussed. Even though a valid representative is appointed to secret talks, the main armed protagonists may find it difficult to understand the other party's desire for a solution as the talks are carried out secretly and thus it is difficult to commit to them without knowing whether they comply with the agreed points for a political settlement.[135]

Initiatives by Peace and Conflict Resolution Organisations (P/CROs)

The term P/CROs describes non-governmental organisations (NGOs) who are involved in a conflict resolution process to broker a political settlement. This research investigates P/CROs' initiatives in relation to their role in facilitating, promoting or preventing conflict resolution efforts towards peace.[136] There has been increasing interest in the efforts of non-governmental peace organisations towards ending ethno-nationalist conflicts.[137] Although peace groups have operated in many conflicts since the end of WWII, as Taylor notes, a focus on conflict resolution and peacemaking has been noticed through the proactive peace efforts of South African P/CROs such as the Institute for a Democratic Alternative for South Africa and the Centre for Intergroup Studies.[138] Although there is some literature on the role of peace groups at the societal level as peacebuilding and social movement organisations, there is little focus on their role in making political agreements during existing violence.[139] This section aims to close this gap in our knowledge by providing a framework for understanding P/CROs' role in conflict resolution processes in Northern Ireland and Turkey. It investigates the relevance of conflict resolution theory for analysing peace organisations, the role of P/CROs as middle-range groups, and track-two diplomacy as an unofficial interaction concept for assessing P/CROs.

The existing literature on peace groups assesses them within four major theoretical areas: organisational theories, social movements, third sector, and conflict resolution and peacemaking studies.[140] The studies which aim to assess peace groups as organisational bodies describe the endogenous and exogenous characteristics of these bodies, whose main focus is organisation-environment relations, as the determinant of organisational behaviour.[141] These characteristics include: responsibilities regarding decision-making mechanisms in the organisation; a set of rules that define the administrating motivations for the members; and the operational goals of the organisation.[142] However, this book does not assess peace groups' organisational entities.

Social movement theories are frequently applied to research which analyses non-institutionalised collective events.[143] The existing social movement literature suggests three analytical forms for social movements. While the 'political opportunity structures' describe how the groups escalate or de-escalate the political environment regarding the role of state and political elites, 'mobilising structures' define the capacity of social movement groups.[144] Lastly, 'framing' examines social movement organisations that aim to mobilise potential supporters and to demobilise potential antagonists.[145] However, these theories hold little interest in these organisations as peacemaking efforts.[146] Similarly, the theories which analyse peace organisations as the third, voluntary or non-profit sector intend to understand where these groups operate and how these groups provide support regarding funding and personnel. Although these features are significant in defining the survival of P/CROs, they mostly focus on their relationship with the state actors and the notion of civil society in the context of NGOs.[147] In contrast, this book aims to understand P/CROs' role in facilitating, encouraging or obstructing peacemaking efforts during an existing conflict instead of a sector analysis for understanding their voluntary structure or funding conditions.

Conflict resolution and peacemaking studies describe the substance, characteristics and philosophy of P/CROs in contrast to other theories. Peace and conflict studies scholars argue that conflicts are not usually isolated, but are connected to other issues in accordance with endogenous or exogenous causes of the conflict.[148] These issues define the characteristics of P/CROs, which choose their strategies to promote peace and the resolution of conflict. P/CROs are influenced by peacemaking and conflict resolution studies as peacemaking addresses peace efforts to seek resolutions or de-escalation of conflicts.[149] This influence helps frame conflict resolution organisations' interests and how they frame the conflict in which they operate. For example, while many of the P/CROs focus on social justice in South Africa, they concentrate on mutual recognition of the rights of both nations in the Israeli–Palestinian conflict.[150] They also aim to facilitate a successful negotiation process through the use of a peaceful language and cultural symbols that bring conflicting parties closer to each other, which underlines the importance of trust and mutual respect.[151] Regarding the use of a peaceful language, Women in Black in Serbia built a network against violence by advocating human rights. However, their focus on feminism and commemoration of the Serbian victims limited their role in peacekeeping.[152] These aims reveal a significant concept in the conflict resolution and peacemaking literature: readiness, which describes a characteristic of one party of a conflict reflecting the attitude of its top leadership to prepare for conciliatory solutions.[153] P/CROs can play a critical role in encouraging parties for readiness to negotiate by developing bridges between parties and between the elite and societal levels of conflict resolution, through independent bodies such as the Peace People in Northern Ireland and the Wise People Committee in Turkey.[154] Therefore, they act as middle-range actors between these two levels during conflict resolution processes.

The 'middle-range' approach is a term coined by Lederach and Kelman and has been used to refer to peace attempts of unofficial groups and actors that encourage, promote and facilitate a non-violent resolution.[155] These groups have mostly been reviewed as important actors in extending the impact of political efforts to society.[156] Although the leaders of this level are generally known by the formal authorities, the position of the middle-level leaders is not necessarily controlled by political elites. Similarly, as the nature of their work does not depend on publicity and/or visibility, they have flexibility to move or act without any permission from top-level leaders. The middle-range actors are connected with various people in positions of power affiliated with the conflict.[157] Middle-range approaches can take a number of forms, such as problem-solving workshops,[158] training in conflict resolution, consultative and conciliation meetings, and cooperation to develop and produce other types of conflict resolution methods consistent with local norms and culture during the pre-negotiation and negotiation stages.[159]

Problem-solving workshops as a process-oriented approach bring participants together who have knowledge about the issue but who cannot be top-level initiators. These are informal discussions which make interactive conversations possible without any prejudices.[160] For example, problem-solving workshops between two Israeli academics and Palestinian Liberation Organisation (PLO) members were successful as they were converted to formal negotiations at a later stage.[161] Training programmes differ from problem-solving workshops as these programmes provide training facilities to increase awareness by educating people about de-escalation of a conflict. Their aim is to motivate internal factors such as developing the skills of participants and adapting different discussion topics into the conflict.[162] Also, peace organisations contribute to peace processes by encouraging conflicting parties to join peace talks, influencing public opinion towards peace, and through cross-community events to oppose armed struggle.[163] However, academic conferences, training programmes and workshops, such as the academic workshops held in Cyprus, Kashmir, Northern Ireland and the Israeli–Palestinian conflicts, are not the focus of my research, since such workshops have little influence in ending a violent conflict.[164]

This research differentiates between these three activities according to their scale. While problem-solving workshops organised by academics and training programmes are micro-scale aims, as they focus on small-group activities, macro-scale aims are to encourage conflicting parties engaging in a political process as opposed to armed struggle, promoting peace at both the elite and societal levels, and suggesting possible ways for resolution, which are the topics of this research.[165] The groups with macro-scale aims assist political parties and actors towards sustainable peace by providing a strong link between elite and grassroots efforts, accessing the members of both levels and rebuilding trust.[166]

The middle-range approaches of conflict resolution explore ethno-nationalist conflicts in a wider context, providing a close link between the effectiveness of peace institutions and the decisions of political elites. Hancock states that these organisations help reduce individual actors' autonomous role in facilitating conflict resolution processes.[167] Since political elites' personalities influence decision-making, reducing their role may foster a suitable environment to reach a peace agreement. As both the Northern Irish and Turkey's Kurdish conflicts have ethnic and nationalist origins, decreasing the role of political elites' personalities illustrates the importance of the P/CROs' role.

Track-two diplomacy, as defined by Montville is 'an unofficial, informal interaction between members of adversary groups or nations that aims to develop strategies, influence public opinion, and organise human and material resources in ways that might help resolve their conflict', but it is not a substitution 'for official, "track-one" government-to-government or leader-to-leader relationships'.[168] Instead, track-two diplomacy is intended to bridge or complement official negotiations.[169] Track-two activities supplement an official negotiation process by producing inputs at each stage of a conflict resolution process into the decision-making mechanism and thoughts of policy makers and the society.[170] P/CROs produce inputs by insisting upon and encouraging changes that originated in the attitudes, approaches and thoughts of the political parties and actors during the pre-negotiation and negotiation stages.[171] They also enable unofficial discussions between non-state actors, those who are 'close enough to the centre of power to have some sort of influence over decision makers, political elites and/or public opinion'.[172]

Track-two activities can influence public opinion by reducing the sense of victimhood of both sides, 'rehumanising' the figures of opponents and providing incentives, institutional support and persistence of the political and psychological process, which constitutes the route of the track-two approach to assist official negotiations.[173] The Israeli–Palestinian and Cyprus peace processes witnessed several track-two initiatives to help political leaders manage these conflicts, which were organised by academics, journalists and other intellectuals.[174] The Dartmouth Conference of 1960 is a successful example of track-two dialogue where US and Soviet citizens came together to improve the US–Soviet relationship.[175]

Track-two diplomacy can serve as a forum to bring together different aspects of a conflict and connect with a wider section of society that demonstrates some expertise regarding this aim.[176] The British–Irish Association (BIA) is a clear example of track-two efforts as it organised annual conferences each year from 1972, which hosted eminent people in public settings in the UK and Republic of Ireland. The conferences were organised with invitations from the Association 'to discuss in private urgent, controversial and often sensitive political, social and economic issues'.[177] The confidentiality and informality of these forums make a deeper conversation and exchange of views possible compared to events that are more public. Chapter 5 will analyse the impact of these forums in peacemaking initiatives.

This book recommends that track-two diplomacy is vital for a conflict resolution process for three reasons. First, traditional negotiation and mediation processes focus on resolving resource-based issues, for example, territorial and power-sharing issues and distribution of economic facilities. In contrast, identity and survival issues, and fears of the opponents can only be undertaken by focusing on human relationships, eliminating prejudices and encouraging a reciprocal understanding in line with the constructivist school of thought.[178] Second, the experience of threats in ethno-nationalist conflicts is a dominant factor, effective at the societal level. The traditional negotiation process alone cannot transform this threat which permeates the society.[179] Last, a conflict consists of both objective and subjective factors, which together intensify and escalate the situation; for instance, the perception of the opponent with deepening mistrust and dehumanisation.[180] The Neemrana Process of 1991 is another significant example organised between Indian and Pakistani academics, and former military officials and diplomats to discuss the conflict in Kashmir.[181] Although the Indian and Pakistani governments did not attend this initiative, the influential elites from both sides who attended the conferences built a sustainable link with both governments and presented their policy papers to the two governments.[182] Official negotiations are not sufficient to cover these issues. Therefore, it is essential to engage in track-two dialogue through P/CROs' initiatives for confidence-building measures. Chapter 5 will assess whether P/CROs met with these assumptions in the Northern Irish and Turkey's Kurdish peace processes.

Track-two diplomacy aims to strengthen conflict resolution processes through a number of major ways. First, parties in a track-two dialogue are not restricted by political decision makers; hence, they are able to express their views freely.[183] Second, track-two agencies do not fear losing a constituency, as they represent the constituency. Third, track-two diplomacy encourages social, political and economic developments in conflict-affected societies through peace groups, which enable them to discuss how to reach a peace agreement.[184] Lastly, these initiatives are led by middle-range leaders who have direct contact with the decision-making mechanism.[185] Despite these strengths, the existing literature suggests that these initiatives also have some weaknesses: Mapendere argues that track-two diplomacy has a limited capacity to influence foreign policy and political structures due to the agencies' lack of political power, which makes them unaccountable to the public.[186] This assumption does not affect the question posed by this book as it aims to understand the role of peace groups as catalysts in the Northern Irish and Kurdish cases. However, this supposition is important to analyse as it might affect the influence of P/CROs at the societal level. Track-two diplomacy is also criticised because its initiatives can take too long to achieve their aims and they have limited influence in transforming a conflict from war to peace. This research addresses these groups and actors' roles with regard to whether they helped transform a violent conflict. The last major criticism is related to the power of these initiatives. It is argued that these peace organisations lack unity, which might be a result of talking to the 'wrong' people.[187] Chapter 5 will analyse these assumptions to understand their contribution to peace by looking at the strengths and weaknesses of track-two groups.

Official Negotiations

Official negotiations involve both supporters and opponents of a political resolution, and address the role played by parties and actors at both national and international levels.[188] This book examines this approach under the nature of negotiations and their role in transforming conflicts, the role of a third party as a mediator and the importance of 'ripeness'. Although ripeness is crucial in both the pre-negotiation and negotiation stages, there is no doubt that these aspects are more sensitive during negotiations.

After advancing the grounds for a peace settlement during the pre-negotiation stage, analysing the characteristics of a negotiation process becomes important. Negotiation has different classifications in distinctive fields.[189] It is identified as a useful tool for handling disputes, which describes not a single process or one discrete dispute; rather, it is a framework of relevant acts involving disputants, decisions and conditions.[190] Therefore, it needs a sustainable process to end a violent conflict. Fisher and Ury went further and developed a model called 'principled negotiation',[191] which focuses on interests and inventing choices for the mutual benefit of conflicting parties (rather than focusing on people in trouble), and insists on objective criteria to investigate resolutions. Applying the term 'mutual benefit' can have an impact on equality in a decision-making process.

Diplomacy is a crucial dimension of a negotiation process, and it remains the key point of peacemaking action despite the possible change in negotiation efforts from one condition to another. This describes 'track-one' diplomacy that defines problem solving efforts at the state level through official resolution attempts.[192] Although these diplomatic efforts do not provide an outcome for a political settlement, they can be seen as steps towards the final agreement. For instance, in Northern Ireland, almost all track-one initiatives had ended in failure until the GFA of 1998, such as the power-sharing assembly of 1974 and the AIA of 1985.[193] Similarly, the Kurdish peace process witnessed different track-one interventions through the Turkish government's negotiations with the pro-Kurdish movement, some of the outcomes of which were the Dolmabahçe Declaration and constitutional reforms such as the democratisation package.[194] According to Fisher, official (track-one) and informal (track-two) diplomatic interventions together provide a positive outcome through the complementarity of these conflict resolution efforts.[195] It can add a value to negotiations through expanding the agreed points to the grassroots level, which helps to reach sustainable peace in some cases, but not in others.[196] This provides an understanding of why some ethno-nationalist conflicts reach agreements (e.g. the Northern Irish conflict), while others do not (e.g. Turkey's Kurdish conflict).

Official negotiations can be achieved through either bilateral or multilateral resolution efforts to reach a political settlement. While bilateral conversations have a limited number of participants and no pressure (e.g. a deadline), multilateral negotiations are more comprehensive as they include all conflicting parties and third parties in official negotiations.[197] This book will use this classification as it helps to distinguish different political actors' influence on the negotiation stage. Multilateral negotiations describe the inclusiveness of official negotiations both at the national and international levels. The national level includes the parties in a conflict consisting of governments, political wings of sub-state armed groups and other political parties in a war-affected society, which embraces the greater majority of conflicting parties. In addition to these actors, the international level involves international mediation, to facilitate a peace process.[198] However, the inclusion of all disputing parties in political resolution attempts may not result in a successful outcome due to the intentions of the parties in negotiations. For example, the multilateral negotiations between the Greek and Turkish Cypriots in the Cyprus conflict, with the UN as international mediator, failed to establish an agreement and the parties remained locked in an adversarial frame due to the refusal of the political settlement by the Greek-Cypriot community.[199]

Ikle and Leites argue that 'governments often enter negotiations without being conscious of their minimum disposition and without making an effort to estimate the opponent's minimum disposition'.[200] This disposition and minimum will of conflicting sides are characterised in an intractable ethno-nationalist conflict, as the two sides in a conflict are assumed equal. There is a moral hazard when a party joins negotiations in bad faith, which suggests the will for confrontation in a negotiation.[201] Hence, although the timing of negotiations may be convenient, an unexpected situation can emerge, as one party does not join discussions with good will. Echoing Steadman, this hazard emerges when extremists involved in a conflict join discussions but are not interested in the arrangement and try to destroy negotiations; these parties are called 'spoilers'.[202] To prevent these spoilers' actions, it is necessary to apply an effective spoiler management policy,[203] with reciprocity between disputing sides to understand each other's demands for ending violent conflicts. Chapter 6 investigates these assumptions and the spoilers who aim to hinder a political resolution.

The negotiation process has two basic perspectives in addition to the functions and assumptions. The perspectives provide an understanding of conflict situations and possible drawbacks during peace negotiations. On the one hand, the relationship-based perspective underlines that a sustainable communication process can overcome the concerns related to 'trust' and 'reciprocal bargaining'. Although negotiators claim that they represent society, the masses might not agree with them if their demands are not being raised or reconciled during the meetings.[204] According to George Mitchell, the mediator of the official negotiations in Northern Ireland, the Ulster talks broke down as there was no trust between the parties.[205] Therefore, an *ad hoc* process was applied to break down the barriers, which provided an interaction between conflicting sides to allow them to understand each other's perceptions. As Pearson states,

> Previously implacable enemies can, given the right circumstances of exhaustion or stalemate, raise hopes by initial agreements or concessions and by forthcoming statements, as when hardened IRA and Unionist fighters apologised for past transgressions in 1997.[206]

On the other hand, the political-risk perspective highlights that the parties in a conflict will not be interested in joining negotiations unless they think that they can achieve their goals without an armed struggle. Besides, even if these groups sit at the negotiating table, they may experience problems in gaining the trust of the other.[207] This perspective gives prominence to 'costing' negotiations. The costs of negotiations and elite bargaining outcomes should be compared with the costs of armed conflict itself, along with future expected costs for an ethno-nationalist conflict. It is argued that if conflict pays, the parties in a civil conflict will not be willing to negotiate.[208] This book considers both perspectives throughout the analysis of the negotiations between government officials, and the IRA and PKK.

Official negotiations are not only utilised for bargaining or establishing a political agreement. Scholars of conflict resolution address the significance of transforming underlying reasons for a conflict in order to make peace.[209] This transformation refers to a 'positive peace',[210] to eliminate the major causes of a violent conflict, instead of 'negative peace', which describes a lack of violence only.[211] Official negotiations should play a role in this transformation. Conflict transformation has five major aspects to transform a violent conflict: structural, actor, issue, personal–group and context transformation.[212] Context transformation addresses social, regional and international contexts that determine the continuation of a conflict. Changes in a context can influence a conflict more than changes in parties or their relationships. A significant example of this transformation is the end of the Cold War, which resulted in unblocking protracted conflicts in Central America and Southern Africa.[213] These internationally fuelled local conflicts could not be resolved, unless the context of these conflicts changed.[214] The end of the Cold War changed the terms of the threat and so facilitated nonviolent resolutions. However, context transformation is not the topic of this book as the Northern Irish and Turkey's Kurdish conflicts have not been affected by this transformation since secret peace efforts are almost as old as these conflicts themselves.[215]

Structural transformation addresses the underlying reasons for a conflict; in particular, if a conflict originates from the relationships within conflicting parties, a structural change is crucial to resolve this conflict.[216] The power relationship within one side of the conflict might be decisive in defining their strategy. For example, dissociation (withdrawal from an unbalanced relationship) is a possible result that was an issue when Kosovar Albanians decided to boycott the Serbian elections and assembled a 'quasi-state' in the 1990s.[217] The power balance within a movement between dominant and weaker parties is another important issue, which was evident in the relationship between the pro-Kurdish parties and the PKK that determined the route of the ethno-nationalist conflict in Turkey for most of its history. Despite the willingness of the pro-Kurdish parties to achieve a negotiated settlement, the PKK was reluctant to pursue a non-violent resolution.[218] Chapter 6 investigates the influence of this transformation in both conflicts.

Actor transformation refers to the requirement for changes in the attitudes of conflicting parties and actors to bring a violent conflict to an end. This transformation focuses on transitions in the current direction, goals and thoughts of parties in a conflict.[219] While the purpose is to eliminate factors that are against making peace, this transformation might create division in conflicting parties, by producing more veto players. The result of efforts to change the thoughts of conflicting parties is significant to understanding the route of a conflict resolution process. For instance, the transformation in the thoughts of the pro-Kurdish side from only armed struggle to both armed and political struggle resulted in a division within the pro-Kurdish movement, which will be investigated in the subsequent chapters.

Issue transformation emerges in two ways. It can emerge due to a change in the positions of conflicting parties. It can also occur when the issues of concern lose their importance and neither conflicting party concentrates on these specific issues any more. When the issues lose their importance, new issues arise, which means that the previous issues are transformed.[220] Issue transformation played an important role in the Northern Irish and Kurdish conflicts through the choice between the armed campaign and political resolution. This choice is also related to trust and gain issues, and a dilemma between zero-sum and win-win approaches as explained in the previous section. By transforming these issues, conflict resolution theory aims to overcome realist theory's zero-sum approaches. As realist scholars argue that realism is the only means of thinking about an anarchical world, as well as issues relating to war, peace, tyranny and freedom between states over the control of resources, conflict resolution theory differs from this win-lose approach.[221]

Finally, personal–group transformation depends on the leadership of the main protagonists of a violent conflict. For example, leaders of sub-state armed groups can apply different strategies, including official or secret negotiations, to reach their ultimate goals.[222] The leaderships of the IRA and PKK have dominated the conflict on behalf of the republican and pro-Kurdish movements, which resulted in determining their strategies according to armed groups instead of political actors. This book will examine whether their strategies helped or obstructed the peace processes.

The role of third parties is also important in the negotiation stage as there is a change in the formulation of mediation.[223] Unlike many of the conflicts in the past, the majority of conflicts in the 1990s were resolved by negotiated settlements and with the support of a third party.[224] The concept of mediation is illustrated as a dispute settlement, requiring an independent party's intervention as invited by the disputants.[225] Mediation has two conceptual approaches. As a social approach, mediation makes interpersonal, intergroup and international negotiations possible.[226] While the role of international actors was decisive in dealing with conflicts with a liberal perspective, it is not the only major factor in ending violent conflicts. It is in line with the liberal view, as liberals believe that one party in a conflict situation can choose to deal with other parties, and thus cooperation is possible through international institutions that aid the flow of information between them.[227] For example, establishing negotiation protocols can lead to reaching a political settlement by considering distinctive relationships, such as inter-negotiator and mediator-negotiator relationships.[228] This approach will be assessed to understand ethno-nationalist conflicts and their resolution attempts in terms of identifying problems, composing requirements of negotiation procedures and informing negotiators to clarify the real issues. Mediation as a transformational approach is identified as a unique capability to transform people's perceptions by supporting them in their fight in difficult situations and to fill the gap that exists between people due to their differences during conflicts.[229] Related to its transformative capability, it embraces consensus and independent decision-making.[230] The role of mediator in leading resolution efforts or assisting disputing sides only determines the route of a peace process.

There are various aims for mediators to achieve resolution of conflicts with sub-state armed groups. For many scholars, the primary aim of the mediator is to reach an agreement between conflicting sides.²³¹ This goal can be achieved by offering an international perspective with no force or arbitrative rules.²³² The mediation of the US Senator George Mitchell in Northern Ireland and the British mediation in Turkey are significant examples that will be assessed in Chapter 6. For example, Mitchell did not concentrate on creating any coalition between political parties in Northern Ireland or establishing the credibility of these negotiations by pushing for a deadline.²³³ Instead, he focused on incorporating the major parties that represented the majority in the Northern Irish conflict into negotiations.²³⁴ The role of British intelligence agents during covert peacemaking efforts in the Kurdish conflict is also of note; the actors in the negotiation process were different (direct representatives of the PKK), but the role of the mediators was the same during the Oslo talks.²³⁵ These principles and the influence of the mediators are crucial to understanding the contribution of this concept to the conflict resolution process.

In this respect, how this influence is shaped between opponents can be questionable. Herein, the response of a mediator is not to only help one side of the conflict but to come up with a solution by mutual agreement.²³⁶ The International Contact Group's mediation in the Mindanao conflict played a complementary role in negotiations for more than fifteen years by mobilising international support for the peace process and providing the link between the conflicting parties through the reduction of trust issues.²³⁷ Yet, the response of mediation cannot be limited to organising relations between conflicting parties. The role of a mediator can begin with negotiations or during the pre-negotiation stage. It means that a mediator can take responsibility for bringing conflicting sides to the negotiating table. Alternatively, his/her responsibility can start with the beginning of negotiations if conflicting parties so desire.

The responsibilities of mediators also depend on their experiences, both in the selection of the mediator and the operation of the process.²³⁸ This research addresses the personality of a mediator. It is suggested that trust between people brings mediators to the foreground and the language of mediation has analytical importance.²³⁹ Even though these are essential issues, a lack of power balance between the two sides is still a matter of importance. Indeed, the stronger sides in a conflict may have difficulties in accepting a mediator.²⁴⁰

In this case, a mediator's responsibility is to preserve the balance between stronger and weaker parties.[241]

In relation to personality, the power of a mediator is also important. It is argued that when third parties offer a payment and/or deadlines or penalties, these conditions may not work for a negotiated settlement. In this case, these conditions may need mediators 'with muscle' who use leverage and coercion regarding promised rewards or threatened punishments.[242] If a third party has 'less muscle', it is more likely that it will move away from the conflict or act more weakly to resolve the conflict.[243] In this context, defining deadlines for each section of negotiations and encouraging conflicting parties to identify their fears and expectations may possibly increase the reliability of this process. The contradictions on the characteristics of a mediator are important for a negotiation process. Chapter 6 will explore this influence by examining the characteristics of the mediation in both chosen conflicts, their process of joining or organising negotiations, and their influence in bringing ethno-nationalist conflicts to an end.

There is an idea that certain times are better for beginning negotiations than others. These starting points address pre-negotiations, clandestine negotiations, negotiating to a settlement, acquiring endorsement, application and institutionalisation.[244] The framework of 'ripeness' can be used as a predictive tool. However, it is claimed that to demonstrate whether a specific time for negotiation is a ripe moment or not depends on whether a conflict has successfully been resolved.[245] A ripe moment shows the suitable time to de-escalate violence created by intractable terrorist groups. This moment has three conditions: a 'hurting stalemate', when the combatants should feel that it imposes unacceptable costs to all conflicting sides; the existence of valid interlocutors who are able to bring the majority of their followers to achieve a settlement; and a framework for an agreement for the basis for negotiations.[246] Mediators have to explore this moment for resolving conflicts successfully, since intervening in a conflict at a non-ripe time may be devastating (e.g. undermining trust or escalating the conflict); unripe moments cannot be changed to ripe moments even by skilful third parties.[247] It means that even though a mediator is powerful and has influence with conflicting parties, this may not be enough to successfully settle agreements, as other psychological and motivational factors are also crucial.[248] Identifying the moments to intervene is essential when analysing ethno-nationalist conflicts. The Northern Ireland and Turkey cases are suitable examples, as negotiations between state officials and representatives of sub-state groups have been interrupted several times.

Concluding Remarks

This chapter has given an overview of conflict resolution by describing the characteristics of three levels of approaches and their influence on resolution attempts. It has demonstrated the relevance of the elite level of conflict resolution processes through a comparison with grassroots initiatives. It has been stated that conflict resolution is convenient for understanding peace attempts during ethno-nationalist conflicts as it addresses the pre-negotiation and negotiation stages towards ending violence. To investigate political resolution efforts in both conflicts, this chapter has suggested a tripartite framework for the conflict resolution process: backchannel communications, peace organisations and official negotiations. This framework provides complementarity not only between track-one and track-two initiatives, but also expands this approach by including track 1.5 diplomacy. It brings together track-one, track 1.5 and track-two diplomacy for a successful conflict resolution process.

This chapter has argued that conflicts between states and sub-state armed groups should be mediated by national and/or international third parties. While this process involves secret and informal peace attempts at the pre-negotiation stage, it has official negotiations and mediation at the negotiation stage. The following chapters will analyse the roles of political parties, government officials, opposition leaders and independent third parties – forming the political interventions by the British and Turkish governments; political parties that represent the views of the IRA and PKK; and the P/CROs, which support de-escalating and resolving these conflicts.

Notes

1. Galtung, 'What Does Professionalization Mean in Peace Research?', p. 361.
2. Bercovitch *et al.*, *The SAGE Handbook of Conflict Resolution*, p. 1.
3. Babbitt and Hampson, 'Conflict Resolution as a Field of Inquiry', p. 46.
4. Ramsbotham *et al.*, *Contemporary Conflict Resolution*, p. 24.
5. Ibid. p. 31.
6. Ibid. p. 31.

7. Austin, 'Introduction', p. 10.
8. Kriesberg, 'The State of the Art in Conflict Transformation', p. 50.
9. Bendana, 'Conflict Resolution', pp. 69–70.
10. Ibid. pp. 69–70.
11. Bar-Siman-Tov, *From Conflict Resolution to Reconciliation*.
12. Bar-Siman-Tov, 'The Arab-Israeli Conflict'; Kuenne, 'Conflict Management in Mature Rivalry'; Lebow, 'Generating Learning and Conflict Management'; Nardin, 'Theories of Conflict Management'; Prei, 'Empathy in Conflict Management'; Stein, 'A Common Aversion to War'.
13. Gartner and Bercovitch, 'Overcoming Obstacles to Peace'.
14. Ibid. p. 825.
15. Kriesberg, *Constructive Conflicts: From Escalation to Resolution*, p. 306.
16. Kelman, 'Reconciliation as Identity Change', pp. 112–19; Rouhana, 'Key Issues in Reconciliation', pp. 294–5.
17. Bercovitch *et al.*, 'Some Conceptual Issues and Empirical Trends in the Study of Successful Mediation in International Relations', pp. 7–17.
18. Lederach, *Building Peace*.
19. Carayannis *et al.*, *Practice Without Evidence*; Kelman, 'Interactive Problem Solving: An Approach to Conflict Resolution'.
20. Hancock, 'The Northern Irish Peace Process'.
21. Boulding, 'Organization and Conflict', p. 133; Boulding, *Conflict and Defense*.
22. Boulding, 'Is Peace Researchable?', p. 76; Boulding, 'Future Directions in Conflict and Peace Studies', p. 343.
23. Galtung, 'Violence, Peace, and Peace Research'; Galtung, 'Twenty-Five Years of Peace Research'.
24. Galtung, 'Institutionalized Conflict Resolution', p. 354; Galtung, *Peace by Peaceful Means*.
25. Burton, *Conflict & Communication*, p. 324; Burton, *World Society*, p. 159.
26. Burton, *Conflict: Human Needs Theory*; Burton, *Conflict: Resolution and Provention*.
27. Fisher, 'The Problem-Solving Workshop in Conflict Resolution'.
28. Fisher, *The Social Psychology of Intergroup and International Conflict Resolution*; Fisher, 'Developing the Field of Interactive Conflict Resolution', p. 124.
29. Ibid. p. 124; Fisher, *Interactive Conflict Resolution*.
30. Kelman, 'Interactive Problem-Solving', p. 200.
31. Kelman, 'Group Processes in the Resolution of International Conflicts', pp. 212–20.
32. Holsti, 'Resolving International Conflicts'; Holsti, *Peace and War*.
33. Wallensteen, *Understanding Conflict Resolution*, p. 153.

34. Boulding, 'Organization and Conflict'; Boulding, 'Is Peace Researchable?'; Burton, *Conflict & Communication*; Burton, *World Society*; Galtung, 'Institutionalized Conflict Resolution'; Galtung, 'Twenty-Five Years of Peace Research'.
35. Fisher, 'Third Party Consultation as a Method of Intergroup Conflict Resolution'; Kelman, 'The Interactive Problem-Solving Approach'.
36. Ikle, *How Nations Negotiate*.
37. Babbitt and Hampson, 'Conflict Resolution as a Field of Inquiry', p. 46.
38. Jackson, 'Constructivism and Conflict Resolution', p. 173.
39. Lederach, *Building Peace*.
40. The terminology of 'top-level, 'middle-out' and 'bottom-level' has been established by a number of frameworks for analysing peace processes. David Bloomfield's structural and cultural aspects (Bloomfield, *Peacemaking Strategies in Northern Ireland*), Lederach's sub-categories under the three-level classification (Lederach, *Building Peace*), Landon Hancock's examination from top-down to middle-out and bottom-up approaches (Hancock, 'The Northern Irish Peace Process') and Harold Saunders's from the official to civil society approaches (Saunders, 'Prenegotiation and Circum-Negotiation') are significant frameworks.
41. Lederach, *Building Peace*, p. 39.
42. Coleman, 'Conflict, Complexity, and Change'.
43. Ibid.
44. Gersick recommends a three-level approach (episodic, developmental and radical) which addresses top-down, middle-out and bottom-up approaches of conflict resolution (see Gersick, 'Revolutionary Change Theories'). This three-level approach is also recommended as bottom-up grassroots, middle-out influential and top-down structure (see Bennis *et al.*, *The Planning of Change*; Coleman, 'Paradigmatic Framing of Protracted, Intractable Conflict').
45. Kelman, 'Creating the Conditions for Israeli–Palestinian Negotiations'.
46. Kriesberg, *Constructive Conflicts*; Nan and Strimling, 'Coordination in Conflict Prevention, Conflict Resolution and Peacebuilding', pp. 1–6; Richter-Devroe, 'Gender, Culture, and Conflict Resolution in Palestine'.
47. Carayannis *et al.*, *Practice Without Evidence*.
48. Lederach, *Building Peace*, p. 43.
49. Hancock, 'The Northern Irish Peace Process'.
50. Ibid.
51. Lederach, *Building Peace*, p. 55.
52. Byrne, 'Consociational and Civic Society Approaches to Peacebuilding in Northern Ireland'; Güller, *Hükümet-PKK Görüşmeleri*.

53. Özerdem, 'Insurgency, Militias and DDR as Part of Security Sector Reconstruction in Iraq'.
54. Byrne, 'Consociational and Civic Society Approaches'; Kriesberg, *Constructive Conflicts*; Rothman, *Resolving Identity-Based Conflict*.
55. Byrne, 'Conflict Regulation or Conflict Resolution'; Love, *Peace Building through Reconciliation in Northern Ireland*; Ruane and Todd, *The Dynamics of Conflict in Northern Ireland*; Woolpert et al., *Transformational Politics*.
56. Kelman, 'Interactive Problem Solving: Changing Political Culture'.
57. Ibid. p. 394.
58. Hancock, 'The Northern Irish Peace Process', p. 205.
59. There are many scholars arguing about the dominance of grassroots initiatives. For example, Sapio and Zamperini focus on bottom-up procedures rather than top-down settings (see 'Peace Psychology, Theory and Practice'). Similarly, Doob and Foltz underline the influence of the grassroots level in the Northern Ireland conflict through their experiments with grassroots leaders (see 'The Impact of a Workshop upon Grassroots Leaders in Belfast'). Likewise, O'Dowd and McCall examine the grassroots level as the significant factor of a resolution effort (see 'Escaping the Cage of Ethno-National Conflict in Northern Ireland?').
60. Druckman, 'Dimensions of International Negotiations'; Guelke, 'Negotiations and Peace Processes'.
61. Lederach, *Building Peace*.
62. Ibid.; Hancock, 'The Northern Irish Peace Process'.
63. Cochrane, 'Unsung Heroes or Muddle-Headed Peaceniks?'; Gidron *et al.*, *Mobilizing for Peace*; Pruitt, 'Negotiation with Terrorists'; Wanis-St John, 'Back-Channel Negotiation'.
64. Potapchuk, 'Building Sustainable Community Politics', p. 56.
65. Carayannis *et al.*, *Practice Without Evidence*, p. 17.
66. Ibid. p. 17.
67. Van der Merwe, *The South African Truth and Reconciliation Commission*.
68. Ibid.
69. Pearson, 'Dimensions of Conflict Resolution in Ethnopolitical Disputes', p. 277.
70. Keyman, 'Çözüm Süreci, Müzakere, Güven ve Demokrasi'.
71. Lederach, *Building Peace*, p. 39.
72. Ibid. p. 38.
73. Angelo, 'The Colombian Peace Process', p. 135.
74. Lederach, *Building Peace*, p. 38.
75. Ibid. p. 40.

76. Ibid. p. 45.
77. Ibid. p.45.
78. Ibid. p. 45.
79. Ibid. p. 45; Kriesberg, *International Conflict Resolution*.
80. Wanis-St John, 'Back-Channel Negotiation'.
81. Ibid.; Kriesberg, *International Conflict Resolution*; Pruitt, 'Negotiation with Terrorists'; Rubin, *Dynamics of Third Party Intervention*.
82. Pruitt, 'Back-channel Communication'.
83. Pruitt, 'Escalation, Readiness for Negotiation'; Spector, 'Negotiating with Villains Revisited'.
84. Pruitt, 'Back-channel Communication'.
85. Kriesberg, *International Conflict Resolution*, p. 123.
86. The term 'front channels' means open discussions between lower-ranking diplomats which are unofficial talks and can be undertaken at any time prior to official negotiations (Wanis-St John, 'Back-Channel Negotiation').
87. Ibid. p. 120.
88. Rubin, *Dynamics of Third Party Intervention*.
89. Savir, *The Process*.
90. Zartman and Berman, *The Practical Negotiator*.
91. Sebenius and Kogan, 'Henry Kissinger's Negotiation Campaign'.
92. Pruitt, 'Negotiation with Terrorists'.
93. Nan, 'Track I Diplomacy'; Nan, 'Track One-and-a-Half Diplomacy'.
94. Mapendere, 'Track One and a Half Diplomacy and the Complementarity of Tracks'.
95. Aall, 'What do NGOs Bring to Peacemaking?'; Agha *et al.*, *Track 2 Diplomacy*; Schiff, '"Quasi Track-One" Diplomacy', p. 95.
96. Mapendere, 'Track One and a Half Diplomacy', p. 70.
97. Ibid. p. 77.
98. Nan, 'Track One and a Half Diplomacy'.
99. Pruitt, 'Negotiation with Terrorists'.
100. Ibid. p. 381.
101. Ben-Porat, 'Introduction'; Demir, 'Debates over "Negotiations in Oslo"'; Lieberfeld, 'Evaluating the Contributions of Track-two Diplomacy'.
102. Wanis-St John, 'Back-Channel Negotiation'.
103. Pruitt, 'Negotiation with Terrorists', p. 382.
104. Pruitt, 'Back-channel Communication', p. 39.
105. Wanis-St John, 'Back-Channel Negotiation'.

106. Gardner and Gittinger, 'The Search for Peace in Vietnam'; Kraslow and Loory, *The Secret Search for Peace in Vietnam*.
107. Crocker *et al.*, 'Introduction'.
108. Kriesberg, 'Coordinating Intermediary Peace Efforts'.
109. Pruitt, 'Negotiation with Terrorists', p. 385.
110. Ibid. p. 385.
111. Ibid. p. 384.
112. Hayes *et al.*, 'Negotiating the Non-negotiable'.
113. Moloney, *A Secret History of the IRA*.
114. Wanis-St John, 'Back-Channel Negotiation', pp. 125–6.
115. Ibid. pp. 125–6.
116. Pruitt, 'Negotiation with Terrorists'.
117. Wanis-St John, 'Back-Channel Negotiation'.
118. Smith and Neumann, 'Motorman's Long Journey'.
119. Çandar, *Mezopotamya Ekspresi*.
120. Pruitt, 'Escalation, Readiness for Negotiation'.
121. Wanis-St John, 'Back-Channel Negotiation'.
122. Pruitt, 'Negotiation Between Organizations'; Pruitt, 'Negotiation with Terrorists'.
123. Renwick, 'FARC, ELN'.
124. Dochartaigh, 'Together in the Middle', p. 768.
125. Pruitt, 'Negotiation with Terrorists'; Pruitt, 'Back-channel Communication', p. 41.
126. Pruitt, 'Back-channel Communication', p. 41.
127. Ibid. p. 41; Crocker *et al.*, 'Introduction'; Wanis-St John, 'Back Channel Diplomacy – Implications'; Wanis-St John, 'Back-Channel Negotiation'.
128. Wanis-St John, 'Back Channel Diplomacy – Implications'; Pruitt, 'Back-channel Communication'.
129. Ikle, *How Nations Negotiate*, p. 134.
130. Brown, *Group Processes*.
131. Bartoli, 'Mediating Peace in Mozambique'.
132. Pruitt, 'Back-channel Communication'; Wanis-St John, 'Back-Channel Negotiation'.
133. Çandar, *Mezopotamya Ekspresi*.
134. Pruitt, 'Negotiation with Terrorists'.
135. Wanis-St John, 'Back-Channel Negotiation'.
136. Byrne, 'Consociational and Civic Society Approaches'.
137. Fisher and Keashly, 'Third Party Consultation'; Kelman, 'Interactive Problem Solving: Changing Political Culture'; Lederach, *Building Peace*.
138. Taylor, 'South Africa', pp. 71–6.

139. Cochrane, 'Unsung Heroes or Muddle-Headed Peaceniks?'; Donnelly-Cox *et al.*, 'Conceptualizing the Third Sector in Ireland'; Gidron *et al.*, *Mobilizing for Peace*; Giugni *et al.*, *How Social Movements Matter*; Slim and Saunders, 'The Inter-Tajik Dialogue'.
140. Gidron and Katz, 'The International Study of Peace/Conflict Resolution Organizations'.
141. Ibid. p. 7.
142. Benson, 'The Interorganizational Network as a Political Economy'; Gidron and Katz, 'The International Study of Peace/Conflict Resolution Organizations'; Hasenfeld, *Human Services as Complex Organizations*; Pfeffer and Salancik, *The External Control of Organizations*.
143. McAdam *et al.*, *Comparative Perspectives on Social Movements*.
144. Eisinger, 'The Conditions of Protest Behavior in American Cities'; Gidron *et al.*, *Mobilizing for Peace*.
145. Snow and Benford, 'Ideology, Frame Resonance, and Participant Mobilization'.
146. Gidron and Katz, 'The International Study of Peace/Conflict Resolution Organizations'; McAdam *et al.*, *Comparative Perspectives on Social Movements*.
147. Cochrane, 'Peace and Conflict Resolution Organisations in Northern Ireland'.
148. Fitzduff, 'Managing Community Relations and Conflict'; Gidron and Katz, 'The International Study of Peace/Conflict Resolution Organizations'; Kriesberg, *International Conflict Resolution*.
149. Galtung, *Peace by Peaceful Means*; Gidron and Katz, 'The International Study of Peace/Conflict Resolution Organizations', p. 19.
150. Ibid. p. 19.
151. Mayer, 'The Dynamics of Power in Mediation and Negotiation'.
152. Stephenson and Zanotti, *Peacebuilding through Community-based NGOs*.
153. Pruitt, 'Readiness Theory and the Northern Ireland Conflict', p. 1525.
154. Knox and Hughes, 'Crossing the Divide'; Oran, *'Ben Ege'de Akilken . . .'*
155. Kelman, 'Interactive Problem Solving: An Approach to Conflict Resolution'; Lederach, *Building Peace*.
156. Lederach, *Building Peace*.
157. Ibid. pp. 41–2.
158. Problem-solving workshops are called 'interactive problem-solving' (Kelman, 'Interactive Problem Solving: Changing Political Culture'), 'third-party consultation' (Fisher, 'The Problem-Solving Workshop in Conflict Resolution') or 'creative problem-solving' (Carnevale and Pruitt, 'Negotiation and Mediation'; Pruitt and Rubin, *Social Conflict*; Sanson and Bretherton, 'Conflict Resolution') in the existing literature.

159. Babbitt and Hampson, 'Conflict Resolution as a Field of Inquiry', p. 51.
160. Coleman, 'Conflict, Complexity, and Change'; Fisher, *Interactive Conflict Resolution*; Richmond, 'Rethinking Conflict Resolution'.
161. Egeland, 'The Oslo Accord'.
162. Lederach, *Preparing for Peace*; Schultz, 'Conflict Resolution Training Programs'.
163. Gidron and Katz, 'The International Study of Peace/Conflict Resolution Organizations'.
164. Azar, 'Protracted Social Conflicts and Second Track Diplomacy'; Burton, *Conflict & Communication*; Fisher, 'The Problem-Solving Workshop in Conflict Resolution'; Fisher, 'Assessing the Contingency Model'; Kaye, 'Track Two Diplomacy and Regional Security in the Middle East'; Kaye, *Talking to the Enemy*; Kelman, 'The Political Psychology of the Israeli-Palestinian Conflict'.
165. Fisher, 'The Problem-Solving Workshop in Conflict Resolution'; Kelman, 'Interactive Problem Solving: Changing Political Culture'; Gidron and Katz, 'The International Study of Peace/Conflict Resolution Organizations'; Sanson and Bretherton, 'Conflict Resolution'.
166. Knox and Quirk, *Peace Building in Northern Ireland*.
167. Hancock, 'The Northern Irish Peace Process', p. 214.
168. Montville, 'The Arrow and the Olive Branch', p. 162.
169. Nan, 'Complementarity and Coordination of Conflict Resolution Efforts'.
170. Kelman, 'Informal Mediation by the Scholar/Practitioner', p. 68.
171. Azar, 'Protracted Social Conflicts and Second Track Diplomacy'; Burton, *Resolving Deep-Rooted Conflict*; Fisher, 'Assessing the Contingency Model'; Kelman, 'Interactive Problem Solving as a Tool for Second Track Diplomacy'; Schiff, '"Quasi Track-One" Diplomacy'.
172. Kaufman, 'Sharing the Experience of Citizens' Diplomacy'.
173. Davidson and Montville, 'Foreign Policy according to Freud', pp. 145–9; McDonald and Bendahmane, *Conflict Resolution*; Montville, 'The Arrow and the Olive Branch', pp. 163–4.
174. Kelman, 'The Political Psychology of the Israeli–Palestinian Conflict'; van der Merwe, *The South African Truth and Reconciliation Commission*.
175. McDonald, 'Further Exploration of Track Two Diplomacy'; Montville, 'Track Two Diplomacy'.
176. Arthur, 'Negotiating the Northern Ireland Problem', p. 415.
177. Ibid. p. 415.
178. Kelman, 'Social-psychological Dimensions of International Conflict'; Rothman, *Resolving Identity-Based Conflict*.
179. Saunders, 'Prenegotiation and Circum-Negotiation'.

180. Fisher and Keashly, 'Third Party Consultation'.
181. Kaye, *Talking to the Enemy*, p. 78.
182. Waslekar, *Track-two Diplomacy in South Asia*, p. 5.
183. Mapendere, 'Track One and a Half Diplomacy', pp. 68–9.
184. Chigas, 'Negotiating Intractable Conflicts', p. 128.
185. Lederach, *Building Peace*; Mapendere, 'Track One and a Half Diplomacy'; Sanders, *Inside the IRA*.
186. Mapendere, 'Track One and a Half Diplomacy'.
187. Kaye, *Talking to the Enemy*, p. 25.
188. Hancock, 'The Northern Irish Peace Process', p. 214.
189. The term 'negotiation' has been used in various disciplines for many years such as in the area of psychology (Chertkoff and Conley, 'Opening Offer and Frequency of Concessions'; Carnevale and Pruitt, 'Negotiation and Mediation'). It has also been used for ending conflicts since the beginning of states' relations (Jackson, 'Successful Negotiation in International Violent Conflict', p. 324.).
190. Ibid. p. 324.
191. Fisher and Ury, *Getting to Yes*.
192. Richmond, 'Rethinking Conflict Resolution'.
193. Fitzduff, *Beyond Violence*, pp. 122–4.
194. Al Jazeera, 'Ortak Açıklamanın Tam Metni'; UPOS, *Demokratikleşme Paketi* [Democratisation Package].
195. Fisher, 'Coordination between Track Two and Track One Diplomacy'.
196. Hartzell, 'Explaining the Stability of Negotiated Settlements'; Licklider, 'The Consequences of Negotiated Settlements in Civil Wars'.
197. Druckman, 'Dimensions of International Negotiations'; Druckman *et al.*, 'A Test of Ikle's Typology'.
198. Hancock, 'The Northern Irish Peace Process'; Hopmann, 'Two Paradigms of Negotiation'.
199. Sözen and Özersay, 'The Annan Plan'.
200. Ikle and Leites, 'Political Negotiation', p. 22.
201. Babbitt and Hampson, 'Conflict Resolution as a Field of Inquiry', p. 49.
202. Stedman, 'Spoiler Problems in the Peace Process.
203. Ibid.; Babbitt and Hampson, 'Conflict Resolution as a Field of Inquiry'.
204. Byrne, 'Consociational and Civic Society Approaches'; Pearson, 'Dimensions of Conflict Resolution', p. 279.
205. Mitchell, *Making Peace*.
206. Pearson, 'Dimensions of Conflict Resolution', p. 277.
207. Babbitt and Hampson, 'Conflict Resolution as a Field of Inquiry', p. 52.

208. Zartman, *Ripe for Resolution*; Zartman and Touval, 'International Mediation'.
209. Boulding, *Conflict and Defense*; Burton, *Resolving Deep-Rooted Conflict*; Galtung, 'Institutionalized Conflict Resolution'; Ramsbotham *et al.*, *Contemporary Conflict Resolution*.
210. In order to achieve a positive peace, social justice, sustainable development, the equal distribution of resources, prevention of structural, social and cultural violence, women rights and a secular administration are vital (Özerdem and Özerdem, 'Introduction', p. 28).
211. Galtung, *Peace by Peaceful Means*.
212. Vayrynen, 'To Settle or to Transform?'; Ramsbotham *et al.*, *Contemporary Conflict Resolution*.
213. Ramsbotham *et al.*, *Contemporary Conflict Resolution*.
214. Holsti, *The State, War, and the State of War*.
215. Güller, *Hükümet-PKK Görüşmeleri*; Taylor, *Provos*.
216. Ramsbotham *et al.*, *Contemporary Conflict Resolution*.
217. Ibid. p. 176.
218. Birand and Yalçın, *The Özal*.
219. Cunningham, 'Veto Players and Civil War Duration', p. 875.
220. Vayrynen, 'To Settle or to Transform?'
221. Keohane, *Neorealism and Its Critics*; Morgenthau, 'Six Principles of Political Realism'; Waltz, *Man, the State and War*.
222. Curle, 'New Challenges for Citizen Peacemaking'.
223. Mediation is one of the oldest settings of conflict resolution (see Wall *et al.*, 'Mediation', p. 370). It has been used by various disciplines such as sociology, psychology and politics. According to a general definition, mediation means to assist two or more conflicting sides by third parties who have no authority to rule and influence anyone or settle an outcome (Kressel and Pruitt, *Mediation Research*). As Read and Michelson note, the concept of mediation should be thought of within the broader perspectives of political acts (Read and Michelson, 'Mediating the Mediation Debate', p. 742).
224. Babbitt, 'The Evolution of International Conflict Resolution'; Babbitt and Hampson, 'Conflict Resolution as a Field of Inquiry'. The focus of this study is official mediation, which refers to solving disputes between and within states. In this context, mediation is applied to many cases such as Japan (Cortazzi, *The Japanese Achievement*), Malaysia (Ott, 'Mediation as a Method of Conflict Resolution'), China (Diamant, 'Conflict and Conflict Resolution in China'), Israel (Abu-Nimer, 'Conflict Resolution Approaches'), Korea (Sohn and Wall, 'Community Mediation in South-Korea'), Poland (Olszanska *et al.*, 'Do

Peaceful Conflict Management Methods Pose Problems') and Norway (Polley, 'Intervention and Cultural Context').
225. Bercovitch and Langley, 'The Nature of the Dispute'; Koch, *War and Peace in Jalemo*.
226. Wall, 'Mediation: An Analysis'; Wall *et al.*, 'Mediation'.
227. Doyle, 'Liberalism and World Politics'.
228. Wall, 'Mediation: An Analysis', pp. 171–5.
229. Bush and Folger, *The Promise of Mediation*, p. 2.
230. Bercovitch, 'International Mediation' (1991), p. 4.
231. Kochan and Jick, 'The Public Sector Mediation Process'; Pruitt, 'Indirect Communication'; Wall, 'Mediation: A Current Review'; Warren, 'Mediation and Fact Finding'.
232. Bercovitch, 'International Mediation' (1991), p. 3.
233. Mitchell, *Making Peace*.
234. Ibid.
235. Demir, 'Debates over "Negotiations in Oslo"'.
236. Jeong, *Peace and Conflict Studies*, p. 180.
237. Herbolzheimer and Leslie, *Innovation in Mediation Support*.
238. Bercovitch *et al.*, 'Some Conceptual Issues and Empirical Trends', pp. 9–10; Bercovitch and Houston, 'Influence of Mediator Characteristics', p. 303.
239. Felstiner, 'Influences of Social Organization', pp. 74–83; Greenhouse, 'Mediation', p. 111.
240. Modelski, 'International Settlement', p. 131.
241. Assefa, *Mediation of Civil Wars*, p. 19.
242. Fisher and Keashly, 'The Potential Complementarity'; Touval and Zartman, *International Mediation*.
243. Babbitt and Hampson, 'Conflict Resolution as a Field of Enquiry'; Zartman, *Ripe for Resolution*; Zartman and Touval, 'International Mediation'.
244. Guelke, 'Negotiations and Peace Processes', p. 56; Kriesberg, 'Timing and the Initiation of De-Escalation Moves'.
245. O'Kane, 'When Can Conflicts Be Resolved?', p. 281.
246. O'Duffy, 'British and Irish Conflict Regulation'; Zartman, *Elusive Peace*.
247. Haas, *Conflicts Unending*, p. 139; Hancock, 'To Act or Wait'.
248. Coleman, 'Redefining Ripeness'; Kleiboer, 'Ripeness of Conflict'; Pruitt, 'Ripeness Theory and the Oslo Talks'.

3

CONFLICT AND PEACE: HISTORY OF THE NORTHERN IRISH AND TURKEY'S KURDISH PEACE PROCESSES

The strongest is never strong enough to be always the master, unless he transforms strength into right and obedience into duty. Hence the right of the strongest, which, though to all seeming meant ironically, is really laid down as a fundamental principle.[1]

The conflicts in Northern Ireland and Turkey have had political, ethnic and nationalist angles for decades. While the roots of these positions are more than a century old, the modern conflicts have taken place in the late 1960s in Northern Ireland and in 1984 in Turkey. The intractable conflicts in Turkey and Northern Ireland encompass not only ethno-nationalist claims, territorial issues, armed campaigns and political attempts to resolve these disputes, but also similar conflict resolution processes. Both the IRA and PKK primarily aim to change the political systems of the UK and Turkey, respectively, by using terrorism as a tool to reach their political goals.[2] These primary purposes address their separatist aspirations. While the primary aim of the IRA was the reunification of Ireland, the PKK's goal has differed from an independent Kurdish state to autonomy and democratic confederalism.[3] These goals have determined the evolution of these conflicts and peace processes, which are assessed in this chapter.

Having developed a conceptual and theoretical framework in order to assess the two ethno-nationalist conflicts in question, it is significant to identify the history and evolution of both peace processes. When assessing the background of both cases, the aim was to distinguish the issues and actors who played a role in the evolution of these conflicts and conflict resolution processes. Based on the assumptions of conflict resolution theory, different types of events will be demonstrated, namely, backchannel communications, initiatives of peace and conflict resolution organisations, and official negotiations. While secret talks were achieved between the conflicting parties and intermediaries, official negotiations were carried out between the major political parties, governments and political representatives of the PKK and IRA. Therefore, the events organised by other agents, for instance within the nationalist and unionist communities aiming to create pan-nationalist and pan-unionist approaches, were not examined as their influence was deemed to be limited in both peace processes. For example, although Father Alec Reid is an important figure in the Northern Irish peace process, his influence in peacemaking efforts was limited because he focused on bringing nationalist groups together and creating a shared democratic approach.[4] The perceptions and initiatives of representatives of disputing parties, namely the pro-Kurdish and republican movements on the one hand, and the Turkish and British governments on the other, determined the position of the conflicting communities. The intensity of these conflicts and major issues also affected deep-rooted ethnic concerns of the nationalist community in Northern Ireland and the Kurdish community in Turkey. The reaction of society and reluctance of conflicting parties negatively affected the progress in both peace processes when the level of violence increased. Also, even though peacebuilding efforts were influential at the grassroots level, their influence on peacemaking initiatives was limited (as discussed in the section 'Conflict Resolution Approaches for Understanding Non-Violent Resolution' in Chapter 2), so they are not discussed in this chapter. In addition, insufficient or no progress in political resolution efforts resulted in the application of an armed campaign. The correlation between armed and political struggle determined the success of the peace processes. These complicated relationships are discussed in both conflicts by focusing on their effects on de-escalating conflict, ending violence and establishing a political agreement.

The chapter is split into three parts. First, it describes the background of the Northern Irish conflict from the beginning of 'the Troubles' in 1969, to the final accord termed the Good Friday Agreement (GFA) of 1998. It focuses on non-violent, political resolution attempts at peacemaking – including ceasefires, secret and official talks between the British government and republican movement, political parties in Northern Ireland and the representatives of the IRA – and the armed conflict between the security forces and IRA. Second, it defines the background of the Kurdish conflict from 1984 to 2015 when the peace process collapsed and violence returned. In contrast to the Northern Irish conflict, the Kurdish conflict remains active.[5] Both cases are divided into three periods determined by the intensity of the conflicts, and the frequency and efficiency of resolution attempts. Although both cases followed a similar path from escalation to de-escalation together with official negotiations, the final periods were decisive in bringing these conflicts to an end. Therefore, the section on Turkey explains the evolution of the peace efforts since there is no agreement to end the conflict. The last section compares the evolution in both cases and the balance between armed and political struggle.

The Background of the Northern Ireland Peace Process

The Anglo-Irish War between 1919 and 1921 caused a division in Ireland. The Anglo-Irish Treaty of 1921 gave twenty-six of the thirty-two counties of Ireland independence (the Republic of Ireland). The other six counties remained in the UK as their majority preferred union with Britain. After the division, Northern Ireland was ruled from the parliament at Stormont. From this time, the violence in Northern Ireland increased with the armed campaign of the PIRA.[6] The violent conflict continued until the signing of the GFA. The IRA did not hesitate to kill people and damage financial interests to end British authority, according to the rules set out in their Green Book.[7] According to Catholic nationalists, the main cause of the conflict was the involvement of the British state.[8] In addition, Article 2 and 3 of the Irish constitution deepened the political violence as it maintained the constitutional claim of the Republic to Ireland as a whole by addressing citizens of Ireland and the Irish nation. The opposition between the nationalist and unionist sides extended the degree of violence. By the 1960s, inspired by the Civil Rights Movement in the US, Catholics founded the Civil Rights Association in 1967 for social justice and reform. The main concern of the Catholic community was to get some sort of equality under the law. Although protests began with sit-ins and media engagement, they were transformed into an uprising due to Catholic and Protestant extremists. The situation became worse, which led to civil violence known as 'the Troubles'.[9] As conflict resolution efforts were predominantly initiated after the beginning of the Troubles, the appearance of this term is the starting point of this research.

This section is divided into three periods. The first period defines the origins of the modern Troubles and escalation of the conflict. It also describes the backchannel communications between the main armed protagonists, which were the first step of the peace process. The second period illustrates a change in the characteristic of the conflict when political initiatives were on the rise as opposed to counter-terrorism measures. The last period witnessed comprehensive official negotiations and mediation that resulted in the signing of the final agreement.

Inception: From Emergence to Escalation (1969–76)

The modern Troubles in Northern Ireland began in the late 1960s; subsequently, almost 3,500 people died as a result of the political violence until 1999.[10] Both Catholic and Protestant communities resorted to violence during the civil rights marches in the mid-1960s. Before the Troubles, on the one hand, the IRA's view was 'when the guns came out and people were being shot, the only ones who could protect [the Catholic community] were the IRA'.[11] Similarly, Catholics assumed that the IRA could defend them against the British troops before the intervention of the British Army.[12] On the other hand, the British government arranged meetings through the Joint Intelligence Committee (JIC)[13] to prevent clashes between Catholic marchers and Protestant communities.[14] In addition, it established the Community Relations Commission (CRC) to bring Catholic and Protestant communities together to encourage societal development.[15] The British government's initiatives to close the gap between these two communities were not sufficient to prevent the Troubles. Repression of peaceful protest may cause an angry reaction in society leading to protesters applying violent methods. The peaceful protesters were faced with repression from the British security forces. This repressive politics resulted in radicalisation of the communities.[16]

During 1969, the degree of violence in Northern Ireland rapidly increased. The reason for this was the conflict between the Catholic and Protestant communities over the future of Northern Ireland: reunification of the whole island or Northern Ireland remaining part of the UK. The British government followed two paths to end the Troubles. The first path was the military intervention by British forces in Northern Ireland. The intervention created different expectations on the unionist and nationalist sides. The Catholic community initially welcomed the influx of British troops as it halted Protestant attacks on their communities. However, the IRA militants blamed their leaders for their inability to secure Catholics and Republicans in Northern Ireland. The division of the IRA stemmed from a group within them which sought to participate in the political system instead of organising violent attacks. This dissidence led to division. While the new group named itself the Provisional IRA (PIRA or Provos), the original IRA became known as the Official IRA. The dissidence emerged over decisions on maintaining the armed campaign or appealing to the political struggle. While the Official IRA was inclined to declare a ceasefire in 1972, the PIRA (henceforth IRA) began its campaign of violence in 1970.[17] The violent campaign was dominated by bombings, murders and violent protests. Though marches had been brought to an end by the British Army in 1969,[18] the intensity of the violence did not decline because the British government and the republicans both believed that they could defeat their respective enemies through military means.

In the early 1970s, SF began to play an active role in the Northern Ireland conflict. It unveiled its manifesto, called *Eire Nua*, written by David O'Connell (vice president of the IRA) and Ruairi O'Bradaigh (president of the IRA), in January 1971. This was its first attempt to consider a unified Irish people and their independence. It has been argued that the manifesto was not a successful strategy, as it overlooked the importance of Ulster Unionism – a greater obstacle to its goals than the British authorities. However, it is an important document since it illustrates the IRA's negotiation aim.[19] Nevertheless, this intention did not stop clashes between unionists and nationalists, which coincided with the unionist government of Northern Ireland's introduction of an 'internment policy'. Although the Northern Irish government introduced this policy for ending violence, it was used for the internment of IRA suspects without trial in 1971.[20] Despite the opposition of the Catholic community, 2,447 people were arrested between 9 August 1971 and 14 February 1972, and this triggered republican violence.[21] British troops interfered in a march on 30 January 1972, a day that became known as 'Bloody Sunday' as thirteen unarmed Catholics were killed by British soldiers.[22] This disaster caused the situation to deteriorate: an Official IRA bombing caused three civilian deaths; this was followed by an attempt to assassinate a Northern Ireland government minister. Immediately after this attack, British PM Edward Heath introduced the 'direct rule' system from Westminster. Although the purpose was to bring violence to an end, it dramatically increased following the events of 21 July 1972, known as 'Bloody Friday', when nine civilians were killed and 130 people injured by IRA bombings across Belfast. The direct rule of the British government was maintained until the GFA.[23] In addition, the IRA set off nineteen car bombs in Belfast. The British troops intervened in the situation, aiming to crush the IRA and to break the link with its supporters. 'Operation Motorman', launched on 31 July 1972, was organised to intervene in the 'No Go' areas of Londonderry[24] and Belfast, ending the presence of IRA safe houses. According to Craig, Frank Steele (the SIS Officer and UK Representative, henceforth UKREP) had allowed the IRA to be warned in advance, so the risk to their lives was minimised.[25] Although Steele's notification helped to make further talks possible for both sides, it was his personal intention instead of the government's decision. Arguably, the reason for applying traditional military tactics was to destroy the enemy, which resulted in dividing the Catholic and Protestant communities. This was because of the belief that the British Army was defending the Protestant community and the IRA was fighting to defend the rights of the Catholic community.

The second path that the British government followed was political intervention. In August 1969, the British government was suspicious of the Stormont administration and hence, established the Office of the UKREP to monitor Stormont's reform programme. This was led by three officials: Oliver Wright, Ronnie Burroughs and Howard Smith. The purpose of the UKREP was to gather political intelligence and to begin discussions about Northern Ireland politics. Wright obtained information by creating a 'backdoor' channel to talk to the IRA, which was completely separate from the Northern Ireland government sources.[26] These backchannels were initiated by intermediaries during the period of intense violence of the early Troubles. For example, Tom Caldwell, a former British Army officer, was the first intermediary between the

British government and IRA whose personal intention helped the declaration of the first IRA ceasefire in March 1972, which will be discussed in Chapter 4. Why the British resorted to secret communication channels is a crucial question. Arguably, it can be said that it was because of the difficulty of initiating official talks due to the ongoing violence. While the aim of the British government in attending these talks was to stop the violence, potential outcry in society against talking to the enemy was the reason for confidentiality.

Even though 1972 was the bloodiest year of the Troubles, two of the three peace attempts were launched after Bloody Sunday, even if the hope for peace tended to be low. For example, secret talks between the leaders of the IRA and British officials brought about the IRA's temporary ceasefire on 26 June 1972 by calling for a 'bi-lateral truce'. In the end, the IRA declared a temporary ceasefire on 26 June 1972. Nevertheless, the ceasefire ended after only thirteen days. The critical point was that even though the ceasefire ended, both sides were willing to talk to each other, which was evident when the IRA senior members (led by Joe Cahill) talked again with the Labour Party leader Harold Wilson in the UK.[27] This backchannel was the first direct contact between the republicans and the British. This contact was a chance for understanding the desires of both sides for peace, the result of which will be examined through the pre-negotiation stage of this conflict resolution process. However, it was not the only secret meeting. Mumford notes that the most meaningful secret talks were the meetings between six senior IRA members and the Northern Ireland Secretary William Whitelaw, on 7 July 1972.[28] According to the IRA, this event was organised as a test to determine whether the British officials were ready for negotiations.[29] Hence, it was clear that the IRA attended these meetings seeking to understand the willingness of the British government to negotiate. This event was of paramount importance in the pre-negotiation stage. There were various disagreements during the Whitelaw talks, such as the question of self-determination and the British Army's withdrawal from Northern Ireland. Therefore, the ceasefire lasted just two days. However, PM Edward Heath defended talking with the IRA.[30] Despite the lack of an agreement, the secret talks were vital as they were the commencing stage of a conflict resolution process. The important point is that the IRA called 1972 its 'year of victory' for their military campaign, but did not interrupt communications with British officials.[31] Therefore, it is said that there was a shift in the policy of SF and the IRA to develop a political strategy other than the armed struggle and short-term military tactics.[32] However, the increased militarisation of both sides resulted in the failure of this political strategy, leading the IRA to a long-war strategy in the late 1970s.[33] The aim of this strategy was to worsen the economic problems in the region.[34] Chapters 4 and 6 will analyse the role of major political actors to establish, promote or maintain peace initiatives. Further, the decisive role of political elites in preventing and precluding the evolution of the process will be a significant factor for the analysis.

Another series of peace attempts were achieved by the Londonderry businessperson Brendan Duddy, who played an intermediary role between British officials and the IRA. The intermediary and messenger role of Duddy in 1974 and 1975 between MI6 (Military Intelligence Section 6, also known as the Secret Intelligence Service) and the Provisionals' Army Council helped extend the IRA ceasefire in 1975.[35] Duddy was also an intermediary between the MI6 officers Frank Steele and Michael Oatley (successor of Steele) and the IRA. These communications were significant as they strengthened the peace talks. For example, Steele played an important role in extending Laneside's[36] contacts further into war-affected communities in Northern Ireland thanks to Duddy's successful part as an intermediary. The underlying reason for building these communication channels are at the forefront of the peace process at the pre-negotiation stage, which was the intention of the intermediaries such as Brendan Duddy and Tom Caldwell. Chapter 4 will examine these secret initiatives with regard to the indirect communications in greater detail.

Finally, with the participation of Whitelaw, the Sunningdale Agreement was signed on 9 December 1973. At Sunningdale, the Irish government recognised Northern Ireland for the first time.[37] However, the Sunningdale Agreement collapsed in 1974 resulting in a change of the approach to talking to armed groups. James Allan of the Foreign and Commonwealth Office (FCO) and Michael Oatley followed a low-level discussion strategy and organised meetings with loyalists instead of republicans. As Craig notes, Allan and Oatley played an important role in talks by communicating with loyalist paramilitaries within the Ulster Workers' Council (UWC) before and after the UWC strike in relation to prisoners and community politics.[38] As these talks were achieved within the unionist bloc, their influence in changing the nature of the conflict and reducing the level of violence was limited. However, the British government maintained its standpoint on peaceful resolution despite the lack of significant success. The Feakle Talks were a cover story between the political wing of the republican movement and Sir Frank Cooper, the Permanent Secretary to the NIO in Stormont, and were mediated by Protestant clergymen that facilitated the IRA ceasefire in December 1974. Wilson and Merlyn Rees (the British Secretary of State for Northern Ireland) had personally met with the leaders of the IRA and negotiated a ceasefire.[39]

Secret talks between the representatives of the British government and the republican movement were not the only resolution attempts. Constitutional reforms were also applied to facilitate the peace process. For example, the White Paper published in March 1973 by the Callaghan government and entitled the 'Northern Ireland Constitutional Proposals', determined specific issues such as direct rule, ethnic divisions and civil violence since 1969. Although the White Paper was published through a majority of votes, there was strong opposition from the Ulster Unionist Party (UUP) and Ulster Unionist Council (UUC).[40] These constitutional changes did not contribute to progress, as a majority of the constitutional reforms were only put into action after the GFA. Thus, these efforts are not a major topic of this book.

Peace efforts were not only conducted by the armed protagonists in the 1970s. There were two other facilitators for organising peace talks. Firstly, peace groups played an important role in promoting and encouraging peace, such as the British–Irish Association (BIA), which facilitated peace by bringing the representatives of the British and Irish governments and the Northern Irish parties together in an unofficial environment. For example, the BIA's Oxford Conference of 1974 brought together Merlyn Rees, Garrett Fitzgerald (the Irish Minister for Foreign Affairs) and deputies from the Republic of Ireland in a space which created an informal and confidential atmosphere for exchanging views at a point when it was not possible to achieve formal negotiations.[41] Chapter 5 will assess the contribution of the BIA to the resolution efforts. Secondly, international actors were involved in the peace process. For example, the US's involvement in the process became visible during the late 1970s, when the Carter administration's soft power efforts and the

Irish-American civil society's political role began to influence the course of the conflict and helped shift the focus more onto conflict resolution efforts rather than 'hard power'.[42] The continuous peace efforts illustrate that the early stage of the Northern Irish peace process was dominated by backchannel communications. A common characteristic of all efforts to create a path towards peace is to arrange non-violent resolution efforts continuously.

Mitigation: From Escalation to De-escalation (1976–94)

The characteristics of the conflict began to change gradually in the second half of the 1970s, as the republican movement was increasingly aware of the importance of the political struggle. In 1976, the status of political prisoners was changed and they no longer had the same status as prisoners of war. At the same time, the violence remained; the IRA organised bomb attacks which killed eighteen British soldiers on 27 August 1979 in Warrenpoint. On the same day, Lord Mountbatten (the Queen's cousin), along with three other people, were killed by an IRA bomb in his boat.[43] The bombings affected the peace process, along with the protests of prisoners through a hunger strike. The first 'hunger strike' began in the Maze Prison on 27 October 1980 and was led by an IRA member, Brendan Hughes. After a short time, Bobby Sands took over the leadership from Hughes. As the British government did not recognise the strikes, Sands organised the second hunger strike in 1981. This act enabled Sands to be elected to a seat in Parliament, but he died on the sixty-sixth day of the strike.[44] Although these strikes helped increase the popularity of the IRA and SF, British PM Thatcher refused to step back. Thatcher's position was that of not treating terrorists differently from other prisoners.[45] After nine more prisoners died in the hunger strikes, families of other strikers accepted medical support. The prisoners, afterwards, declared an end to the strike on 3 October 1981 and Thatcher made concessions to their requests.[46] Although the hunger strikes were examined as a hard-line policy of the British government, this book reveals that there was a secret channel built by Brendan Duddy whose influence will be assessed in the next chapter.

The hunger strikes led to the formation of the 'New Ireland Forum' (NIF) in 1983, with the attendance of all major nationalist parties from both north and south. It was enabled by SF's policy change from rejecting any political initiatives to participating in elections. The reason for this policy change was the belief amongst republicans that it could be possible to reach their aim through political campaign, particularly following the success of resistance in the hunger strikes, which had resulted in the strikes' leader, Bobby Sands, being elected in the national election of 1981.[47] In addition, SF decided that outright rejection and using only military tactics were insufficient to achieve their aims, and so electoral participation was strategically chosen.[48] The NIF helped the parties to think of alternative ways to move forward beyond merely Irish unification, such as the rights and interests of Northern Ireland Catholics/nationalists.[49] The NIF also opened the way to an agreement, that was followed by Thatcher and Taoiseach[50] Charles Haughey's assignment of a commission to work on the future of the UK, Republic of Ireland and Northern Ireland. The commission's reports on the future of Northern Ireland had an influence on the later talks between the British and Irish governments. After discussions, the AIA of 1985 was signed with the declaration of Britain and Ireland on the possible change of Northern Ireland's status if only the majority demanded it. These meetings aimed to create an agreement between the two governments by highlighting the requirement of self-determination and the right of Irish people to decide their future. The agreement has paramount importance as it ended the unionist veto and included the Irish government in the conflict resolution process. The agreement also included marginal political organisations in the non-violent, political process for the subsequent peace attempts.[51] However, the agreement was opposed through mass protests by both republicans and unionists.[52]

During the mass protests and violence, high-level confidential talks were organised between the Social Democratic and Labour Party (SDLP; John Hume), which represented the majority of Catholics and always stood against violence, and SF (Gerry Adams), which is the political wing of the IRA and represented around one third of Catholics.[53] The negotiations continued for a long time and they were publicly known by late 1987. Despite the ongoing talks, the violence continued, including the IRA bombing in November 1987, which killed eleven people and wounded sixty-three, while thousands of people attended the memorial in the centre of Enniskillen on Remembrance Day.[54] The talks between Hume and Adams, called the 'Hume–Adams Principles', helped create the 'Downing Street Declaration' (DSD) as it determined the demands of Catholic nationalists. This attempt and other initiatives will be examined in Chapter 6 to understand the influence of political elites on reaching an agreement. During the same years, the British government organised a series of pre-negotiations with various constitutional parties in Northern Ireland that were known as 'talks about talks'. However, as Hauss states, these talks did not bring any success because the parties representing the paramilitary groups were not included.[55]

The DSD (the Joint Declaration) was signed between PM John Major and Taoiseach Albert Reynolds on 15 December 1993, affirming the right of self-determination for Northern Ireland citizens. It also affirmed that 'Northern Ireland would be transferred to the Republic of Ireland if the majority of the island's population favoured this move; and parties associated with paramilitaries could play a role with the governments in seeking a peaceful solution, if they renounced violence'.[56] On the one hand, the Declaration was an indicator of political dialogue, on the other, it needed the support of both nationalists and unionists. The recommendation of including the political wings of armed groups demonstrated the intention of the British government, but did not meet with approval from the republican movement due to their reluctance to renounce violence. Although there were several negotiation attempts and an effort made by Gerry Adams, he defended the primary importance of the armed campaign of the IRA: 'The tactic of armed struggle is of primary importance because it provides a vital cutting edge. Without it, the issue of Ireland would not even be an issue. So, in effect, the armed struggle becomes armed propaganda.'[57] In contrast, Richard McAuley from SF underlined the importance of electoral politics for resolving the Northern Ireland conflict during the early 1990s:

> We are not going to realise our full potential as long as the war is going on in the north and as long as SF is presented the way it is with regard to armed struggle and violence. I think that is a reality that perhaps we were not conscious or aware of back in the early 80s when we first got involved in electoral politics.[58]

These views demonstrated a shift between political and armed tactics, and were an indicator of using the ballot box in one hand and an Armalite in the other.

Settlement: From De-escalation to Agreement (1994–8)

By August 1994, the IRA declared a ceasefire in the hope that it would lead to an agreement. However, the loyalist paramilitary groups did not announce a ceasefire due to a lack of trust in the IRA's ceasefire. The Combined Loyalist Military Command eventually declared a ceasefire six weeks later. The peace environment lasted eighteen months until the IRA declared the end of the ceasefire in February 1996, blaming the British government for not stepping forward in negotiations. However, this had helped decrease the level of violence (Figure 3.1). Fortunately, the eighteen-month ceasefire helped improve the relationship between loyalists and republicans and led to the GFA.[59]

During the ceasefire, the international mediation of the US again played a part in the process through the Clinton administration's granting of a visa to Gerry Adams to attend a conference in 1994. Irish commentator Deaglen de Breadun perceived this moment as a fundamental change in US policy that had a great influence on advancing the peace process.[60] However, British diplomats were affronted by the granting of a visa to Adams, which caused a rupture in Anglo-American relations and caused Clinton–Major relations to become 'frosty'.[61] Fortunately, this confrontation did not bring the peace attempts to an end in Northern Ireland. In addition, the ceasefire of 1994 provided Adams with another visa in March 1995 to attend the St Patrick Day celebrations in the US for fundraising activities.[62] Additionally, the European Union (EU) conducted the Peace-I (1994–9) and Peace-II (2000–6) Programmes. While the Peace-I focused on paramilitary ceasefires,

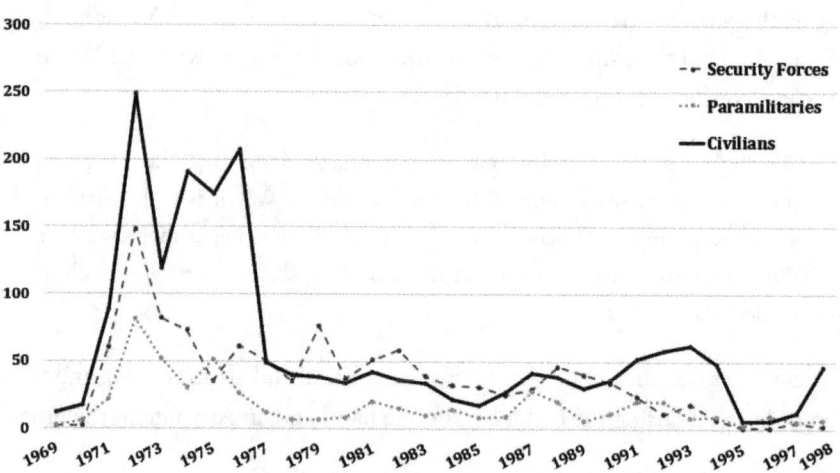

Figure 3.1 The casualties in Northern Ireland (1969–98). Source: data on conflict-related deaths were taken from McKittrick *et al.*, *Lost Lives* and Melaugh, 'Sutton Index of Deaths'.

the Peace-II emphasised the legacy of the conflict and proceeding negotiations in the post-violence period.[63] However, the major focus of these programmes was cross-border cooperation between the north and south of Ireland, and they were to complement political efforts at peacebuilding by implementing projects at the grassroots level.[64]

Inter-party talks were organised very intensively during the ceasefire. The aim of the British and Irish governments was to facilitate the progress, which was maintained with the British and Irish governments' announcement of 'A New Framework for Agreement' in February 1995. Actually, the Framework was not a blueprint for both sides, but it demonstrated a commitment including expectations of self-determination. The Framework recommended three strands for both communities: North/South structures (in Northern Ireland and the Republic of Ireland), East/West structures (in the Republic of Ireland and UK) and internal Northern Ireland structures.[65]

Official and high-level secret talks between the British government and SF were maintained during 1995. Nevertheless, there was no significant success in these negotiations. The end of the IRA's ceasefire in February 1996 interrupted the peace process. However, it was not a long-term interruption, since multilateral peace efforts coincided with the beginning of all-party meetings with the declaration of the Irish and British governments. The meetings were followed by a by-election in May 1996 to determine the parties to join the peace negotiations. Although SF polled 15.5 per cent of the vote, the party was not permitted to attend negotiations as republican violence remained and SF did not sign the Mitchell Principles of democracy and non-violence. There were six major principles that parties had to affirm:

a) To democratic and exclusively peaceful means of resolving political issues, b) to the total disarmament of all paramilitary organisations, c) to agree that such disarmament must be verifiable to the satisfaction of an independent commission, d) to renounce for themselves and to oppose any effort by others to use force, or threaten to use force, to influence the course or the outcome of all-party negotiations, e) to agree to abide by the terms of any agreement reached in all-party negotiations and to resort to democratic and exclusively peaceful methods it trying to alter any aspect of that out come with which they may disagree, and f) to urge that 'punishment' killings and beatings stop and to take effective, steps to prevent such actions.[66]

The Principles were the key element of negotiations, indicating an obligation to move forward politically. The former US senator George Mitchell suggested that all-party negotiations must declare their agreement to the principles for 'democratic and exclusively peaceful means of resolving political issues'.[67] The multi-party talks could not reach an agreement in the first year. In the UK general election of 1997, a Labour government was elected and this created a perception, particularly among nationalists, regarding a change of the British government's approach to Northern Ireland. The IRA therefore renewed the ceasefire and SF signed up to the Mitchell Principles. Therefore, it can be said that two expectations had primary importance in changing the perceptions of both sides: the prospect of the republicans regarding the British government to include SF in the official negotiations, and the expectation of the British government related to SF to force the IRA to accept disarmament. SF was then permitted to join the multi-party talks at Stormont – which resulted in the UUP and the Democratic Unionist Party (DUP) leaving the talks. Intensive negotiations took place for more than six months among the British and Irish governments and eight Northern Irish parties, resulting in the GFA (the Belfast Agreement).[68] The position of the British and Irish governments, the Northern Irish parties, and particularly SF, will be examined, and the reasons for preventing SF from joining negotiations, its results, and the shift in the policies of the British government and SF will be analysed in Chapter 6. Mitchell's focus on gathering political parties with different views on the future of Northern Ireland provided for the majority of Northern Irish people to be represented.[69] During the negotiations for the GFA, he strove to stick with the principles and deadlines, and this focus resulted in a successful agreement.

The multi-party negotiations provided a comprehensive approach and both the views of nationalist and unionist communities from north and south were discussed. The GFA was conducted by President Bill Clinton, PM Tony Blair, Senator Mitchell and Taoiseach Bertie Ahern and created a semi-autonomous government body in Northern Ireland.[70] It brought various changes. First, the GFA recognised ethno-national cultures, accepting nationalists as nationalists not simply as Catholics.[71] Second, the GFA declared that Northern Ireland citizens should decide their constitutional future. For this purpose, the Agreement was voted in both in Northern Ireland and in the Republic of

Ireland in 1998. After violence for hundreds of years in Ireland, the unionist and nationalist parties were united in support for the agreement.[72] Third, the GFA contained the transfer of power from London to Belfast through the Northern Ireland Assembly and Executive Committee. The Committee oversees power sharing between nationalists and unionists. Fourth, the GFA also addressed questions related to decommissioning, policing, disarmament, human rights, the UK's demilitarisation in Northern Ireland and the status of prisoners in terms of being war criminals.[73] It addressed the issues of civil rights and the political condition for a semi-autonomous Northern Ireland system as well. Last, the Agreement created two councils; a North–South Ministerial Council which enables the northern and southern leaders to consult on cross-border issues, and a British–Irish Council which allows the examination of regional issues by the representatives of the two governments, the devolved governments of Scotland, Wales, the Channel Islands, the Isle of Man and Northern Ireland.[74]

The Background of Turkey's Kurdish Peace Process

The contemporary conflict in Turkey emerged in 1984 and has been dominated by the PKK. Although the Turkish state's relation with its Kurdish citizens has been problematic since the 1920s,[75] this research focuses on the contemporary Kurdish conflict, which is the most protracted armed conflict in Turkey's history.[76] The PKK was established by a small group of people who came together in Lice, Diyarbakır in November 1978 and called themselves 'Kurdistan revolutionaries'. Abdullah Öcalan was selected as the secretary of the PKK and leader of the group.[77] The PKK focused on forming its ideology and recruiting personnel for armed attacks in its early years by eliminating other Kurdish groups in eastern Turkey and putting pressure on local people to join the PKK.[78] In addition, Öcalan admitted that the PKK also killed its members who disagreed with the leadership, who did not deserve to be killed.[79]

The PKK's aims have differed over time, from creating an independent Kurdish state to federalism, and cultural and political rights.[80] To achieve these aims, the PKK's violent campaign has claimed more than 35,000 lives and maintains its importance as a major and long-standing problem for Turkey.[81] According to the US Department of State's Country Report, the

Turkish government carried out evacuation due to the conflict of 3,236 villages in the early years of the conflict, and eventually, 362,915 Kurds were obliged to leave their homes due to the threat of terrorist attacks.[82] According to Özerdem and Jacoby, the internal displacement was due to both the claim of the Turkish Army that local populations (voluntarily or involuntarily) supported the PKK logistically, and the PKK's pressure on the people of the region who did not support the insurgency's armed campaign.[83] In addition, the repressive politics of the Turkish government and the army on the Kurdish population caused a strengthening of the support for the PKK, instead of eliminating it.[84]

Turkey's attempts to end the ongoing armed conflict contain both armed and political resolution efforts. The Kurdish situation has been accepted as a terrorism problem through most of its history. This has resulted in counter-terrorism and denial policies, in particular the denial of the existence of Kurdish ethnic identity by the Turkish state officials and the labelling of the conflict as an 'eastern' or 'south-eastern' problem instead.[85] Similar to the Northern Irish peace process, the Turkish case is divided into three periods: the first period describes the rise of the military conflict and secret peace efforts. The next period defines the rise of the political struggle, and the last demonstrates official and secret conflict resolution efforts and informal initiatives of independent third parties, as well as the failure of these attempts. In contrast to the Northern Irish peace process, this peace process was led by the Turkish government instead of different political parties. It has been led by the personal aims of presidents and prime ministers from the early stages of the conflict. The characteristics of these efforts changed when the AKP identified it as an ethnic problem to be resolved through official initiatives. The peace efforts in Turkey, initiated by Turgut Özal during his second term as PM (1987–9) and then as President (1989-1993), have been continued by Süleyman Demirel as PM (1991–3), Tansu Çiller as PM (1993–6), Necmettin Erbakan as PM (1996–7) and Tayyip Erdoğan as PM (2003–14) and President (2014–present) under AKP rule.

Inception: From Emergence to Escalation (1984–95)

The PKK organised its first attack on the Gendarmerie Station in Eruh, Siirt, on 15 August 1984, in which one soldier was killed, three of them injured, and also three civilians were killed in Turkey's southeast. The PKK's second attack was one of the most lethal of the whole conflict, killing twenty-nine people including five children and eight women in Pınarcık, Mardin, in June 1987.[86] In 1988, in order to respond to the PKK's hit-and-run tactics, the Turkish state established a special counter-insurgency strike force consisting of 5,000 well-trained soldiers to fight against the PKK.[87] However, the PKK increased the number of its militants to nearly 8,000 operating inside Turkey, using Syria, Lebanon, Iran and northern Iraq for training grounds, camps and launching pads for organising attacks in Turkey very quickly by the mid-1990s.[88] This regional and international support helped the PKK to survive. In the 1980s and early 1990s, Syria's support was the most comprehensive, including both weapon supply and financial support. The Syrian government also gave permission for the PKK to use the Bekaa Valley for training purposes and for Öcalan to live in Syria.[89] The reason for Syria's support for the PKK was to use this insurgency campaign in order to force Turkey to consent to Syria's demands regarding fresh water sources in the region.[90] In addition to regional support, the PKK received a great amount of financial support from Kurdish immigrants in Europe.[91]

Despite the dominance of the military struggle, there were some political attempts to interrupt violence. For this purpose, the first contact between the Turkish government and PKK was provided in 1988 by the Özal administration. Özal sent intermediaries to meet with Öcalan to gauge the views of the PKK and to ask for a PKK ceasefire.[92] These indirect communications resulted in the first PKK ceasefire, beginning on 17 March 1993, thanks to Jalal Talabani's[93] intermediary work to exchange messages between Özal and the PKK that will be examined in the next chapter. The ceasefire was then extended indefinitely on 16 April, at the request of Özal.[94] Unfortunately, forty days after Özal's death, the PKK killed thirty-three unarmed soldiers in Bingöl who had completed their army duty and were returning home.[95] This attack brought the first ceasefire to an end.

During this period, peace attempts remained in the shadow of the military struggle due to the high intensity of armed conflict and the mostly armed response by Turkish authorities. The Turkish government had adopted a traditional military response and repressive politics to fight against 'Kurdish terrorism as a zero-sum game'.[96] The PKK's deadly attacks in eastern Turkey obliged Turkey to seek alternative policies in the 1980s. Firstly, the government declared a 'State of Emergency' (*Olağanüstü Hal*, henceforth OHAL) in thirteen eastern cities in 1987, which lasted until 2002. As stated by the Turkish Armed Forces' (*Türk Silahlı Kuvvetleri*, henceforth TSK) General Staff, the aim of the OHAL rule was to secure these provinces and to provide decisions quickly for countering terrorism.[97]

The other political pressure was the closure of the pro-Kurdish parties in the 1990s. The People's Labour Party (*Halkın Emek Partisi*, henceforth HEP) had been founded as a predominantly Kurdish party. Since the HEP lacked enough support to reach the election threshold,[98] it formed an electoral pact with the left-of-centre Social Democratic People's Party (*Sosyal Demokrat Halkçı Parti*, henceforth SHP) in the 1991 national election, which provided it with twenty-two deputies in the Turkish Grand National Assembly.[99] However, the HEP was banned due to the deputies of the party choosing to speak in Kurdish and for promoting the PKK's insurgency campaign in 1993. The Democracy Party (*Demokrasi Partisi*, henceforth DEP) was founded to replace the HEP in the same year. Yet, the DEP was also shut down by the Constitutional Court because of the claim of it being an extension of the PKK. However, it did not stop pro-Kurdish political actors founding a new party called the People's Democratic Party (*Halkın Demokrasi Partisi*, henceforth HADEP) in 1994. The HADEP took part in the 1995 national election, but could not reach the electoral threshold with only 4.2 per cent of the votes.[100] Its successor, the Freedom and Democracy Party (*Özgürlük ve Demokrasi Partisi*, henceforth ÖZDEP) was also closed by the Constitutional Court.[101]

Overall, there were two problems with Kurdish politics in Turkey. First, many pro-Kurdish parties were shut down by the Constitutional Court, which prevented them using their rights to present themselves in the parliament. The reason for the closure of these parties was the claim of the Constitutional Court that they advocated the PKK's armed campaign. Even though they did not advocate the PKK's violence, apparently being Kurdish was sufficient to be accused of defending the PKK.[102] These events also resulted in the Kurdish community losing their trust in the Turkish government and caused a breakdown in relations since they were not allowed to be represented in the political arena. Second, electoral support for the pro-Kurdish parties was limited during the 1990s. Ergil noted that this insufficient support was because of the lack of a political agenda and the influence of the PKK over the Kurdish community.[103]

Alongside the problems over pro-Kurdish parties, the Turkish government carried out some amendments regarding Kurdish rights. For example, in 1991, the government allowed publications in the Kurdish language.[104] In addition, Kurds had also been permitted to bring court cases against the crimes of the TSK during the violent conflict between the PKK and Turkish security forces.[105] Furthermore, the Özal administration sought to modify the constitutional meaning of the monolithic Turkish identity. Özal wanted to change Kemalist[106] policy and aimed to follow a constructivist approach by identifying the existence of each ethnic identity in the country. Özal followed the structure of the Ottoman Empire, which had several ethnic groups and those groups were brought together under different religious groups. Ethnic identities were aimed to be classified as cultural and ethnic dimensions.[107] However, these changes could not be accomplished as Özal died in 1993. His successor, Demirel, failed to continue political overtures due to his belief in the success of military tactics rather than a political resolution.[108]

The 1990s witnessed intensive armed conflict between the Turkish state and PKK through which thousands of people lost their lives.[109] The Turkish state had responded to the PKK's mortal attacks through the designation of 'the village guard system'. This system consisted of local militia groups loosely or closely affiliated with the state with the purpose of preventing village raids and massacres by the PKK.[110] These guards were paid and armed by the state for the war against the PKK. Most of them were Kurds, so they were forming a barrier between the PKK militants and local people.[111] Jacoby and Özerdem argue that 'the village guards reduced accountability and increased the polarisation of Kurdish society'.[112] Political, non-violent efforts, such as secret talks and minor amendments to Kurdish rights, were overshadowed during the early stage of the conflict by the armed struggle, the influence of which will be assessed in the subsequent chapters.

Mitigation: From Escalation to De-escalation (1995–2005)

The political attempts towards peace during this period witnessed both indirect communications through intermediaries and direct talks through political actors. PM Tansu Çiller, successor of Demirel, focused more on non-violent resolution attempts and called for a political solution in 1995.

She declared that she was against the so-called military solution.[113] She sent her advisor Ercan Vuralhan to meet with Talabani to forward her letter to Öcalan asking for a PKK ceasefire. Öcalan replied through Talabani and said that if the Turkish government developed a dialogue with the PKK, he would declare a ceasefire.[114] After this indirect dialogue, Öcalan declared a ceasefire on 15 December 1995 that was broken immediately; the PKK blamed the Turkish government for not stopping air strikes and not taking any steps forward towards peace.[115]

The first direct talks between the Turkish government and the PKK were achieved in 1996. The initial step was the intermediary work of İsmail Nacar.[116] In June 1996, Zübeyir Aydar, one of the leading members of the PKK, called Nacar and wanted him to provide the connection between them and the Turkish government. Nacar then met with PM Necmettin Erbakan, successor of Çiller, and forwarded Aydar's message. Erbakan responded positively to this request and appointed one of his deputies, Fethullah Erbaş, to conduct negotiations along with Nacar. Erbaş met with Öcalan claiming to release Turkish soldiers who had been taken captive by the PKK. The negotiation resulted in the release of eight soldiers. However, they could not be moved on due to the opposition of political parties and the TSK.[117] It was important to understand the underlying reason of the PKK initiating secret negotiations. Although the PKK was generally in favour of talking to the Turkish government, it could be said that the reason for building this communication channel was the TSK's oppressive counter-terrorism measures which had resulted in the increase in deaths of PKK militants from 1,340 in 1992 to 4,111 in 1994, and 3,007 in 1995.[118] Although they were direct talks, the negotiations were achieved secretly and the purpose of the negotiations was limited to releasing Turkish soldiers who had been taken by the PKK. The next chapter will discuss the outcome of these efforts.

The mid-1990s were dominated by political efforts. However, it did not stop the violent conflict. In order to stop the PKK's attacks in Turkey's southeast, Turkish officials started to put diplomatic pressure on Syria, threatening that it was a *casus belli* if Syria continued to harbour Öcalan. Hence, Syria had to deport Öcalan in the autumn of 1998. After moving from Russia to Italy, Turkey's diplomatic efforts to extradite Öcalan continued. He sought political asylum status to turn his military defeat into a political victory and applied for political asylum in European states. For example, when he was arrested in Rome's Da Vinci Airport, he immediately applied for political asylum.[119] However, Turkey's diplomatic efforts through the North Atlantic Treaty Organization (NATO) compelled first Italy and then Greece to reject his application.[120] His last stop was Kenya, where he was located in the Greek Embassy. With the help of US intelligence, Öcalan was captured in Kenya on 16 February 1999 and imprisoned in the İmralı Prison where he is serving a life sentence.[121]

After the capture and imprisonment of Öcalan, the term between 1999 and 2004 witnessed several peace attempts to de-escalate the conflict. This term provided a great chance to offer a non-violent resolution to the Kurdish movement.[122] According to Baser and Özerdem, the Kurdish movement started to act as a political power more actively, especially in eastern Turkey.[123] Immediately after Öcalan's capture, a secret channel between the Turkish authorities and the PKK was built by the MIT. Deputy Undersecretary of the MIT, Emre Taner, secretly met with Öcalan and put forward his demand for the PKK's dissolution. In addition, MIT officers talked with Cevat Soysal, one of the leading members of the PKK, after his capture in Moldova. While the MIT requested the disarmament of the PKK, Öcalan responded to this request by asking for legal arrangements in which constitutional changes should be included for each PKK militant.[124] As a result of these meetings, Öcalan commanded the PKK militants to move out of Turkey in 1999. Although it seemed like a positive step for the peace process, Öcalan did not want the PKK militants to lay down their arms.[125] Instead of disarmament, the PKK changed its organisational structure: in 2002, it changed its name to the Kurdish Freedom and Democracy Congress (KADEK), claiming that the PKK had completed its historical mission and would now be operated as a political group. In late 2003, the organisation again changed its name, to the Kurdistan People's Congress (*Kongra-Gel*), but none of these changes resulted in a change of either strategy or tactics.[126] Instead, according to Öcalan, Kongra-Gel declared the ideal of an Independent United Kurdistan by including Turkey's southeast.[127]

As Cagaptay has suggested, to re-establish the PKK under different names was related to the pressure of international society.[128] The EU and US declared the KADEK and Kongra-Gel as terrorist organisations shortly after their foundations, thanks to diplomatic efforts from Turkey. In response to these changes, the Turkish government passed an amnesty law to provide a suitable environment for the PKK militants to lay down their arms in August 2003, in response to the PKK's organisational change. It followed the PKK's unilateral ceasefire on 29 May 2004. One year later, the group restored the name PKK. The PKK announced another ceasefire in 2004, which slowed down the intensity of its attacks, but did not bring them to an end. The PKK's attacks and the Turkish government's response were maintained in the following years.[129] However, neither the amnesty law nor ceasefires were sufficient to cease the armed campaign of the PKK. Even though the amnesty was a great effort on the government's side, it was not in demand amongst PKK militants. The initiative, therefore, remained as an unsuccessful resolution effort. The root causes of the tactics of the Turkish government and PKK in the early 2000s are imperative here. On the one hand, the PKK's aim in changing the name of the group was to illustrate to Western countries that they had departed from the armed campaign and would continue to exist as a political organisation only.[130] On the other hand, the reason for the efforts of Turkish officials can be examined as a quest for responding to Öcalan's call for the withdrawal of the PKK militants from Turkey. This was because it was seen as part of these discussions, and the hope that these talks could lead to substantive negotiations, eventually leading to the end of the Kurdish conflict. However, these were insufficient efforts towards ending a deep-rooted ethno-nationalist conflict.

This period also witnessed the PKK's change of strategy and the beginnings of 'communalising' the Kurdish question through new opportunities offered by EU regulations. In fact, the EU asked Turkey to reform its legal system and provide the Kurdish minority rights on the basis of the Copenhagen Criteria.[131] In addition, the reforms required abolishing the State of Emergency and the State Security Courts, decreasing detention periods pending trial and lifting the ban on Kurdish publications.[132] According to Özerdem, the EU accession criteria played a facilitating role to create a suitable environment to initiate peace talks.[133] However, these developments did not prevent violence, as Öcalan called upon the PKK to return to Turkey to develop the Kurdish forces.[134] In 2003, the PKK had approximately 1,500 members within the borders of Turkey.[135] As a result, another positive step did not have a successful outcome for the peace process.

The Iraq War of 2003 was another important incident which affected the nature of the region and precipitated the establishment of a Kurdish province in northern Iraq. Turkey's loss of control after the US operation caused the rise of the PKK again. The Kurdistan Regional Government's establishment in Northern Iraq after 2003 has made the situation more complicated and helped foster cooperation between Kurdish militant groups in Iraq.[136] For the Turkish government, it was an indicator of the insufficiency of traditional security tactics and so it was necessary to produce more comprehensive policies. The rise of Kurdish nationalism in the region began to undermine the moral basis of Turkey's monolithic Turkish identity. Additionally, the rise of Kurdish nationalism in Iraq was affecting claims and expectations of Turkey's Kurdish citizens.[137]

Intensification: From De-escalation to Deterioration (2005–15)

The period between 2005 and 2015 witnessed an increase in both political and security efforts to end the conflict. From 2005 to 2008, the PKK organised several attacks on Turkish security forces and civilians (for example, targeting tourist resorts), which together caused 1,500 deaths.[138] The PKK's attacks in 2007 raised an issue of how to stop their militants based in northern Iraq. Turkish politicians and military authorities began to discuss the need for a 'cross-border military operation' into northern Iraq in order to demolish the PKK camps and to prevent the establishment of an independent Kurdish state in the region. After a serious discussion and cooperation with the US, Turkey launched cross-border operations including many air strikes and land operations.[139]

Alongside its violent attacks, the PKK established a congress called the Kurdistan Communities Union (*Koma Civakên Kurdistan*, henceforth KCK) by bringing the PKK members in Turkey, Iran, Iraq and Syria together. The KCK is an umbrella group constituting of both youth and women's councils; the PKK; the Party of Free Life of Kurdistan (*Partiya Jiyana Azad a Kurdistanê*, henceforth PJAK), which operates in Iran; PYD/YPG, which operates in Syria; and the PKK's other armed group, the People's Defence Forces (*Hêzên Parastina Gel*, henceforth HPG). Although the KCK claims that its formation is not related to either power or state, its policy and aim to compete with the Turkish state demonstrates that the it has clear ambitions on politics and power.[140] The KCK incorporated so-called legislative

(Kongra-Gel), executive and jurisdiction systems that aim to serve as a state form. These groups were a clear sign of the PKK's aim to maintain its ultimate goal of establishing an independent Kurdish state. This was responded to by the Turkish government through military operations and detentions of the members of these terrorist groups.[141]

In 2009, political resolution efforts again increased, but of a different character. The Turkish government, for the first time, launched an official 'opening' policy to bring the conflict to an end. The policy was called the 'Kurdish opening' by PM Erdoğan. It was later broadened under the title of the 'democratic opening' and afterwards, 'the national unity project'.[142] The project was a sign that armed struggle alone was not sufficient to achieve the disarmament of the PKK. An insight into the government's democratic opening project was announced by Beşir Atalay, Minister for Internal Affairs: opening the first official Kurdish TV channel (TRT-6), giving back the ancient Kurdish names of villages, Kurdish courses in private schools and opening many institutions for other languages used in Turkey.[143] Öcalan found this project insufficient: he threatened the government that if the collective rights of the Kurdish people were not recognised, the war would be maintained for another fifty years.[144] It was clear that this was the greatest effort towards ending this conflict in a non-violent way in Turkey's history. The reason for the failure of this initiative was that the country was too divided. On the one hand, many Kurds in Turkey were following the lead of Öcalan. On the other hand, there was a vast population strongly criticising the democratic opening project.[145] The Resolution Commission was an outcome of this project, which aimed to provide a suitable environment for peace talks. It was a significant sign that, after prolonged troubles, the Turkish authorities were now demanding a solution to the conflict in a non-violent way through political parties. The outcomes of the democratic opening project and initiatives of the Resolution Commission will be analysed in Chapter 6.

The government's aim was to solve the problem in parliament during the late 2000s. However, despite the Democratic Society Party's (*Demokratik Toplum Partisi*, henceforth DTP)[146] claim to represent the Kurdish community, it was blamed for being a mouthpiece for the PKK. It was argued that the party was founded 'under the instructions of Abdullah Öcalan and was controlled mainly by the PKK leadership'.[147] According to Çandar, since the pro-Kurdish party had no experience of formulating policies, the Kurdish opening was led by the PKK leadership, which put in question the role of the DTP as a political party.[148] As a result, the Constitutional Court closed the DTP by declaring the party to be a centre for acts 'against the indivisible integrity of the state with its country and nation, considering its actions and also ties with the terrorist organisation'.[149] This was a step back from the use of democratic rights, to party closures similar to those of the 1990s, and so negatively affected the environment for a non-violent resolution. Fortunately, it did not stop the intention of the Turkish government to achieve a political resolution, unlike in the previous decade.

Another milestone in the conflict were the secret talks between the MIT and PKK leaders under the mediation of the British SIS in Oslo, known as the 'Oslo talks'. These were the beginning of official negotiations with the PKK. Although negotiations had been held secretly since 2006, they were leaked through a news agency in Turkey in 2011. It triggered pressure from the majority in Turkey to end the talks. The pro-Kurdish movement then put pressure on the government to make constitutional reforms.[150] However, these talks had made an important contribution; direct talks (even if organised secretly) between the Turkish government and the PKK provided hope for both sides of the possibility of solving the military-dominated conflict with political, non-violent attempts.[151] While Chapter 4 will examine the Oslo talks in detail, since these are the most comprehensive secret talks, Chapter 6 will assess the impact of the involvement of international mediation.

As an outcome of these clandestine initiatives, the Turkish government and the PKK organised an event where a PKK group would surrender at Turkey's Habur border. Thus, eight PKK members were chosen from the Qandil Mountain area and twenty-six of them from the Makhmour Refugee Camp in northern Iraq. These militants were called the 'peace group'. Although their arrival was presented as a further step in the peace process, it led to different responses from different communities in Turkey. On the one hand, it was celebrated at the Habur border by PKK sympathisers. On the other hand, their arrival and the celebrations triggered angry protests across Turkey and caused a drawback in the peace process.[152] This unsuccessful attempt proved that the government had not thought out the results of the Kurdish opening in practice and could not manage its fulfilment, let alone its consequences.[153] Chapter 4 will investigate the Habur event as an outcome of backchannel communications.

In 2012, the PKK's increased attacks led the state to undertake more military operations. At the same time, hundreds of inmates, convicted of being PKK militants, organised hunger strikes calling upon the government to end Öcalan's isolation on İmralı Island. The government gave permission for prisoners to make contact with Öcalan and hunger strikes ceased following Öcalan's press release. A few months later, PM Erdoğan stated that 'the state would re-initiate talks with Öcalan if necessary'.[154] Peace talks then started between the government, the BDP and Öcalan in late 2012, and resulted in a ceasefire. In March 2013, Öcalan called on the PKK to lay down their arms; the next day, the PKK declared a unilateral ceasefire indefinitely. The first group of PKK members retreated from Turkey to northern Iraq in May 2013.[155] This date was also called the beginning of the 'solution process', which lasted until July 2015. The solution process involved different levels of bilateral negotiations – whose only outcome was the Dolmabahçe Declaration of 2015 comprising a statement on the social-economic dimensions, and national and local dimensions of democratic rights.[156] Chapter 6 will assess these negotiations in greater detail.

The peace organisations in Turkey have been active only in this period. Some of these organisations have concentrated on peacemaking efforts, promoting and encouraging peace. For instance, the Wise People Committee (WPC), which was introduced in April 2013, was initiated to contribute to the decision-making mechanism. The members of the Committee were journalists, academics, experts and other public figures who organised hundreds of meetings, peace events and conferences.[157] The influence of these attempts and the underlying reasons for their outcomes will be examined in Chapter 5.

Nevertheless, neither the democratic opening project nor other changes in the law and other peace efforts were sufficient to solve the problem. There were a few reasons for the unsuccessful outcome: first, the government did not seek consensus amongst major political parties in the parliament. In addition to the reluctance of the government to insist on opposition parties joining peace initiatives, the opposition parties the Republican People's Party (*Cumhuriyet Halk Partisi*, henceforth CHP) and Nationalist Movement Party (*Milliyetçi Hareket Partisi*, henceforth MHP) were against the peace process.[158] The lack

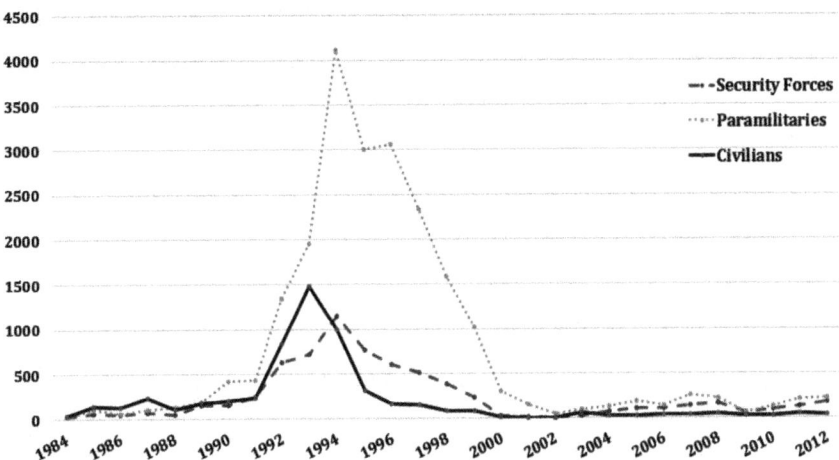

Figure 3.2 The casualties in Turkey (1984–2012).[a] Source: 21YYTE, *Terörle Mücadelede Verdiğimiz Şehitler*, and TBMM, *Terör ve Şiddet Olayları Kapsamında Yaşam Hakkı İhlallerini İnceleme Raporu*.

[a] There is no concrete data for the lives lost between 2013 and 2015. However, after the ceasefire ended in 2015, 532 security personnel (army personnel and police officers) lost their lives in only one year as of June 2016 (Çiçek, 'Elimination or Integration of Pro-Kurdish Politics').

of consensus on even basic premises resulted in polarisation between autonomy-seeking Kurds and other Turkish citizens. The Turkish government did not talk to the pro-Kurdish DTP, which caused some concerns about the representativeness of the Kurds. It triggered the radical components of the party to turn to the lead of the PKK.[159] Second, Figure 3.2 illustrates that there was no positive development towards a solution of the Kurdish problem and, as a result, violence remains. There were only a few attempts made: the surrender of the PKK members, known as the Habur event; the return of the ancient Kurdish names of villages; and the introduction of education in languages other than Turkish in private schools.[160] Further, it was the Copenhagen criteria for Turkey's EU membership that were the driving force for political reforms instead of the Turkish government.[161] Lastly, the talks between the Turkish government and HDP continued until the ceasefire was broken. However, all these pro-Kurdish political parties were accused of being spokespersons for the PKK, which made the situation more complicated since Turkish authorities did not want to negotiate with the PKK. In addition, the PKK established another armed group, called the Patriotic Revolutionary Youth Movement

(*Yurtsever Devrimci Gençlik Hareketi*, henceforth YDG-H), to organise attacks in urban areas that threatened the solution process. After more than thirty years, the PKK still exists and is one of the major security problems facing Turkey. The Turkish government has failed to disband the PKK or stop its attacks.

From Armed to Political Struggle

This chapter has explained the Northern Irish and Kurdish peace processes, together with the violent conflicts, which have provided a detailed understanding of the dilemma between the armed and political struggle. The discussion on the application of these methods has helped understand the transition from armed to political struggle. It has demonstrated that political resolution initiatives have been applied since the early stages of these conflicts. These initiatives illustrate different levels of resolution efforts, including direct and indirect talks, secret and official negotiations, intermediaries and initiatives of P/CROs. The Northern Ireland and Turkey cases have various similarities regarding conflict resolution efforts. First, both peace processes demonstrated similar political efforts in their early stages. Both conflicts witnessed secret and indirect talks to interrupt violence, declare ceasefires and give way to peace negotiations. Namely, the British government and IRA achieved several secret talks during the early phase of the Troubles, even when violence was at its peak. Secret talks led to the IRA ceasefire of 1972. Similarly, the Turkish government and the PKK organised secret talks which resulted in the PKK ceasefires when the violence rapidly increased in the early 1990s. In both conflicts, secret and indirect talks played a significant role in order to interrupt violence and to move the peace talks forward from the pre-negotiation to the negotiation stages.

Second, indirect talks through intermediaries were used in both conflicts. During the 1970s and early 1980s, the British government and IRA used intermediaries to keep in contact with each other. Brendan Duddy was one of those who met with the republican prisoners during the hunger strikes. The next chapter will assess his efforts, which led to the extension of the IRA ceasefire in 1975. Similarly, the Turkish government and PKK used intermediaries to make contact with each other. In particular, the early years of the conflict witnessed Cengiz Çandar and Jalal Talabani's peace attempts. The influence of indirect talks in both cases demonstrates similar characteristics because they were organised when there was no suitable ground for direct talks between the conflicting parties. In addition, they helped the British and Turkish government officials to move towards direct talks. Therefore, although the impact of intermediaries is limited in terms of conflict resolution approaches, they have been successful in making progress in both cases.

Third, official negotiations were achieved in the later stages in both conflicts. Whilst these talks provided different agreements, official talks could not lead to any accord in the Kurdish conflict. In the Northern Irish conflict, it started with the Sunningdale Agreement and lasted until the GFA. Nevertheless, official talks between the Turkish government and the PKK (and its political wings) did not reach any agreement, except for the Dolmabahçe Declaration. In this sense, two important aspects need to be discussed. The first point is that even though the Northern Irish conflict has ceased, it witnessed a few agreements over almost thirty years. As explained earlier in this chapter, the reason the previous agreements did not terminate the conflict was the fact that they did not include all conflicting sides. Although their wills were claimed to be represented, the AIA was massively opposed by the Catholic and Protestant communities. In contrast to the previous accords, the GFA's success can be explained through the involvement of all political views in the agreement. The other point is the different outcomes of the two conflicts even though they have similar conflict resolution processes. It shows that the impact of conflict resolution processes may change from one case to another when attempting to understand the implications of these procedures. Hence, it is necessary to look at other conflict resolution initiatives (e.g. mediation) related to official negotiations.

Fourth, international mediation is an essential determinant of official negotiations. It played a significant role in both peace processes, but it was reflected differently in each conflict. On the one hand, the US administration's efforts and George Mitchell's mediation led to official negotiations and helped in reaching the GFA in the Northern Irish peace process. The major condition for the process was the participation of almost all political views in the official talks. In addition, Mitchell's strong mediation role was crucial to keep on track the British government and Northern Irish political parties. The involvement of Mitchell in the peace negotiations was both due to the intentions of the US towards halting this conflict and the consent of both the British and republicans for Mitchell being accepted as the 'mediator' of the official negotiations. As discussed in the Northern Ireland section, the intention of the US was formed by pressure from Irish-Americans to end this conflict in a non-violent way. On the other hand, Turkey's peace process also had mediation initiatives in the 2000s. However, the mediation of British intelligence was achieved as secret negotiations and organised with the participation of Turkish officials and representatives of the PKK. Although the negotiations demonstrated two sides with the authority to bargain on behalf of their communities, the nature of negotiations did not illustrate a complete success since it was not officially accepted as a declaration in the end. It was an unsuccessful initiative due to the mass protests and angry reaction of wider Turkish society. The underlying reason for the Turkish government not to declare the outcome of these negotiations can be explained through the traditional approach of 'we do not talk to terrorists'. It is clear that implementation of the decisions made in secret negotiations was not always easy. This difficulty created a dilemma for the Turkish government and resulted in an outcry in society against talking to the PKK. As the very existence of talks was enough to create anger in society, it was very difficult to discuss the outcome of these meetings. The implications of these initiatives in Northern Ireland and Turkey will be analysed in Chapter 6.

Fifth, both conflicts involved P/CROs that played a significant role in facilitating the peace processes. Different P/CROs were established from the early 1970s to assist peacemaking efforts in Northern Ireland. For example, the BIA and Peace People (PP) played a role in closing gaps between conflicting communities, encouraging both the British government and republican movement towards a non-violent, political resolution. Similar types of groups were established in Turkey in order to strengthen the influence of political actors. The WPC, for instance, was established to bring together the participants from conflicting communities to discuss their demands and carry out talks about the peace process. Chapter 5 will investigate all these political resolution initiatives, which have affected the two peace processes differently. While some of them have had a direct influence on the peace processes (to move them forward to official talks), the impact of others was limited.

Last, political parties in both conflicts played a crucial role in conducting, maintaining or interrupting the peace processes. The British and Turkish governments followed different strategies against nationalist/republican parties in Northern Ireland and pro-Kurdish parties in Turkey. While the approach was to exclude extreme parties from the peace process in Northern Ireland, it was to close pro-Kurdish parties in Turkey. This approach resulted in radicalising the pro-Kurdish movement in Turkey, because there was no opportunity for representatives of this movement to express their thoughts in the political arena. While it caused the Kurdish community to feel sceptical towards the government, these events did not create an ethnicity gap between the Kurdish and Turkish communities because ethnic groups in Turkey were intertwined with each other even before the foundation of the Turkish Republic. In contrast, the British government chose not to include SF in the political resolution process. However, both peace processes moved forward when SF and the HDP (and its predecessors) joined peace talks. Whilst political peace attempts in Northern Ireland were conducted by several political parties including republicans, nationalists, unionists and the British government, the political peace efforts in Turkey were dominated by the Turkish government and representatives of the PKK. The influence of the perception changes of the conflicting sides and their consequences regarding the conflict resolution approaches will now be investigated, along with the empirical evidence of both cases.

Notes

1. Rousseau, *The Social Contract or Principles of Political Right*.
2. Crenshaw, *Explaining Terrorism*; Guelke, *The Age of Terrorism*.
3. Laqueur, *No End to War*; Sanchez-Cuenca, 'The Dynamics of Nationalist Terrorism'; Stavenhagen, *Ethnic Conflicts*.
4. Alonso, 'Pathways out of Terrorism'.
5. Although the Northern Irish peace process reached an agreement and violence came to an end, the dissident republican groups have not been dissolved.
6. Cairns and Darby, 'The Conflict in Northern Ireland', p. 755.
7. The Green Book was a blueprint to give trainees the ability to keep the IRA's political aims in mind and to oppose external pressures. The book described all trainee aspects and the purpose of the republican movement (Coogan, *The IRA*, p. 544).

8. Byrne, 'Toward Tractability', pp. 140–1; Wolff, 'Conflict Management in Northern Ireland', p. 43.
9. Little, *Peacemakers in Action*, p. 58.
10. Archick, *Northern Ireland*, pp. 1–2; Lavery, 'I.R.A. Apologizes for Civilian Deaths in its 30-Year Campaign'.
11. Hanley, 'I Ran Away', p. 27.
12. Bell, 'The Escalation of Insurgency', p. 402.
13. The JIC is part of the British Cabinet Office which handles events and situations relating to external affairs, international criminal activities, defence, terrorism, and other transnational issues, focusing on secret intelligence (Goodman, *The Official History of the Joint Intelligence Committee*).
14. Charters, 'Have a Go', p. 206.
15. McVeigh and Rolston, 'From Good Friday to Good Relation', p. 13.
16. White, 'From Peaceful Protest to Guerrilla War', p. 1410.
17. Little, *Peacemakers in Action*, p. 60.
18. Ibid. p. 59.
19. Craig, 'From Backdoors and Back Lanes', p. 99.
20. Moore, 'Paramilitary Prisoners', p. 85.
21. Kennedy-Pipe and Mumford, 'Is Torture Ever Justified?', p. 59.
22. Little, *Peacemakers in Action*, p. 60.
23. Ibid. p. 61.
24. The official name of the city is Londonderry. However, many residents call it Derry. While the unionists prefer to use Londonderry, the nationalists use Derry.
25. Craig, 'From Backdoors and Back Lanes', p. 106.
26. Ibid. p. 101.
27. Ibid. pp. 105–6.
28. Mumford, 'Covert Peacemaking', p. 636.
29. Taylor, *Provos*, p. 136.
30. Mumford, 'Covert Peacemaking', pp. 637–8.
31. Craig, 'From Backdoors and Back Lanes', p. 104.
32. Bishop and Mallie, *The Provisional IRA*.
33. Darby and MacGinty, 'Northern Ireland'.
34. Arthur, *Government and Politics of Northern Ireland*.
35. Craig, 'From Backdoors and Back Lanes', p. 99.
36. Laneside is a house which was suspected of being a station of the British Intelligence in Northern Ireland. It was officially the residence of the British political reporting service. Many secret talks were achieved in the Laneside House between British officials and the members of the IRA (Craig, 'From Backdoors and Back Lanes', p. 102).

37. McDaid, *Template for Peace*, p. 25.
38. Craig, 'From Backdoors and Back Lanes', p. 108.
39. Muircheartaigh, 'The Death of Ruairí O Bradaigh and the Feakle Peace talks of 1974'; Powell, *Great Hatred, Little Room*, p. 69.
40. Arthur, *Government and Politics of Northern Ireland*, p. 1232.
41. Arthur, 'Negotiating the Northern Ireland Problem'.
42. Cochrane, 'Irish-America', p. 220.
43. Cochrane, *Northern Ireland*, p. 117.
44. Little, *Peacemakers in Action*, pp. 65–6; Sanders, *Inside the IRA*, p. 132.
45. Mallie and McKittrick, *The Fight for Peace*, p. 20.
46. Little, *Peacemakers in Action*, p. 66.
47. Ibid. pp. 66–7.
48. Whiting, *Sinn Féin and the IRA*, p. 36.
49. Boyle and Hadden, 'The Peace Process in Northern Ireland', p. 274.
50. Taoiseach is the Gaelic name of the prime minister of the Republic of Ireland.
51. Byrne, 'Consociational and Civic Society Approaches', p. 327.
52. Little, *Peacemakers in Action*, p. 68.
53. Boyle and Hadden, 'The Peace Process in Northern Ireland', p. 271.
54. Remembrance Day is a memorial day observed in the Commonwealth of Nations member states since the end of WWI to commemorate their soldiers who lost their lives (Little, *Peacemakers in Action*, p. 72).
55. Hauss, *International Conflict Resolution*, p. 87.
56. Little, *Peacemakers in Action*, p. 77.
57. Adams, *Free Ireland*, p. 51.
58. McAuley, quoted in Wilson, 'Time for Magnanimity', p. 5.
59. Little, *Peacemakers in Action*, p. 79–80.
60. De Breadun, *The Far Side of Revenge*, p. 11.
61. Lynch, 'The Gerry Adams Visa'.
62. Cochrane, 'Irish-America', p. 220; Cochrane, *Northern Ireland*, p. 154.
63. O'Dowd and McCall, 'Escaping the Cage', p. 87.
64. Ibid. p. 87.
65. Ingraham, 'The Irish Peace Process'.
66. Mitchell *et al.*, *Report of the International Body on Arms Decommissioning*.
67. Mitchell, quoted in Knox, 'See No Evil, Hear No Evil', p. 170.
68. Wolff, 'Conflict Management in Northern Ireland', p. 55.
69. Mitchell, *Making Peace*, p. 57.
70. Hammer, 'In Northern Ireland'.
71. Evans and Tonge, 'Catholic, Irish and Nationalist'; McGarry and O'Leary, 'Power Shared', p. 34.

72. Little, *Peacemakers in Action*, p. 81.
73. Galtung and Duffy, 'Northern Ireland'; Archick, *Northern Ireland*.
74. Archick, *Northern Ireland*, pp. 1–2.
75. There are seventeen Kurdish rebellions in the history of the Republic of Turkey. Three of them, those of 1925, 1930 and 1937, were the major ones (Heper, *The State and Kurds in Turkey*).
76. Ibid.
77. Mango, *Turkey and the War on Terror*, p. 34.
78. İmset, *The PKK*.
79. Öcalan, *PKK IV. Kongresi'ne Sunulan Politik Rapor*.
80. Beriker-Atiyas, 'The Kurdish Conflict in Turkey', p. 439.
81. Mango, *Turkey and the War on Terror*, p. 31.
82. US Department of State, *Country Reports on Human Rights Practices*.
83. Özerdem and Jacoby, 'Conflict-Induced Internal Displacement', pp. 162–3.
84. Van Bruinessen, 'Shifting National and Ethnic Identities'.
85. Başbuğ, *Terör Örgütlerinin Sonu*; Marcus, *Kan ve İnanç*; Tan, *Kürt Sorunu*; van Bruinessen, *Ağa, Şeyh, Devlet*.
86. Mango, *Turkey and the War on Terror*, p. 38.
87. Entessar, 'The Kurdish Mosaic of Discord', p. 95.
88. Kaliber and Tocci, 'Civil Society', pp. 195–6.
89. Barkey, 'Turkey's Kurdish Dilemma', p. 53.
90. Hinnebusch and Tür, *Turkey-Syria Relations*.
91. Abramowitz, 'Dateline Ankara', p. 174.
92. Aslan, 'TC'nin PKK ile Görüşmeleri' [The Republic of Turkey's Talks with the PKK]; Donat, 'Anılar Denizi' [The Sea of Memories].
93. The leader of the Patriotic Union of Kurdistan. He was the president of Iraq between 2005 and 2014.
94. Aslan, 'TC'nin PKK ile Görüşmeleri'; Birand and Yalçın, *The Özal*; Romano, *The Kurdish Nationalist Movement*.
95. Ensaroğlu, 'Turkey's Kurdish Question', p. 11.
96. Cizre, 'The Emergence of the Government's Perspective', p. 3.
97. TSKA-EK/980/26, *Report about Implementation of the State of Emergency*.
98. In Turkey, the electoral threshold in national elections is 10%.
99. Turkish: *Türkiye Büyük Millet Meclisi* (TBMM). This book uses the terms TBMM and parliament interchangeably to refer to the Turkish Assembly.
100. Ergil, 'The Kurdish Question in Turkey', p. 129.
101. Beriker-Atiyas, 'The Kurdish Conflict', p. 448.

102. White, *Primitive Rebels*, p. 171.
103. Ergil, 'The Kurdish Question in Turkey', p. 129.
104. Bozarslan, 'Turkey's Elections and the Kurds', p. 16.
105. Blum, 'The Futures of Conflict', p. 349.
106. Kemalist reforms and the ideology of Kemalism has seen the emergence of the modern Turkish society and state. The major aim was to bring Turkey to a level even above contemporary civilisation. There are six principles of Kemalism: republicanism, nationalism, populism, secularism, statism and reformism. These aims would be achieved through national unity. Kemalism formed the ideological basis of the commitment to modernisation, and the reforms contained the practical application of the basic principles of this ideology (Kili, 'Kemalism in Contemporary Turkey', p. 387).
107. Ataman, 'Özal Leadership', p. 128.
108. Barkey and Fuller, 'Turkey's Kurdish Question', p. 69.
109. 21YYTE, *Terörle Mücadelede Verdiğimiz Şehitler*; Özcan, *PKK*.
110. TSKA-EK/984/34, *Report about the Village Guard System*.
111. Barkey and Fuller, 'Turkey's Kurdish Question', p. 69.
112. Jacoby and Özerdem, *Peace in Turkey 2023*, p. 78.
113. Bozarslan, 'Turkey's Elections', p. 16.
114. Aslan, 'TC'nin PKK ile Görüşmeleri'; Birand and Yalçın, *The Özal*.
115. CNNTürk, 'Geçmişten Bugüne PKK Ateşkesleri'; Öcalan, 'Önümüzde İki Yol Var'.
116. İsmail Nacar is a Kurdish writer and NGO spokesperson from the Committee of Peace, Fraternity and Solidarity.
117. Beriker-Atiyas, 'The Kurdish Conflict in Turkey', pp. 446–7; Yeni Çağ, 'Özal'dan Sonra Hoca da Apo'yla Temas Kurmuş'.
118. 21YYTE, *Terörle Mücadelede Verdiğimiz Şehitler*.
119. Aliboni and Pioppi, 'The Öcalan Affair Revisited', p. 37.
120. Gunter, 'The Continuing Kurdish Problem', p. 850.
121. Ergil, 'The Kurdish Question in Turkey', p. 128.
122. Gurses, *Anatomy of a Civil War*, p. 129.
123. Baser and Özerdem, 'Turkey'.
124. ANF, 'Öcalan: Kürtlerin Kellesine Karşı ABD-Türkiye Anlaştı' [Öcalan: The USA and Turkey Made an Agreement to Slaughter Kurds]; Güller, *Hükümet-PKK Görüşmeleri*; Kapmaz, *Öcalan'ın İmralı Günleri*, pp. 91–2.
125. Ibid. pp. 92–3.
126. Baybars-Hawks, 'Will Peace Flourish in the End?', p. 279.

127. Öcalan, *Özgür İnsan Savunması*.
128. Cagaptay, 'Can the PKK Renounce Violence?'
129. Baybars-Hawks, 'Will Peace Flourish in the End?', p. 279.
130. Bahar, *Çözüm Süreci*.
131. Yavuz and Özcan, 'The Kurdish Question', p. 103.
132. Ensaroğlu, 'Turkey's Kurdish Question', p. 12.
133. Özerdem, 'Türkiye'ye Barış Gelir Mi?', p. 26.
134. Çandar, *Dağdan İniş-PKK Nasıl Silah Bırakır?*, p. 81.
135. Kapmaz, *Öcalan'ın İmralı Günleri*, p. 202.
136. Özcan, *Araf'taki Çözüm Süreci*.
137. Çiçek, 'Elimination or Integration of Pro-Kurdish Politics', p. 19.
138. Barrinha, 'The Political Importance of Labelling', p. 170.
139. Efegil, 'Turkey's New Approaches', p. 54.
140. Saeed, *Kurdish Politics in Turkey*, p. 126.
141. BiaNet, 'İki Buçuk Yıldır Gündemdeki "KCK" nedir?' [What is the 'KCK' Which is in Question for Two and a Half Years?]; Deligöz, *KCK: Demokrasi Kılıfında Terör*.
142. Milliyet, 'Bakan Atalay "Kürt Açılımını" Açıkladı'.
143. Ibid.
144. Sendika, 'Öcalan'la Görüşme Notu'.
145. Abramowitz and Barkey, 'Turkey's Transformers', p. 122.
146. The DTP was closed by the decision of the Constitutional Court in December 2009. The Peace and Democracy Party (*Barış ve Demokrasi Partisi*, henceforth BDP) was the successor of the DTP, which was dissolved to join the HDP on 22 April 2014. The latest and current pro-Kurdish party is the HDP (Celep, 'Can the Kurdish Left').
147. Çandar, 'The Kurdish Question', p. 18.
148. Ibid. p. 18.
149. Official Gazette, *Anayasa Mahkemesi'nin 11.12.2009 Tarih E. 2007/1, K. 2009/4 Sayılı Kararı*.
150. Öcalan, 'Demokratik Anayasal Çözüm Gelişmezse Halkın Direnme Hakkı Vardır!'
151. Ensaroğlu, 'Turkey's Kurdish Question', p. 13.
152. Ibid. p. 13.
153. Gunter, 'Reopening Turkey's Closed Kurdish Opening?', p. 89.
154. Ensaroğlu, 'Turkey's Kurdish Question', p. 14.
155. Tocci, 'Turkey's Kurdish Gamble', p. 74.

156. HDN, 'Kurdish Peace Call'.
157. KDGM, *Demokratikleşme Paketi*.
158. Although the CHP did not support the peace process, the first reports regarding the Kurdish question were published by the CHP during the 1990s (Yayman, *Türkiye'nin Kürt Sorunu Hafızası*). The MHP has always defended counter-terrorism measures against the PKK (Özdağ, *PKK ile Pazarlık*).
159. Criss, 'Parameters of Turkish Foreign Policy', p. 15.
160. Çiçek, 'Elimination or Integration of Pro-Kurdish Politics', p. 15.
161. Baser and Öztürk, 'In Lieu of an Introduction', p. 5.

4

BACKCHANNEL COMMUNICATIONS: TALKING TO THE ENEMY BEHIND THE SCENES

> Without the possibility of back-channel communication, there would be little front-channel negotiation and very few settlements of the major conflicts in the world.[1]

This chapter assesses the role of backchannel negotiations in the Northern Irish and Turkey's Kurdish peace processes. Backchannels are one of the three major aspects of this analysis due to their role in initiating a peace process and forming the pre-negotiation stage of a conflict resolution process. This chapter examines the secret channels which were opened to make contact between the British government and republican movement that included both SF and the IRA, and between the Turkish government and pro-Kurdish movement that contained both the HDP and its predecessors, and the PKK. These channels were active for more than twenty years in both conflicts.

The chapter argues that secret negotiations in Northern Ireland and Turkey reduced the concerns of disputing parties about trust and reliability. Therefore, these negotiations facilitated a level of understanding when it was not possible to meet officially. It states that direct and indirect backchannels made it possible to carry out official negotiations and played a significant role towards de-escalating both conflicts. These kind of talks enable a discussion of conflicting parties' demands in a flexible environment, with no preconditions applied to the meeting.[2] There has been relatively little exploration in either case of the influence of backchannel talks in these conflict resolution processes.³ There has also been little interest shown in how these secret initiatives defined the nature of official negotiations. This chapter asks the following question to explore these areas: How did backchannel initiatives play a role in de-escalating the violent acts carried out by the IRA and PKK during the pre-negotiation stage?

To answer this question, the chapter first assesses the impact of direct and indirect secret talks in the Northern Irish peace process. It then analyses how direct and indirect backchannel communications worked to reduce the level of violence and facilitate the conflict resolution process in Turkey. It frames backchannel communications in these two major cases and analyses the under-explored pre-negotiation stage of conflict resolution. The impact of secret talks is described through the role of intermediaries in building trust and exchanging information between the two conflicting parties, as well as the structures and outcomes of the direct talks. It also aims to understand how these secret talks were transformed into official negotiations. Afterwards, the influence of the talks in the two studied cases is compared by examining their major components.

Backchannels in Northern Ireland

The Northern Ireland peace process was initially started with a dialogue between the SDLP and SF in the mid-1980s.⁴ However, when the secret contact between the British government and republican movement, and the intermediaries' role in establishing communication and facilitating the progress, were revealed after archival sources were investigated, it was clear that the peace process needed to be examined in a wider context. This section reveals the secret contact between the British government and the republican movement, and assesses the role of backchannels in the whole peace process.

Indirect Communications

In the early 1970s, an anonymous letter written on behalf of the Northern Ireland Office revealed that British authorities had rejected contact with the IRA by claiming 'there was not any one man or group in the IRA who were both willing and able to deliver an efficient and lasting ceasefire'.⁵ Therefore, they initially tested each other's authority on minor issues such as releasing hostages or the transfer of prisoners. These minor issues in the early 1970s helped establish an understanding that both sides had the authority to deliver their promises. Indirect communications initiated secret contact between the British government and republican movement through intermediaries.

The first intermediary in the Northern Irish peace process was Tom Caldwell, a former British Army officer. Although his contact with the republican movement began at the Dublin Horse Show when he bumped into a senior Provisional in 1971 and 'exchanged pleasantries but nothing more', the nature of these talks changed after the Abercorn explosion on 4 March 1972, which killed two women and injured more than a hundred people.[6] This explosion triggered Caldwell's initiation of a secret dialogue. The structure and consequence of Caldwell's initiatives are crucial for understanding the impact of the first covert peace effort. Regarding the structure, as Caldwell states, it was his own intention to make contact with SF leader Ruairi O'Bradaigh, and was not a negotiation on behalf of anyone.[7] However, the information gained was being passed on to British officials. Therefore, there was no binding discussion between the two sides, but it was still helpful in understanding both sides' demands. His contact with the IRA was only known by Harold Wilson, leader of the opposition, not the British government.[8] Although Caldwell was the only intermediary for this channel, his mediation was supported by Wilson, which demonstrates that it was a collective attempt between an unofficial intermediary and a British politician. However, it was not supported by the British government, and this affected the result.

Regarding the discussion and outcome, Caldwell's meeting with O'Bradaigh concerned the republicans' plan for peace, but it was also about a truce.[9] Caldwell forced the republicans to think about the inadequacy of their strategy of daytime bombing as it resulted in more civilian casualties.[10] Even though he put pressure on the republican movement to reduce the level of violence, this effort was not a powerful mediation because it was limited to violence and was not related to peace efforts. His meetings with O'Bradaigh and Chief-of-Staff of the IRA, Sean MacStiofain, created a political perspective since Caldwell passed their messages to London. Therefore, Caldwell's mediation was weak intermediary work, but, fortunately, as it was stated in a meeting note between Caldwell and William Whitelaw (the British Secretary of State for Northern Ireland), he provided the first backchannel between the two sides.[11] As a result of his efforts, the IRA declared its first ceasefire lasting for three days beginning on Friday, 10 March 1972. This demonstrates that despite the limited authority of weak intermediaries, suggested in the existing literature,[12] Caldwell was successful in facilitating the ceasefire. The critical point was the republican movement's intention to test the water for their political claims for the first time in the Troubles. As a defector from the republican movement, Maria McGuire in her memoirs stated, 'we were by now sure that the British government would be compelled to ask where we stood politically, such was the success of our military campaign'.[13] McGuire's statement was evidence of their intention for a political resolution, but was also a statement of their aim for an armed campaign victory. Because Caldwell's contact with the republican movement was his personal initiative, it can be said that the ceasefire was a one-sided event by the IRA, which did not get a response from the British.

After the ceasefire ended and the level of violence dramatically increased, the British government sent in troops and carried out the largest military operation in the entire history of the Troubles, called Operation Motorman. Fortunately, the operation on 31 July 1972 did not result in a cessation of secret talks as the former General Officer Commanding (GOC) Northern Ireland, General Sir John Hackett, contacted the Provisional IRA Army Council member David O'Connell after this incident. It was a personal initiative and the communication channel was built by only one intermediary, just like Caldwell's attempt. The letters between Whitelaw and Hackett illustrated that Whitelaw was reluctant to talk to O'Connell and was unhappy about Hackett's dialogue with him; he said that Hackett's contact with an IRA member was very damaging and dangerous.[14] There is an important question here: although the existing backchannel literature assumes that there is no cost of entry to indirect communications,[15] why was the British government reluctant to engage in these initiatives?

The failure of Hackett's efforts stemmed from two factors. Firstly, these initiatives were achieved immediately after unsuccessful talks undertaken by Whitelaw himself. Thus, the British government was reluctant to carry out another covert initiative immediately. The disagreement between Whitelaw and senior republicans made it difficult to organise another set of meetings in a short time period. Therefore, it was not a ripe moment to start dialogue between the conflicting parties even though it was initiated by a mediator.

As Zartman argues, even if communication is commenced by a third party, it cannot be turned into negotiations if parties in a conflict are not in favour of a non-violent resolution.[16] Secondly, although ongoing violence did not cease covert initiatives, it created mistrust between the parties. This situation could only be overcome by an intermediary who was accepted by both sides.[17] Hackett's mediation was clearly not accepted by the British side.

The last and most comprehensive indirect communications were built by Brendan Duddy,[18] a Londonderry businessperson. Duddy's intermediary role began when he was asked by Steele and Oatley, senior SIS officers, to make contact with O'Bradaigh.[19] As Duddy personally knew O'Bradaigh, he played a key role in passing the messages between the British and republican sides.[20] Therefore, even though Duddy was the only intermediary between the two sides, the communication channel was initiated by the SIS officers. It was a clear sign of the need of the British officials to communicate with the republican movement. However, it was not only the British government's intention, but also that of the republicans, as the collapse of the political arrangements of Sunningdale aroused the 'dovish' component of the republican movement.[21] Duddy's intermediary efforts can be examined in three periods: the mid-1970s, early 1980s and early 1990s.

His personal archive acknowledges that 'the contact'[22] played a key role in extending the 1975 IRA ceasefire, since he acted as both a messenger and an intermediary between Wilson, Oatley and the IRA Army Council by hosting several meetings in his home.[23] The importance of Duddy's role was explained by Oatley later on, as the primary problem for him was 'how to begin a dialogue and then contact with the IRA leadership without doing so directly. If there were to be negotiations at some stage, the ground had to be prepared.'[24] It was also essential for the IRA leadership to feel that there was an ongoing and secure contact with the government. It is evident through the statement of Frank Cooper, a senior British official in Northern Ireland, that it was necessary for 'O'Bradaigh and, to some extent, O'Connell to feel that they were in contact with part of the British government which might, at some stage, help them to move in a political direction'.[25] However, it was still very risky for the government to contact the IRA directly. Even Whitelaw was not informed about these talks.[26] Therefore, it can be said that the reason for the secrecy of these meetings was the difficulty to consider it government policy during the early stage of the conflict. As Pruitt indicates, secrecy might help disputing sides to discuss their demands without any preconditions.[27] It would have been harder to conduct covert negotiations by including or informing a government representative. Therefore, this initiative provided a twofold advantage to making progress: it firstly reduced uncertainty on both sides, as both parties were feeling that they were in contact with their opponents. It was also successful on the government's side as it did not mean that they gave de facto legitimacy to the IRA.

Concerning the content of the discussions, Duddy put pressure on the British government to make concessions that would help the IRA leaders who took a pro-ceasefire position. At that time, Billy McKee, Commander of the Belfast IRA, was in the position of declaring a unilateral ceasefire. Duddy told his British contact,

> Be generous, give McKee a chance. Consider his position; he needs help . . . He is not a miracle worker . . . Pull out some mar[ine] comm[andos]. Release his buddy from Purdysburn. Release nineteen internees on Tuesday; give the names to McKee . . . We are all in this together.[28]

Even though Duddy's intention of bringing the British closer was not successful, it was clear evidence of Duddy's active role as a powerful intermediary in the secret negotiations. As Princen indicates, intermediaries can put pressure on the conflicting sides and insist on applying the requirements of secret dialogue,[29] which was clearly seen in Duddy's efforts.

Yet, the violent campaign of the IRA eventually returned, for a number of reasons. First, the 1975 ceasefire negotiations demonstrate that the British government aimed to weaken the IRA militarily instead of carrying out non-violent resolution efforts. This was admitted by the government. An anonymous British official said 'we know that the Provisionals fear that we may be stringing them along' and 'if the Provisionals stop violence, they must not now expect immediately to raise the process of talking to new levels'.[30] Therefore, Duddy's great effort at building the backchannel could not help focus political resolution efforts. This was because of the British government's intention to use the ceasefire as an opportunity for weakening the IRA. As Merlyn Rees, the new Secretary of State for Northern Ireland stated: 'The importance of a ceasefire is that it offers us the opportunity to create the conditions in which the Provisionals' "military" organisation and structure may be weakened. They would not find it easy to start a campaign again from scratch.'[31] Second, lack of trust prevented a better outcome as the British government did not rely on the IRA ceasefire. Rees pointed out in a private Cabinet discussion:

> There is the risk that the Provisionals can rest, re-supply and regroup so as to re-emerge more strongly . . . They badly needed a ceasefire if only in order to reorganise after a long period of attrition and disruptions at the hands of the Security Forces. But they are not beaten. Their cohesion and discipline are remarkable.[32]

These statements are clear evidence of the British government's aim to defeat the IRA. Therefore, these contacts did not bring a positive outcome towards peace. Finally, the IRA Army Council's letter in the Duddy papers asserted that the insufficient response of the British government, ongoing pressure from British troops and the inadequate numbers of prisoners released brought the ceasefire to an end.[33] However, General Sir Frank King, GOC of Northern Ireland, revealed just a few months after the announcement of the ceasefire, in May 1975: 'The PIRA was becoming stronger every day, but the Security Forces were becoming weaker . . . It would take a considerable time now to reverse the PIRA's new-found strength.'[34] In fact, the ceasefire did not weaken, but helped to strengthen the IRA. As former Belfast IRA member Anthony McIntyre told Moloney:

> I cannot understand these people who say that the truce wrecked us. In my view, it strengthened us. We had a lot of internees coming back in for active service. It was so unlike the situation in 1974 when we had four active volunteers. By the start of 1976, we were bursting at the seams.[35]

This initiative demonstrates that despite the credibility, powerful mediation and reduction in uncertainty, it did not provide a clear outcome towards peace. Therefore, this research reveals that the success of backchannels is not reliant only on the inclusiveness of the initiative, but also the intentions of disputing parties. It can be said that these negotiations were not 'serious' talks intended to lead the discussion to a broader level by discussing the underlying causes of the conflict. The British government's intention to use this dialogue as an opportunity to defeat the IRA by declaring a ceasefire, proved that it was a 'false' motive for a ripe moment. This is in line with Zartman's argument that the intention of all conflicting parties is crucial for resolution of conflict.[36] Although the secrecy of these talks secured them from the effect of wider and external issues, for instance national and international politics, it also created an environment in which the intentions of the parties were difficult to understand by each other.

Duddy's second major initiative was during the republican hunger strikes in 1980 and 1981. The Duddy papers reveal an intense and accelerating series of phone calls between Duddy and an anonymous representative of the British government. He met the strikers several times in the Maze Prison and forwarded their messages to his contact in the British government. According to the records, Duddy insisted on a negotiated settlement of the hunger strikes. In response to his petition, the British officials stated that 'the British government is prepared to issue a statement only if there is an immediate end to the hunger strike'.[37] However, the hunger strikers made a number of demands of the government to end the strike: civilian clothing, the right of the prisoners to decide what work should be done and visits for prisoners.[38] While the backchannel communications were being conducted, PM Thatcher refused to negotiate with the strikers as her position was that of not treating terrorists differently to other prisoners.[39] Hence, there was nothing to discuss with the republican strikers. However, while the government continued its opposition in public, the secret negotiations helped to pursue ways to weaken the conflict behind the scenes. This outcome verifies Wanis-St John's assumption that backchannels make it possible to maintain the governments' opposition to talking to terrorists while they are talking to them behind the scenes.[40] This situation helped both sides to understand each other's major demands, which also hindered any potential spoilers from destroying this channel.

Duddy sought possible ways to end the strike by contacting both strikers and their families. According to Duddy, the hunger strikers' lives could only be saved through a mutual understanding regarding the strikers' required conditions.[41] Eventually, after ten prisoners died in the strike, other strikers' families accepted medical support. The prisoners finally declared an end to the strike on 3 October 1981 and Thatcher made concessions to their requests.[42] Undoubtedly, it was not only Duddy's efforts, but also the government and strikers' perception of change that brought this about. Together with these developments, the 1980s witnessed more active political resolution efforts.

Duddy's last intermediary attempt was in the early 1990s, which led to the 1994 IRA ceasefire. When Duddy's mediation between John Major's government and the IRA was leaked to the media in 1993, it caused a political storm.[43] Although maintaining the backchannel initiatives was threatened, these secret talks led to the IRA's 1994 ceasefire. It can be said that a satisfactory dialogue had been built between the British government and republican movement that facilitated official negotiations. A similar situation emerged in Turkey when the secret Oslo talks were leaked to the press. Fortunately, neither of these incidents caused an interruption in conflict resolution efforts. The reaction in wider society was because of the content of the meetings. Duddy pointed out that there was an agreement during the discussions between the two sides:

> Walter's [IRA representative] position has been accepted and a new draft British paper has been formulated and approved by Mayhew [when he was Secretary of State for Northern Ireland] which is to be put in a special meeting on Tuesday May 18th 1993 to Mr Major in Downing Street.[44]

These covert negotiations resulted in finding common ground which was evident through the message of the British representative Robert McLarnon to Duddy to facilitate peace efforts: 'We are appalled at the present mess. We are trying to think of questions that you could put that will give you all the assurance of our goodwill and good intentions that you need.'[45] Although the message did not find an immediate response from the government's side, the process brought about the IRA's 1994 ceasefire after protracted negotiations. There were some other initiatives which facilitated the IRA's ceasefire together with Duddy's efforts. Haughey, the chairperson of the SDLP, notes that the SDLP worked hard in the late 1980s and early 1990s to make contact with the IRA, through SF, to stop its armed campaign. The secret talks between the two parties helped build a closer relationship between republicans and nationalists.[46] Together with these attempts, Duddy's efforts contributed to an understanding between the main armed protagonists.

Direct Talks

The first direct contact occurred on the last day of the first IRA ceasefire in March 1972 between Harold Wilson, his press secretary, Joe Haines, and

Merlyn Rees, the Labour Party's Shadow Secretary of State for Northern Ireland on the one hand, and the IRA Army Council member Joe Cahill and the IRA's Belfast Brigade Commander, John Kelly, on the other. The meeting was facilitated by another intermediary, John O'Connell, a Labour Party MP in the Irish government, which was a clear sign of the Irish government's facilitating role in the resolution efforts.[47] This secret meeting signalled a change towards both sides creating a path to peace. Haines later described the extent of the difficulty facing this meeting, saying: 'a meeting of minds was clearly impossible. We were planets apart; words had different meanings.'[48] However, he also highlighted the importance of the talks: 'We had broken the taboo of talks with the IRA, and thus held a door ajar for the future.'[49] Nonetheless, the difference in the focus of the two sides made it impossible to move these talks forward. The British side's focus was limited to only a ceasefire, with Wilson insisting on an extension of the ceasefire that would provide space for non-violent efforts. This claim was not responded to by the IRA.[50] In contrast, the IRA aimed to reach a satisfactory level of discussion that would lead to the recognition of their demands before declaring a ceasefire. Thus, the violence returned on the following day, with the IRA shooting at the British Army in the Bogside area of Londonderry. Although the British government announced that the Stormont parliament was suspended on 24 March 1972, this suspension did not result in breaking off the secret talks between the main armed protagonists, thanks to the lack of an official link. As Pruitt argues, these talks are easier for both states and sub-state armed groups to deny,[51] so neither side were reluctant to meet in this dispute.

As discussed in the previous section, the efforts at indirect contact by Caldwell helped bring the British government and senior republicans together, which was the second direct contact between the British and republican sides. The Prime Minister's Office noted that their first meeting was on 20 June 1972 between the IRA representatives David O'Connell and Gerry Adams on the one hand, and officials from William Whitelaw's office – Sir Phillip Woodfield and Frank Steele – on the other.[52] It was a step towards the meeting with Whitelaw. As a result of Steele's initiatives, Whitelaw had a meeting with six IRA leaders on 7 July 1972. This talk was offered to Whitelaw by a public IRA statement, with the group inviting him to Londonderry on 13 June 1972 through the republican media. Although the invitation was officially refused by Whitelaw, John Hume, the leader of the SDLP, and a senior member of the SDLP, Paddy Devlin, convinced the government that the offer was genuine.[53] Hence, Whitelaw agreed to meet the republicans secretly.

The structure of the IRA negotiating team gives a clue to the importance attached to these clandestine talks. The six members comprised three senior members of the IRA's Belfast Command: Gerry Adams, Seamus Twomey and Ivor Bell, and the IRA's Londonderry battalion commander Martin McGuinness, the IRA's Army Council member David O'Connell and Chief-of-Staff Sean MacStiofain.[54] On the other side, Whitelaw and Paul Channon, Minister of State in the Northern Ireland Office (NIO), represented the British government. Despite the high-level representatives in the talks, mistrust was revealed when Whitelaw focused on attrition instead of conciliation. An anonymous attendee of the talks informed Coogan that Whitelaw said; 'we can accept the casualties' and continued by asserting 'we probably lose as many soldiers in accidents in Germany'.[55] As discussed in Chapter 2, trust between disputing parties is one of the most salient aspects of a successful negotiation process. Due to the lack of trust, there were many disagreements during the meeting, such as over self-determination and the withdrawal of British troops. However, there was minor progress in the form of an agreement between the two sides on a week-long bilateral ceasefire with immediate effect and on arranging another set of negotiations after this ceasefire. According to an anonymous meeting note of the NIO of the British government, after the Whitelaw talks had come into effect, the ceasefire was immediately announced, but lasted only two days.[56] Fortunately, the intensive discussions between warring parties is a sign that these talks provided a flexible environment by encouraging informality and discussions about both sides' fears, aims and proposals.[57] Even though this initiative was unsuccessful, it illustrated the British government's intention to conduct political resolution efforts, as Whitelaw defended secret negotiations by saying that 'a refusal to talk would leave the political initiative in the hands of the IRA'.[58] Overall, the Whitelaw talks were a constructive effort to reach a mutual understanding. The talks strengthened the position of the Provisionals since they sat at the negotiating table with the government. They also used this initiative as a chance to understand the position of the British side: 'It was time to test the water and see if the British were prepared to negotiate.'[59]

Although the violence was ongoing, this initiative embodied the advantage of the two sides' intention for a non-violent resolution, which is one of the major requirements for a conflict resolution process. On the one hand, Whitelaw points out his demand in the application of peace talks in February 1972: 'our aim is not to conquer or occupy the city but to bring it back permanently and with as little rancour as possible in a peaceful and orderly state'.[60] On the other hand, the IRA also demanded a meeting with the British government to discuss the IRA's peace plan, which encapsulated the Irish people's right for self-determination, the British troops' withdrawal from Northern Ireland and a general amnesty for prisoners in Britain and Ireland.[61] Even though the two sides intended to conduct negotiations, the underlying reason for the lack of success was a great gap in their desires. McGuinness explained that the republican movement's only interest in meeting with Whitelaw was 'to secure a binding agreement from the British declaring their intention to leave Ireland at some date in the future'.[62] In contrast, even though Whitelaw's approach during the secret meetings was criticised, he aimed to create conditions of political bargaining instead of a violent campaign, unlike Rees and some other British officials. This was evident through the British government's statement in a Cabinet discussion: 'Recent developments offered an opportunity for a political advance that the government could not afford to miss.'[63] The difference between the two sides' desires prevented progress. Whitelaw later examined the meeting in his memoirs as 'a non-event', he continued: 'The IRA leaders simply made impossible demands which I told them the British Government could never concede. They were in fact still in a mood of defiance and determination to carry on until their absurd ultimatums were met.'[64] Therefore, initiating the dialogue was not a 'hurting stalemate' for both sides. As Zartman indicates, a hurting stalemate emerges when disputing parties are locked in a conflict and cannot reach victory, and hence seek a way out of the conflict to end this deadlock.[65] Whitelaw's attrition policy, instead of conciliation, demonstrated that it was not a ripe moment for resolution from the British side. In addition, it is also critical that objective elements (conflicting parties' refusal to recognise the facts as accurate) are necessary but not sufficient for a political resolution. Subjective elements were also necessary, which are not only a hurting stalemate for both sides and their intention towards a negotiated settlement, but also other parties that can cultivate these dialogues from a painful situation to a preferable alternative.[66] The Northern Irish parties were not included in the process due to the secrecy of the meetings and so the agents who were in favour of the peace initiatives did not play an encouraging role in the progress. Thus, the discussion in this backchannel can be examined not as a 'false' event, but as an event in appearance only due to the great gap between the perceptions of both sides.

The last significant secret initiative was arranged by a group of Protestant clergymen from the Irish Council of Churches in Feakle on 10 December 1974. According to English, the Feakle talks were made possible because the British were keen to send signals to the IRA that they were thinking of withdrawing from Northern Ireland.[67] There was a clear intention to conduct peace attempts by the British as the talks were achieved three weeks after the Birmingham pub bombings, which killed nineteen people and injured 182.[68] Political parties in the UK were against a political resolution due to their anger over the IRA's violent campaign that had resulted in the killing of many civilians.[69] Ending the IRA's armed campaign was a national policy and at the top of the British government's agenda. However, there is little evidence that the backchannel communications were affected by international politics. Instead, they were defined by the nature of the conflict, and intentions of the British and republican sides. However, despite the intensity of the conflict, the meeting was carried out due to the change of government and thanks to the willingness of PM Harold Wilson's minority government for a political resolution in March 1974.[70] The change of government created a positive environment in which to apply peace initiatives; hence, the change in the national political environment in the UK aided non-violent, political resolution attempts. It can be said that national politics played an encouraging role during the Feakle talks, in contrast to the previous secret dialogues, because this time Wilson's government aimed to discuss a political settlement.

The declassified secret TNA papers revealed that Merilyn Rees, the Secretary of State for Northern Ireland, stated that even though Wilson was willing to talk to the IRA about a cessation of violence, this minority government was reluctant to respond to any of the IRA's demands as they would lead to a misunderstanding in public regarding negotiations with SF.[71] Therefore, the reluctance of the British government was because of the possibility of this channel being revealed; the channel seemed vital for the government in order to prevent a public outcry against an agreement with the IRA.[72] Arguably, it could be said that the change in the ruling party facilitated the peace efforts between the IRA and British government. It was a ripe moment for initiating peace negotiations since both the British government and republican movement were in favour of the peace talks. In addition, the efforts of the mediators to bring together both sides facilitated the dialogue and determined an approachable agenda for the talks that prevented this event from looking like a simulation exercise. Instead, it was a 'serious' event because it was motivated by 'true' motives,[73] specifically, the intention of both conflicting parties and attempts of intermediaries as internal factors, and the change in the political environment in the UK as national development. As Ikle[74] and Zartman[75] indicate, true motives might help reach a ripe moment to turn into negotiations to establish a political resolution. This was also a 'hurting stalemate' because the pub bombings were one of the most lethal attacks in IRA history. After this attack, both sides started to think that they could not reach victory by armed campaign. The loss of civilian lives created anger in the society and caused a deeper divide between the Catholic and Protestant communities in Northern Ireland. This belief also helped advance non-violent, political resolution efforts. The insight of the discussions demonstrates that the topics discussed in the Feakle talks were at the core of the Northern Ireland conflict.

The Feakle talks were carried out between the political wing of the republican movement, which was represented by the leader O'Bradaigh, vice-leader Maire Drumm and Seamus Loughran, SF's Belfast organiser, and the IRA wing that was represented by Billy McKee, David O'Connell and three helicopter escapees from Mountjoy prison: O'Hagan, Twomey and Mallon. Sir Frank Cooper, the Permanent Secretary to the NIO in Stormont represented the British side.[76] Four factors are crucial to understanding the significance of these talks. First, reducing audience effects helped build a stronger communication channel.[77] As these discussions excluded audiences, they made it possible for the British government to meet with the IRA escapees. It was also a sign of the intention of the two sides for a non-violent resolution. Second, it helped overcome mistrust on the republican side as it was a face-to-face discussion.[78] Similarly, the IRA's ceasefire encouraged the British side to think about further steps for peace.[79] Third, it was an obvious example of how spoilers could undermine a backchannel. As Stedman argues, a spoiler threat emerges when extremist elements of a conflict-affected environment intervene in the situation.[80] It was a well-organised event because the clergymen had prepared a document and aimed to get the IRA's agreement, then to present it to the British government as a framework for ending violence. However, the meetings did not have an immediate outcome as they were stopped when the Irish Special Branch raided the hotel where they were being conducted.

Despite this obstacle, the IRA's statement demonstrated that they later informed Oatley about their declaration of a ten-day ceasefire from midnight on 22 December, hoping to create a climate in which a more productive dialogue might be achieved.[81] The clergymen undoubtedly played their role in crystallising the IRA's thinking towards a political discussion. The ceasefire was then extended until 16 January through another intermediary, Brendan Duddy, as discussed in the previous section. Finally, the discussion gives the clue of the underlying reason for the ceasefire. McKee asserted that 'I asked what was on the agenda and he [Oatley] said "Withdrawal"[82] and he said that he needed our help . . . They said, that is what they wanted.'[83] McKee continued: 'If they had not mentioned withdrawal, there would have been no ceasefire and no truce at that time.'[84] So, the withdrawal was the primary reason for the republicans to come together with the British and to declare the ceasefire. Therefore, it is important to understand that secret talks are not the only important factors in leading the way towards official negotiations and a political settlement; more importantly, it is the promises given by the conflicting sides related to their major demands, such as withdrawal.

Backchannels in Turkey

Turkey's Kurdish question has witnessed several secret initiatives through intermediaries and direct talks. While different intermediaries played a role in exchanging messages between the Turkish government and the PKK, secret talks were carried out between the leading members of the MIT and PKK. The influence of these channels was determined by different factors, which are discussed in this section.

Indirect Communications

The secret contact between the Turkish government and the PKK was initiated by different intermediaries. The first secret contact was initiated by Jalal Talabani, who was the leader of the Patriotic Union of Kurdistan (PUK), when President Özal asked him to make contact with Öcalan between the late 1980s and 1993.[85] The content of these messages was revealed through the interview data. Cengiz Çandar, who was Özal's chief advisor, stated that Özal's message to Öcalan was a request for a ceasefire.[86] Similarly, it was also admitted by Öcalan during his interview with a Turkish journalist, Oral Çalışlar,[87] that he met with Talabani and Çandar in an attempt to de-escalate the conflict.[88] Özal asked the PKK to declare a ceasefire, which he believed was the first step towards a non-violent resolution. Talabani's contact with Öcalan in the Bekaa Valley in Syria (where the PKK's headquarters were located) was the first initiative towards a non-violent peace.[89] As Pruitt puts it, the role of intermediaries can only be to pass messages, including the desires and demands of parties, between each other.[90] Talabani's role was also limited to passing on Özal and Öcalan's messages to each other, which makes his effort that of a weak intermediary. Despite his limited involvement, Talabani's messenger role was successful in decreasing the level of violence and understanding both sides' desires. It is evident that even though Talabani did not play a key role, his messenger role facilitated the PKK's first ceasefire, which was one of the major aims of the backchannel communications. Özal informed the TSK about these indirect dialogues in 1988.[91] However, he was faced with a strong reaction from the Chief of the General Staff, Necip Torumtay, who said 'the state does not talk with the bandits'.[92] This reaction prevented the expansion of the framework the indirect dialogues were based on.

Talabani then began to make contact with PM Süleyman Demirel. Birand and Yalçın's interview with Talabani reveals insight of his contact with Demirel. According to Talabani, when he asked Demirel about his demand, Demirel replied: 'I do not want to negotiate with him [Öcalan]. But, you [Talabani] can contact him and ask to stop violent attacks. The ceasefire is crucial for us to achieve political reforms in the south-east of Turkey.'[93] These talks and initiatives are a sign of the intention of both sides to conduct political resolution efforts instead of an armed campaign. Both Demirel and

Özal thought that a ceasefire was the precondition for initiating dialogue. The exchange of messages resulted in the PKK's first ceasefire starting on 20 March 1993. Öcalan declared that the PKK was ready for a political resolution and the Nevruz[94] celebration would be held in peace.[95] The ceasefire was a result of Talabani's efforts, based on his trustworthiness as seen by both sides. As Princen notes, intermediaries are expected to be trustworthy or, at least, more trustworthy than one's opponent.[96] Therefore, they can improve communication and enhance the disputing parties' understanding of each other's intentions and desires.[97] It can be said that President Özal's trust in Talabani's mediation encouraged him to initiate the process, while Öcalan's reliance helped him to improve communication between the warring parties. It was also due to the intention of the PKK, which was to resolve the conflict through negotiations as Öcalan noted, the first choice for the PKK being to reach their aim through political struggle.[98]

The second intermediary during the early peace efforts was Cengiz Çandar. Çandar met with Öcalan a few times before and after the 1993 ceasefire. Çandar's first contact was before the ceasefire when he went to the Bekaa Valley. According to Çandar, Öcalan was not reluctant about either a ceasefire or a political resolution, but asked for the cessation of an intimidation policy against the PKK; otherwise, the PKK would respond to it with an armed campaign.[99] After the declaration of the ceasefire, he contacted Öcalan through Talabani and asked for the ceasefire to be extended indefinitely and without preconditions. Three days later, Talabani called Çandar and agreed that Öcalan had accepted to extend the ceasefire indefinitely. However, as President Özal died a few days later, the dialogue ceased.[100] The ceasefire was ended by a dreadful terrorist attack in which the PKK executed thirty-three unarmed off-duty soldiers and five civilians on 24 May 1993.[101] Overall, Çandar's mediation contained more than one link in the chain as he contacted Öcalan via Talabani. It can be said that this effort created a more chaotic situation since it resulted in both sides blaming each other. For example, Öcalan later blamed the Turkish government for the failure of this initiative: 'We declared a ceasefire. However, the Turkish state was not ready for resolution. Özal did not prepare the security forces and his party for peace. He could not convince them.'[102]

These initiatives illustrate two important factors of secret talks. First, it was evident that both sides were willing to discuss the future of the Kurdish question in a non-violent context. Çandar stated that 'both Özal and Öcalan were willing to solve the conflict in a political way'.[103] The intention of the conflicting parties formed the starting point of the peace process. Next, as Wanis-St John indicates, the personal initiatives of intermediaries made officially sanctioned communications possible.[104] Although Çandar was the advisor to Özal, it was his personal initiative to communicate with Öcalan. Çandar explained that he was not asked by Özal or any other Turkish officials to do so.[105] Therefore, both contacts were achieved thanks to the intermediaries' personal efforts. Talabani's initiative resulted in the PKK ceasefire, while Çandar played a facilitating role to achieve this backchannel.

The contact between the two sides was maintained through Talabani in the mid-1990s, despite the political pressure of the Chief of the General Staff Doğan Güreş. He pointed out that the only place to discuss the Kurdish issue was the National Security Council[106] (*Milli Güvenlik Kurulu*, henceforth MGK).[107] Even though it was never attested to in public, the analysis on the declassified secret documents revealed that Özal informed the MGK about the indirect talks and asked the Chief of the General Staff to stop counter-terrorism operations. Güreş's reply is a clear indicator of the Army's opposition to a political resolution:

> We are not going to cease operations. I am not following your order in this regard. Otherwise, what would I say to my soldiers on duty at the operation theatre? You can dismiss me from the office if you can afford to. Then, you can do whatever you want.[108]

The reaction of Güreş prevented peace efforts being conducted as government policy, and thus resulted in secret initiatives being personally maintained by political leaders. As a ripe moment is also affected by national politics, it is clear that it was not the right time to conduct official negotiations towards ending the Kurdish conflict – because of the dominant role of the MGK in national politics at the time and it being one of the major executive bodies in Turkish politics on security issues, even if a political decision was being discussed.

Talabani was again the key messenger between PM Tansu Çiller and Öcalan. However, this indirect initiative had a different structure as Çiller took great care that this channel was not revealed by spoilers. Çiller, therefore, sent her chief advisor, Ercan Vuralhan (who later became Minister of

National Defence) to meet with Talabani. The significant point of this backchannel was the length of the communication chain as this channel contained two intermediaries, just like Çandar's mediation. While Vuralhan acted as a messenger between Talabani and Çiller, Talabani played a pivotal role as he was the direct contact with the two principal actors. It can be said that the length of backchannels in the Turkish case has been used to ensure that these dialogues remain secret.

In terms of insight into the backchannel, Günay Aslan,[109] the director of the PKK's Med-TV, revealed PM Çiller's dialogue with Talabani through his letter to Öcalan on 14 March 1995, 'Tansu Çiller seeks a political resolution'.[110] As Aslan stated, Çiller asked the PKK to declare a ceasefire for a year and later to end the armed campaign.[111] Öcalan responded to this call by focusing on a bilateral truce. In Öcalan's words, 'if the government avoids any attacks against the people [in the south-east of Turkey] and [armed] operations against the PKK, I am ready to declare a ceasefire'.[112] The exchange of demands finally resulted in a ceasefire, which was announced by Öcalan during a live broadcast of Aslan's Med-TV programme. Nevertheless, the ceasefire was broken by the PKK after only three days. The PKK blamed this on the government for not responding to its demands and for organising a cross-border operation in northern Iraq, where the PKK's camps were located.[113] The reason for the failure of this dialogue was the TSK's hard-line policies.[114] The TSK, as the spoiler of this effort, aimed to prevent building a communication channel after Öcalan's live broadcast. This backchannel illustrated that it was not a 'hurting stalemate' on the Turkish Army's side since the TSK was willing to maintain traditional counter-terrorism measures instead of conflict resolution procedures through intermediaries. This indirect communication channel illustrates that trust in the intermediary facilitated the building of communication channels between the conflicting parties, but the role of intermediaries was restricted to transmitting messages.

There was also an unsanctioned backchannel initiated by Seyyit Haşim Haşimi, a deputy of the Welfare Party (*Refah Partisi*, henceforth RP). Although Haşimi was a deputy of the coalition party in government, it was not an RP initiative. It was Öcalan's demand to talk to Haşimi as he is a Kurdish politician and a well-known figure in Turkey's southeast. This was an untold and overlooked issue, but was important in the conflict resolution process since it illustrated the intention of the pro-Kurdish side to conduct peace talks despite the high-intensity conflict. Haşimi noted that Öcalan called him and asked to contact Erbakan for a political settlement.[115] Haşimi and Mukadder Başeğmez, who later became a deputy of the Virtue Party (the successor of the RP; *Fazilet Partisi*, henceforth FP), talked with PM Necmettin Erbakan. Erbakan accepted this recommendation and decided to commence secret talks with the PKK. Nevertheless, Erbakan deployed İsmail Nacar, who was an NGO leader, as an intermediary.[116] The reason for Erbakan's choice of Nacar instead of Haşimi was explained through Nacar's earlier meetings with Erbakan on the Kurdish question.[117] Although this attempt was not successful, it provided paramount information on the Turkish government's perception of secret communications. This issue can be explained through mistrust of Haşimi, which resulted in the lack of an outcome. The existing backchannel communication literature addresses the requirement to overcome trust and credibility issues regarding the implementation of secret talks.[118] In this context, while Haşimi's attempt was not a credible contact from the government's side, Nacar's effort helped build the first direct contact between the government and the PKK. His involvement in this initiative will be assessed in the next section as he became part of direct talks.

İlhami Işık[119] was the last intermediary who played a role from 1998 to 2004. Işık's early efforts between the government and senior members of the PKK resulted in a PKK ceasefire on 1 September 1998.[120] It proved critical, as the ceasefire dramatically decreased the casualties from more than a thousand to less than a hundred in a year (see Figure 3.2). According to Işık, both the Turkish officials and PKK leaders were not ready to come together.[121] Therefore, Işık exchanged information between these two sides. Işık's mediation was weak intermediary work as he only exchanged messages between the Turkish government and PKK. Işık met with leading members of the PKK: Karayılan, Karasu and Ok on the one hand, and the MIT members on the other, who later attended the Oslo talks.[122] The significant point was that the PKK leadership asked Işık to send messages to the government for the sake of non-violent resolution. Therefore, he made contact with the leading members of both sides. He even met with Öcalan in İmralı prison. In contrast to Haşimi, Işık's intermediary role between the two sides has never been denied by either the Turkish government or the PKK. Hence, it can be said that he met with the expectations of an intermediary in this conflict, who, in Princen's words, is required to be 'neutral or impartial, or, at least, to act to preserve one's expected – and deserved – outcome'.[123]

In terms of insight into the discussions, after his intermediary role, the PKK fulfilled the major claims of the Turkish government as it changed its name, withdrew its militants from Turkey and did not apply an armed struggle. Nevertheless, the Turkish government did not amend issues regarding human rights and democratic changes for equality and self-governance.[124] Işık revealed that, during his mediation, Öcalan's primary claim was that the Turkish government should have recognised that the PKK did not create the problem, but that there had been an existing Kurdish issue before the PKK.[125] However, as discussed in the previous chapter, these changes did not help the progress. The reason why this backchannel failed after six years of exchanging demands and claims on both sides should be analysed. In 2004, the PKK brought its ceasefire to an end by blaming the TSK for maintaining military operations and the AKP rule for not making any political reforms related to the Kurdish question.[126] After declaring the ceasefire, the PKK changed its name to KADEK and then Kongra-Gel. In response, the government did not discuss a political resolution. Therefore, as Yayla notes, Turkey could not use this five-year ceasefire to its advantage.[127] This was because of not only the reluctance of politicians, but also the 'deep state'.[128] Although it is not the topic of this research, many unresolved crimes were alleged to have been related to the deep state in the 1990s and early 2000s. However, while Işık's intermediary work facilitated the communication between the conflicting sides, the failure of the process was due to the perceptions of the disputing parties.[129] Even though the government was blamed for being reluctant, two factors have been paid little attention: the division within the PKK and regional factors. On the one hand, Coşkun noted that the PKK came to a crossroads in 2004.[130] While one side wanted a political struggle instead of an armed conflict, the other defended carrying out an armed campaign. As a result, the group that advocated armed conflict eliminated the other side and the PKK returned to a violent campaign in June 2004.[131] On the other hand, the PKK's end of ceasefire and cessation of conflict resolution efforts were also due to the Iraq War of 2003. The US's invasion of Iraq changed the nature of the region, and the PKK used the authority gap in Iraq to their advantage. When Saddam Hussein's regime was ended, and the US army left northern Iraq, the PKK found great ammunition supplies in Iraq from the Saddam regime. The group wanted to use this opportunity to fight against Turkey as its government was not willing to take steps towards a political settlement.[132] Even though the Iraq War seems an external issue for Turkey's Kurdish question, it had a direct effect on the nature of the peace process due to the PKK's use of northern Iraq as its headquarter and for its camps. The war in Iraq therefore resulted in the reluctance of the PKK to maintain the peaceful dialogue. As a result, the intermediaries' efforts in the 1990s and 2000s did not have a major effect on the peace process.

Direct Talks

The first direct contact between the Turkish government and the PKK occurred during Erbakan's RP rule in 1996.[133] Zübeyir Aydar, president of the executive committee of the Kurdish parliament-in-exile, made contact with Nacar and asked Nacar to make contact with the government. Nacar's personal contact with PM Erbakan led him into being selected as the intermediary of this channel on 27 July 1996.[134] Erbakan then appointed Fethullah Erbaş, the then RP deputy, to conduct secret negotiations with Nacar. Öcalan later related, during his interrogation, that 'Nacar was one of the intermediaries during the RP rule who contacted me on the phone from time to time' and 'Erbakan claimed the PKK to end the violent conflict in order to achieve political, economic and cultural reforms in the south-east of Turkey'.[135] When this backchannel was leaked to the press, an outcry emerged from the other parties in the parliament.[136] During the secret talks, Öcalan demanded amnesty for Kurdish deputies and other prisoners, Kurdish broadcasting on state television, and Kurdish education in private schools. Erbaş's request on behalf of the government was an immediate ceasefire, the release of eight captured Turkish soldiers, and an end to border violations.[137] Erbaş later described the secret talks as partially successful as they led to the release of captured Turkish soldiers, even though they also caused an outcry from the TSK and MGK.[138] Although the government was defending the argument 'we do not talk to terrorists' in public, due to the lack of cost of entry to this talk, the spoilers' reaction resulted in ending this peace initiative. The outcome of the talks was a result of their secrecy, but the process was then prevented from continuing due to the spoilers, namely the TSK and opposition parties. Although Dochartaigh suggests that it is easier to keep these channels secret and to exclude both internal and external spoilers,[139] it was not possible in the Turkish case in the late 1990s due to the dominance of the TSK.

Furthermore, the TSK's role in Turkey's national politics diminished the influence of this direct communication channel, just as it had the impact of indirect dialogues. Fortunately, this initiative did not remain as a 'simulation exercise' since it contributed to the peace process by testing the willingness of both sides to work towards a political resolution. However, even though Turkish soldiers were captured by the PKK, it was not a 'hurting stalemate' for resolution because the major political agents in Turkey, including the Turkish Army and political parties, were in favour of maintaining an armed struggle. This was due to the belief that a predominantly armed response by the Turkish Army would be adequate to destroy the PKK. Later, the Turkish government realised that it was an insufficient policy, as it largely overlooked the fact that it was an ethnic conflict. This change appeared in the final secret communication channel.

The last and most comprehensive secret talks between the Turkish government and the PKK were achieved during AKP rule. The significance of the Oslo talks derived from a number of major factors: the duration of the talks, participants, insights and outcome. The duration of the talks has been a contested issue since the talks leaked to the public. It is largely understood that these talks were carried out between 2009 and 2011, despite some disagreement. For example, the CHP spokesperson, Haluk Koç, asserted that the meetings began in 2009.[140] However, Etyen Mahçupyan, the chief advisor to the PM, revealed that the talks were first launched in 2006 and lasted until 2011, being conducted in different locations including Brussels and Oslo, until some parts of the records were leaked to the media.[141] Similarly, a senior member of the PKK, Nuriye Kesebir, who attended the talks, stated that the talks began in 2006.[142] The start date of the talks is very significant, as 2006 was a dreadful year in the conflict, seeing 111 security officers, 149 PKK members and 38 civilians losing their lives with many more injured.[143] Murat Karayılan, one of the five top leaders of the PKK, argues that the process transformed into the official peace negotiations, which took place in September 2008.[144] It was an indicator of the government's demand to conduct a political strategy rather than an armed campaign. In parallel to Pruitt's assumption of backchannels' positive role during existing violence,[145] these initiatives provided a suitable environment for paving the way to official negotiations.

It is also significant that the year 2006 witnessed a 'hurting stalemate' for not only the Turkish government, but also the PKK, due to the high-intensity violence. Although 1996 was one of the most devastating years of the Kurdish conflict, the belief of the political and military agents in armed struggle to defeat the PKK prevented the success of the Erbakan administration's backchannel communication. The change in the perception of the Turkish government and the application of negotiations illustrate a situation similar to Zartman's argument that both sides were locked in a conflict from which they cannot reach victory through armed struggle.[146] The data on the lives lost (298 in total) demonstrate the intensity of the violence, which was the highest number of security service members and civilians lost and second highest number of members on the PKK's side lost in the 2000s.[147] The casualties demonstrated the cost of the escalation of the conflict and proved the inability of both sides to de-escalate the violence. From this mutually hurting stalemate, a sense of a way out emerged in both parties. This stalemate was a subjective element leading towards a peaceful process, together with events in an international context. International politics were important to initiate peace events in the mid-2000s. The EU's support for the resolution of the Kurdish conflict in a political way was an incentive to talk to the PKK and learn their demands in order to resolve the conflict.[148] These talks also opened the way for political changes through reforms to the constitution. Although the reason for the British, Norwegian and Swedish governments to organise the secret talks as mediators and facilitators is not clear due to a lack of primary sources, their involvement was a clear indication of their intention and help towards the resolution of the conflict in a non-violent way. Also, the agreement between Turkey and the US on organising joint operations and appointing reciprocal private representatives against the PKK militants in northern Iraq was a trigger factor for the PKK to be willing to negotiate. More importantly, the meetings between the two states witnessed the US's insistence on the resolution of the conflict only being reached through negotiations. These factors helped both sides to apply conflict resolution efforts as opposed to maintaining the violent conflict.

The participants of the talks illustrate high-level representation, which shows the importance given to the talks by both sides. They were carried out between the Undersecretary (head) of the MIT, Emre Taner (later on by Hakan Fidan, the successor of Taner), alongside Deputy Undersecretary of the MIT, Afet Güneş, and the leadership of the PKK: Sabri Ok, Mustafa Karasu, Adem Uzun and Zübeyir Aydar.[149] There was also a third party to mediate the talks. Although these actors have never been declared by the Turkish government, Karasu later noted that while British intelligence was the mediator of the meetings, the Norwegian government attended the talks as a facilitator.[150] Hence, the role of mediation is significant for a peace process. As Bercovitch indicates, a mediator's role can be to form an international perspective with no force or arbitrative rules.[151] Similarly, British intelligence did not define a route for negotiations, but organised the meetings and brought both sides together in independent locations.[152] Related to the representatives of the disputing parties, the high-level representation helped make progress. On the one hand, the attendance of the head of the MIT illustrates the significance of the secret talks. Further, Hakan Fidan,[153] later appointed the Undersecretary of the MIT, pointed out the importance of PM Tayyip Erdoğan being represented in the talks stating; 'I am the Deputy Undersecretary of the MIT, but I am here as the private representative of PM [Erdoğan]'.[154] Fidan also declared that he had the authority to make political decisions on behalf of the Turkish government.[155] The high-level attendance at the talks demonstrates that the political authorities were willing to resolve this problem in a non-violent way. Compare this to the secret talks in Northern Ireland, where although Steele and Oatley were senior officers, neither were the key decision makers – this is a great difference between the two cases. On the other hand, the PKK members who attended the talks were leading members of the group. Similar to the backchannels in Northern Ireland, the PKK's negotiators are officially on the wanted terrorist lists.[156] In both initiatives, the high-level representation in these talks played a promoting role for overcoming trust issues. In addition, the HDP deputies Altan Tan, Sırrı Süreyya Önder and Pervin Buldan also played a messenger role, forwarding the result of the meetings to the PKK's imprisoned leader Öcalan.

The discussion topics of the meetings are also crucial to understanding the role of secret talks in the peace process. During the meetings, Fidan encouraged the PKK side to support a political resolution by noting that if a communal movement is supported by the people, it will achieve its aim sooner or later – so, he offered a model of direct societal support for the political environment instead of an armed campaign.[157] In addition, the purpose of the Oslo talks was to demonstrate that even if the armed struggle was maintained, the government and the PKK would keep talking behind the scenes. Further, the insight of these talks illustrates a secret agreement between the two sides, since Fidan underlined that he was involved in the talks. This was because the dimension of the talks changed from only a technical channel to establish the groundwork of negotiations, to a political discussion including major dimensions for the future of the conflict and political reforms. He then followed with one of the most important statements of the secret talks as a whole, stating that there was 90–95 per cent agreement between the government and PKK on their general demands.[158] The agreed topics were constitutional changes repealing ethnic differences in the rule of law, and Öcalan's amnesty.[159] It means that the Turkish government and the PKK agreed on the main issues for resolving the conflict[160] and was clear evidence of the success of the Oslo talks. However, the government was careful to secure this initiative by not declaring the agreement in public. Arguably, keeping the agreement secret could have been used to gain time to destroy the PKK through armed struggle. Koç revealed the agreement between the AKP leaders and the PKK. According to the agreement:

> The parties agree to work on the names to be included in commissions that were to be founded as per Öcalan's drafts, namely the 'Constitution Council', the 'Peace Council' and the 'Truth and Justice Commission'.[161] The Turkish government promises to have two people representing the PKK meet with Öcalan right after the elections, apparently the general elections on June 12, 2011, and have some sub-commission members meet him after the foundation of the commissions mentioned above . . . the release of people arrested on allegations of ties to the KCK would be an appropriate step to resolution. In this context, the Turkish side promises to release arrested Kurdish politicians after Nevruz as a first step. The parties also promise each other to halt military operations mutually until June 15, 2011, while planning to meet once again in the second half of June 2011.

Referring to this revealed document when made public, the CHP, the leading opposition party, blamed the AKP for making an agreement with the PKK. In fact, even though the spokesperson of the AKP, Ömer Çelik, refused to acknowledge the existence of an agreement, it had been accepted earlier by the Minister of Internal Affairs, Efkan Ala: 'The problem was caused by the PKK. We had an agreement in Oslo. It was collapsed by the PKK.'[162] While a series of secret negotiations were maintained, PM Erdoğan denied the claims of talking to terrorists with harsh language and even called people who made the allegations 'dishonoured slanderers'.[163] It was in line with Pruitt's assumption that these backchannels enable parties to continue their opposition in public whilst they are seeking ways to de-escalate the conflict secretly.[164] When the secret talks were revealed in the media, the CHP's leader, Kemal Kılıçdaroğlu, blamed the government: 'It is understood that the meetings took place with the desire of PM Erdoğan. The language behind closed doors and in public is 180 degrees different.'[165] However, many of the agreed points were never implemented as the process ended due to the negative reaction of wider Turkish society.

The 'Habur event' was a clear outcome of the Oslo talks. Fidan called the Habur event the consequence of the agreement between the government and the PKK.[166] According to the agreement between the MIT and PKK, a symbolic surrender of thirty-four PKK members was organised at the Habur border checkpoint of Turkey in 2009. The two groups, one from the Makhmour Refugee Camp in northern Iraq and the other from Qandil Mountain, surrendered. The Turkish government had agreed to arrange an investigation at the border and to release these militants. After the government had kept its promise, the militants were released. They were welcomed by great celebration, victory marches and propaganda for the PKK. These marches resulted in an outcry in the wider Turkish society.[167] Algan, a witness to the event, stated that the Habur event was a clear sign that the Turkish government was taking steps towards resolution of the conflict.[168] The event illustrated a significant effort on the government's side, since a court was established just to investigate the surrenders at the border, the judges were brought in via helicopter, and everything was settled to release these militants prior to their investigation. The first impression of the residents of Turkey's southeast was very positive as they felt that peace was not impossible anymore. Nevertheless, the pro-Kurdish movement introduced the event as the PKK's triumph, claiming the PKK was successful in the war against Turkey. These PKK members travelled around many cities in the south-east of Turkey in an open-topped bus. This show resulted in strong opposition in the wider population of Turkey, and so interrupted the peace process.[169] It can be said that although the Habur event was a remarkable effort on the government's side to legalise the conflict resolution process, the pro-Kurdish movement's aim to demonstrate it as their victory negatively affected the success of this event. The Kurdish politicians also attested this, as Tan, a deputy of pro-Kurdish HDP, stated that the Habur celebrations in different cities did not help the peace process.[170] As a result, the Habur event did not have a positive outcome for the peace process.

Peacemaking in Progress?

Secret communications between the British government and IRA, and between the Turkish government and PKK are as old as the history of these conflicts. This was possible through strong leaderships in the two governments and terrorist groups respectively. Therefore, Cronin was right regarding strong leadership in terrorist groups as a major reason for initiating these talks.[171] In contrast, this book contradicts his argument on terrorist groups regarding the Northern Irish and Kurdish conflicts in that they are more likely to engage in negotiations if conflicts exist for a long time, since backchannel communications were initiated shortly after the conflicts began.[172] The backchannels in Northern Ireland and Turkey were determined by the contact of the intermediaries in indirect dialogue and by the actors who aimed to resolve these conflicts in non-violent ways during direct talks. The success of these channels depended on different factors, including: the desires of disputing parties, the influence of spoilers, whether a violent conflict existed, and on these parties keeping their promises.

Table 4.1 Characteristics of intermediaries in Northern Ireland and Turkey.

Outcome	Northern Ireland		Turkey	
Partial consent	Caldwell:	Weak Collective	Talabani:	Weak Precondition
Consent	Duddy:	Powerful Collective Extend ceasefire	Işık:	Weak Collective Ceasefire
Reaction	Hackett:	Individual Weak Mistrust	Haşimi:	Individual Weak Mistrust

In terms of the influence of indirect dialogue, both conflicts embodied personal and official actions to make contact between the main armed protagonists. The first backchannels in both conflicts aimed to decrease the level of violence. While Caldwell's intermediary work was his personal initiative, but was known to Wilson, Talabani was asked by Özal to exchange messages between him and Öcalan (Table 4.1). Both resulted in the armed groups' ceasefires to show their intention for a political resolution. What was important was that neither side gave promises to each other, not to lay down arms on the part of the IRA and PKK, nor an immediate political reform by the British and Turkish governments. Although both intermediaries had contact with the leaders of the IRA and PKK, this contact did not lead to the same outcome. It can be said that the British government's lack of intention to form a communication channel with the IRA prevented a better outcome. However, it was still significant that this contact was sufficient to make direct contact possible. As Özal initiated the backchannel in the Turkish case, it provided a much stronger link between the conflicting sides and helped overcome trust issues. Therefore, this chapter reveals that when the officials of the governments initiated a communication channel, these talks were more successful than the channels provided by independent third parties with regard to moving towards official negotiations and conflict de-escalation. However, both dialogues were conducted as personal initiatives, and were not the policy of the British and Turkish governments. Any overt attempts at political resolution aroused the anger of wider society. This anger demonstrated that these were not ripe moments for resolution.

Moreover, two other intermediaries had direct contact with leaders of the republican and pro-Kurdish movements. While Duddy was asked by SIS officers to make contact with the IRA, Işık was requested by the PKK in contrast to Talabani's mediation.[173] As Table 4.1 indicates, both intermediaries played a more extensive role than only exchanging messages because of the consent of the conflicting parties. Duddy's facilitating role turned into an encouraging action to make progress when he put pressure on his British contact to give McKee a chance to de-escalate the conflict by pulling out some of the British troops from Northern Ireland.[174] This was also due to both sides' implicit consent for Duddy's mediation. Although Steele and Oatley forwarded the messages to British officials, their role was to represent the

British government during the secret talks. Similarly, Işık was also accepted as an intermediary by both sides, as his peace efforts were maintained even after Öcalan's capture. More specifically, Işık was one of the few people who went to the İmralı prison to discuss the PKK's demands on the nature of the conflict and helped to bring the PKK's violent campaign to an end.[175]

Duddy and Işık were not only messengers, but also facilitators, as they were involved in the discussions and aimed to keep the communication channels open. However, this was not always possible since the perceptions of the governments and armed groups were not always in favour of political resolution. For example, as discussed in the section 'Backchannels in Northern Ireland', the 1975 ceasefire was used as an opportunity by the British government to weaken the IRA. It was evident through Rees's statement during a secret Cabinet discussion: 'The importance of a ceasefire is that it offers us the opportunity to create the conditions in which the Provisionals' "military" organisation and structure may be weakened.'[176] In parallel, Işık had difficulties keeping the ongoing secret channel open, due to the TSK's oppressive military strategy. Hence, both initiatives witnessed non-ripe moments for resolution. However, the political actors' willingness to politically resolve the conflict helped Işık to maintain contacts even though they were not officially sanctioned.

In terms of the direct talks, both Wilson and Erbakan's efforts were low-level talks with regard to the profile of attendees and their aims (Table 4.2). However, as stated previously, even though Wilson's initiative seemed to fail, unlike Erbakan's efforts, the outcomes of both attempts were opposite to each

Table 4.2 Characteristics and outcomes of direct talks in Northern Ireland and Turkey.

Outcome	Northern Ireland		Turkey	
Little progress	Wilson:	Low-level No outcome No precondition	Erbakan:	Low-level Limited agenda No precondition
	Whitelaw:	High-level Ceasefire Little progress		
Substantial progress	Feakle:	High-level (lower) Consent Ten-day ceasefire Spoilers	Oslo:	High-level Consent Democratisation Decision makers

other. That is, after the talks were revealed in Turkey, there was a reaction by both opposition parties and the TSK. The reaction of spoilers affected the process in a significant way, and resulted in the hard-line policies of the 1990s. In contrast, the suspension of the Stormont parliament and the IRA's statements on their victory did not break the chain in Northern Ireland. Instead, it continued with more comprehensive communication: the Whitelaw talks. Although there was disagreement on the major demands of both sides, such as on self-determination and withdrawal of the British troops, they agreed to a bilateral ceasefire for one week and promised another set of negotiations. The PKK's major dispute during the negotiations was the government's recognition of their existence as a Kurdish authority. In the end, both the IRA and PKK's ultimate aims were to secure a binding agreement from the British and Turkish governments, which were unsuccessful. It can be said that whilst the disagreement between the republican movement and British government did not result in breaking the chain, Erbakan's initiative in the Turkish–Kurdish peace process helped make more progress.

Last, both the Feakle and Oslo talks had similar structures in terms of participants, methods and outcomes. The secret talks with the wanted members of the IRA and PKK were risky for both the British and Turkish governments, but illustrate that both governments prioritised the secret negotiations. For example, a leaked secret meeting record revealed that Fidan stated, during the talks, that there was a high risk for him being involved in these meetings, and if the discussions were revealed, it would have been a disaster for the AKP.[177] While the Oslo talks were mediated by British intelligence, the Feakle talks were mediated by Protestant clergymen. Also, the level of violence demonstrated a 'hurting stalemate' in both conflicts to bring on secret negotiations. This chapter has found that the influence of both mediation parties was limited, since they did not propose a route for these meetings or any deadlines that provided a reduction in the level of violence through a ceasefire. However, without their efforts, it would not have been possible to initiate the process. In addition, even though both talks witnessed the discussions of the main armed protagonists of their major demands, there was no concrete outcome in the Feakle talks, other than a temporary ceasefire. In contrast, as was stated in the leaked records of the Oslo talks, there was a general agreement on the future of the conflict between the Turkish officials and the PKK.[178] Further, the specific outcome of the talks was the Habur event, which was a great opportunity for the Kurdish community to reach a non-violent resolution, but the talks collapsed. The interview data reveals that one of the main problems during this event was that even though the HDP and PKK manipulated the initiative by announcing it as their victory, it could still have been successful if the media had not stirred up trouble instead of calling for society to stay calm.[179] Thus, it can be said that both the pro-Kurdish movement and the media's devastating reaction prevented this initiative from helping to de-escalate the conflict. As a result, despite the lack of an agreement after both initiatives, the Oslo talks can be labelled as more successful, since it is believed that all official efforts that were initiated after these discussions (such as the İmralı talks and Resolution Commission) applied the contacts and framework of these talks through the Democratisation Package of 2013, which will be discussed in Chapter 6.

To sum up, the direct talks' collective attempts were more successful than the indirect communications' personal efforts as high-level attendance aided discussion of major demands and so facilitated official negotiations. Both the British and Turkish governments and the republican and pro-Kurdish movements had a chance to discuss their claims and demands for the future of the two conflicts. While the indirect talks focused on interrupting violence, the direct talks witnessed a bargaining process including the limits of applicability of the demands of conflicting sides. Therefore, the interviews and declassified secret archival material demonstrates that while the intermediaries formed the basis of communication, the direct talks were built upon these indirect dialogues. Hence, the influence of direct talks towards ending ethno-nationalist conflicts is broader than indirect communications.

Notes

1. Pruitt, 'Back-channel Communication', p. 51.
2. Wanis-St John, 'Back Channel Diplomacy'.
3. Dochartaigh, 'Together in the Middle'; Güller, *Hükümet-PKK Görüşmeleri*; Mumford, 'Covert Peacemaking'.
4. Spencer, 'The Northern Ireland Peace Process'.
5. TNA-PREM/15/1016, *Frank Steele*.
6. Taylor, *Provos*.

7. Caldwell, cited in Fortnight, 'Tom Caldwell's Initiative'.
8. Taylor, *Brits*.
9. TNA-CJ/4/4245, *Account of Meeting with Tom Caldwell MP and R O'Bradaigh*.
10. Fortnight, 'Tom Caldwell's Initiative', p. 6.
11. TNA-PREM/15/1127, *Correspondence with Tom Caldwell MP*.
12. For an example, see Pruitt, 'Negotiation with Terrorists'.
13. McGuire, *To Take Arms*, p. 100.
14. TNA-CJ/4/319, *From the Principal Sir John Hackett to O'Connell*.
15. Wanis-St John, 'Back-Channel Negotiation'.
16. Zartman, 'Ripeness', p. 227.
17. Princen, *Intermediaries in International Conflict*, p. 10.
18. Brendan Duddy was an intermediary between the British government and the IRA between the mid-1970s and 1993. The Brendan Duddy papers were archived at the James Hardiman Library Archives, National University of Ireland in the Republic of Ireland.
19. Taylor, *Brits*.
20. Dochartaigh, 'The Role of an Intermediary', p. 227.
21. Mumford, *The Counter-insurgency Myth*, p. 103; Taylor, *Brits*, p. 170.
22. Jonathan Powell, one of the key architects of the GFA, revealed that Duddy was the key in the secret talks and was called 'the contact' during the secret initiatives (Powell, *Great Hatred, Little Room*).
23. Craig, 'From Backdoors and Back Lanes to Backchannels'.
24. Oatley, quoted in Taylor, *Brits*, p. 170.
25. Cooper, quoted in Taylor, *Brits*, p. 170.
26. Taylor, *Brits*.
27. Pruitt, 'Negotiation with Terrorists'.
28. NUI-POL/35/4/62, *Duddy Papers*.
29. Princen, *Intermediaries in International Conflict*.
30. NUI-POL/35/69, *The Gardiner Report*.
31. TNA-CAB/134/3921, *Memo on IRA ceasefire from Merlyn Rees to IRN*.
32. Ibid.
33. NUI-POL/35/68/1, *A Letter from the IRA to the British Prime Minister*.
34. TNA-CJ/4/839, *Force Levels and the Ceasefire*.
35. Moloney, *A Secret History of the IRA*, pp. 177–8.
36. Zartman, 'The Timing of Peace Initiatives'.
37. NUI-POL/35/166/2, *The Red Book*.
38. NUI-POL/35/166/3, *The Red Book*.
39. Thatcher, *The Downing Street Years*, p. 389.

40. Wanis-St John, 'Back-Channel Negotiation'.
41. NUI-POL/35/167/3, *The Red Book*.
42. Little, *Peacemakers in Action*, p. 66.
43. Spencer, 'The Northern Ireland Peace Process'.
44. NUI-POL/35/266/1, *IRA Ceasefire Offer*.
45. NUI-POL/35/9/279, *Robert McLarnon's Message to Brendan Duddy*.
46. Interview with Haughey, founder member of the Social Democratic and Labour Party, 19 January 2015.
47. Taylor, *Provos*, p. 182.
48. Haines, *The Politics of Power*, p. 128.
49. Ibid. p. 129.
50. Taylor, *Provos*, p. 133.
51. Pruitt, 'Escalation, Readiness for Negotiation'.
52. TNA-PREM/15/1009, *Note of a Meeting with Representatives of the Provisional IRA*.
53. Taylor, *Provos*, p. 136.
54. Mumford, 'Covert Peacemaking', p. 636.
55. Whitelaw, quoted in Coogan, *The IRA*, pp. 393–4; Smith, *Fighting for Ireland?*
56. TNA-CJ/4/1456, *The IRA Truce*.
57. Pruitt, 'Negotiation with Terrorists'; Pruitt, 'Back-channel Communication'.
58. Whitelaw, *The Whitelaw Memoirs*, p. 100.
59. Taylor, *Provos*, p. 136.
60. HC Deb, *House of Commons Debates*.
61. Sinn Féin, *Freedom Struggle by the Provisional IRA*.
62. McGuinness, quoted in McKool, 'Valuable Lessons in British Duplicity'.
63. TNA-CAB/128/48/3, *Confidential Annex*.
64. Whitelaw, *The Whitelaw Memoirs*, p. 100.
65. Zartman, 'The Timing of Peace Initiatives'.
66. Zartman, 'Ripeness', p. 229.
67. English, *Armed Struggle*.
68. McKittrick *et al.*, *Lost Lives*.
69. Dixon, *Northern Ireland*.
70. Mumford, 'Covert Peacemaking', p. 640.
71. TNA-PREM/16/158, *Principal Private Secretary*.
72. Dochartaigh, 'Together in the Middle'.
73. The terms 'serious' events and 'true' motives were coined by Zartman, to describe the sincere contribution of negotiations into resolution of a conflict (Zartman, 'The Timing of Peace Initiatives').
74. Ikle, *How Nations Negotiate*.

75. Zartman, 'Ripeness'.
76. Megahey, *The Irish Protestant Churches*; Taylor, *Brits*.
77. Wanis-St John, 'Back Channel Diplomacy'.
78. Bartoli, 'Mediating Peace in Mozambique'.
79. Hennessey, *The First Northern Ireland Peace Process*; TNA-CJ/4/860, *Church Leader's Meeting with the IRA*.
80. Stedman, 'Spoiler Problems in the Peace Processes'.
81. TNA-CJ/4/2263, *Statement by the IRA*.
82. Double quotation mark and capital are in original.
83. McKee, quoted in Taylor, *Provos*, p. 179.
84. McKee, quoted in Taylor, *Brits*, p. 180.
85. Aslan, 'TC'nin PKK ile Görüşmeleri'.
86. Interview with Çandar, chief advisor to President Turgut Özal (1991–3), 29–30 June 2015.
87. Çalışlar is a journalist who met with Öcalan in the Bekaa Valley. The purpose of the meeting was not part of a peace initiative, but for an interview, which was later published as a book (Çalışlar, *Öcalan ve Burkay'la Kürt Sorunu*).
88. Ibid.
89. Interview with Çalışlar, member of the WPC's Black Sea Region, journalist and author, 7 July 2015.
90. Pruitt, 'Negotiation with Terrorists'.
91. TSKA-MGK/989/4, *Meeting of the National Security Council*.
92. TSKA-MGK/988/9, *Meeting of the National Security Council*.
93. Demirel, quoted in Birand and Yalçın, *The Özal*, p. 474.
94. Nevruz is a traditional celebration day of spring for both the Kurdish and Turkish people. It is also called Nowruz and Newroz. Nevruz is chosen as this is the official form used in Turkish.
95. Öcalan, cited in Birand and Yalçın, *The Özal*, p. 476.
96. Princen, *Intermediaries in International Conflict*.
97. Ibid. p. 29.
98. Perinçek, *Abdullah Öcalan'la Görüşmeler*, p. 87.
99. Interview with Çandar, 29–30 June 2015.
100. Çandar, *Mezopotamya Ekspresi*.
101. Hürriyet, '33 Şehitli O Günden Beri Hiç Kahkaha Atamadım'.
102. ANF, 'Öcalan: Kürtlerin Kellesine Karşı ABD-Türkiye Anlaştı'.
103. Interview with Çandar, 29–30 June 2015.
104. Wanis-St John, 'Back-channel Negotiation'.

105. Interview with Çandar, 29–30 June 2015.
106. The MGK was a Council consisting of President, PM, National Defence, Internal and External Affairs Ministers and the chiefs of the Turkish Army. The Act 2945 assigned great power to the MGK; 'not just in the defence of Turkey's territory and its political and economic interests, but also the preservation of its Kemalist legacy' (Cizre, 'Demythologyzing the National Security Concept', p. 221; Jenkins, *Context and Circumstance*, p. 46).
107. Saybaşılı, *DYP-SHP Koalisyonu'nun Üç Yılı*, pp. 62–3.
108. TSKA-MGK/993/4, *Meeting of the National Security Council*.
109. Günay Aslan is a Kurdish journalist and a moderator of a TV programme on Kurdish Med-TV. During the programme, Öcalan was hosted on the phone in many of his live broadcasts. He gave messages to Kurdish people and Turkish political actors. Aslan also went to the Bekaa Valley to meet Öcalan (Oğur, 'Asker Üç Yıl Boyunca PKK ile Görüştü'; Tayyar, 'Apo'ya 'Acil' Kodlu Mesaj'.
110. Aslan, 'TC'nin PKK ile Görüşmeleri'.
111. Ibid.
112. Öcalan, quoted in ibid.
113. CNNTürk, 'Geçmişten Bugüne PKK Ateşkesleri'.
114. Cemal, *Kürtler.*
115. Interview with Haşimi, Kurdish politician, former deputy of the RP and FP, 3 July 2015.
116. Ibid.
117. Alphan and Albayrak, *Erbakan'ın Gizli PKK Zirvesi.*
118. Pruitt, 'Back-channel Communication'; Wanis-St John, 'Back-channel Negotiation'.
119. The details of Işık's intermediary work were revealed later on (he was called 'the fisherman'), and illustrated his pivotal role during the secret initiatives (HaberTürk, 'Barış ve Çözüm Sürecinde Geri Dönmek Mümkün Değil').
120. Interview with Işık, intermediary between the Turkish government and pro-Kurdish movement, 19 June 2015.
121. Ibid.
122. Ibid.
123. Princen, *Intermediaries in International Conflict*, p. 60.
124. Interview with Işık, 19 June 2015.
125. Ibid.
126. CNNTürk, 'Geçmişten Bugüne PKK Ateşkesleri'.

127. Interview with Yayla, member of the LPP, professor at İstanbul Ticaret University, 7 July 2015.
128. Ibid. The term 'deep state' (*derin devlet*) is used to describe powerful anti-democratic coalition groups within the Turkish political system, composed of high-level elements within the intelligence services (domestic and foreign), Turkish military, security, judiciary and mafia (Kanlı, 'The Turkish Deep State'). The existence of the deep state was even admitted by Erdoğan: 'I do not agree with those who say the deep state does not exist. It does exist. It has always had – and it did not start with the Republic; it dates back to Ottoman times. It is simply a tradition. It must be minimised, and if possible even annihilated' (Erdoğan, quoted in Barlas, 'Osmanlı'da Oyun Bitmez: Derin Devlet').
129. Kadıoğlu, 'The Oslo Talks: Revealing the Turkish Government's Secret Negotiations with the PKK', p. 926.
130. Interview with Coşkun, member of the WPC's Central Anatolia Region, 4 September 2015.
131. Ibid.
132. Interview with Oğur, member of the WPC's Black Sea Region, columnist, 25 June 2015.
133. Alphan and Albayrak, *Erbakan'ın Gizli PKK Zirvesi*.
134. Beriker-Atiyas, 'The Kurdish Conflict in Turkey', p. 446.
135. Uğur, *Abdullah Öcalan'ı Nasıl Sorguladım*, p. 42.
136. Radikal, 'CHP'den Ömer Çelik'e Yanıt'.
137. Beriker-Atiyas, 'The Kurdish Conflict in Turkey', p. 447.
138. Erbaş, 'Farkında Bile Olmadan Karayılan'la Öpüşmüşüm'; Yeni Çağ, 'Özal'dan Sonra Hoca da Apo'yla Temas Kurmuş'.
139. Dochartaigh, 'Together in the Middle'.
140. HDN, 'Kurdish Peace Call'.
141. Interview with Mahçupyan, member of the WPC's Southeastern Anatolia Region, the chief advisor to PM Ahmet Davutoğlu, 22 June 2015.
142. Kesebir, cited in Söylemez, 'Oslo'daki o Kadın Konuştu'.
143. 21YYTE, *Terörle Mücadelede Verdiğimiz Şehitler*; TBMM, *Terör ve Şiddet Olayları Kapsamında Yaşam Hakkı İhlallerini İnceleme Raporu*.
144. Karayılan, cited in Cemal, *Kürtler*.
145. Pruitt, 'Negotiation with Terrorists', p. 382.
146. Zartman, 'Ripeness'.
147. 21YYTE, *Terörle Mücadelede Verdiğimiz Şehitler*.

148. Interview with Yüksekdağ, Co-Leader of the HDP, 13 July 2015.
149. Başaran, 'Oslo, Çözüm Süreci ve Hepimizin Bilmesi Gerekenler'; Taraf, 'PKK-MİT Görüşmeleri Tam Metin'.
150. Karasu, cited in Akşam, 'PKK İlk Kez Açıkladı . . . Oslo'da Neler Oldu?'.
151. Bercovitch, 'International Mediation' (1991), p. 3.
152. The role of this mediation will be assessed in Chapter 6, with regard to international mediations.
153. Although the date of the meeting was not stated in the leaked record, there are a few indicators illustrating that the meeting was achieved in early 2010. During the meeting, the Habur crisis and Reşadiye attack of December 2009 were talked about (Taraf, 'PKK-MİT Görüşmeleri Tam Metin'). In addition, Hakan Fidan introduced himself as the Deputy Undersecretary of the MIT. So, the leaked meeting must have taken place in 2010, but before April when Fidan took the office.
154. Fidan, cited in Taraf, 'PKK-MİT Görüşmeleri Tam Metin'.
155. Fidan, cited in Uğur, *Abdullah Öcalan'ı Nasıl Sorguladım*.
156. EGM, 'Aranan Teröristler: Kırmızı Liste'; EGM, 'Aranan Teröristler: Mavi Liste'.
157. Taraf, 'PKK-MİT Görüşmeleri Tam Metin'.
158. Fidan, cited in Taraf, 'PKK-MİT Görüşmeleri Tam Metin'.
159. Uğur, *Abdullah Öcalan'ı Nasıl Sorguladım*.
160. Kadıoğlu, 'The Oslo Talks: Revealing the Turkish Government's Secret Negotiations with the PKK', p. 924.
161. Double quotation marks are in original.
162. Çelik, cited in NTV, 'Ömer Çelik'; Ala, quoted in Selvi, 'Çözüm Süreci Stres Altında'.
163. HDN, 'Chronology of Oslo Dialogues with PKK'.
164. Pruitt, 'Escalation, Readiness for Negotiation'.
165. HDN, 'Chronology of Oslo Dialogues with PKK'.
166. Taraf, 'PKK-MİT Görüşmeleri Tam Metin'.
167. Interview with Oğur, 25 June 2015.
168. Interview with Algan, Chairperson of the LPP, journalist and civil society activist, 30 June 2015.
169. Ibid.
170. Interview with Tan, Deputy of the HDP, Ankara, 24 June 2015.
171. Cronin, *How Terrorism Ends*.
172. Cronin, *When Should We Talk to Terrorists?*

173. NUI-POL/35/69, *The Gardiner Report*.
174. NUI-POL/35/4/62, *Duddy Papers*.
175. Interview with Işık, 19 June 2015.
176. TNA-CAB/134/3921, *Memo on IRA Ceasefire*.
177. Fidan, cited in Taraf, 'PKK-MİT Görüşmeleri Tam Metin'.
178. Ibid.
179. Interview with Haşimi, 3 July 2015.

5

PEACE AND CONFLICT RESOLUTION ORGANISATIONS: CATALYSTS FOR PEACE?

The best agent for a peace initiative is one who is known to have access to his government's leaders and can convey their intentions accurately, but who holds no official position.[1]

Unofficial peace groups are significant players in a peace process, who have been widely assessed with regard to their role in community relations. However, the peace and conflict resolution organisations (P/CROs) have been paid little attention in the existing literature in relation to their role in shaping, promoting or precluding a conflict resolution process. This book aims to close this gap by focusing on the relevant peace groups that played a role both in reducing the level of violence and maintaining the peace processes in Northern Ireland and Turkey. There has been little focus on the peace groups' role in shaping and promoting the Northern Irish and Turkey's Kurdish peace processes.[2] This chapter argues that official negotiations are not enough on their own as it is more complicated to bring ethno-nationalist conflicts to an end through official negotiations only. Therefore, I suggest complementing official negotiations (track-one diplomacy) with peace organisations in order to create unofficial conflict resolution approaches (track-two diplomacy) by exploring ethno-nationalist conflicts in a wider context. It is imperative because P/CROs may provide a close link between the effectiveness of peace institutions and the decisions of the political elite.[3]

P/CROs can influence decision-making mechanisms through public and non-public conferences, forums and events with the participation of current or former politicians; representatives of conflicting parties and actors; important figures and intellectuals in the conflict-affected society; and other grassroots initiatives. The role of peace organisations may begin in the pre-negotiation stage and continue until an agreement between conflicting parties is reached. This chapter argues that the efficiency of these organisations has facilitated progress in ending violence in both of the chosen peace processes. Thus, it is crucial to understand their influence in both conflicts. This chapter aims to answer the following question: To what extent have peace and conflict resolution organisations facilitated peacemaking efforts during existing violence in Northern Ireland and Turkey? The chapter first describes the rationale behind the selection of peace groups in Northern Ireland and Turkey. Then, it focuses on the groups which have had an influence on political decisions. Finally, it compares the influence of these groups on the conflict resolution processes.

Rationale Behind the Selection of P/CROs

To investigate the influence of P/CROs towards ending violence and reaching a political settlement, the analysis begins by setting out key criteria to select the relevant groups. First, peace organisations must be national, so they should have national demands. Second, these groups should reflect the perceptions of the conflicting sides. Therefore, the groups which contain only one side's opinion are not relevant. One such example is the Ulster Community Action Network (UCAN) in Northern Ireland, which was perceived to be exclusively pushing the Ulster Protestant community's demands.[4] Similarly, the Islamic Resolution Committee for the Kurdish Question (*Kürt Meselesine İslami Çözüm Çalıştayı*) was not used since it operated within a religious context and therefore overlooks the demands of both communities.[5] Third, groups should aim for peacemaking rather than other contexts such as training or peace education. The groups such as All Children Together and the Northern Ireland Council for Integrated Education were not included in the analysis since they focused only on peace education in the Northern Irish peace process.[6] Similarly, the Children under Single Roof Association (*Çocuklar Aynı Çatının Altında Derneği*) was not analysed as its remit is not peacemaking in Turkey.[7] Fourth, the relevant peace groups should play a role in elite-level decision-making, rather than grassroots initiatives: for instance, community relations. Therefore, the Community Relations Council (CRC) in Northern Ireland was not investigated, even though it was established by political actors. As the CRC promotes relations between communities only, it has not worked on establishing a peace agreement. Although it is an important part of peace efforts, this book only assesses the groups which have been active in the elite-driven process, but not peacebuilding institutions. Last, the selected peace groups need to have been active during the time frame of the research. The peace groups should have been active between 1969 and 1998 in the Northern Irish conflict, and between 1984 and 2015 in the Kurdish question of Turkey.

Following these criteria, peace groups in Northern Ireland and Turkey were investigated. It was seen that several peace and reconciliation groups were active during the time frame in both cases. Those groups operating in Northern Ireland are within 'the voluntary sector', with a large turnover (over £400 million).[8] Although there are no specific figures for the Turkish case, peace organisations do not act independently of the government due to insufficient internal and international funding. However, the economic foundations of the peace groups are not the topic of this chapter, as the intention is to investigate conflict resolution initiatives. The initial stage was to distinguish peace groups from other groups concerned with such issues as community relations, reconciliation, training and education. The second stage was to eliminate groups which had been established to defend specific groups' interests. The research could now concentrate on groups which meet with the demands and interests of both conflicting parties. The final stage was to investigate peace groups in regard to their contribution to the peace processes in Northern Ireland and Turkey. In this context, groups that emerged in reaction to a specific event or incident were included in the discussion due to their influence on the peace process.[9] Thus, these criteria led to the selection of the Peace People and the British–Irish Association (BIA) in Northern Ireland, and the Wise People Committee (*Akil İnsanlar Heyeti*) and the Look at Peace Platform (*Barışa Bak Platformu*) in Turkey.

P/CROs in Northern Ireland

The P/CROs in the Northern Irish peace process aimed to contribute to the peacemaking process. Blackwell's letter to James Prior (the Secretary of State for Northern Ireland) revealed that the BIA was formed in 1972 by a group of academics, journalists, politicians and others who sought to contribute to the resolution of the political problems of Ireland by advancing Anglo-Irish understanding.[10] The Peace People (PP) was established in August 1976 in reaction to an incident in which a terrorist crashed his car and killed three children when he was escaping from security forces. According to the PP's statement, the children's aunt Mairead Corrigan founded the movement with Betty Williams who was a local person and a witness of this incident.[11] Hence, both groups were founded to play an active role in resolving the Northern Irish conflict. The BIA aimed to promote common understanding between the British and Irish people, to describe concerns and to enable them to be solved in a positive manner. It brought official and unofficial actors together, who were senior politicians, government officials, former paramilitaries and community leaders; and provided a suitable environment to discuss the conflict without any restraints.[12] It illustrates that the BIA's major characteristic is to create a flexible environment for political parties and actors by bringing them together in an unofficial environment as a track-two initiative, thanks to their direct contact with government officials. Therefore, the BIA aims to fill the gap of official negotiations as a middle-range organisation. In contrast, the PP aimed to aid the conflict resolution process by directing peace from below: from the society to the elite level. Although it was a reactive peace group, its aims were not limited to local or regional events. Instead, as stated in the PP's declaration, the group's aim was 'to give peace a chance to solve problems which all the politics and all the violence have failed to solve'.[13] With respect to this aim, the PP announced that 'All we want is to show the terrorists – and that includes all paramilitaries – that the vast majority of people want them off our backs.'[14] This section investigates the contribution of these groups to the Northern Irish peace process.

The British–Irish Association

The BIA aimed to contribute to the peace process by creating an environment in which private discussions by governmental and non-governmental bodies could take place on sensitive political issues through its annual conferences, as noted by the BIA leadership.[15] The significant feature of the BIA is its ability to bring together current or former political actors from the

British and Irish governments and Northern Irish parties. As the BIA was founded and has been active since 1972, its activities during the intense violent conflict were crucial to the contribution of P/CROs. Its initial events were the Cambridge Conference of 1973 and the Oxford Conference of 1974, which hosted high-level politicians, journalists and civil servants. For example, Lyons's (a Minister from the Northern Ireland office) letter to Roy Hattersley (the Shadow Secretary of State for Foreign and Commonwealth Affairs) revealed that Merlyn Rees (the British Secretary of State for Northern Ireland), Garrett Fitzgerald (the Irish Minister for Foreign Affairs) and deputies from the Republic of Ireland attended the conference in Oxford.[16] This illustrates the influence of the BIA in bringing influential officials together, those who were reluctant to come together at official events. This was the first initiative to bring Rees and Fitzgerald together at an unofficial event, which was a chance for increasing the attention paid to political resolution attempts. In the early 1970s, political parties and actors were brought together by these unofficial events as it was not possible to achieve official negotiations without first de-escalating the conflict.

Looking at the contribution of the BIA, the political events organised by the members of the BIA's personal contacts were a significant dimension of track-two diplomacy. They enabled informal discussions between the people who were close enough to the centre of power, which is an important step to having a degree of influence over decision makers.[17] For example, as Merlyn Rees was one of the founders of the BIA, he successfully built the communication channels with political actors and facilitated political parties and actors to attend the BIA's events. Although these events did not change the nature of the conflict, they helped create a flexible environment through informal interaction during a period of minimal political communication efforts due to the intense conflict, as explained in Chapter 3. In contrast, Rees's successor Roy Mason kept his distance from the Association as he said that it would be better for him and other ministers not to attend the BIA's events unless they received official invitations from the BIA.[18] As a middle-range peace organisation, the BIA facilitated discussions between not only the British and Irish governments, but also the Northern Irish parties. However, Rees and Mason's positions demonstrated that this contribution depended on the members of the BIA's links with political elites. Although Rees played an encouraging role for the BIA events, Mason was reluctant to contribute to its initiatives. As this bridge was not successfully formed during Mason's term (1976–9), this period did not witness the facilitating role of the BIA. However, the British government maintained its willingness to attend the BIA's events in the following years, which illustrates that the British wanted to support the BIA's activities explicitly, unlike the PP's events. The situation undoubtedly increased the reliability of the Association within the island. It therefore fostered greater understanding by reinforcing peace attempts in the UK and Republic of Ireland.[19]

The events of the BIA witnessed important discussions for the future of the island. Humphrey Atkins, the Secretary of State for Northern Ireland, echoed the prospects of political progress in the conferences of 1979 and 1980. In addition, Lord Gowrie, then a NIO minister, spoke about the Northern Ireland policy of the British government in 1981. Gowrie's speech was evidence of the confidentiality of the BIA's events, as he said that 'Direct Rule was not very British' and dual citizenship consisting of Britain and the Republic of Ireland should be recognised for the people who identify themselves as Irish.[20] It would have been very difficult to make this statement in public, but was possible through the informal and confidential discussions of the BIA, which provided a better atmosphere for exchanging views compared to public events.[21] Moreover, the discussions at the BIA's events helped not only to facilitate a political process, but also to direct decision makers towards a political solution. For example, the BIA insisted on the establishment of a new local government in Northern Ireland, a government which would contain more than one regional council. The BIA suggested that several Northern Ireland Departments should be split up between new regional councils in relation to different centres throughout the region.[22] This suggestion is important as it demonstrates the outcome-oriented discussion at the BIA's meetings. In particular, the BIA conference in 1979 was important, since the discussion at the conference addressed political changes in the province. The BIA noted that a simple majority rule regime would not be acceptable in Northern Ireland due to the ethnic division of the province, since it would mean that one-third of the province would be overlooked. In addition, Northern Ireland would not be able to be fully integrated into either the South or the UK.[23] These suggestions made by the BIA were intended to solve the conflict in a political way by considering different views and demands. This approach helped the group, as Kaufman notes, to stay close enough to the centre of political power to influence decision makers.[24]

The BIA is a unique organisation in the Northern Irish peace process since it has brought together high-level politicians from all disputing parties. Gee's letter to Lane (Northern Ireland ministers) revealed that the discussions at the BIA events were very helpful in political debates.[25] In particular, the BIA's Lambeth Conference of 1981 hosted both nationalists and official unionists and witnessed their opposition regarding power sharing. Nevertheless, there was no representative from the republicans and 'Paisleyites'. Arguably, it can be said that despite the unofficial character of the meetings, the opposition of both parties to this peace initiative was due to the BIA's semi-official structure, gathering political actors in an unofficial environment. It was a sign that both parties were unwilling to solve the problem in a political way. Regarding the discussion, while the unionists were defending majority rule, the nationalists were demanding Catholics' political rights. Also, Harold McCusker, a member of Parliament for the UUP, argued that Direct Rule had failed and the only possible way was to return a Northern Ireland government.[26] However, the discussions raised a question about whether unionists might walk away from meetings. The declassified secret meeting notes revealed that the discussions even resulted in polemics between John Hume and unionists, a great example of the insight of the BIA discussions: 'John Hume also enunciated a stripped-down version of unity. He was strongly attacked on Fermanagh/South Tyrone elections and was both uncomfortable and unconvincing.'[27] More generally, these activities provided unofficial discussions between political actors that contributed to political resolution attempts.

The BIA's events helped change the nature of the peace process by criticising the political environment in Northern Ireland. For example, its proposals on political development in Northern Ireland were passed into law and were implemented. Another important topic that was discussed in the Association's meetings was elections in Northern Ireland. After long-standing debates, elections were held for the first time after eight years and a locally elected Assembly met in Belfast in 1982.[28] Although these were political decisions, according to the declassified secret meeting note of the British government, the Association's conferences helped change these policies by bringing together the official representatives of the British government, Republic of Ireland and Northern Irish parties, and pushing them to seek political means to resolution.[29] The BIA as a middle-range group created a suitable environment for discussion and so affected political decisions about the future of Northern Ireland. In addition, the BIA underlined the importance of different identities' existence in the Northern Ireland Assembly. The Secretary of State, James Prior, attested that different identities in Northern Ireland needed to be represented in the political environment.[30] The Association helped to underline these differences, through informal discussions amongst the official representatives of disputing parties. These track-two initiatives were influential also because of the fact that the participants were representives of the conflicting communities.[31] The BIA also facilitated political agreements through its policy reports that were prepared after long-standing discussions between current and former politicians, academics and journalists. For example, one of the BIA's reports, the Kilbrandon Report, helped modify the AIA of 1985 in terms of the demands of Catholics and Protestants, since both communities were represented in the talks.[32] More significantly, the Kilbrandon Report suggested a number of reforms regarding political arrangements which would help to establish a middle ground between the Catholic and Protestant communities. Even though the British government did not take into account the Kilbrandon Report immediately, the suggested reforms by the BIA were reflected in the AIA. Reforms included a bill of rights to guarantee the rights of the minority, and a reform of the justice system with the introduction of trial by two judges, one from the UK and the other from the Republic of Ireland.[33]

The Association complemented the peace process even after the beginning of the official efforts. For example, the BIA's conference in 1993 witnessed intense discussion about the competition between the British and Irish governments.[34] Dick Spring, Minister for Foreign Affairs in the Republic of Ireland, made a speech, which revealed the rivalry between the two governments:

> I would like . . . to see Britain rivalling with Ireland in its eagerness to build bridges, "to abolish the memory of past dissensions"[35] and to enable all those who inhabit Ireland to find, by agreement among themselves and without external hindrance, arrangements and institutions which all could endorse

and support as their own. I would like to see Ireland rivalling with Britain to make sure that unionists felt certain that political change in Ireland was irrevocably conditional on respect for their rights and their sense of identity and allegiance.[36]

These intense discussions were proof of the flexibility that these events provided, but could not encourage the disputing parties to change. Instead, they revealed more disputes in the 1990s as the BIA focused more on the intractability of the conflict. For example, Sir Patrick Mayhew, the Secretary of State for Northern Ireland, argued about the deep-rooted characteristic of the conflict in his speech to the BIA in September 1996.[37] Therefore, it can be said that the BIA complemented the progress in the 1970s and 1980s more than in the 1990s.

Despite the comprehensiveness of the BIA's events, it was criticised by political parties in Northern Ireland. However, in contrast to the assumptions of track-two diplomacy, this criticism was not related to the question of the influence of the group.[38] Instead, the major criticism levelled towards the BIA was made by unionist ministers who thought that the BIA was supporting and attracting moderate nationalists.[39] However, the Association's efforts to bring disputing sides together and to create a suitable environment for discussions on possible ways for peace demonstrate that the group has been a useful body for both unionists and nationalists. Overall, the British government thought that the BIA was a useful body that deserved official support and encouragement. This was provided through the representation of the British and Irish governments at ministerial and official levels at conferences between 1973 and 1976.[40] To conclude, the BIA's efforts to make peace and to bring the violent conflict to an end were significant and helped maintain the peace process.

The Peace People

In contrast to the BIA, the PP aimed to promote and encourage peace attempts through bottom-up approaches. The Peace Movement[41] recommended bringing conflicting sides together, and avoiding sectarian and confrontational politics.[42] Community support was vital for the success of the group and this support increased due to its rejection of any type of discrimination or violence and its aim of keeping a distance from both communities.[43]

The group contributed to the peace process in three major ways. The PP initially weakened the emotional popular support for the IRA in Catholic areas. The NIO's report on the PP stated that the group facilitated a decrease in the level of sectarian attacks and indiscriminate bombings (see Table 5.1). The report states that the PP helped de-escalate terrorism by encouraging people to come together against violent attacks.[44] Although the NIO argued that the PP played a role in reducing the level of violence, it was not the only actor in de-escalating the conflict, since the backchannel communications between the British government and IRA were also influential, as discussed in the previous chapter. That said, this secret report of the NIO is clear evidence of the British government's awareness of the PP's encouraging role in de-escalating the conflict, as is seen through the total incident numbers. For example, according to the British government, the Movement had a direct impact on facilitating peacemaking attempts through its marches and so was successful in creating a united voice against violence in Northern Ireland in 1977.[45] Its focus on both communities' identities and fears resulted in reducing the prejudices of both sides, as is suggested by track-two scholars.[46] The PP was successful in changing the view of people in Northern Ireland in relation to the IRA. They encouraged the Catholics to speak out against the IRA defending them and their rights. The Movement asked for the same from Protestants in relation to the Ulster Defence Association (UDA).[47]

The PP's attempts to close the gap between the two communities facilitated both Catholics and Protestants turning against violence. Their opposition to any type of violence and their peace efforts led to Williams and Corrigan

Table 5.1 Consequences of incidents between 1973 and 1978. Source: TNA-CJ/4/2380, *Emergency Provision Legislation in Northern Ireland*.

Year	Deaths	Injuries	Shooting incidents	Explosions
1973	250	2,651	5,018	978
1974	216	2,398	3,206	685
1975	247	2,474	1,803	399
1976	297	2,729	1,908	766
1977	112	1,398	1,081	366
1978 (to 31 October)	70	753	658	285

winning the Nobel Peace Prize in 1976. The Movement's success was also praised by the Queen in her Christmas Broadcast and was described as a glimmer of hope for the people in Northern Ireland.[48] In addition, as noted in an anonymous NIO paper, while the British government did not openly support the PP, they chose to get in touch with them secretly.[49] Hence, the British government did not have a major influence on the Movement's events. In contrast, the Movement began to influence the peace process through its well-supported protests.

The PP contributed to the peace process through their clear position towards violence deployed by security forces. They met with the British government several times to discuss political decisions and their implications in Northern Ireland. The Movement criticised the approach of both the British Army and the Royal Ulster Constabulary (RUC) towards the conflict. It was opposed to any internment without trial, and to violence from any of the nine armies in Northern Ireland; 'one British, three Roman Catholic and five Protestant'.[50] For example, the group was strongly opposed to the British Army's arrest policy. The leading members of the group discussed it with the Secretary of State for Northern Ireland, Roy Mason. Although the Army was displeased, the Army agreed with the PP's suggestions and their publicity claims.[51] The declassified secret paper of the British government revealed that the Army was unhappy about both the PP's policy on accompanying troops when people were arrested and the group's visit to the prisons of Port Monagh.[52] However, in contrast to the theoretical assumption about parties with insufficient approval/power possibly ending up talking to the 'wrong' people,[53] the leaders of the PP reached political parties and actors, and put pressure on the government to reconsider the actions of security forces. These situations illustrate the PP's contribution to changing the region's environment.

The PP contributed to the conflict resolution process by getting involved in political decisions in different ways. The blanket protest of the prisoners (the H-Block issue) is an important event in which the PP was involved, talking to prisoners to understand their demands. According to Seanna Walsh, the leader of the blanket protest and former member of the IRA, this protest was a political event organised to take a stand against British rule.[54] The leading member of the PP, Ciaran McKeown, requested an amnesty for political prisoners from the British government once a peace agreement had been settled.⁵⁵ Although there were different types of peace groups, an anonymous declassified secret NIO paper noted that the PP was the only group that crossed the sectarian divide and created links between the divided communities.⁵⁶ In particular, two members of the PP, McLachlan and Campbell, met with the Minister of State for Northern Ireland, Don Concannon, on 30 November 1978 and discussed the H-Block protest, which was assisting the IRA's propaganda war. Furthermore, the Movement lobbied for reforms in the methods of fighting terrorism. For example, it lobbied for the renewal of the Emergency Provisional Act in 1979; the PP demanded the removal of this Act since it had not decreased the level of violence in Northern Ireland.⁵⁷ The group complemented this progress through an exchange of information, which provided a mutual understanding between the societal and elite level. They also suggested that the RUC was more helpful than the Army in relation to supplying information about suspects. However, the Minister insisted that the Act was necessary. Campbell suggested two things: first, the Bennett Inquiry might not be useful anymore due to police brutality in the province. Second, she recommended political status for prisoners related to the Act.⁵⁸ The Minister agreed that there would not be a return to the Special Category.⁵⁹ Thus, it can be said that in contrast to Mapendere's assumption on the limited influence of track-two interventions, the lack of political power did not restrict the PP's impact.⁶⁰ This was because the group focused on the major reasons for the ongoing violence and the disagreement between both communities and so truly represented their constituency.

The PP's attempts were not limited to the discussion with the Northern Ireland Minister. The insight they gained from their meetings with the H-Block protesters resulted in contact with Thatcher. According to the PP's letter to Thatcher, three of the five demands of the prisoners were resolved as of 23 January 1981.⁶¹ The remaining issues were related to work and clothing. However, resolution of these two issues could not have guaranteed political status. According to the PP, 'it is a red herring: the objection to political status is that it implies an amnesty, which is to encourage violence on the promise of eventual absolution'.⁶² Further, the Movement sent a letter to Thatcher on 19 March 1981 suggesting that the political status term had lost its meaning and had been transformed into a device for manipulating public opinion.⁶³ However, the letter was sent forty-seven days before Bobby

Sands died. In particular, the deteriorating condition of the strikers caused an outraged reaction in society and the death of Bobby Sands on 5 May 1981 changed the political environment in Northern Ireland. An estimated one hundred-thousand people attended his funeral in Belfast, illustrating the level of reaction.[64] In addition to this, the PP said that Direct Rule was unacceptable. James Galway, one of the leading members of the group, noted that the establishment of a non-legislative administration with all the powers previously administrated by central government resulted, in the end, in the 'political sterility' of Northern Ireland.[65] These initiatives demonstrate that the PP was actively involved in political elites' decisions, which facilitated progress towards peace by complementing official initiatives by including the demands and claims of general society.

The PP was, however, criticised by the DUP and SF. The DUP's reaction was two-fold. While the DUP's media organ, the *Protestant Telegraph*, described the Peace Movement as 'spurious', the DUP blamed the Movement for playing into the IRA's hands.[66] In addition, SF condemned the PP and claimed that the group was not objective. The declassified archival documents demonstrate that the British government thought that these parties' criticisms were not related to the help of the Movement, but to the impartiality of the group.[67] However, the disputing sides had little influence on the PP's activities. In contrast, the group acted as an independent organisation by bringing the Catholic and Protestant communities together at each of the PP's events. Its neutral role resulted in no strong opposition to the existence and activities of the group. Finally, the British government noted that the PP contributed to the peace process through bringing hope to Northern Ireland by underlining the aspiration for peace and reconciliation.[68] Similar to other reactive groups, the support for the PP rapidly increased, mass protests organised by the group demonstrating the support for its peace events. Hence, it has been influential in de-escalating violence and changing political decisions related to the Northern Irish problem.

P/CROs in Turkey

Two Turkish peace organisations have been chosen for analysis: the Wise People Committee (WPC) and the Look at Peace Platform (LPP). The WPC was founded by the Turkish government and announced after the meeting between the members of the Committee and PM Erdoğan on 3 April 2013.[69] The Committee was composed of seven groups, which represented the seven regions of Turkey and consisted of sixty-three members. The LPP was founded as a reaction to the increasing level of violence. The LPP's level of action against violence increased after a slaughter in the south-east of Turkey, known as the 6–7 October Incidents, which claimed fifty lives.[70] Cengiz Algan, the chairperson of the LPP, noted that the group intensified their peace initiatives immediately after this incident.[71] Therefore, both P/CROs were established to complement the conflict resolution process towards a peaceful settlement. The initial purpose of the WPC was to understand the society's demand for a non-violent resolution. The Committee, therefore, aimed to forward the Turkish and Kurdish communities' views to political actors.[72] The WPC then aimed to play an active role in the peace process by influencing the decisions of the Turkish government and promoting a non-violent resolution.[73] Although the government founded the Committee, it was not an official body. Its members were intellectuals, opinion leaders, academics, authors, journalists and other well-liked[74] public figures, but not officials or politicians. Yılmaz Ensaroğlu, the chairperson of the Committee's South Eastern Region, who was later appointed as chief advisor to the PM, confirmed that even though the WPC was founded by the Turkish government, the activities and events of the Committee were completely independent from the government.[75] Similarly, PM Erdoğan stipulated that the Committee should work independently without being influenced by either governmental or non-governmental authorities.[76] However, these special characteristics negatively affected its role in the peace process. Although the members of the Committee were independent in organising any types of events and meetings, they were reporting the outcome of their events to the Turkish government. While these reports provided them with a unique opportunity to contact political parties and actors, arguably it can be said that it laid a burden on the group with regard to the promotion of government's peace initiatives. This diminished the critical thoughts and different opinions in the Committee, which will be analysed in the next section. Keeping this feature in mind, the WPC was the most fitting peace group for this investigation within Turkey's Kurdish peace process. The differences in structure between the WPC and the Northern Irish peace groups were considered during the analysis.

However, in contrast to the WPC's unique advantage at the elite level, due to its direct contact with the government, this did not give it an exceptional role in peacemaking initiatives. The characteristics of the WPC and the outcome of its events will be assessed in the next section.

Furthermore, the LPP was formed by journalists, academics, former politicians and activists who declared the existence of a threat to cease the peace process. Therefore, it was vital to keep supporting a non-violent, political resolution. Atilla Yayla, a member of the LPP, stated that the Kurdish problem affects Turkey's developmental, economic, social and cultural issues.[77] The LPP aims to help solve this problem by creating a suitable environment for disputing communities to come together. This section firstly assesses the influence of the WPC and then analyses the LPP to understand their contribution to the peace process.

The Wise People Committee

The mode of foundation of the WPC gave the group a great advantage because it could contact the government, which is a vital aspect for the success of a middle-range peace group.[78] The WPC aimed to contribute to the peace process by three methods. The first method was to organise panels, public talks, small town meetings and visits to opinion formers to understand the society's demands and to increase their support for resolving the conflict in a non-violent way.[79] These events uncovered each community's lack of trust in the government in a few key areas: the fear of partition and Öcalan's amnesty; the government's negotiations with the PKK; and opening discussions about the Turkish flag and national anthem, which were perceived as a threat towards the unitary system.[80] In addition, Ensaroğlu said that society's major problem was trust in the government in relation to carrying out legal regulations to solve the Kurdish question of Turkey.[81] As Mayer indicates, trust and mutual respect are necessary conditions for a successful negotiation process.[82] These concerns emerged in the Kurdish community during the official negotiations. The P/CROs aimed to overcome this issue to facilitate the process. On the one hand, these concerns highlighted the difference between the Turkish and Kurdish communities' views of the peace process. For example, the main concerns of the Turkish community were whether Öcalan would be released and what promises were given to the PKK.[83] On the other hand, the

WPC was a unique initiative, which revealed these concerns and thus helped maintain the conflict resolution process by creating a suitable environment in which to discuss the Kurdish question at the societal level. It also helped to eliminate these issues through not only public talks and small town meetings, but also meetings with several different associations, groups and people such as NGOs, and representatives of people who were ethnically Kurdish but did not support the PKK.[84] Beril Dedeoğlu, vice chairperson of the Central Anatolia Region, noted that their expectations helped the Committee to draw up a road map for how to maintain the peace process and how to help achieve a political agreement.[85] Thus, in line with Montville[86] and Nan's[87] suggestions on track-two initiatives, it can be said that the WPC complemented official negotiations by overcoming trust and fear issues, and by drawing up a framework for how to reach a political settlement.

These meetings revealed a very significant aspect related to the nature of the peace process: it was stated that many people in the south-east of Turkey thought that the PKK was not the Kurdish people's representative. Therefore, as Ensaroğlu points out, the government should consider all communities' demands in the region including Kurdish, pro-Kurdish, Sunni and Alevi people in order to reach a successful settlement.[88] These outcomes of the meetings raised awareness in society of the peace process.[89] Ayhan Oğan, Secretary of the Eastern Anatolia Region, noted that the WPC's efforts helped the public initially to believe that there was an acceptable degree of support for a political agreement. After society's support was gained, the group expressed the people's demands in public and so aimed to influence political decisions. The Committee successfully built a communication channel between the Turkish and Kurdish communities and encouraged society in supporting a political resolution.[90] This was clear evidence of the WPC's success in promoting the peace process through the use of peaceful language and encouraging the government and pro-Kurdish side to use a common language for a peaceful resolution.[91] As Mayer indicates, it is crucial to close the gap between conflicting communities in order for peacemaking to take place.[92] Hence, the WPC played a role as a middle-range group to increase support for peace at the societal level. It also identified that the reason there was high support for political resolution in eastern Turkey was due to the weariness, tedium and demoralisation of the people. The WPC was seen as an organisation to help decrease violence by creating hope in people's minds.[93]

The WPC was a useful group for promoting peace and understanding the demands and requests of different communities within society. However, as mentioned in the previous section, it is not a typical peace group, which aims to close the gap between conflicting communities and to contribute to peace through public pressure on political agents. Instead, even though the special characteristics of the WPC show an independent organisation with regard to its membership and mechanism, the group operated as a quasi-governmental body since it was responsible for forwarding the demands of society to the government. This make-up caused the group to act as a body to promote peace negotiations between the Turkish government and pro-Kurdish movement. This resulted in reducing the critical voice of the WPC concerning how the peace process should be defined and made in action. Instead of this, the WPC was perceived as promoting the government's peace agenda, which was to end the PKK's armed campaign. The public talks and small-town meetings of the WPC demonstrated that the audiences and civil society representatives acted as if they were talking to a governmental body. This was evident through the interview data. Members of the WPC stated that the audiences wanted to learn how the government aimed to reach a political settlement.[94] Therefore, an outcry was directed at the WPC members themselves, through protests aiming to prevent their meetings and by attacking members of the group during their meetings and visits. For example, a two-hundred-strong group attacked WPC members in Amasya city, intending to beat them, because they were believed to be the government's spokespersons.[95]

Another method of the WPC was to promote the attempts at non-violent, political resolution by the political parties and actors. The Committee played a role in maintaining the peace process and promoting talks between the Turkish government and PKK leaders. It developed a positive environment even for those opposed to a political agreement. The Committee's efforts became apparent with the leak of the secret Oslo Talks between the government and PKK members. As discussed in the previous chapter, the Oslo Talks created a negative reaction in wider Turkish society, since it was perceived as bargaining between the government and a terrorist group. Ironically, the greater reaction in society was related to the claim of reaching an agreement with a terrorist group, not on building a communication channel, hence, the Committee also aimed to understand society's perception of these talks and to increase support for a non-violent resolution.[96] Similarly, Hatem Ete, the chief advisor to the PM, stated that the outcome of WPC events was used by the Turkish government during the negotiations with regard to the concerns of both communities.[97]

The characteristics and structure of the WPC helped increase public support and promote the peace process through its varied membership, who were ethnically Turkish, Kurdish or had different religious and other backgrounds such as non-Muslim citizens.[98] The variety of backgrounds facilitated public support and acted as a bottom-up initiative focusing on bringing about a political resolution, a new constitution and peace project that encompassed the demands of the rival communities.[99] The WPC's aim to close the gap between different ethnic identities was vital in reducing prejudices. To achieve this aim, the WPC focused on reciprocal understanding by encouraging each community to be introduced not as a threat or enemy, but as human beings. This facilitated public support for the group.

The variety in the WPC members' ethnic and religious backgrounds garnered support for the group at the grassroots level. However, it did not prevent them from being considered representatives of the government. Even the leader of the nationalist MHP, Devlet Bahçeli, accused PM Erdoğan of manipulating the WPC, 'that delegation members were AKP and PKK sympathisers, that they are acting as PKK spokespersons and that they were aiming at dividing the Turkish nation'.[100] Whether the events and aims of the WPC could have been different if it had not been set up by the government, and its members not selected by governmental bodies, remains as a question mark. Although this feature gave the group a unique opportunity to contact political agents directly, this emerged as a threat to the impartiality of the group. Despite this criticism, the WPC was successful in promoting peace at the grassroots level. It was the only peace group that enabled different communities to talk about their demands towards a political resolution. These discussions successfully increased conflicting communities' support for a non-violent resolution. However, this was viewed as the only clear contribution of the group; it can be said that this was because of their lack of an agenda. This was attested to by Dedeoğlu, as she said that the lack of an agenda during their events caused uncertainty about the potential outcome of their activities with regard to contributing to the peace process.[101] Nevertheless, the promising support for the group by both Kurdish and Turkish communities and its encouraging role in peacemaking did not lead to it contributing to the peace process in any greater detail.

The last method of the WPC was to meet with the Turkish government and political parties in order to further contribute to the peace process. The Committee insisted on a new constitution, one of the most notable demands from society, to resolve the conflict.[102] The report written by the WPC's Black Sea Group revealed that the Turkish and Kurdish communities believed that the new constitution would eliminate all restrictions in terms of ethnic identity, fundamental rights of freedom, the definition of citizenship, religious and linguistic restrictions, and participatory and pluralistic democracy that are the principles of human security.[103] The group also demanded the repeal of the Counter-terrorism Legislation, and Police Duty and Authority Law, since these two items of legislation seemed to be causing an increase in the level of violence. Furthermore, the group suggested that the Law on the Compensation of Damages Arising from Counter-terrorism (Legislation Number 5233) was insufficient to amend the conditions of people who were exposed to violence.[104] However, none of these laws were changed or amended to help decrease the effect of terrorism on society. Hence, the group was unsuccessful in facilitating change in any legislation. Despite its foundation process (initiated by the government with proximity to political agents), the group was lacking power in pushing the government for constitutional reforms by using their support at the grassroots level. Compared to the Northern Irish P/CROs, it can be said that the WPC's different nature and function within the peace process in Turkey meant that it did not work as a catalyst for a positive outcome in the peace process.

Finally, the group aimed to persuade the government to accept the European Charter of Local Self-Government, and to repeal its reservations about this act.[105] The Charter suggested increasing local governments' authority.[106] The WPC believed that this was an important step towards decreasing the tension in the south-east of Turkey.[107] However, the group, again, was unsuccessful in influencing the government to change its perceptions in relation to this legislation, as the government believed that it would be a restriction of its authority.

The only achievement related to constitutional changes was to help the declaration of the democratisation package of 2013. The package contained the regulations on political rights, the fight against discrimination and hate crimes, steps to guarantee the respect of different lifestyles and an expansion of the rights of meeting and demonstration.[108] The package was a great opportunity for reducing the discrimination which had caused the ethnic conflict. The changes included the repeal of the law to fight against terrorism in Specially Authorised Courts (*Özel Yetkili Mahkeme*), which had been authorised to try cases only involving terrorism and organised crime. It also decreased long detention periods, the requirement of concrete evidence for custody and arrest, and allowed political parties to use Kurdish and other languages for election campaigns, and for education in private schools in languages other than Turkish. It also allowed former non-Turkish names of villages to be reinstated, which enabled the use of Kurdish names again.[109] Although the democratisation law helped progress, the pro-Kurdish BDP berated the government for the insufficiency of this reform as there were still cases pending against Kurdish politicians for using Kurdish in their election campaigns.

Furthermore, the WPC was criticised by some groups in Turkish society and political parties. On one hand, the WPC was protested against during its events and meetings. Although they were small protests, they were extensively discussed in the media. Oğur and Sayman, members of the WPC, admitted that the protests affected the WPC's activities during public talks.[110] On the other hand, the WPC was also criticised by political parties. Tan, a deputy of the pro-Kurdish HDP, argued that the WPC promoted the government's decisions and policies.[111] Thus, he said, the group did not serve the peace process, but the government. Fortunately, these situations did not prevent the WPC's activities from taking place.

Lastly, there was an unexpected and unintended outcome of the WPC events. Şükrü Karatepe, a member of the WPC's Mediterranean Region, said that the WPC played a barrier role between the Turkish government and society. This was not the intention of the government or the Committee, but the group's function was unique in facilitating the progress of resolution efforts. In particular, the group changed the perception of people who had previously refused to engage with a political resolution process as they thought that the unitary system would always remain the same, and this eased the peace process.[112] In fact, there was no sign of partition of the state. In addition, the then chief advisor to the PM, Etyen Mahçupyan, indicated that the Committee was a group which was successful in increasing the support for a non-violent resolution to the Kurdish question. It successfully brought together people who had never had contact with each other before, and discussed their demands in order to end the conflict. The reaction towards the Committee was not very strong and, overall, it increased the support for a political resolution, as opposed to an armed struggle.[113]

The Look at Peace Platform

The first action of the LPP was to publish a statement in relation to the peace process, a call to all citizens of Turkey to support a political resolution.[114] This call was also a protest against any type of violence and the killing of innocent people.[115] The statement insisted on maintaining the peace process, which was the major purpose of the Platform.[116] The LPP contributed to the peace process by two methods. The first major method of the group was to organise public events, panels and protests against any type of violence deployed by the PKK and responded to by the security forces. The group's biggest event was a peace train that started in İstanbul and completed its trip in Diyarbakır in 2015. The Peace Train Organisation (PTO) aimed to take the peace message to society, on a train that stopped at eleven cities between İstanbul and Diyarbakır and where they organised different activities, such as a petition drive. The train arrived in Diyarbakır on Nevruz, which is a traditional celebration day of spring for both Kurdish and Turkish citizens.[117] The deputies of the political parties in parliament and people from different ethnic backgrounds, both Turkish and Kurdish, attended this event, demonstrating the political actors' support for the peace process.[118] The LPP brought the two communities together through the PTO since many people from both Kurdish and Turkish communities attended these events as neutral spaces. This is in line with Chigas's assumption that track-two agencies can bring disputing communities together.[119] Also, even though it was an informal group, the deputies of political parties attended the events of the PTO in order to stand against violence. Although political parties did not express their support for the group explicitly, it was a unifying event which brought people with different views together.

The group also organised other events. For instance, they organised meetings in many cities and marches against both the security forces and PKK to end violence. More specifically, the group organised conferences such as 'Samsun Barışa Bakıyor' and 'Uşak Barışa Bakıyor' (Samsun/Uşak are Looking at Peace).[120] Through these events, the LPP not only aimed to bring the Turkish and Kurdish communities closer to each other and to discuss possible solutions, but also encouraged disputing communities and other groups in society, who were reluctant about a political agreement, towards resolving the root causes of the conflict.[121] Therefore, the LPP helped transform society's perception of a non-violent resolution by convincing them of the possibility of ending the Kurdish conflict.

The other major method of the LPP was direct contact with political parties and actors to encourage them to make political reforms and thus forward the peace process. This was possible through direct contact with the political parties in the parliament. The leading members of the LPP met with four major political parties in the Assembly. The group met with the deputy chairpersons of the AKP, CHP, MHP and HDP. Contacting political parties increased both the reliability of the LPP and the possibility of their contribution to the peace process. Moreover, Algan said that the group even witnessed a softer and more approachable attitude from Yusuf Halaçoglu (the then vice chairperson of pro-Turkish MHP). Halaçoglu was supportive and positive towards the LPP even though the MHP as a whole was completely against the peace process.[122] However, the LPP did not play a role in putting pressure on the political actors for political change. Its main purpose was to promote peace. Hence, its contribution related to political decisions was only through facilitating peace talks between the government on the one hand, and the HDP and Öcalan on the other. In this way, the group acted as a catalyst to maintain official negotiations. Nevertheless, in contrast to the existing literature, which suggests that this type of contact results in a contribution to the decisions of political actors,[123] the LPP's direct contact with political parties did not result in their suggestions being considered by the main protagonists of the conflict. The LPP's limited contribution to political decisions was because of its inadequate influence on transforming issues at the root of the conflict, not because they were talking to the wrong people.

The LPP was also faced with protests from nationalists and some pro-Kurdish groups. For example, the group was exposed to some aggression from local people in the cities of Sivas and Kırıkkale.[124] Algan said that the LPP was also criticised by the HDP for being an initiative of the government.[125] Fortunately, these claims did not interrupt the group's events and did not create a reaction against it in society because it had a mix of Kurdish, leftist, religious, non-religious and feminist members.[126] Even though the HDP supported the peace process, it opposed the LPP's peace events. This is a situation which illustrates that the peace process contains misunderstandings and a lack of trust even between political actors and P/CROs. Finally, even though the LPP aimed to create change and to facilitate the peace process, it could only influence society to support a non-violent, political resolution. Its aim to reduce the level of violence could not be achieved. Similarly, Mahçupyan said that the LPP's activities remained very limited with regard to reducing the level of violence and changing regulations on ethnic discrimination.[127] Their communications with all political parties in the parliament did not result in a change in the peace process. It can be said that the limited contribution of the group was due to the lack of political and constitutional demands, as well as the focus of action being solely on public support. Therefore, the influence of the LPP's events, meetings and protests remained limited.

Great Attempt, Limited Help?

This chapter has demonstrated the role played by P/CROs during the conflict resolution processes in Northern Ireland and Turkey. While the peace groups in Northern Ireland illustrated a wider contribution, peace groups in Turkey had limited influence on bringing the violence to an end and making a peace agreement.

The BIA in Northern Ireland and WPC in Turkey have similar characteristics, because political actors played a significant role in establishing or assisting both these groups. Considering the distinctive nature of the WPC due to its initiation process by the Turkish government, it was the closest P/CRO in the Kurdish peace process to use to assess the effectiveness of the peace groups, as analysed in the previous section. Fortunately, the similarities between these groups helped in the comparison of their influence. The Turkish government founded the WPC and political actors were actively involved in the establishment of the BIA. Also, both P/CROs were led by academics, journalists and other intellectuals.[128] While the PP was founded as a reaction to a specific incident caused by an IRA member, the LPP was established as

Table 5.2 Methods and results of the initiatives of the P/CROs in Northern Ireland and Turkey.

Conflict	Northern Ireland		Turkey	
Groups	BIA	PP	WPC	LPP
Foundation	Political and unofficial actors	Reactive groups (unofficial)	Political and unofficial actors	Reactive groups (unofficial)
Support	Publicly supported by the government	Covert support by the government	Publicly supported by the government	Covert support by the government
Method	Panels, high-level conferences, meetings	Meetings with communities, marches	Panels, low-level conferences, meetings	Meetings with communities, demonstrations
Goal	Changing the legal arrangements	De-escalating the conflict, promoting peace	Changing the legal arrangements	De-escalating the conflict, promoting peace
Outcome	Successful in changing some regulations	Partially successful in changing regulations	Partially successful in changing regulations	Unsuccessful in changing regulations

a general reaction to an increasing level of violence; however, the LPP's most influential event, the Peace Train Organisation, was a reaction to an incident that caused the loss of fifty civilians' lives.[129] The PP and LPP have many similarities in terms of their *raisons d'être*, characteristics and demands. The comprehensiveness of these four groups with regard to the inclusion of all disputing views resulted in them gaining the governments' support publicly or secretly (Table 5.2). While both governments assisted the BIA and WPC publicly, by being involved in their foundation, they preferred to give covert support to the PP and LPP. It can be said that the communication between these groups and the governments helped the groups to contribute to the peace process.

In relation to the methods and results of the BIA and WPC's activities, they organised very similar events: for instance, panels, conferences, meetings between disputing communities and with political parties and government officials. Regarding their activities at the grassroots level, they respectively organised panels and meetings between the Catholic and Protestant communities in Northern Ireland, and between the Kurdish and Turkish communities in Turkey. As a result of these bottom-up activities, they successfully increased public support for the conflict resolution processes. Solely top-down changes are likely to maintain ongoing issues or create other grievances; the activities of the P/CROs complemented those of the political elites by encouraging all communities to take part in the peace processes.[130] This success was attested to by the British and Turkish governments, underlining the contribution of the two groups in facilitating the peace processes and gaining public support.[131] Both groups' conferences had similar types of structures and attendees, with one exception. While the BIA organised private conferences, the WPC organised public conferences, but participation was by invitation only. The interview with Dedeoğlu revealed that the reason for this was to preclude the intervention of potential spoilers.[132] Although they had similar structures and participants – such as academics, representatives of NGOs, experts and opinion leaders – there was an important difference between the BIA and WPC: the BIA's conferences hosted high-level politicians during the 1970s and 1980s. This difference affected the contribution of these conferences. For example, as the declassified secret meeting notes indicated, the Cambridge Conference of 1973 and Oxford Conference of 1974 witnessed salient discussions on power-sharing between Merlyn Rees, Garrett Fitzgerald and the deputies of the Republic of Ireland.[133] In contrast, the WPC's conferences were organised to identify the demands of society and to determine the requirements of a peace agreement.[134] Therefore, the WPC's conferences achieved little when compared to the BIA's conferences. The track-two initiatives of the BIA created an informal dialogue between political parties and actors, and other participants who had knowledge on this conflict, while official negotiations were impossible due to ongoing violent clashes.

The final method of the two groups was to make contact with government officials. The meetings between the members of the BIA and WPC, and the British and Turkish governments respectively, were significant opportunities to contribute to the peace processes and to decrease the level of violence. Whilst the BIA was aiming for change in relation to majority rule, the establishment of a new local government and constitutional politics, the WPC had the objectives of changing counter-terrorism policy, and strengthening local governments' rights and the articles in law related to ethnic identities.[135] As a result of its activities, the BIA was successful in changing some legal arrangements through the Association's conferences and meetings with the British government. For example, the then Secretary of State for Northern Ireland, James Prior, argued that the BIA helped re-establish the basis of the Northern Irish government through local elections and a locally elected Assembly after eight years.[136] Its informal and flexible environment, as Lederach suggests, facilitated this, by bringing together official representatives of the Northern Irish parties in an unofficial environment.[137] In contrast, the WPC's activities did not result in any altered legal arrangements. The only change made was through the Democratisation Package of the Turkish government, which contained the Committee's suggestions, including regulations related to the ethnic discrimination between communities.[138] The majority of the WPC's suggestions were not considered by the government; therefore, the activities of the WPC were of limited help to the progress of peace. Overall, both groups were beneficial in promoting and maintaining the peace processes. However, the NIO minister Marshall's letter to Lord Melchett revealed that the BIA made a clear contribution as it facilitated not only the progress but also improved the rule of law.[139]

The PP and LPP followed similar methods, namely meetings between the communities and with governments and political actors, as well as organising marches that were well supported by both disputing sides in the two conflicts. The PP and LPP easily gained public support compared to the BIA and WPC. Correspondingly, an anonymous declassified secret TNA paper demonstrated that the highly supported P/CROs in Northern Ireland were focusing on the promotion of peace at the grassroots level.[140] The PP and LPP in particular aimed to influence the British and Turkish governments in respect to maintaining non-violent, political resolution efforts. The leaders of the PP, Corrigan and Williams, met with the then Secretary of State for Northern Ireland and some other officials in the British government to initiate a change in the rule of law, and to de-escalate the conflicts. The PP insisted on a change in the British Army's internment policy and of the Army's visibility, an amnesty for political prisoners and the Emergency Provisions Act. Although the British government did not change its internment policy, it agreed with the PP on the visibility of the Army. The British government's declassified secret meeting note revealed that the government decided to inform the public about the internment of terrorist suspects, which undoubtedly helped decrease the level of the unionist and nationalist communities' opposition towards the Army's actions.[141] In addition, the PP's efforts regarding political prisoners allowed them to talk directly to the prisoners in H-Block. They played an intermediary role between the government and the prisoners, which added value to the peace process. They also informed society of the H-Block issue, which helped minimise the reaction of the Catholic community.

Furthermore, the leading members of the LPP met with the chairpersons of the four parties in parliament, including the government's chairperson, during their events. Although both the PP and LPP were not supported explicitly by the governments, they were supported implicitly, which differentiates them from other peace groups. The governments' covert support for the groups, for example for the PTO's activities, and the ongoing communication and cooperation between them, make their activities significant. This support is evident through the conferences and peace talks that were organised during the PTO's trip from İstanbul to Diyarbakır, and which were promoted by the Turkish government.[142] However, the LPP's aim to help bring about a more democratic constitution, with no discrimination, could not be achieved because its events were not continued. The previous section provided evidence that this was also because of the limited aim of the LPP: to promote peace.

The PP and LPP were active during violent conflicts and their aim to help reduce the level of violence facilitated progress towards peace. While the LPP had a positive influence on increasing public support for the peace process, the PP provided a change in the Province. Therefore, they contributed to positive peace through the restoration of relationships in society. This was acknowledged by the British government and revealed through David Goodall's letter to Peter Foster (Northern Ireland ministers), that the Movement was successful in bringing hope to Northern Ireland.[143] The personal reputations of the leaders were also used to advantage, extensively by the PP and partially by the LPP, since they were not administered by political actors, but they had some effect on these actors' decisions. In particular, the personal reputations of the PP's leaders (they won the Nobel Peace Prize and met with the Pope) resulted in the Queen's support for the Movement.[144] It can be said that these aspects helped the Movement to be seen as a successful peace group.

The influence of these four peace organisations on the Northern Irish and Turkey's Kurdish peace processes can be explained in two major ways: as an impact on reducing or ending violence, and in encouraging political actors to reach a peace agreement. Initially, all four groups helped de-escalate the

Northern Irish and Turkey's Kurdish conflicts. While the PP's influence in reducing the violent attacks of unionists, republicans and the British government was very effective through its well-supported marches, the BIA, LPP and WPC had less influence. Although the WPC's aim was to understand society's demands, it was perceived as an elite-driven group, since the public used the group to forward their messages to the AKP government. Hence, reducing the level of violence was an indirect outcome of the group through their promotion of peace, and by closing the gap between the Kurdish and Turkish communities thanks to its events as a civil society organisation. Here, the proximity of these groups to society – that is, the communities in conflict – is an important factor, which was measured through the peace groups' focus on the demands of the societies and whether they were successful in bringing disputing communities together. Thus, the closer the peace commissions were to society, the more successful they were in helping to reduce the level of violence in the Northern Irish and Turkey's Kurdish peace processes.

The four groups' influence on political actors is another salient aspect. All four groups had the chance to communicate with high-level politicians. This gave them an opportunity to influence political decisions. However, as they were not official representatives or elected people, their potential impact on the peace processes could be limited. In this context, the BIA and WPC had a greater influence than the PP and LPP, because political actors played a role in establishing the former two P/CROs. On the one hand, the BIA and WPC brought high-level politicians, experts and opinion leaders together in an unofficial environment, providing them freedom to express their ideas and thoughts. The British and Turkish governments took into account the outcome of these conferences and meetings. However, the BIA's political events were much more effective than the WPC's activities due to the nature of these initiatives. The BIA's conferences hosted far more politicians of different political views, such as the unionist and nationalist parties and British government, than the WPC's events; this was undoubtedly a significant factor in determining the outcome of these events. The WPC could contact the government, but not the republican and nationalist parties as they refused to attend any peace attempts. Undeniably, the lack of a political contribution restricted the peace groups talking only to the government, which affected the acceptability of any political resolution. Although it was an external factor for the WPC, it affected the efficiency of the group. Moreover, the foundation of the WPC by the Turkish government affected the perception of wider Turkish society and opposition parties of the impartiality of this group. On the other hand, the PP and LPP also contacted political actors who were important people in the peace processes. However, their contribution was very limited compared to the BIA and WPC's impact. It can be said that the closer the peace groups were to the decision-making mechanism, the more they could influence political actors in order to maintain the conflict resolution processes in Northern Ireland and Turkey.

To sum up, it can be said that the contribution of the P/CROs in Northern Ireland was more comprehensive than the P/CROs in Turkey's Kurdish peace process. Even though they influenced political actors, these groups were not the key players in political decisions. Instead, they were supplementary groups whose great attempts resulted in only limited help to the peace processes. Fortunately, they played a far better role in helping to reduce the level of violence, since the reaction of society had an influence on this in both cases. These two aspects illustrate the fact that these four groups acted as a bridge between society and political actors. Therefore, they successfully brought these two levels of the conflict resolution processes closer, facilitating official negotiations, which will be discussed in the next chapter.

Notes

1. Pillar, 'Ending Limited War', p. 254.
2. The peace groups related to the topic of this research have only been analysed by a few sources in Northern Ireland (Arthur, 'Negotiating the Northern Ireland Problem'; Hadfield, 'The Anglo-Irish Agreement'; Hughes and Knox, 'For Better or Worse'; Hylton, 'The Peace-making Role of Christians'). Similarly, there are only a few sources related to the peace organisations in Turkey (Çıtak and Alkan, 'Terörden Kaynaklı Çatışmaların Çözümü'; Kızılkaya, *Barışa Katlanmak*; Oran, 'Ben Ege'de Akilken . . .'). None of this research underlines the importance of peace groups' role as conflict resolution organisations.
3. Knox and Hughes, 'Crossing the Divide'.
4. Cochrane and Dunn, 'CAIN: CSC Report'.
5. Radikal, '"Kürt Meselesine İslami Çözüm" Çalıştayı'.
6. Duffy, 'Peace Education in a Divided Society'; McGlynn *et al.*, 'Moving out of Conflict'.

7. Hafıza Merkezi, 'Çocuklar Aynı Çatının Altında Derneği'.
8. Cochrane and Dunn, 'CAIN: CSC Report'.
9. Hughes and Knox, 'For Better or Worse?'
10. TNA-CJ/4/4173, *B.A. Blackwell's letter to Mr Abbott and Secretary of State*.
11. McKeown and McLachlan, *Strategy for Peace*; TNA-CJ/4/1549/2, *Community of the Peace People*.
12. Arthur, 'Negotiating the Northern Ireland Problem'; BIA, 'The British–Irish Association'.
13. TNA-CJ/4/1549/1, *Mr David Goodall's letter to Peter Foster*.
14. TNA-CJ/4/4025, *J.H.G. Leahy's letter to Graham Greene Attachment*.
15. TNA-CJ/4/296, *Nick Stadlen's letter to Mr Howell*; TNA-CJ/4/4169, *D. Chesterton's letter to Lord Gowrie*.
16. TNA-CJ/4/582, *F.S.L. Lyons letter to Roy Hattersley*.
17. Kaufman, 'Sharing the Experience of Citizens' Diplomacy'.
18. TNA-CJ/4/4169, *N.C. Abbott's letter to Mr Merifield*.
19. Hylton, 'The Peace-making Role of Christians', p. 333; Hylton, 'Opportunities for Peacemaking', p. 32.
20. TNA-CJ/4/4169, *Minister's Case 7849*.
21. Arthur, 'Negotiating the Northern Ireland Problem', p. 415.
22. TNA-CJ/4/2228, *British–Irish Association Conference*.
23. TNA-CJ/4/2580, *A.P. Wilson's letter to Secretary of State*.
24. Kaufman, 'Sharing the Experience of Citizens' Diplomacy'.
25. TNA-CJ/4/2580, *British–Irish Association Conference*.
26. TNA-CJ/4/4169, *R.A. Harrington's letter to Mr Chesterton*.
27. TNA-CJ/4/4174, *Hayes's letter to Mr Bell*.
28. TNA-CJ/4/4173, *Secretary of State's BIA Speech*.
29. Ibid.; TNA-FCO/87/1303, *The Irish Association*.
30. TNA-CJ/4/4173, *Secretary of State's BIA Speech*.
31. Montville, 'The Arrow and the Olive Branch'.
32. Hadfield, 'The Anglo-Irish Agreement', p. 18.
33. Cochrane, *Unionist Politics and the Politics of Unionism*, pp. 8–10.
34. Kadıoğlu, 'Great Effort, Little Help?', p. 216.
35. Double quotation marks are in the original.
36. Spring, quoted in Rea, 'The Political Dimension of Northern Ireland', p. 40.
37. Mayhew, cited in Aughey, 'A State of Exception', p. 2.
38. Mapendere, 'Track One and a Half Diplomacy'.
39. TNA-CJ/4/4173, *C.L. Angel's letter to Miss Mulligan*.
40. TNA-CJ/4/1947, *J.A. Marshall's letter to Lord Melchett*.

41. The Peace People is also known as the Peace Movement (TNA-CJ/4/1549/1, *Northern Ireland Peace People*; TNA-CJ/4/4025, *J.H.G. Leahy's letter to Graham Greene*).
42. Fairmichael, 'The Peace People Experience', p. 5.
43. O'Donnell, *The Peace People of Northern Ireland*; TNA-CJ/4/1549/1, *Peace Leader Denies Helping Killers*.
44. TNA-CJ/4/1549/2, *Northern Ireland Office's Report*.
45. TNA-CJ/4/1549/2, *N.N. Cowling's letter to Mr Wilson*.
46. Kelman, 'Social-psychological Dimensions of International Conflict'; Rothman, *Resolving Identity-Based Conflict*.
47. TNA-CJ/4/4025, *Ulster Woman Advocates Peace*.
48. TNA-CJ/4/1549/1, *Mr David Goodall's letter to Peter Foster*.
49. TNA-CJ/4/1549/1, *Northern Ireland Peace People*.
50. The Republican paramilitary groups are the Provisional IRA, Official IRA and INLA. The loyalist paramilitary groups are the Ulster Volunteer Force, UDA, Red Hand Commando, Ulster Freedom Fighters and Ulster Young Militants (TNA-CJ/4/1549/2, *J.E. Henderson's letter to Abbott*).
51. TNA-CJ/4/1549/2, *M.W.J. Buxton's letter to the Secretary of State*.
52. Ibid.
53. Kaye, *Talking to the Enemy*.
54. Interview with Walsh, member of SF, former member of the PIRA and the leader of the Blanket Protest, 19 January 2015.
55. TNA-CJ/4/2380, *Peace Leader Ciaran McKeown*.
56. TNA-CJ/4/2380, *Note for the Record*.
57. TNA-CJ/4/3706, *Community of the Peace People's Report*; TNA-CJ/4/3706, *Marshall's letter to A.P. Wilson*.
58. TNA-CJ/4/2380, *Note of a Meeting between the Peace People and Mr Concannon*.
59. Ibid.
60. Mapendere, 'Track One and a Half Diplomacy'.
61. TNA-CJ/4/3706, *Mairead Corrigan's letter to Prime Minister Margaret Thatcher*.
62. Ibid.
63. Ibid.
64. O'Hagan, 'The Real Maze Men Speak'.
65. TNA-CJ/4/4024, *Direct Rule Not Acceptable*.
66. TNA-CJ/4/1549/2, *N.N. Cowling's letter to Mr Wilson*.
67. Ibid.
68. TNA-CJ/4/1549/1, *Mr David Goodall's letter to Peter Foster*.
69. WPCCAG, *Akil İnsanlar Heyeti İç Anadolu Bölgesi Raporu*.

70. Hürriyet, '6-7 Ekim'in Bilançosu 50 Ölü'.
71. Interview with Algan, 30 June 2015.
72. WPCEAG, *Akil İnsanlar Heyeti Doğu Anadolu Bölgesi Raporu*.
73. Hürriyet, '"Akil" Rapor Tamam'.
74. The description 'well-liked' public figures refers to well-known academics, members of labour and trade unions, journalists, lawyers, actors, and some other public figures (ibid.).
75. Interview with Ensaroğlu, Chairperson of the WPC's Southeastern Anatolia Region, the chief advisor to PM Ahmet Davutoğlu on the peace process, 2 July 2015.
76. WPCSG, *Akil İnsanlar Heyeti Güneydoğu Bölgesi Raporu*.
77. Interview with Yayla, 7 July 2015.
78. Lederach, *Building Peace*; Sanders, *Inside the IRA*.
79. Interview with Uçum, Deputy of the AKP, 2 July 2015.
80. WPCMG, *Akil İnsanlar Heyeti Marmara Bölgesi Raporu*.
81. Interview with Ensaroğlu, 2 July 2015.
82. Mayer, 'The Dynamics of Power'.
83. Kızılkaya, *Barışa Katlanmak*.
84. Interview with Erdem, Chairperson of the WPC's Aegean Region, former Deputy of the CHP, 10 July 2015; interview with Oran, member of the WPC's Aegean Region, 18 June 2015.
85. Interview with Dedeoğlu, Vice Chairperson of the WPC's Central Anatolia Region, later appointed the Minister for the EU, 17 June 2015.
86. Montville, 'The Arrow and the Olive Branch'.
87. Nan, 'Complementarity and Coordination of Conflict Resolution Efforts'.
88. Interview with Ensaroğlu, 2 July 2015.
89. Interview with Belge, member of the WPC's Southeastern Region, 30 June 2015.
90. Interview with Oğan, Secretary of the WPC's Eastern Anatolia Region, 18 June 2015.
91. Oran, *'Ben Ege'de Akilken . . .'*
92. Mayer, 'The Dynamics of Power'.
93. Interview with Oğan, 18 June 2015.
94. Interview with Can, member of the WPC's Central Anatolia Region, 25 June 2015; interview with Dedeoğlu, 17 June 2015.
95. Vatan, 'Akil İnsanlar Heyeti'ne Amasya'da Protesto'.
96. Interview with Oğur, 25 June 2015; interview with Korkut, Secretary of the WPC's Marmara Region, Chairperson of the Association of Civil Society Development Centre, 10 July 2015.

97. Interview with Ete, chief advisor to PM Ahmet Davutoğlu, on behalf of the AKP government, 03 July 2015.
98. Interview with Çalışlar, 07 July 2015.
99. WPCEAG, *Akil İnsanlar Heyeti Doğu Anadolu Bölgesi Raporu*; WPCMRG, *Akil İnsanlar Heyeti Akdeniz Bölgesi Raporu*.
100. Bahçeli, quoted in Gursel, 'Erdogan Asks "Wise People" to Make Case for Peace'.
101. Interview with Dedeoğlu, 17 June 2015.
102. Interview with Can, 25 June 2015.
103. WPCEAG, *Akil İnsanlar Heyeti Doğu Anadolu Bölgesi Raporu*; WPCBSG, *Akil İnsanlar Heyeti Karadeniz Bölgesi Raporu*. Although human security is not the focus of this research, it is significant for resolving ethno-nationalist conflicts. The three basic principles of human security are freedom from fear, freedom from want, and freedom to live in dignity (Annan, 'We are the Peoples', p. 17; Özerdem, 'Türkiye'ye Barış Gelir Mi?', p. 2).
104. WPCSG, *Akil İnsanlar Heyeti Güneydoğu Bölgesi Raporu*.
105. Ibid.
106. EU, *European Charter of Local Self-Governments*.
107. Interview with Arıboğan, Chairperson of the WPC's Marmara Region, 8 September 2015.
108. UPOS, *Demokratikleşme Paketi*.
109. TBMM, *Temel Hak ve Hürriyetlerin Geliştirilmesi Amacıyla Çeşitli Kanunlarda Değişiklik Yapılmasına Dair Kanun*.
110. Interview with Oğur, 25 June 2015; interview with Sayman, member of the WPC's Marmara Region, 3 July 2015.
111. Interview with Tan, 24 June 2015.
112. Interview with Karatepe, member of the WPC's Mediterranean Region, former Mayor of Kayseri, 13 July 2015.
113. Interview with Mahçupyan, 22 June 2015.
114. Interview with Algan, 30 June 2015.
115. BarışaBak Platformu, 'Barışa Bak!'.
116. BiaNet, 'Barışa Bak Kampanyası 69 İmzayla Başladı'.
117. Interview with Algan, 30 June 2015.
118. Interview with Yayla, 7 July 2015.
119. Chigas, 'Negotiating Intractable Conflicts'.
120. Interview with Algan, 30 June 2015.
121. Interview with Yayla, 7 July 2015.
122. Interview with Algan, 30 June 2015.

123. Kaye, *Talking to the Enemy*.
124. Interview with Algan, 30 June 2015.
125. Ibid.
126. Interview with Yayla, 7 July 2015.
127. Interview with Mahçupyan, 22 June 2015.
128. TNA-CJ/4/4173, *B.A. Blackwell's Letter;* WPCAG, *Akil İnsanlar Heyeti Ege Bölgesi Raporu*.
129. Interview with Algan, 30 June 2015.
130. Jacoby and Özerdem, *Peace in Turkey 2023*, p. 136.
131. Interview with Uçum, 2 July 2015; TNA-CJ/4/1947, *J.A. Marshall's letter to Lord Melchett*.
132. Interview with Dedeoğlu, 17 June 2015.
133. TNA-CJ/4/582, *F.S.L. Lyons letter to Roy Hattersley*.
134. Interview with Ensaroğlu, 2 July 2015.
135. TNA-CJ/4/2228, *British–Irish Association Conference*; TNA-CJ/4/2580, *A.P. Wilson's letter to Secretary of State;* WPCSG, *Akil İnsanlar Heyeti Güneydoğu Bölgesi Raporu*.
136. TNA-CJ/4/4173, *Secretary of State's BIA Speech*.
137. Lederach, *Building Peace*.
138. UPOS, *Demokratikleşme Paketi*.
139. TNA-CJ/4/1947, *J.A. Marshall's letter to Lord Melchett*.
140. TNA-CJ/4/1549/1, *Northern Ireland Peace People*.
141. TNA-CJ/4/1549/2, *M.W.J. Buxton's letter to the Secretary of State;* TNA-CJ/4/2380, *Note of a meeting between the Peace People and Mr Concannon*.
142. Sabah, 'Barış Treni Yola Çıktı'.
143. TNA-CJ/4/1549/1, *Mr David Goodall's letter to Peter Foster*.
144. Ibid.

6

OFFICIAL NEGOTIATIONS: THE LONG, NARROW ROAD TO PEACE

If you cannot kill them all [terrorists], then sooner or later you come back to the same point, and it is a question of when, not whether, you talk. If there is a political cause then there has to be a political solution.[1]

Jonathan Powell, one of the architects of the GFA and the chief advisor to PM Blair, states that political conflicts require non-violent resolutions, which can best be achieved through official negotiations. The focus of this chapter is to examine the role of these negotiations through bilateral talks, multilateral initiatives and third-party approaches towards bringing the Northern Irish and Turkey's Kurdish conflicts to an end. It also aims to understand how political parties and actors have determined these two peace processes. The chapter aims to answer the following question: What has been the impact of the official negotiations towards ending violence and reaching peace agreements in the Northern Irish and Kurdish conflicts?

The chapter first investigates the official negotiations in Northern Ireland and then in Turkey through a two-focus analysis: bilateral talks and multilateral initiatives, including mediation efforts. While bilateral talks were largely used as the initial stage of the official negotiations in both peace processes, the multilateral efforts were implemented at the later stage. It then compares the findings of the two cases and the underlying reasons for the successful or unsuccessful outcomes of the peace initiatives. It concludes with an explanation of how these initiatives helped achieve a political resolution.

The Official Negotiations in the Northern Irish Peace Process

Bilateral Talks

The official negotiations in the Northern Irish peace process began in the early 1980s through bilateral talks between the British and Irish governments, and between Northern Irish parties. The first peace effort was initiated between the British and Irish governments. According to the Anglo-Irish Summit's Draft Communique, this was because the British government believed that a solution in Northern Ireland could only be reached through cooperation with the Irish government.[2] Therefore, the 1980s was dominated by Anglo-Irish talks. The Anglo-Irish Intergovernmental Summit of 1981 between PM Thatcher and Taoiseach Haughey was the first official peace initiative between the two governments. Although the governments' different concerns prevented a better outcome (e.g. creating more comprehensive negotiations with the Northern Irish parties), the Summit helped to establish a discussion environment for political resolution efforts. It was a significant initiative since the British government accepted that there were two different traditions with religious and cultural backgrounds in Ireland. The NIO recorded that 'the Prime Minister and the Taoiseach agreed on the need for efforts to diminish the divisions between the two sections of the community in Northern Ireland and to reconcile the two major traditions in Ireland'.[3] Yet, the Irish government was reluctant to talk about security issues due to the negative reaction of the nationalist community in the South. Even though political cooperation was not the priority of the British government, Thatcher accepted Haughey's suggestion to move relations forward. At the end of their meeting, Thatcher and Haughey declared a communiqué helping to form joint working groups between the two states with regard to new institutional structures, namely the Anglo-Irish Intergovernmental Council (AIIC), which was established on 6 November 1981.[4]

The AIIC witnessed disagreement between the two governments over the Irish government's proposal for establishing an inter-parliamentary body and the British government's recommendation for founding a joint security commission.[5] These initiatives demonstrate that even though there was a disagreement between the two sides over security and political cooperation, there were still some changes. It is evident that there was a change in the position of the British government, as it admitted the existence of two different traditions within Northern Ireland. As Vayrynen notes, a change in the identification of the problem is a sign of issue transformation.[6] This occurred by recognising the existence of the Catholic and Protestant communities. It was a significant point in the negotiations, but did not end the British government's coercive measures and security policies, which did not help conduct resolution efforts in a peaceful environment. For example, the hunger strikes of 1980–1 demonstrate that the government was willing to maintain coercive policies, as Thatcher declared the triumphalism of the British government when she went to Belfast on 28 May 1981. She said: 'Faced with the failure of their [the IRA] discredited cause, the men of violence have chosen in recent months to play what *may well be their last card.*'[7] Similarly, Moore describes the British government's position as consistent regarding the refusal to concede to any of the political demands of the hunger strikers.[8] However, the government's approach was not consistent with official statements, as the government and republican movement were negotiating secretly (as outlined in the section 'Indirect Communications in Northern Ireland'). This demonstrates that even though there was a change in the political context, this change did not create a transformation in the official security policy of the British government.

The AIIC's failure in de-escalating the conflict through political reforms did not help to end the IRA's 'long war' strategy, just like the British government's coercive policies. However, as discussed in Chapter 4, the secret talks between the British government and republican movement resulted in a change in the republican strategy, as they began to believe in the possible success of political resolution efforts. This was seen as a change in the republican view, as noted by Danny Morrison, a senior republican; 'Who here really believes we can win the war through the ballot box? But will anyone here object if, with a ballot paper in one hand and the Armalite in the other, we take power in Ireland?'[9] The strategy changes from predominantly armed struggle to both ballot and bullet led to the republicans' involvement in political resolution efforts. However, it did not lead to de-escalation of the conflict.

The AIA was eventually signed by the British and Irish governments on 15 November 1985. The Agreement widened the scope of the root cause of the conflict's definition from only an ethnic to both an ethnic and constitutional problem. While the definition of the Irish government determined *de jure* sovereignty over the whole island, which was close to the SDLP and SF's positions, the British government defined the problem as identical to the unionist definition with some concessions to the nationalist view. The AIA widened both governments' views on the conflict. Irish nationalists conceded by 'recognising and respecting the identities of the two communities in Northern Ireland, and the right of each community to pursue its aspirations by peaceful and constitutional means'.[10] Together with the change in perception of Irish nationalists, the British government widened its understanding to include constitutional nationalists and recognised the existence of two communities with different cultures and political aspirations.[11] This was different from the early Anglo-Irish talks, since the British government's perception began to introduce political rights for the two communities instead of only cultural traditions. The Agreement also considered the demands of unionists by stating that there would be no change in the status of Northern Ireland without the consent of the majority.[12] The change in perceptions of the two governments was a significant step for the negotiation process; it helped close the gap between them and made sitting at the negotiating table possible. The inclusiveness of peace attempts is vital for their success as official negotiations need to embrace both supporters and opponents of the resolution process.

The British government's consideration of the unionists' main concern in the AIA did not prevent an outcry from the unionist community. Their initial reaction was strongly hostile and was not expected by Thatcher: she described it 'as much worse than [she] expected'.[13] The unionist community reacted to the AIA with protests and marches.[14] In addition, all the unionist MPs resigned from their seats at Westminster, aiming to use by-elections as a mini-referendum.[15] Their purpose was to gauge the demands of the Northern Irish people as a whole. However, as Table 6.1 shows, the result of the election disappointed the unionists as they could not achieve their aim of 500,000 votes: the UUP, DUP and UPUP's combined vote was only 418,230. As a result, they lost one seat to the SDLP. As described in Chapter 2, spoilers can emerge to undermine a peace process, and sometimes after an agreement has

Table 6.1 Westminster by-election results in 1986. Source: ARK, 'Westminster by-elections, 23 January 1986', http://www.ark.ac.uk/elections/fw86.htm.

Parties	Votes	Percentage	MPs
UUP	302,198	51.7	10
DUP	85,239	14.6	3
SDLP	70,917	12.1	1
SF	38,821	6.6	–
Alliance	32,095	5.5	–
UPUP	30,793	5.2	1
Workers Party	18,148	3.1	–
Peter Barry (AIA)	6,777	1.2	–

been made.[16] The unionist parties played a spoiler role in interrupting the progress, which affected the sustainability of the peace process by demolishing the AIA. In addition, as the main protagonists did not attend the official negotiations, personal and group, structure and actor transformations were not applicable to reaching a successful result, so did not lead to a positive peace in the 1980s.

After different attempts by the British and Irish governments, official peace efforts were shaped around the Northern Irish parties after 1993. As discussed in the section 'Backchannels in Northern Ireland', it was not a volte-face, but a smooth transition thanks to the secret talks. After many years of unsuccessful attempts, it was understood that the talks on the framework for a political resolution could only be achieved through the involvement of the Northern Irish parties. The first peace initiative that changed the nature of negotiations in the 1990s was between John Hume and Gerry Adams in April 1993. The two-party dialogue on self-determination drew up a mutual understanding between nationalists and republicans on the future of Northern Ireland. It addressed the SDLP and SF's claims for the Northern Irish people to decide their political future.[17] Although it was not a new claim, this was important in illustrating the intention of the two leaders to make progress. In addition, Hume stressed the collective benefit of nationalists and republicans for a non-violent resolution perspective, and in particular, for SF to give up its 'ballot box and Armalite together' strategy. Therefore, the SDLP pressed for laying down arms and tried 'to persuade the Provos to bring their campaign of violence to an end'.[18] The Hume–Adams dialogue demonstrates that it is vital to include all conflicting parties in the peace process, as it needs to be complemented with sustainable political attempts. Hence, it can be said that the continuity of different political efforts helped increase the contribution of republicans and nationalists to the official negotiations.

The negotiations resulted in the Downing Street Declaration on 15 December 1993, which witnessed the Irish government's insistence on self-determination for the Northern Irish people. As the British government did not accept this demand, the British and Irish governments' mutual declaration stated that the status of Northern Ireland could only be changed 'if a majority of the people of Northern Ireland are so persuaded'.[19] These discussions illustrated that both governments constantly defended contrasting issues that made it impossible for them to change their perceptions. As Vayrynen suggests, it is difficult to transform issues unless they lose their importance or new issues emerge.[20] In this case, there was no change in the ultimate goals of the republican movement or the British government so the level of conflict could not be mitigated. Peter Brooke, the then Secretary of State for Northern Ireland's statement that Britain had 'no selfish, strategic or economic interest in Northern Ireland' was published in the Declaration.[21] Nonetheless, it can be said that the lack of the phrase 'no political interest' of Britain towards Northern Ireland in this affected the trust of the republican community.[22] In addition, the Brooke–Mayhew talks, which aimed to establish a settlement by creating new structures for governing Northern Ireland viaa series of negotiations with the different Northern Irish parties, helped towards the signing of the DSD.[23] As a result of these attempts, the document presented a structure in which a political agreement could be settled. According to Rev. Gary Mason, Methodist Minister of the Belfast Mission, the DSD illustrates that 'the door was beginning to open to allow some to sit around in order for peace to be built. But, the door was not fully opened.'[24] Even SF accepted that it was progress, which showed hope for peace. Jim Gibney, a senior member of SF, states that there was clear progress from the AIA to the DSD that encouraged the people of Northern Ireland to believe in peace.[25] In contrast, according to Mason, despite John Major's reasonable and approachable political stance, the Declaration's ultimate aim, which was to reach a peace settlement, could not be achieved because of the lack of a ceasefire during the negotiations.[26] After the announcement of the DSD, both nationalist and unionist communities were expecting republican and loyalist ceasefires.

According to the republican movement, to stop using arms was possible after the change in the British government's perception and decision to negotiate with republicans instead of focusing on destroying them, in addition to the Hume–Adams dialogue.[27] After the announcement of the Declaration, Adams gave a speech to a republican event and said:

> I am especially confident that after twenty-five years of unparalleled courage and self-sacrifice, the nationalist people of this part of Ireland are prepared to show the way to a new future while at the same time reaching out the hand of friendship to unionists.[28]

As both sides realised that they could not achieve their goals through armed struggle, it was a 'hurting stalemate' and thus a ripe moment for a negotiated resolution. As described in Chapter 2, the phrase hurting stalemate, coined by Stedman[29] and Zartman,[30] refers to a stalemate that forces an armed group to choose political efforts as opposed to an armed struggle; this situation was evident in Northern Ireland in the 1990s.

The loyalist paramilitary groups also had different expectations of the British government. In line with the unionist community, loyalists wanted a guarantee from the British government to remain part of the UK.[31] Perhaps they were comforted by the phrase that the union was safe 'until a majority of people want otherwise'.[32] Therefore, the DSD was significant in many contexts. On the one hand, the two-party dialogue opened the way to further negotiations and helped SF to believe in politics instead of armed struggle. The change in SF's perception led the IRA to declare an eighteen-month ceasefire. On the other hand, loyalists' claim on securing the current situation was also mentioned in the Declaration. After all, it can be said that both republican and loyalist ceasefires saw significant improvements in the 1990s. From the republican perspective, the war was over by the mid-1990s and that removed the barriers from the peace process.[33] This emerged not only in the Northern Irish context, but also in an international context with Adams' visa from the Clinton administration, which is discussed in the next section.

Multilateral Efforts

After the bilateral talks provided the basis for more comprehensive initiatives, the multi-party and all-party negotiations and mediation efforts were applied in the 1990s. The first significant issue was Gerry Adams's visa. Adams was granted a visa from the US in January 1994, which changed the nature of the process for two interrelated reasons. First, it was a chance for Adams to explain the problem in the US and to meet with Irish-Americans who had been a great help and supported the reunification of Ireland. As Gibney notes, 'the Gerry Adams visa was one of the most important gestures of bringing peace to Ireland'.[34] When Adams visited the US, he saw a high degree of support and sympathy for the Northern Irish peace process. Even the unionists admitted that this visit brought about a change in the perception of the Clinton administration and helped make the president look at it differently.[35] It was also a significant point in relation to structural transformation. As Vayrynen suggests, the scale and nature of a national violent conflict can be altered through the inclusion of a regional or an international actor,[36] which may result in a transformation in the structure of a conflict. In the Northern Irish conflict, this transformation facilitated the conflict resolution process and helped create a positive peace within which to overcome the root causes of the conflict, by changing the context from national to international. Second, even though the US administration was always interested in the Northern Irish conflict, they only became directly involved through Adams's visa. Unlike the previous leaders, Clinton had a great interest in ending the violence in Northern Ireland and in solving the problem in a peaceful way by bringing in SF. However, the British government resisted this idea, as is seen by PM Major's fury at Clinton offering a visa in the first place. Major explained his resistance by stating 'on my instructions Rod Lyne, my Foreign Affairs Private Secretary, told the White House *forcefully* that we believed the offer of a visa should be held open until there was an end to violence'.[37] In contrast, the Irish-American lobby applied intense pressure for the visa to be granted.[38] In the end, this was also a sign to the British government that it was not just Britain's problem anymore. It was attested to by republicans, as Walsh states, that until the involvement of the Clinton administration, the British government had believed it was an internal issue of the UK.[39]

Another issue that triggered multilateral efforts was the lack of trust in the British government. There was a general desire for a political settlement after secret talks in the 1990s, contrary to the previous decade. However, there was still opposition from the unionist community. Referring to the DSD, Lord Reginald Empey, the former leader of the UUP and member of the House of Lords, said that 'we traditionally relied on the British government but they proved to be unreliable; then, the only way forward was to do this, ourselves'.[40] The unionist community decided to defend their rights on their own, believing it was the only way to get what they wanted. As discussed in Chapter 2, mistrust between parties in a conflict can intensify and escalate the problem.[41] The empirical analysis showed that trust issues existed in two ways in the Northern Irish negotiations: not only during the talks, which resulted in walking out from negotiations, but also as a determinant to 'joint' discussions. The UUP's decision to be more involved in negotiations was due to their lack of trust in the British government. In contrast to the literature on conflict resolution that suggests that there is a negative influence to a lack of trust in maintaining a peace process,[42] this issue helped towards the success of negotiations by increasing participation in each peace initiative.

The peace efforts in the mid-1990s were maintained through the mutual work of PM Major and Taoiseach Bruton. The republican and loyalist ceasefires moved the discussion forward to the decommissioning of paramilitary groups and the framework for negotiations. The discussion between the two leaders led to the Joint Communiqué of 28 November 1995, which announced a two-fold approach: 'to make parallel progress on decommissioning and all-party negotiations'.[43] The agreement between the two governments provided two critical developments in the peace process: the establishment of an international commission for decommissioning, which aimed to end the armed struggle; and the appointment of former US Senator George Mitchell to chair the all-party talks, which were one of the major elements of the conflict resolution attempts in Northern Ireland.

One of the significant situations that changed the direction of the peace process was the report of the International Body on Arms Decommissioning in 1997 whose members were Mitchell, General John de Chastelain from Canada and Harri Holkeri, former PM of Finland. Despite the opposition of the unionist community and British government, the report declared that decommissioning was part of the all-party negotiations, but did not contain rules requiring decommissioning prior to such negotiations.[44] The declaration of the report was a call to all parties to carry out negotiations without any prerequisites. Nevertheless, the British government accepted the UUP's proposal for an elected assembly.[45] This caused a great division between Britain and the Republic of Ireland. While it was welcomed by Britain with statements such as 'the most creative proposal yet advanced for moving the peace process forward', it was criticised by the Irish Republic as a 'serious breach of faith'.[46] The political gridlock between the two states interrupted the peace process and caused it to lose momentum. This was a significant point as it triggered the IRA to use violence again. The IRA's Canary Wharf bombing in London (9 February 1996) ended its ceasefire, blaming the British government for preventing progress in the peace process: 'The resolution of the conflict in our country demands justice. It demands an inclusive negotiated settlement. That is not possible unless and until the British government faces up to its responsibilities.'[47] It was clear that the IRA was not interested in maintaining negotiations, as the cost of negotiations was higher than the armed struggle. This is in line with Zartman's assumption, since the direction of the talks was not moving as the IRA demanded.[48] In this context, it is revealed that a lack of transformation in actors from the military to the political wing of the republican movement was the result of the IRA standing as the only decision maker.

The significant point here was the aim of the parties to maintain the negotiations despite the return of paramilitary violence. A close deadline (30 May 1996) for the Northern Ireland Forum[49] election for the parties who would be involved in the negotiations was a motivation to illustrate that peace was possible. Furthermore, the desire to maintain the peace process was opened through bilateral talks between the British and Irish governments, and was a hidden, but critical element of the peace process. The track-one initiative between Major and Bruton provided the Irish government with a joint coordinator role in the negotiations.[50] In spite of the opposition from the unionists, the change helped conduct the Forum election. Furthermore, it became a more comprehensive process, with the inclusion of the demands of the Republic of Ireland. After the Forum election, the last and final stage of negotiations began on 10 June 1996. Although ten parties[51] in Northern Ireland were invited to the negotiations, SF was not invited due to the ongoing IRA violence. This revealed the fact that even though the dialogue between the British and Irish governments was helping the progress, the major component of the peace process were the negotiations between the Northern Irish parties and British government. The controversy between SF and other parties could not be overcome by the British government and this demonstrated the vital importance of an independent third party in the negotiations.

The efforts in 1996 illustrated that one of the most complicated aspects of this negotiation process was bringing conflicting sides together. Mitchell interpreted these negotiations as 'a serious effort to address and resolve the many substantial obstacles to agreement'[52]. Another critical aspect was the victory of Tony Blair's Labour Party in the general election of 1997. Immediately after the election, PM Tony Blair focused on establishing an independent commission on decommissioning in August 1997. In his words: 'the issue of decommissioning was one very unfortunate legacy from the previous administration which was to become a big ball and chain round our legs in the years to come'.[53] The establishment of the Independent International Commission on Decommissioning (IICD)[54] helped maintain peace negotiations within a more peaceful environment. In addition, the Mitchell Report's key recommendation to begin all-party talks and arms decommissioning in parallel helped SF to attend the negotiations.[55] Hence, this peace process illustrates that a powerful mediator broke down one of the greatest taboos of the political efforts by including SF in the official negotiations. This issue illustrates a similar direction with Touval and Zartman's assumption that a mediator with 'muscles' can break the barriers between the conflicting parties even if these are the major concerns, such as preconditions to reject any type of violence and to declare a ceasefire.[56] This will be compared with the mediation in the Kurdish peace process at the end of this chapter.

While the negotiations were being held between all parties (except SF), there was another important initiative between Hume and Adams. The negotiation stage was again shaped by bilateral talks, which demonstrates how bilateral and multilateral talks interlocked with one another and were applied interchangeably during the official negotiations. Hume and Adams's talks on 18 July 1997 and their joint statement pointed to democracy and equality. These elements became the two major aims of the two parties in the peace process. They stated that 'a just and lasting commitment will only be achieved if it is based on principles of democracy and equality and has the allegiance of both traditions'.[57] The IRA declared a ceasefire just two days after the statement, which led to resumption of the negotiation process. As happened in the 1994 ceasefire, the republican ceasefire played a fundamental role in facilitating the talks. It is important to bear in mind that the IRA ceasefire statement was addressing the progress in the political situation.[58] Therefore, this book has revealed that there is a dual relationship between conflicting parties: whilst the British government and other parties in conflict were insisting on a peaceful environment to conduct peace efforts, the IRA waited for political progress that included its demands as a condition to lay down arms. The Northern Irish peace process gained its momentum when these two aspects were brought together. It was because the ceasefire led to the invitation of SF to attend peace negotiations, one of the most important aspects of official negotiations, that a comprehensive peace accord was able to be reached. SF signed the Mitchell Principles that addressed abandoning and condemning the use of arms. However, this caused a deadlock in the negotiations since DUP leader, Ian Paisley, urged Blair to scrap the negotiations and asserted that he would leave for good if SF were let in. Paisley's approach here can be explained through the long-standing opposition of the DUP towards any political attempts. Further, as Mitchell states, the three unionist parties (the DUP, UUP and UKUP) insisted on the IRA's decommissioning prior to SF's inclusion in negotiations.[59] After the British and Irish governments' proposal on maintaining negotiations without prior decommissioning had been accepted, the DUP and UKUP walked out and never returned. Yet, the DUP and UKUP blamed the UUP for 'selling-out the union' as the UUP did not walk out.[60]

The existing violence also negatively affected multi-party negotiations. After the renewal of the loyalist groups' violence, the UUP resigned from negotiations immediately before its suspension. Similarly, SF was suspended after the IRA's violent attacks. The two parties were allowed back before the deadline of the agreement. Mitchell's effort to include all parties in the negotiations was promising since he successfully established 'an outwardly rippling, relatively inclusive, coalition of the centre against extremes'.[61] As a former US senator, he knew that all conflicting sides should join the negotiations and hence, their supporters should be represented in the peace negotiations. Therefore, the influence of the agreement was broad.[62] As Jeong suggests, the response of a mediator is not to assist only one side of the conflict, but to come up with a mutually agreed solution.[63] This was successfully carried out during the mediations led by Mitchell.

After several two-party, multi-party and all-party talks, the Good Friday Agreement was declared on 10 April 1998 through the attendance of all parties involved in the talks. The all-party talks before the Agreement helped bring all disputing views together and so addressed all parties' demands.[64] A political agreement in 1998 was possible through the intention of conflicting parties as the political parties in the negotiations were much more approachable than in the 1980s and early 1990s. For example, according to Empey, SF was careful not to refer to the IRA and also softened its language. Therefore, it helped create a positive atmosphere by pushing for non-violence and democracy.[65] The reason for being more approachable is that the parties began to believe that they could not achieve their aims through armed struggle. Similarly, the British government helped to conduct the negotiations by keeping secret the details of the discussions. The desire of the Northern Irish people for a political settlement was another major element for the successful outcome. According to Ben Mallon, the then DUP Councillor for Lisburn and Castlereagh, they were sick and tired of murder on the streets after many years of terrorism.[66] A peace agreement would not be possible without the consent of the people of Northern Ireland. The consent and support for the GFA was clearly seen through the two referendums held in the North and South of the island with a great majority of the people's approval (Table 6.2). A guaranteed referendum was also important to increase public support. It was argued that the difference of these negotiations from previous attempts were their structure (i.e. formed of elected members) and the agreed process, which guaranteed a referendum at the end of the negotiations.[67]

Table 6.2 The 1998 Good Friday Agreement referendums. Source: ARK, 'The 1998 Referendums', http://www.ark.ac.uk/elections/fref98.htmWestminster by-elections.

Referendum	Yes	No
Northern Ireland	676,966 (71.1%)	274,879 (28.9%)
The Republic of Ireland	1,442,583 (94.4%)	85,748 (5.6%)

The international involvement in the peace process was also one of the crucial elements of the peace. Although the US administration was criticised for having a nationalist approach due to the Irish-American population in the US, the Clinton Administration changed the view of the Northern Irish people, which helped Mitchell to mediate the talks in a peaceful environment. In addition, Mitchell carried the authority of the President of the US, which was a significant source of influence. He also informed President Clinton periodically about the developments.[68] This authority strengthened his position as an independent mediator, which is one of the basic characteristics of a mediation approach. He resisted any attempt to interrupt the process of the British and Irish governments since they behaved 'in the mood of the big boys who could do the deal'.[69] Moreover, as mentioned in Chapter 2, mediation as a social approach requires making interpersonal, intergroup and international negotiations possible.[70] In addition to his personality as an international actor, he carried out interpersonal and intergroup negotiations through his talks with all parties himself and with his two colleagues.[71]

The GFA brought a political framework and political institutions which responded to the questions of the people in Northern Ireland. The three strands of the GFA, namely the Northern Ireland Assembly (within Northern Ireland), a North–South ministerial Council (between Northern Ireland and the Republic of Ireland) and a British–Irish Council (between the Republic of Ireland and Britain), offered a comprehensive political approach that included the concepts of self-determination, power-sharing and other constitutional amendments. These institutions successfully addressed unionists, nationalists and republicans' demands.[72]

The Official Negotiations in Turkey's Kurdish Peace Process

The official negotiations in Turkey's Kurdish peace process have witnessed two-party and multilateral negotiations, political reforms and mediation efforts, which have revealed some breaking points, spoilers and changes in the disputing parties' attitudes. As mentioned in the section 'Background of Turkey's Kurdish Peace Process', even though the EU accession criteria facilitated constitutional amendments regarding human rights, civil–military relationships and democratisation, they were subsidiary steps towards peace. Rather, the major events were the bilateral and multilateral initiatives. This section will firstly analyse the influence of bilateral talks through the Democratic Opening Project, the İmralı talks and the Dolmabahçe Declaration. Then, it will assess the impact of the multilateral efforts through the Resolution Commission and Oslo talks.

Bilateral Talks

The official talks in Turkey began after a democratic initiative was announced by the Turkish government. The Democratic Opening Project of 2009 was a critical point for resolution, which was initiated at a meeting in Büyükada, İstanbul and led by Kezban Hatemi, an attorney who had joined many humanitarian initiatives in different countries. This initiative brought different ethnic and religious leaders, and the Turkish government together. It was a declaration which initiated a democratic project related to all ethnic and religious identities in Turkey. As Hatemi noted, the project contained non-Muslim citizens' rights, the right of property, freedom of religion and conscience, and ethnic identity rights.[73] Hence, it was a comprehensive effort to achieve political reforms for not only ethnic identities but also different religious sects. There was also a specific reference to the Kurdish question, which Hatemi argues was: 'let's begin the democratisation project from İmralı'.[74]

However, the Project was not put into action immediately since it was declared that the content needed to be decided upon through a consensus of all political parties in the TBMM (the Turkish Assembly). Although the AKP administration had meetings with all political parties in the TBMM, the opposition parties' unwillingness to attend peace initiatives led the AKP government to conduct law amendments by cooperation with only the pro-Kurdish DTP and its successors BDP and HDP.[75] After the discussions between the parties, PM Erdoğan announced the democratisation package, which contained political reforms related to the Kurdish issue.[76] The package was passed into law in the TBMM in March 2014 and introduced rights, including the right to political campaigning in languages other than Turkish, a co-leadership system of political parties, and punishment for the hate and discrimination of different languages, religions, nationalities and races.[77]

The Project was one of the major steps of the peace process since it emphasised the rights of Kurdish people. The changes in legislation were even acknowledged by pro-Kurdish figures such as Celalettin Can, who noted that the government had brought more democratic rights than all of the previous governments in the history of Turkey.[78] Similarly, Mehmet Uçum, the then AKP deputy, stated that implementation of the reforms – for instance reinstating the ancient Kurdish names of villages, permission to make political speeches in Kurdish, a Kurdish television channel, Kurdish education in private schools, and the opening of Kurdish institutions – all created a peaceful environment in society.[79] The significance of the reforms was to mitigate one of the underlying reasons of the Kurdish question, which was to end assimilation and the denial of Kurdish ethnicity. It was also stated that one of the major advantages of the democratisation project was to demonstrate to society that a political resolution without violence was possible.[80] The Turkish government's recognition of Kurdish ethnicity transformed one of the root causes of the conflict. This was an issue transformation from rejecting the Kurdish conflict's existence to making political reforms in order to eliminate ethnic discrimination. Such a position change is crucial for resolving an ethno-nationalist conflict.[81] This change led to the reframing of issues. As noted by Starkey *et al.*, recognition of Kurdish ethnicity caused a re-examination of other issues related to ethnicity and to the institutionalisation of resolution efforts.[82] However, even though there was an issue transformation, the democratic opening project was not adequate to resolve the conflict, due to the existence of ethnic references in the constitution. As Aydınlı and Özcan put it, the lack of proper preparation before launching the project resulted in the PKK dominating the peace process,[83] as the government did not plan to marginalise radical elements of the PKK that defended the armed struggle. Therefore, the negotiations were mostly conducted between the government and Öcalan.

In order to institutionalise the peace process, the AKP government's democratic opening project established the Undersecretariat of Public Order and Security (*Kamu Düzeni ve Güvenliği Müsteşarlığı*, henceforth KDGM). According to the law passed in June 2014, the KDGM was declared as the official association for conducting the peace process.[84] The KDGM took responsibility for the official resolution attempts. One of the senior officers of the KDGM stated that the democratic opening was a declaration in which the Turkish government admitted the existence of the problem and committed to solving this conflict.[85] As Babbitt and Hampson underline, reciprocity between conflicting parties can change the nature of the conflict by putting agreed points into action.[86] The KDGM played a role in official negotiations on behalf of the government by negotiating the conditions of the peace with Öcalan on İmralı Island, which became known as the İmralı talks.[87]

The İmralı talks were the second bilateral initiative between 2013 and 2015 that was carried out between the Turkish government on the one hand, and the PKK's jailed leader Öcalan and BDP (later on the HDP) on the other. Unlike the secret talks between the MIT and Öcalan in the mid-2000s, these talks were official and publicly known, but the content of the talks remained secret. Before exploring the secret negotiations during the İmralı talks, it is important to understand the components of these talks. Similar to the Northern Irish peace process, the bilateral talks came into effect between the government and the pro-Kurdish BDP. However, the BDP did not play a major role in the negotiations. Instead, it played a communicator or messenger role between the government and Öcalan. It was publicly known that negotiations between the government and BDP followed a framework suggested by Öcalan, as revealed by Sırrı Süreyya Önder during the İmralı Committee's[88] meeting in the İmralı Prison. Önder said to Öcalan: 'you will decide the condition and future of the peace process'.[89] Similarly, another member of the İmralı Committee and the HDP deputy, İdris Baluken, asserted that the transformation of the government's standpoint from destroying the PKK and its leader, to organising official negotiations with him illustrates the importance of Öcalan as the major actor.[90] Therefore, the first thing to understand about the nature of the talks is Öcalan as the leading actor and decision maker on behalf of the Kurdish community, not the pro-Kurdish party.[91] Secondly, although one of the main actors was Öcalan, the government wanted to move the talks into the political environment. Therefore, the government needed the BDP at the negotiating table. This was admitted by the chief advisor to the PM on the peace process, Yılmaz Ensaroğlu, that 'the only way for resolution is to bring the peace efforts into the political framework'.[92]

The framework of the talks was very comprehensive. It was an opportunity to understand the desire of the two sides, their resolution offers and the reciprocal bargaining between the two sides. As Baluken states, the government realised that Öcalan's recommendations for a resolution were moderate and acceptable during the talks.⁹³ This was publicly confirmed by Beşir Atalay, Minister of the Interior, as he noted 'they [the PKK and Öcalan] are more moderate and consistent than the HDP'.⁹⁴ Further, Baluken referred to the change in the position of the government following Öcalan's demands. According to Baluken, Öcalan's recommendation addressed democratic reforms, including constitutional changes in Kurdish rights and equal citizenship, which would be guaranteed in the constitution.⁹⁵ It is also noted that Öcalan's recommendations during the İmralı meetings, such as democratic autonomy for not only the south-east of Turkey but the whole country, was a chance for a non-violent resolution, which nevertheless remained a missed opportunity.⁹⁶ The significant point was that even though the official negotiations were carried out in only the short-term, it helped change the position of the government. As Ramsbotham et al. identify, position changes in an ethno-nationalist conflict are closely related to interest and goal changes.⁹⁷ Turkey's Kurdish question has also witnessed changes in interest, including allowing the leader of the PKK to implicitly act as the chief negotiator. This was not done officially, since he was the imprisoned leader of a terrorist group.

According to the İmralı Committee, there was an agreement between the government and Öcalan. Baluken reveals the insight of this agreement:

> Before the 2013 Nevruz letter from Öcalan, the government and Öcalan agreed on a three-stage plan. The first stage was to withdraw the PKK to create a suitable environment for peace negotiations. After Öcalan's call, the KCK firstly declared a unilateral ceasefire and then the PKK began to withdraw on May 8. The second step was the government's duties. According to the commitment, the Turkish government should have legislated a rule of law related to withdrawal, amendments in democratic rights of Kurdish people, to clear the way and to establish a mechanism which would administer the process in relation to the democratisation process of Turkey. The third step was disarmament. Even though the PKK began to withdraw, the government did not change any regulations, which were the causes of inequality between different ethnic identities of Turkey.⁹⁸

The agreement was a milestone for the process. Öcalan's roadmap indicated three major steps of the process. After the withdrawal of the PKK and implementation of democratic rights by the government, the DDR (disarmament, demobilisation and reintegration) of the PKK members would be put into action. Disarmament is a *sine qua non* for a successfully resolved conflict, which formed the third stage of peace. However, this could not be achieved due to the lack of consensus between the Turkish government and PKK. The first step of the agreement came into effect through Öcalan's Nevruz letter, which was read in Diyarbakır during the Nevruz celebrations and was a call for the PKK's withdrawal.[99] According to Baser and Özerdem, the Turkish government let Kurdish MPs read Öcalan's message, which broke a major taboo.[100] Öcalan stated:

> We are entering the new process in the Turkish Republic on the basis of free and equal constitutional citizenship as a democratic society with democratic identity in the peace and live fraternal. In this way, to get over the ninety years of the Republic's history which is full of conflicts, we are walking into the future with knitted real peace and universal democratic criteria.[101]

Murat Karayılan, one of the leading members of the PKK, respected Öcalan's call and announced that the PKK would withdraw all of its forces from Turkey as of May 8 as part of the peace agreement.[102] Nevertheless, the group halted withdrawal from Turkey in September 2013, this being announced by Cemil Bayık, one of the five founders and among the top leadership of the PKK.[103] So, why did one of the biggest steps of the peace process fail? From the government's perspective, the PKK should have completed withdrawal prior to political reforms.[104] Likewise, a senior officer of the KDGM said that the withdrawal was the first step in the negotiations.[105] It was reported that only 600 PKK members had left Turkey as of September 2013.[106] From the opposing perspective, Baluken asserts that even though the government had guaranteed to legislate the withdrawal process during the İmralı talks, it was not passed into law.[107] If 'clearing the way' had been legislated for, along with preventing the capture of PKK members during the withdrawal process, it is less likely that the PKK's withdrawal would have been interrupted.[108] The term 'clearing the way' was about freedom of thought, association, and media, to eliminate all barriers standing in the way of democratisation and to legislate regulations related to local administrations.[109] As the government did not bring it to the TBMM, the process suffered and an environment 'full of mistrust' emerged.[110] However, as Karayılan admitted, the PKK had problems with its members, as they did not obey the PKK's rules regarding the withdrawal.[111] Therefore, any type of transformation could not be achieved due to the lack of trust between the two sides. Although there was an agreement between them, sustainability of the process could not be maintained (unlike the Northern Irish peace process), as both the government and pro-Kurdish movement believed that the other side would not fulfil their promises. Uçum states that although the government instigated several regulations, the PKK was the spoiler of this initiative since it did not withdraw from Turkey, did not lay down its arms, and did not keep its promise of maintaining non-violent resolution attempts.[112] As Özhan also notes, the unsuccessful peace attempt was related to the PKK's reluctance to both withdraw from Turkey and to disarm.[113] Furthermore, both sides blamed each other for the order of their responsibilities, which also did not help the process. In this context, an independent third party could have been useful in mediating these talks by organising interpersonal and intergroup relations between them, to transform people's objections that were hindering the progress.[114] Nevertheless, this was impossible since both sides did not trust any mediators during official negotiations.

The last two-party initiative was the Dolmabahçe Declaration of 2015. It was the first and only official agreement declared in public between the Turkish government and HDP. During the Declaration, two papers were read by the two sides.[115] Öcalan's statement, which addressed the definition of national and local dimensions of a democratic solution, socio-economic dimensions, the relationship between state and society, and legal and democratic warranties of free citizenship, was accepted by the government.[116] After reading the Declaration on behalf of Öcalan and the HDP, Önder said 'we are closer than ever to achieving peace in Turkey'.[117] Nevertheless, the Declaration did not result in progress due to issues on implications, structure and content of the agreement.

Figen Yüksekdağ, former co-leader of the HDP, notes that the Dolmabahçe Declaration was a commitment between the Turkish government and the HDP, but the Turkish government did not implement its instructions.[118] The negotiations on the implementation of the Declaration should have been conducted by mixed commissions consisting of the Turkish government, state bureaucracy's central associations, and Kurdish party and non-Kurdish democratic society representatives.[119] Moreover, Hatem Ete, the chief advisor to the PM, claims that the Dolmabahçe Declaration was 'a premature declaration' which did not have a strong structure or background.[120] He also blamed the PKK:

> As long as the PKK dominates the south-east of Turkey, there was no point of declaring a statement. Therefore, it was an early and not very-well planned initiative. During that time, the PKK had not withdrawn from Turkey. Hence, there was no point in declaring a statement on this occasion. Therefore, the government did not apply this declaration. Furthermore, the government blamed the HDP for using this situation as a justification of defending armed struggle. However, even if the declaration was not applied, there is no excuse for using arms or killing people.[121]

As a result, although this track-one effort resulted in a declaration, this declaration could not contribute to the peace process, as its conditions were not applied. The reason for the lack of progress was the disagreement between the disputing parties. Çandar asserts that the Dolmabahçe Declaration failed due to the Turkish government's unwillingness to take responsibility for the Declaration.[122] After President Erdoğan's[123] speech his on disagreement with the Declaration, the Turkish government did not take the step forward, so it became void.[124] Therefore, it can be said that the government's reluctance to maintain the negotiations was one of the major reasons for the failure of this initiative.

The Declaration was also criticised in terms of the structure and content of the agreement, and this was another reason for its failure. For example, Kemal Burkay, honorary leader of the pro-Kurdish Rights and Freedoms Party (*Hak ve Özgürlükler Partisi*, henceforth Hak-Par) underlines that the ten articles of the Dolmabahçe Declaration were not related to Kurdish rights.[125] It included women's, environmental and ecological rights, but there was nothing related to Kurdish rights. Burkay also criticised the PKK for minimising its ultimate goal from establishing an independent Kurdish state to a democratic autonomy, which was called 'being from Turkey' (*Türkiyelilik*).[126] Similar to Burkay, Vahap Coşkun, a member of the WPC, argues that Öcalan's ten-point declaration could have been a party's election programme, which could have been applied in the long-term.[127] Nevertheless, it did not offer anything to the peace process. Therefore, it could not be accepted as a framework or roadmap for resolution because some recommendations of the Declaration did not address Kurdish questions. It is important not to equate both sides' announcements of their demands with the resolution of each problem in Turkey. A more concrete framework should have been determined.[128] Overall, the interview data revealed that the Declaration between the disputing sides did not result in a successful outcome due to the content and structure of the Declaration, and the reluctance of both parties to take any steps forward since the process was not moving in the direction they demanded. The outcome of this initiative reveals one of the critical issues in the negotiation stage, that if conflict pays, disputing parties are not willing to negotiate.[129] This problem was intense during the talks leading to the Declaration; there was a conflict of interest instead of a win-win approach.

Multilateral Efforts

There have been two major multilateral initiatives in Turkey's Kurdish peace process. While the Resolution Commission was the TBMM's initiative, the Oslo talks were carried out together with international mediators. The Resolution Commission of 2013 was the result of the pro-Kurdish BDP's insistence on formalising the process. As a result, a commission was founded to decide the future of the peace process and all constitutional parties were invited to join. Nevertheless, the CHP and MHP refused to attend the talks. This affected the official resolution efforts' inclusiveness since it prevented a greater majority of people being represented. This was attested to by Ete, who said that the TBMM would have made progress in a shorter time if the CHP and MHP had joined the peace efforts.[130] As a result, the Commission remained an AKP-BDP initiative, but it was supported by other political parties who were not in the parliament and by other peace institutions. An interview with a member of the Commission, İmran Demir, helps to understand the role of the Commission in the peace process. Demir stated that the Resolution Commission was important to legitimise the peace process, to transform the peace efforts from the unofficial to the political arena.[131] It was a facilitating event for the BDP because the party insisted on maintaining peace efforts in the TBMM rather than by the MIT or individual political actors. By insisting on taking the TBMM as the headquarters of the peace process, the BDP aimed to reach binding decisions for the Turkish government. Demir reveals the approach of the BDP during the meetings:

How are you going to make sure that the political authority will fulfil its promises? The only way to make them to fulfil their promises is to put them under an obligation. The only obligation at that point was to make it as public as possible and to make it as a process that belongs to the Parliament because the Parliament was the voice of the people. I think that was the major concern.[132]

During the negotiations, another deadlock occurred when the BDP insisted on all its claims being included in the report. According to Demir, they would then be able to use the argument that their demands were recognised by the government thanks to the published report.[133] However, the government refused this, as the demands were unacceptable to them. For example, one of the major demands of the BDP (later the HDP) was to stop establishing fortified gendarmerie stations (Turkish: *kalekol*) in Turkey's south-east, which was refused by the AKP government.[134] Yüksekdağ confirms Demir's statement by highlighting that if a problem is discussed in the TBMM, it becomes a national problem. Yüksekdağ states that the pro-Kurdish parties, therefore, insist on bringing issues to the agenda of the parliament and thus, they can be the public's problem instead of only the AKP or pro-Kurdish parties' concern.[135] Following these statements, this book argues that there were two dilemmas here: security and political implementations, and negotiating in private and public. Although the intention of both sides was to maintain negotiations, the lack of trust in each other resulted in the PKK's insistence on not giving up weapons, and the government's concerns about the security of the civilians and security personnel. The dilemma concerning negotiating in private or public centres on both the trust and gain issues, since the pro-Kurdish movement believed that they might achieve their otherwise unattainable demands in public. On the AKP government's side, the concern was the pro-Kurdish movement's demand to put pressure on the government that might affect the future of the conflict. It was clear that the different demands from both sides had resulted in the collapse of the peace process long before violence returned.[136] The Commission also had meetings with academics to learn their view on a peaceful resolution. For example, Alpaslan Özerdem's suggestion for a positive peace to strengthen peace negotiations with the grassroots initiatives through cooperation between the state, private sector and civil society, and Jenny Pearce's information on the peace process between the Colombian Government and the FARC, helped the Committee to draw up a road map for the parliament.[137]

In terms of the negotiation outcomes, the Commission brought more confusion than progress. Tan states that the Resolution Commission worked only as 'a distraction commission'. It did not recommend anything related to the future of the peace process. It only maintained the current situation, without presenting possible solutions.[138] However, the Commission's report produced some important points related to the peace process, including the new constitution, education in the mother tongue, strengthening local administrations and other political reforms related to amnesty, migration and counter-terrorism.[139] The report was not sufficient according to the BDP, so the party prepared an alternative report that contained their demands for the resolution of the conflict. In their report, they declared the PKK's campaign to be the last Kurdish rebellion, and a legitimate action to protect Kurdish people.[140] It was also admitted that it was a symbolic initiative as the peace process was led by the MIT not the TBMM. In sum, it was a great chance to transform the issues which were the major reasons behind the conflict. However, the identification of the different aspects of the conflict did not result in the transformation of these issues.

The other peace initiative was the Oslo talks, which were a milestone in the peace process. Since the talks were carried out secretly, the role of these talks in ending violence and reaching a political settlement were analysed in regard of secret negotiations. However, the Oslo talks are also crucial to assess in terms of their multilateral structure and mediation efforts. The latter are important to analyse in order to understand whether they changed the nature of the conflict or facilitated progress. The Oslo talks are examined under official initiatives, as these talks were mediated by an international and independent third party and led by the government and pro-Kurdish movement. As the outcome of these talks led to the conflict resolution process, it is one of the major aspects of the official negotiations.[141] As Bercovitch points out, a mediation initiative is also possible by bringing parties together, gaining trust and cooperation, and setting out the route of peace talks, which is a fundamental stage of a peace process.[142] The Oslo talks, together with the involvement of a third party, illustrate an important stage within the peace process.

The nature of the Oslo talks was different to previous peace efforts since the Turkish government and PKK were brought together by a third party in a place that was chosen by the British intelligence agency MI6. Therefore, the structure of these talks, the context of the discussions and role of the mediators in relation to the unsuccessful outcome need to be assessed. First of all, the talks were carried out between the head of the MIT, Emre Taner (later replaced by Hakan Fidan), and deputy head of the MIT, Afet Güneş, and the top leadership of the PKK: Sabri Ok, Mustafa Karasu, Adem Uzun and Zübeyir Aydar, plus some third parties.[143] In relation to third parties, while British intelligence was the mediator of the talks, the Norwegian and Swedish governments attended the talks as facilitators. Although Turkish officials did not declare the mediators' nationality, Karayılan admitted, during his interview with Avni Özgürel, a Turkish journalist, that the mediator of the talks was British intelligence.[144] Taner later accepted MI6's mediation during the Oslo talks.[145] In terms of the time frame of the talks, even though it was announced that they were maintained for two-and-a-half years (between 2009 and 2011), Mahçupyan states that the talks were carried out between 2006 and 2011 in different locations in Europe.[146] This reveals the fact that the talks were achieved during one of the most intense periods of conflict.[147] Considering both parties' will to maintain the peace negotiations when there was violence, it can be said that they contributed to the sustainability of the conflict resolution process.

Furthermore, in terms of the role of the mediators, British intelligence brought the conflicting sides together, which is the first step of a mediation attempt. As Koch identifies, a mediation initiative begins with a third party's intervention by inviting disputants to peace talks.[148] This can be achieved only by bringing these parties together and facilitating their negotiations, or by intervening in intractable aspects of a conflict with the aim to transform these aspects. The leaked meeting records reveal the mediator's effort to bring the two sides together. The mediator said:

> We made a suggestion to both sides; there might be some kind of mini package which was surrounded based on Nevruz. The idea of there being this might be a first step to establish the confidence in both sides. I wanted to emphasise that it was our idea. We were not asked by the Kurdish side to propose it and we were not asked by the Turkish side to propose it. So, it was an initiative which was taken on our responsibility, not on the responsibility of either side.[149]

The British mediator's statement demonstrated that the influence of the mediator as a social approach made it possible to internationalise the resolution of this conflict. Furthermore, the British mediators also helped to identify the problem and to compose requirements of negotiation. Nevertheless, the secrecy of the talks prevented the analysis of expectations and objectives of the mediators in more detail. The leaked meeting records demonstrate that it was British intelligence's intention to initiate a series of talks between the Turkish government and the PKK. Whilst the reason for British intelligence building this communication channel is not clear, due to insufficient primary sources, there are some important details in the secret negotiations that were revealed by a news agency. During the talks, the mediator states that the recommendations of Öcalan need to be considered when political reforms are being made in parliament.[150] Hence, the mediators facilitated reaching a solution that is acceptable to both sides, and so a win-win solution. However, this facilitating role did not move forward with regard to transforming the disputing parties' views by focusing on making decisions during the talks. Instead, in line with Bercovitch's assumption, the British mediators focused on a perspective with no force or arbitrative rules,[151] which restricted the benefit of the mediators.

Finally, it was clear that the talks were about gaining more of their demands and moving the outcome of these talks forward to political reforms. Due to the lack of trust between the government and PKK, the mediators were the integrative part of the peace process, but not the primary component. British intelligence helped overcome the concerns of trust and win-lose issues, which made it possible for the parties to sit at the negotiating table and discuss their major claims. As Babbitt and Hampson describe, it is important to overcome these concerns regarding relationship-based issues between warring sides.[152] It is also clear that if one of the conflicting parties is a sub-state armed group, it is always very difficult for a state to sit at the negotiating table with them. This difficulty was overcome thanks to the British mediation. However, as Coşkun underlines, this mediation was only about understanding what they expected from the negotiations.[153] The mediator did not play a role in offering suggestions, presenting different alternatives for a solution or intervening talks.[154] As a result, the mediation did not put pressure on the conflicting parties for a deadline or discussions of specific issues to overcome related problems.

The Kurdish conflict continued; the level of violence rapidly increased, particularly through the 'ditch incidents' of August 2015 when thousands of people lost their lives as a result. This was taken as a sign to return to traditional counter-terrorism measures. Although there have been several national and international calls for resuming the peace process and ending violence,[155] the violent conflict still endures and hope for peace in Turkey is diminishing.

A Road to Peace?

The Northern Irish and Turkey's Kurdish peace processes have been assessed through their different efforts with relation to bilateral and multilateral initiatives. These initiatives illustrate different incentives and barriers which affected the transformation of the underlying reasons for these conflicts (Table 6.3).

Both peace processes witnessed political changes to resolve issues in order to overcome the underlying reasons for these conflicts. While political reforms in the UK were applied together with the negotiations and agreements between the British and Irish governments in the 1980s and early 1990s, the reforms in Turkey were a result of negotiations between the Turkish government and pro-Kurdish movement. The key issues addressed in the AIA and DSD were the recognition of both identities, a bill of rights, intergovernmental cooperation, reform of the policing system and abandonment of violence in Northern Ireland.[156] The political reforms in Turkey addressed similar issues, such as a change in the policing law, bill of rights, and recognition of ethnic identities and their rights.[157] Both cases illustrate a transformation in the issues related to ethno-nationalist identities and recognition of their rights. Although these issue transformations were not sufficient for resolution, they were fundamental pieces of both peace processes. Nevertheless, both initiatives were faced with a reaction: from the unionist parties in Northern Ireland and from the nationalist party in Turkey (Table 6.3). However, the interruption of the peace processes was not because of the outcry, but due to the ongoing violence deployed by the IRA and PKK. In addition, the efforts in the UK also provided a long-term benefit. The benefit of the AIA in the long-term, in Thatcher's words, was that 'the international dimension [of Northern Ireland] became noticeably easier to deal with'.[158] In brief, both cases witnessed similar efforts and experiences, which helped maintain non-violent, political resolution efforts.

Table 6.3 Overview of the influence of official negotiations on Northern Ireland and Turkey.

Conflict	Northern Ireland			Turkey		
Transformers	Initiatives	Incentives	Drawbacks	Initiatives	Incentives	Drawbacks
Issue	*Reforms* Anglo-Irish efforts	Recognition of two traditions	Unionists' opposition Ongoing violence	*Reforms* Democratic opening	Recognition of ethnic difference	Nationalists' opposition Ongoing violence
Actor	Hume–Adams talks	Ripeness Hurting stalemate	–	Imrali talks	Reciprocal bargaining	Lack of trust
Structural	*Change in the nature* Adams's visa	US administration	British government	*Change in the nature* Dolmabahce Declaration	Legitimacy	Timing Spoilers
	Third party intervention All-party talks	Strong mediation	Spoilers	*Third party intervention* Oslo talks	Weak mediation	Spoilers
Personal and Group	*Changes in Adams's perception*	Drop precondition of disarming	–	*Changes in Ocalan's perception*	From partition to integration	The PKK

The two-party talks in Turkey were conducted between the same parties, and resulted in the transformation of the actors over time. The İmralı talks between the Turkish government and pro-Kurdish HDP caused a split within the pro-Kurdish side. While all pro-Kurdish actors appeared to be on the same side at the beginning of the talks, a difference of opinion emerged in the negotiations which created more veto players. The difference was particularly evident between the HDP and PKK. As Cunningham states, more veto players involved in a process makes conflicts more difficult to solve through negotiation.[159] The split within the pro-Kurdish side resulted in the emergence of three veto players: the HDP, Öcalan and the PKK. The different demands of these actors were revealed through the Minister of Interior, Beşir Atalay's statement during the negotiations: 'They [the PKK and Öcalan] are more moderate and consistent than the HDP.'[160] In other words, when the HDP made a statement, the PKK warned them to change their statement, which caused an inconsistency in the negotiation process.[161] This also created a lack of trust between conflicting parties during reciprocal bargaining on whether the withdrawal or political reforms would come first. Hence, it became more difficult to solve the Kurdish problem due to more veto players. In contrast to Turkey's Kurdish question, the Northern Irish peace process was not only conducted by the main armed protagonists but also through other bilateral talks. For example, the Hume–Adams talks allowed SF to join peace negotiations. As described earlier, it facilitated the end of the republican strategy of ballot in one hand and bullet in the other. Together with the great effort made by Hume, both the British government and IRA began to think that they could not destroy each other.[162] It was a ripe moment for joining peace negotiations and resulted in the transformation of the goals of the republicans.

The US administration's visa to Gerry Adams was imperative in the Northern Ireland peace process, which resulted in the US's participation in official negotiations. As Lynch argues, 'the Northern Ireland conflict could more accurately be called a peace process when Clinton became involved'.[163] Similarly, the Dolmabahçe Declaration changed the nature of the Turkish peace process. The Turkish government and HDP presented a political framework for peace, which was the first official declaration made between them. The timing of the initiative was demonstrated as being the reason for its failure.

Ete terms the Declaration 'a premature declaration',[164] emphasising that it was brought in earlier than it should have been. Further, President Erdoğan denounced the Declaration by stating: 'I, by no means, accept the expression of Dolmabahçe Agreement', which thus caused the AKP to renounce the Declaration.[165] This situation created two drawbacks in the peace process: the first one was the reluctance of the government to maintain the process, which affected the sustainability of resolution efforts. The other drawback was the trust issue, which re-emerged during the İmralı talks. Coşkun describes the consequence of the initiative as having 'disappointed Kurds for whom the peace process means a lot'.[166]

Looking at the third-party intervention, whilst George Mitchell's mediation included all conflicting parties in the negotiations, the British mediation did not bring all parties together, since the negotiations were conducted secretly. During the negotiations in Northern Ireland, even though the DUP and UKUP walked out, it did not interrupt the process or affect the inclusiveness, as the unionist community was still represented by the UUP. In contrast, negotiations and mediations did not include the opponent parties in the Kurdish peace process. This was not because of the government's attitude, but mostly due to the opposition and an outraged reaction in the CHP and MHP. This was attested to by the British mediators during the Oslo talks: 'If the CHP and MHP learn these negotiations, how do they react? If they knew about these negotiations, it would have been a great difficulty to maintain these talks.'[167] Furthermore, the role of the mediators was crucial in both peace processes. Echoing Touval and Zartman,[168] and Fisher and Keashly,[169] mediators 'with muscle' are more likely to make a contribution towards ending a conflict by offering deadlines, penalties, focusing on a mutual agreement and leading negotiations than mediators 'with less muscle' as they are unable to control the process or offer deadlines. On the one hand, Mitchell did not concentrate on creating a coalition to establish credibility to push for a deadline.[170] Instead, he focused on incorporating all major parties into the negotiations, which represented the majority in the Northern Irish conflict. During the negotiations for the GFA, he stuck with these principles and this focus resulted in a successful agreement.[171] On the other hand, the British mediators in the Oslo talks did not offer a framework or define the structure of the route of the negotiations, which was, as Mithat Sancar, a deputy of the HDP, argues, 'the major reason for the unsuccessful outcome'.[172] Hence, it can be said that while Mitchell's mediation was about structural prevention consisting of creating organisations and institutionalised rule of law to accommodate conflicting interests and to transform conflicts, British mediation was about facilitating meetings to enable conflicting parties to understand each other's positions and to create an environment for a peaceful resolution.[173] Overall, the structural transformation in the Northern Irish conflict was achieved by bringing SF into the process and through the direct involvement of the Clinton administration, which faciliated reaching the GFA. In contrast, the transformation of the relationship between the Turkish government and HDP was not very strong, and this relationship did not provide an ongoing, sustainable peace process in Turkey.

Personal and group transformation is at the heart of a successful conflict resolution process. The two peace processes contained the same route from armed to political struggle through Adams and Öcalan's position changes. While the change in SF's perception contributed to peacemaking in the short-term, Öcalan's perception did not provide any help. Undoubtedly, the outcomes of their intentions were affected by other actors and issues. For example, the change in SF's perception was gradual through the Hume–Adams talks, the DSD and the Clinton administration's involvement. All these aspects persuaded SF to apply political resolution efforts. In contrast, the leader of the PKK's intention to end the war did not help to make a peace agreement due to the transformation of the actors on the pro-Kurdish side from Öcalan as the only decision maker to a trilateral structure consisting of the HDP, Öcalan and the PKK. This transformation was a result of the competition within the Kurdish movement.

Finally, this chapter has found that the concerns related to trust and gain issues between the Turkish government and pro-Kurdish side did not help towards a successful result. It also appeared that the major concern of the two sides differed during the peace process: while the Turkish government re-determined its ultimate aim to disarm the PKK, the pro-Kurdish side described different goals ranging from federation, to integration with Turkey and democratic rights. Also, both sides blamed each other for the failure of the peace process. One criticism was that the peace process was used by the main protagonists as an opportunity to achieve their differing aims. According to this criticism, Erdoğan's peace aspiration was related to gaining the support of the Kurds for changing the political system to a presidential system; Öcalan's goal was to get a deal that would guarantee his release from prison.[174] Another critic suggested that the Syrian civil war and the hopes of the PYD/YPG to establish a Kurdish state in Northern Syria inspired the PKK to think that they could gain autonomy for Turkish Kurds through armed violence.[175] It is also argued that the possibility of a Kurdish state in the Middle East brought the peace process to an end.[176] However, these criticisms remain just accusations of the main protagonists of the conflict. In the end, this chapter has stated that more veto players made the problem more complicated to resolve and thus caused the unsuccessful outcome in the Turkish case.

Notes

1. Powell, 'How to Talk to Terrorists'.
2. TNA-PREM/19/509, *Anglo-Irish Summit: Draft Communique*.
3. Ibid.
4. TNA-PREM/19/509, *Anglo-Irish Summit: Steering Brief by Foreign and Commonwealth Office*.
5. TNA-PREM/19/814, *Note of a Meeting Held in the Northern Ireland Office*; TNA-PREM/19/1068, *Irish General Election*; TNA-CAB/128/71/17, *Conclusions of a Meeting of the Cabinet*.
6. Vayrynen, 'To Settle or to Transform?'
7. Emphasis added. Thatcher, 'Speech at Stormont Castle Lunch'.
8. Moore, 'Paramilitary Prisoners', p. 87.
9. Morrison, 'By Ballot and Bullet'.
10. Anglo-Irish Agreement.
11. Thatcher, *The Downing Street Years*.
12. Connolly and Loughlin, 'Reflections on the Anglo-Irish Agreement'.
13. Thatcher, *The Downing Street Years*.
14. TNA-CAB/128/83/36, *Conclusions of Meeting of the Cabinet*.
15. TNA-CAB/128/81/34, *Cabinet Conclusion*; TNA-CAB/128/81/37, *Conclusions of a Meeting of the Cabinet*.
16. Stedman, 'Spoiler Problems in the Peace Process'.
17. Interview with Gibney, member of the Executive Committee of SF, 20 January 2015.
18. Interview with Haughey, founder member of the Social Democratic and Labour Party, 19 January 2015.

19. British and Irish Governments, 'Joint Declaration on Peace'.
20. Vayrynen, 'To Settle or to Transform?'
21. Brooke, 'Peter Brooke's "No Selfish Strategic Interest" Speech'.
22. British and Irish Governments, 'Joint Declaration on Peace'.
23. O'Kane, 'Anglo-Irish Relations'.
24. Interview with Mason, Reverend, Methodist Minister of Belfast Mission, 20 January 2015.
25. Interview with Gibney, 20 January 2015.
26. Interview with Mason, 20 January 2015.
27. Interview with Gibney, 20 January 2015; interview with Walsh, 19 January 2015.
28. Adams, quoted in Rowan, *Behind the Lines*, p. 91.
29. Stedman, *Peacemaking in Civil War*.
30. Zartman, 'Ripeness'.
31. Interview with Mason, 20 January 2015.
32. British and Irish Governments, 'Joint Declaration on Peace'.
33. Interview with Mason, 20 January 2015.
34. Interview with Gibney, 20 January 2015.
35. Interview with Empey, Lord, former leader of the UUP and member of the House of Lords, 27 January 2015.
36. Vayrynen, 'To Settle or to Transform?', pp. 3–4.
37. Emphasis added. Major, *John Major: The Autobiography*, p. 456.
38. Ibid. p. 456.
39. Interview with Walsh, 19 January 2015.
40. Interview with Empey, 27 January 2015.
41. Fisher, *The Social Psychology of Intergroup*.
42. Ibid.
43. British and Irish Governments, 'Joint Declaration on Peace'.
44. Mitchell *et al.*, *Report of the International Body on Arms Decommissioning*.
45. Bew and Gillespie, *The Northern Ireland Peace Process*, p. 162.
46. Ibid. p. 154.
47. IRA, 'Statement Ending the Ceasefire'.
48. Zartman, 'Ripe for Resolution'.
49. The Northern Ireland Forum (formally called the Northern Ireland Forum for Political Dialogue) was a body founded in 1996 as part of a process of negotiations that eventually led to the GFA (MacGinty, 'Biting the Bullet', p. 240).
50. British Government, 'Ground Rules for Substantive All-Party Government'.
51. The ten parties who attended the talks were the most successful ten parties in the Forum election: the UUP won thirty seats (24.2%), the DUP won twenty-four seats (18.8%), the SDLP won twenty-one seats (21.4%), SF had its best

ever showing and won seventeen seats (15.5%), the Alliance Party of Northern Ireland (APNI) won seven seats (6.5%), the United Kingdom Unionist Party (UKUP) won three seats (3.7%), the Progressive Unionist Party (PUP) (3.5%), the Ulster Democratic Party (UDP) (2.2%), the Northern Ireland Women's Coalition (NIWC) (1.0%), and a Labour coalition (0.9%) (Bew and Gillespie, *The Northern Ireland Peace Process*, p. 177).
52. Northern Ireland Office, *Statement by the Independent Chairmen of the Northern Ireland Talks*.
53. Blair, *A Journey*, p. 163.
54. The IICD consisted of General John de Chastelain, Brigadier Tauno Nieminen from Finland and Ambassador Donald Johnson from the US, as of 1997.
55. Darby, *Northern Ireland*.
56. Touval and Zartman, *International Mediation*,
57. Hume and Adams, 'Joint statement issued by Sinn Féin President Mr Gerry Adams MP and the SDLP Leader Mr John Hume MP'.
58. IRA, 'Irish Republican Army (IRA) Ceasefire Statement'.
59. Mitchell, *Making Peace*, p. 108.
60. Ibid. p. 109.
61. Curran *et al.*, 'Two Paths to Peace'.
62. Interview with Empey, 27 January 2015.
63. Jeong, *Peace and Conflict Studies*.
64. Interview with Gibney, 20 January 2015.
65. Ibid.
66. Interview with Mallon, Democratic Unionist Party Councillor for Lisburn and Castlereagh, 19 January 2015.
67. Interview with Empey, 27 January 2015.
68. Interview with Gibney, 20 January 2015.
69. Interview with Empey, 27 January 2015.
70. Wall, 'Mediation: An Analysis'; Wall *et al.*, 'Mediation: A Current Review', p. 104.
71. Interview with Empey, 27 January 2015.
72. Interview with Gibney, 20 January 2015.
73. Interview with Hatemi, Vice Chairperson of the WPC's Southeastern Anatolia Region, 7 September 2015.
74. Ibid. Turkey's Kurdish conflict is witness to many issues related to rhetoric. When the peace process is conducted, the term 'the PKK's headquarters' is replaced with 'Qandil' (where their camps are located) and 'Öcalan' (the leader of the PKK) is

replaced with 'İmralı' (where Öcalan is imprisoned). The analysis of these metaphors is not the topic of this research. Having said that, it is crucial to consider that the use of Qandil and İmralı by political actors is a sign of creating space for non-violent resolution efforts.
75. As discussed in Chapter 3, three pro-Kurdish political parties witnessed political resolution efforts. The Constitutional Court closed the DTP in December 2009. The BDP was the successor of the DTP which was dissolved to join the HDP on 22 April 2014. The latest and current pro-Kurdish party is the HDP (Celep, 'Can the Kurdish Left Contribute to Turkey's Democratization?').
76. NTV, 'İşte Demokratikleşme Paketi'.
77. TBMM, *Temel Hak ve Hürriyetlerin Geliştirilmesi Amacıyla Çeşitli Kanunlarda Değişiklik Yapılmasına Dair Kanun.*
78. Interview with Can, 25 June 2015.
79. Interview with Uçum, 2 July 2015.
80. Interview with Arıboğan, 8 September 2015.
81. Ramsbotham *et al.*, *Contemporary Conflict Resolution.*
82. Starkey *et al.*, *Negotiating a Complex World.*
83. Aydınlı and Özcan, 'The Conflict Resolution and Counterterrorism Dilemma'.
84. TBMM, *Terörün Sona Erdirilmesi ve Toplumsal Bütünleşmenin Güçlendirilmesine Dair Kanun.*
85. The interviewee did not want the researcher to use his name: (Name withheld), interview with a Senior Officer of the KDGM, 1 July 2015.
86. Babbitt and Hampson, 'Conflict Resolution as a Field of Inquiry'.
87. Interview with Çandar, 29–30 June 2015.
88. The İmralı Committee was a group within the pro-Kurdish BDP (later on the HDP) who met with Öcalan in the İmralı prison and which comprised three BDP deputies: Sırrı Süreyya Önder, Pervin Buldan and Altan Tan. In 2014, Tan was replaced by İdris Baluken.
89. Öcalan, *Demokratik Kurtuluş ve Özgür Yaşamı İnşa*, p. 26.
90. Interview with Baluken, Deputy and Parliamentary Group leader of the HDP, member of the İmralı Committee, 1 September 2015.
91. Ibid.
92. Interview with Ensaroğlu, 2 July 2015.
93. Interview with Baluken, 1 September 2015.
94. T24, 'Beşir Atalay'dan Öcalan'a Övgü'.
95. Interview with Baluken, 1 September 2015.
96. Interview with Tan, 24 June 2015.

97. Ramsbotham *et al.*, *Contemporary Conflict Resolution*.
98. Interview with Baluken, 1 September 2015.
99. Hürriyet, '"Akil" Rapor Tamam'; Yeğen, 'The Kurdish Peace Process in Turkey'.
100. Baser and Özerdem, 'Conflict Transformation and Asymmetric Conflict', p. 9.
101. Öcalan, 'Öcalan's Newroz Message'.
102. NYT, 'Kurdish Rebel Group to Withdraw from Turkey'.
103. BBC, 'PKK'dan Açıklama'.
104. Interview with Ete, 3 July 2015.
105. Interview with [Name withheld], a Senior Officer of the KDGM, 1 July 2015.
106. Radikal, '"Kürt Meselesine İslami Çözüm" Çalıştayı'.
107. Interview with Baluken, 1 September 2015.
108. Ibid.
109. Ibid.
110. Interview with Tan, 24 June 2015.
111. Karayılan, *Bir Savaşın Anatomisi*, p. 402.
112. Interview with Uçum, 2 July 2015.
113. Özhan, *Normalleşme Sancısı*.
114. Wall, 'Mediation: An Analysis'.
115. Al Jazeera, 'Ortak Açıklamanın Tam Metni'.
116. HDN, 'Kurdish Peace Call'; Daily Sabah, 'Erdoğan Renounces Dolmabahçe Declaration'.
117. Financial Times, 'Turkish Government and Kurds in Bid to Revitalise Peace Talks'.
118. Interview with Yüksekdağ, 13 July 2015.
119. Ibid.
120. Interview with Ete, 3 July 2015.
121. Ibid.
122. Interview with Çandar, 29–30 June 2015.
123. Tayyip Erdoğan was prime minister between 2003 and 2014. He became president on 28 August 2014.
124. Interview with Çandar, 29–30 June 2015.
125. Interview with Burkay, 2 July 2015.
126. Ibid.
127. Interview with Coşkun, 4 September 2015.
128. Ibid.
129. Zartman, *Ripe for Resolution*.
130. Interview with Ete, 3 July 2015.

131. Interview with Demir, 15 September 2015.
132. Ibid.
133. Ibid.
134. Ibid.
135. Interview with Yüksekdağ, 13 July 2015.
136. Kadıoğlu, 'The End of Turkey's Kurdish "Peace Process"?'
137. TBMM, *Toplumsal Barış Yollarının Araştırılması ve Çözüm Sürecinin Değerlendirilmesi Komisyonu Görüşme Tutanakları*.
138. Interview with Tan, 24 June 2015.
139. TBMM, *Toplumsal Barış Yollarının Araştırılması ve Çözüm Sürecinin Değerlendirilmesi Amacıyla Kurulan Meclis Araştırma Komisyonu Raporu*.
140. BDP, *Toplumsal Barış Yollarının Araştırılması ve Çözüm Sürecinin Değerlendirilmesi Komisyonu Raporu*. Although the BDP's report was also presented at the Commission, it was not an official report and was prepared by the BDP only. The report was not published and so was provided by the General Secretary of the BDP.
141. Ural, *Bir Emniyet Müdürünün Kaleminden Oslo Görüşmeleri*.
142. Bercovitch *et al.*, 'International Mediation', pp. 9–10.
143. Başaran, 'Oslo, Çözüm Süreci ve Hepimizin Bilmesi Gerekenler'.
144. Karayılan, cited in Özgürel, 'İşte Avni Özgürel'in Karayılan Röportajı'.
145. Taner, cited in DHA, 'Eski MİT Müsteşarı Emre Taner: Yapamadık, Alamadık'.
146. Interview with Mahçupyan, 22 June 2015.
147. People who lost their lives due to the Kurdish conflict amounted to 1,054 between 2006 and 2011 (TBMM, *Terör ve Şiddet Olayları*). This number includes security force members and civilians, but does not include members of the PKK.
148. Koch, *War and Peace in Jalemo*, p. 28.
149. Özgür Haber, 'İşte AKP ve PKK Arasındaki Yapılan Anlaşmaların Ses Kayıtları'.
150. Taraf, 'PKK-MİT Görüşmeleri Tam Metin'.
151. Bercovitch, 'International Mediation' (1991).
152. Babbitt and Hampson, 'Conflict Resolution as a Field of Inquiry', p. 52.
153. Interview with Coşkun, 4 September 2015.
154. Ibid.
155. After the collapse of the peace process in 2015, many national and international figures called for bringing violence to an end and returning to the Kurdish peace process urgently. For example, the EU Commissioner for Neighbourhood Policy and Enlargement Negotiations, Hahn, called for an immediate ceasefire and resumption of peace efforts claiming 'the peace process remains

the best opportunity in a generation to solve a conflict that has claimed far too many lives' (Hahn, *Situation in the South East of Turkey*). In addition, 1,128 academics signed a peace petition demanding the Turkish state 'abandon its deliberate massacre and deportation of Kurdish and other peoples in the region', who were accused of treason and the propaganda of PKK terrorism (Baser *et al.*, '"Academics for Peace" in Turkey').

156. Wolff, 'Conflict Management in Northern Ireland'.
157. Ensaroğlu, 'Turkey's Kurdish Question'.
158. Thatcher, *The Downing Street Years*, pp. 406–7.
159. Cunningham, 'Veto Players and Civil War Duration'.
160. Atalay, cited in T24, 'Beşir Atalay'dan Öcalan'a Övgü'.
161. Interview with Oğur, 25 June 2015.
162. Interview with Gibney, 20 January 2015.
163. Lynch, 'The Gerry Adams Visa', p. 43.
164. Interview with Ete, 3 July 2015.
165. Erdoğan, quoted in Daily Sabah, 'Erdoğan Renounces Dolmabahçe Declaration'.
166. Coşkun, 'HDP Torn Between Violence and Politics', p. 49.
167. Taraf, 'PKK-MİT Görüşmeleri Tam Metin'.
168. Touval and Zartman, *International Mediation*.
169. Fisher and Keashly, 'The Potential Complementarity of Mediation'.
170. Mitchell, *Making Peace*; Powell, 'Great Hatred, Little Room'.
171. Mitchell, *Making Peace*.
172. Interview with Sancar, 8 July 2015.
173. Beriker, *Çatışmadan Uzlaşmaya*; Stern and Druckman, *International Conflict Resolution*.
174. Hakyemez, 'Turkey's Failed Peace Process with the Kurds', p. 2.
175. Ibid. p. 3.
176. Ozkahraman, 'Failure of Peace Talks between Turkey and the PKK', p. 13.

7

CONCLUSION

> Terrorism cannot be overcome by the use of force because it does not address the complex underlying problems. In fact, the use of force may not only fail to solve the problems, it may exacerbate them and frequently leaves destruction and suffering in its wake.[1]

This book has analysed the influence of conflict resolution processes by focusing on non-violent, political peace efforts to bring the Northern Irish and Turkey's Kurdish conflicts to an end. Even though both ethno-nationalist conflicts have similar characteristics, the Northern Irish conflict was brought to an end, but Turkey's Kurdish conflict is still ongoing. It has been argued that peacemaking efforts in Northern Ireland and Turkey have a broader scope than official negotiations. The conflict resolution processes in these two cases encouraged the conflicting sides to consider talks and to enter into a negotiation process at the pre-negotiation stage. The processes then intended to reach a peace agreement during the negotiation stage. This book has suggested that a peace agreement requires mediation by an independent third party: between the British government and their adversaries, the IRA and their political wings, in one case, and the Turkish government and their adversaries, the PKK, in the other.

To explore the impact of political resolution efforts towards ending ethno-nationalist conflicts, this book has argued that it is crucial to examine three major aspects of conflict resolution processes: backchannel communications, as the unofficial aspect; peace organisations, as the informal and semi-official aspect; and official negotiations, as the official aspect (Table 2.2). There is a complementarity between the unofficial (track 1.5), informal (track-two) and official (track-one) aspects that together constitute a conflict resolution process. Both of the studied peace processes began through backchannels rather than official negotiations. Therefore, this book has demonstrated that it is crucial to engage in pre-negotiation efforts as a component of a peace process. Furthermore, P/CROs that have a direct link with the initiatives of political parties and actors have played a role in the peacemaking efforts. Lastly, negotiations should be considered as an ongoing process instead of single disputes. In this concluding chapter, I first outline the outcomes of the two peace processes. Then, I assess the contribution of this research and implications for theory and policy. Finally, suggestions for future research are discussed.

This book has revealed that peace efforts towards ending ethno-nationalist conflicts require a more comprehensive analysis beyond official negotiations. A tripartite analysis has therefore been constructed here (backchannels, P/CROs and negotiations), within the wider theoretical framework on peacemaking, and there has been a focus on an under-explored dynamic of peacemaking by investigating these three approaches as indispensable components of a conflict resolution process during the pre-negotiation and negotiation stages. These approaches have been led by representatives of the British and Turkish governments and leading members of the republican and pro-Kurdish movements respectively, assisted by national and international third parties. A recommendation is that peace efforts should be analysed from before official negotiations as the process begins at the pre-negotiation stage through backchannels and P/CROs. This can provide a better understanding of the influence of non-violent, political resolution attempts. Here, it has resulted in an analytical framework that can be applied to other similar ethno-nationalist conflicts.

By comparing a successful and an unsuccessful case, this book has embodied a more comprehensive approach than a single case analysis. Comparative analysis provides a better understanding of conflict resolution processes through a comparison of the transformation of issues responsible for the cause of conflicts. Significantly, Chapter 6 has demonstrated that it is crucial to transform the root causes of these conflicts, including personal/group relations, actors and issues related to the restrictions of the British and Turkish governments respectively. It has also illustrated that P/CROs, and national and international third parties, act as catalysts during the conflict resolution processes by bringing disputing parties together to discuss their demands, encouraging them to adopt a non-violent resolution to close the gaps between them. Chapters 4 and 6 have indicated that personal and collective efforts for ending violence or de-escalating conflict and the intervention of international mediators helped to bring about positive outcomes. Although Turkey's Kurdish peace process has not reached an agreement, third parties have contributed to the de-escalation of the conflict.

The results from archival research material, semi-structured interviews, memoirs of major actors, government documents, newspaper articles and reports provided five main findings. The first is that indirect communications through intermediaries played an important role in de-escalating the violent conflicts in Northern Ireland and Turkey. This significant finding relates to the establishment of communication channels, whether they were built by the personal initiatives of intermediaries or by the consent of the principal armed protagonists. On the one hand, this research found that indirect communications in both conflicts between the main armed protagonists were successful when the intermediaries were appointed by one of the conflicting parties. For example, Talabani successfully established dialogue between the Turkish government and PKK via the consent of President Özal and the PKK's leader Öcalan.[2] On the other hand, this book revealed that intermediaries were unsuccessful in building a communication chain and passing on messages when initiating the chain was their personal idea or when their mediation was rejected by one of the parties. Therefore, personal attempts were less successful than the collective efforts of representatives of the conflicting parties. Indeed, Hackett's efforts were unsuccessful as his intermediary role was rejected by Whitelaw because he thought that Hackett's contact was seen as dangerous and damaging.[3] Similarly, Haşimi's intermediary role was denied by PM Erbakan, despite his direct contact with the PKK leadership. This was due to Erbakan's earlier initiative through another intermediary, İsmail Nacar, and the Turkish government's lack of trust in Haşimi, as we saw in Chapter 4. Therefore, this book has revealed that intermediaries whose mediation was accepted by both disputing parties played a role in bringing conflicting parties together, defining the agenda for discussions and establishing a ceasefire.

The analysis of the third parties in covert negotiations also revealed that the communication channels between warring parties remained in place longer if the intermediaries had personal contact with political elites and the opposition leadership. Both Duddy and Işık played a more extensive role than the mere exchange of messages as they helped reduce violence and declare the respective ceasefires.[4] While Duddy contacted SF leader O'Bradaigh, Işık's personal contact with both the PKK's leader Öcalan and the Turkish government enabled him to easily overcome the trust issues, allowing the longest PKK ceasefire in six years. Chapter 4 found that both intermediaries encouraged conflicting parties to carry out face-to-face negotiations. This was achieved several times during violent conflict due to the strength of the communication channels. This book also demonstrated that it was not always possible to maintain open communication channels, since opposing parties were not always in favour of political resolution. It provided evidence of this situation through the declassified secret Cabinet papers showing that indirect dialogue in the mid-1970s was used as an opportunity to weaken the IRA's armed campaign by the British government.

The second main finding of this research is that the initial secret efforts had a similar influence on the two peace processes. However, the secret talks in Turkey were more successful in moving towards peace than in Northern Ireland. There was a negative correlation between the success of secret talks and the outcome of peace efforts. Key direct talks during the first ten years of both conflicts demonstrated that the declaration of a ceasefire by both the IRA and PKK was respected by political elites, as discussed in Chapter 4. This produced a two-way opportunity: while political elites used the advantage of broadening the scope of discussions during the ceasefire terms, the sub-state armed groups achieved their aim of being recognised implicitly by both the British and Turkish governments as they were involved in face-to-face discussions. Since backchannels are pre-negotiation efforts, their success was evaluated through their outcomes. Even though both the IRA and PKK's ultimate aims to secure a binding agreement were unsuccessful, the secret discussions of political actors with the PKK aided the release of captured Turkish soldiers. Yet, the ceasefire in Northern Ireland only lasted two days after the 1972

Whitelaw talks.[5] As backchannels are part of an ongoing peace process, the lack of immediate success in moving towards official negotiations did not break the communication channels in either case.

The differing outcomes of secret initiatives are critical to assess: the Northern Irish conflict was brought to an end, but the Turkish conflict continues. Chapter 4 highlighted that the mediation of third parties resulted in different outcomes in direct talks. It demonstrated that similar peace efforts provided political elites and the leaderships of the sub-state armed groups the opportunity to discuss their major objectives. However, the lack of a concrete outcome to the Feakle talks (other than a temporary ceasefire) and a clear result from the Oslo talks in Turkey (a general agreement on the future of the conflict) meant the two processes diverged as a direct result of secret initiatives. As argued in Chapter 4, the position of the deputy head of MIT as the authority for making political decisions was the primary reason for the success of the Oslo talks. The analysis of the interview data and secret talks that were leaked to the media suggests that the authority of political elites to make agreements in secret talks provided concrete outcomes such as the Habur event and a deal on the commissions established by the Turkish parliament. However, these outcomes did not lead to a successful conflict resolution process in Turkey because of the limited contribution of national and international third parties, and the failure of the negotiation stage.

This book suggests that the strength of parties other than the main armed protagonists to maintain or preclude the peace processes is a significant aspect in determining the route of backchannels. When spoilers are dominant in a violent conflict, the strength of the communication chain might not necessarily facilitate a positive outcome. Besides, the existing literature argues that there are no costs of entry into secret talks.[6] Related to this, indirect dialogues through intermediaries were hard to uncover due to the indirect nature of the communication chain in both conflicts. However, Chapter 4 demonstrated that spoilers affected peacemaking events negatively as regards the recognition of opponents as representatives of the Kurdish community in Turkey and of the Catholic community in Northern Ireland. For example, although covert negotiations were kept secret for a long time, they failed when spoilers (namely the opponent parties and TSK) discovered the secret talks between the Erbakan administration and the PKK.[7] The analysis of the backchannel initiatives also revealed that the secrecy of these talks created mistrust in two ways: on the one hand, between disputing parties when it was used to gain time to destroy adversaries; on the other hand, in the wider social context of a backlash towards a perception of 'talking to terrorists'. For example, Duddy's secret papers demonstrated that the revelations of secret talks between the political elites and the republican movement undermined the credibility of the British government.[8] A similar reaction emerged when the Oslo talks were leaked to the press. Furthermore, the secrecy of these discussions created mistrust especially for the sub-state armed groups and their political wings due to the credibility of these talks. Credibility was under question as it was not possible to implement topics discussed in backchannels. Fortunately, none of these situations prevented the secret talks from continuing.

Overall, indirect communications were used as an initial dialogue step, eventually resulting in face-to-face meetings and bargaining over the demands of the conflicting parties. For example, Caldwell's initial contact with both sides resulted in direct communications, firstly between Wilson and the republicans, and then Whitelaw and the leading members of the republican movement.[9] These conflict resolution attempts evolved into official negotiation processes in both conflicts. The context of the discussions and their outcomes affected the role of backchannels over the formal negotiations. However, there was no correlation between the success of backchannels and the end of violence, since conflict resolution as an ongoing process must be supported by other actors and initiatives, such as those of peace groups.

The third main finding is that while the peace groups in Northern Ireland made a wider contribution, the influence of Turkish peace groups was limited in bringing the violence to an end and establishing political settlement. This book revealed that the peace groups in both conflicts had a role in the conflict resolution processes, but their influence was different. Chapter 5 argued that in both cases peace groups contributed to the peace processes through top-down and bottom-up initiatives. Regarding the bottom-up initiatives, the peace groups acted as a bridge between society and political elites by encouraging the latter to adopt society's demands for a resolution. Support at the societal level had different implications in each conflict. As highlighted in Chapter 3, Northern Ireland is a deeply divided society, which made it problematic in bringing the Catholic and Protestant communities together; many believed that the IRA was defending their rights and legitimacy, while others relied on British security forces for the same reasons. In contrast, there is no sharp division between the Kurdish and Turkish communities in Turkey. The interview data illustrated that despite the high-intensity violence, the support of the Kurdish community for the PKK's armed campaign was limited, as we saw in the section on P/CROs in Turkey. Therefore, to create mutual understanding between the disputing communities was easier for the peace groups in Turkey than the Northern Irish groups. In addition, the analysis of the support for these groups within society illustrated that when public support for the peace groups is high, these groups deliver social demands to political elites more quickly. The comparison of cases has provided the evidence for this: while the PP's events in Northern Ireland hosted several thousands of people from both sides of the conflict, the LPP's panels and other activities in Turkey witnessed less support and could not gain the support of all disputing communities.

The peace groups in Northern Ireland and Turkey helped de-escalate the conflicts. As Cowling's letter to Mr Wilson (NIO Minister) revealed, the PP was influential in reducing the intensity of armed campaigns of the republicans, loyalists and British government through its well-supported marches.[10] The BIA and WPC had relatively weaker influence at the societal level as their major focus was not to unify society. The analysis revealed that the closer the peace organisations were to communities in conflict, the more they were successful in facilitating the de-escalation of the conflicts in both Northern Ireland and Turkey. In addition, existing violence resulted in a reluctance of warring parties to discuss a political settlement. Table 5.2 demonstrated that the P/CROs' protest campaigns, conferences and public talks, which criticised the armed campaign of both sides, made a clear contribution to making peace. The key point of bottom-up initiatives of the peace groups was to defend community rights, which resulted in the British and Turkish governments' support for these groups either publicly or implicitly at the elite level of conflict resolution. However, this support had limited effect in garnering public support for a political settlement in Turkey.

Considering top-down initiatives, the peace groups that had direct contact with political elites and had support in public from the British and Turkish governments contributed to political decisions and reforms more than those peace groups that were only supported implicitly. For example, the analysis of the declassified archival material revealed that the BIA's semi-official structure played a role in re-establishing the Northern Irish government through local elections and a locally elected Assembly in the 1980s.[11] The archival material suggested that the BIA's efforts focused on transforming the anti-political reform views of political elites. Thus, it lobbied for peace during the conferences that hosted nationalist and unionist politicians. As discussed in Chapters 2 and 5, the influence of P/CROs in establishing peace has been mostly overlooked in the existing literature. This book highlighted that the P/CROs made these changes possible by bringing political elites together in an 'unofficial' environment. The lack of political pressure facilitated a discussion of both sides' claims in a peaceful environment in Northern Ireland. Similarly, the WPC's events and relationship with the Turkish government facilitated their initiatives to change regulations related to ethnic discrimination between Turkish and Kurdish identities in the constitution. However, this influence was limited as the WPC was initiated by the Turkish government and so was restricted to peacemaking contributions. The analysis of relationships between peace groups and political elites demonstrated that the closer the peace groups were to the decision-making mechanism, the more they could influence political actors to maintain the peace processes. The proximity of these groups to political agents was a precondition for them to be effective in political reforms. However, this may not have provided an immediate influence unless the P/CROs had a continuous and long-standing relationship with decision makers, which also had public support. Hence, this book revealed that despite the lack of political authority, the P/CROs in these conflicts put pressure on the governments to work towards eliminating ethnic and political discrimination. Although both the BIA and WPC were successful in promoting the resolution efforts at the elite level, the BIA's contribution is more extensive as it not only facilitated the progress but also helped to improve the rule of law. In contrast, the book has demonstrated that the British and Turkish governments implicitly supported the groups that emerged as a reaction to increasing violence (PP and LPP). This implicit support restricted these groups' success in contributing to peace efforts. Overall, this research has found that the Northern Irish peace groups played a more comprehensive role than the Turkish peace groups, as they put pressure on the government to change regulations on discrimination against Catholic groups and to work towards other political reforms such as the internment policy and policies relating to prisoners.

This book has argued that the limited success of peace organisations in Turkey was not due to the perception or pressure of the Turkish government, but as a result of these groups' objectives and actions. Even though peace groups in both conflicts contributed to the peace processes through the involvement and demands of wider society, their impact on the elite level to end the violent conflicts differs. Although the peace groups did not confront high-intensity resistance, their activities contributed to the two conflict resolution processes. Unlike the Turkish case, the peace groups in Northern Ireland were proactive even during the violent conflict, as they played a role in both de-escalating the situation and applying political reforms to overcome the underlying reasons for the conflict. My book has revealed that the P/CROs could also be effective in facilitating peace when there is existing violence. For example, it was impossible to conduct official negotiations during ongoing violence due to the objections of society and opposition parties. These organisations focused on closing the gap between the two communities through their popular public events and demonstrations and so became the voice of society against any form of violence. Therefore, it is necessary to have more engagement between the decision-making mechanisms and those peace groups that have a potential influence on political elites.

The fourth main finding of the book is that the official negotiations were criticised by opposition parties in both conflicts for negotiating with terrorist groups, but this criticism did not prevent the peace processes from moving forward. However, the greater number of veto players that emerged in the peace processes, the more complex the peace processes were to resolve. Regarding the reaction of opposition parties, the Northern Irish and Kurdish peace processes were faced with different spoilers that aimed to destroy negotiations. Chapter 6 has indicated that the unionist parties in Northern Ireland and the nationalist party in Turkey were against political resolution efforts. However, the criticism of these parties did not interrupt the peace processes. The peace conferences, for example, between the Northern Irish parties witnessed the DUP and UUP's anger about changes in legislation and this affected the outcome of these meetings. As these conferences did not affect official negotiations, their influence remained limited. Instead, the interview data revealed that the interruption of the peace efforts was a result of ongoing violence deployed by the IRA and PKK. In addition, as Chapter 6 illustrated, the level of violence was influential over the transformation of political reform issues such as the recognition of ethnic identities, a bill of rights and reforms of the security system. Both the British and Turkish governments made the interruption of the armed campaigns by the IRA and PKK a precondition for achieving political reforms. The interview data provided evidence that the Turkish government credited the PKK's unilateral ceasefire as the reason for carrying out changes in the constitution related to ethnic discrimination.

Regarding the veto players, it is expected that negotiations will take place between the same adversaries throughout the negotiation process. As highlighted in Chapter 2, non-violent resolution efforts need to include major stakeholders, but a possible split within conflicting parties may produce a more complicated negotiation environment. Chapter 6 revealed that Turkey's Kurdish peace process became more intractable when the pro-Kurdish movement's decision mechanism was split into three actors: the HDP, Qandil and Öcalan. While all pro-Kurdish actors appeared to be on the same side at the beginning of the talks, the negotiations eventually created a difference of opinion and thus more veto players. This book has found evidence of disagreement particularly between the PKK and HDP through interviews and public statements. For example, when the HDP made a statement, the PKK warned them to change their statement, which caused inconsistencies in the negotiation process.[12] It resulted in a lack of trust between the government and pro-Kurdish actors during the İmralı talks from 2010 to 2015. In contrast to the Turkish case, the primary stakeholders of the Northern Irish conflict played a facilitator role during the bilateral and multilateral negotiations. For example, the Hume–Adams talks allowed SF to join peace negotiations. Together with the substantive efforts of Hume, both the British government and IRA began to realise their aims could not be achieved through armed struggle alone. It was a 'ripe moment' for joining peace negotiations and resulted in the transformation of the republicans' goals. As the negotiations facilitated a political environment for the Northern Irish parties and British government to discuss their objectives, they also facilitated the progress to peace – in contrast to the Turkish case. The involvement of more veto players in the Turkish case affected progress, but the discussions between the same adversaries helped make progress.

The last main finding of the book is that international mediators in the Northern Irish and Turkish cases played a significant role in facilitating the negotiation processes. However, their impact was different depending on the framework of the mediation. Third parties had different impacts on the two peace processes and their role was dependent on the consent of conflicting parties and arrangements to determine the nature of negotiation processes. The conflicting parties in Northern Ireland and Turkey gave consent for third parties to lead the negotiation processes. The book reveals that the contribution of the mediators was determined through an extensive range of features, from bringing conflicting parties together and setting the context of discussions to determining deadlines for an agreement. While Mitchell's mediation in Northern Ireland brought all Northern Irish parties together (apart from the DUP and UKUP), the British mediation in Turkey was between the government and the pro-Kurdish movement only. The analysis of the characteristics of mediators demonstrated that Mitchell had authority to define the agenda of peace talks due to the power of the US administration, whereas the British mediators in Turkey were not able to offer possible solutions for a political settlement or de-escalate the conflict. The form of the secret Oslo talks demonstrated that it was not possible to bring all conflicting parties together due to the secrecy of the meetings. This was also because of the objection of the opposition parties (the CHP and MHP), which later prevented their inclusion in the multilateral negotiations. During the multilateral negotiations in Northern Ireland, the absence of the DUP and UKUP did not interrupt the process, as the UUP was able to represent the unionist community.

The change in the standpoint of the conflicting parties was another important factor that helped Mitchell during the negotiations, but restricted the contribution of the British mediation. The change in SF's stance in the early 1990s facilitated a political agreement, yet the HDP's insistence on not taking responsibility and addressing Öcalan and the PKK as decision makers did not help progress, as we discussed in Chapter 6. More specifically, this book provides evidence that the transformation of the relationship between the Turkish government and HDP was weak, for two reasons. First, the Turkish government was reluctant to strengthen the position of the HDP against the PKK by negotiating with them on behalf of ethnically Kurdish people. Second, unlike SF's position change, the HDP could not use the advantage of being in parliament and did not condemn the PKK's violent attacks. Hence, this relationship did not provide for an ongoing, sustainable peace process in Turkey. Chapter 6 also found that certain other actors and issues influenced the relative perceptions of conflicting parties. For example, SF's standpoint gradually evolved throughout the Hume–Adams talks, the DSD and the Clinton administration's involvement. All of these aspects persuaded SF to apply political resolution efforts. In contrast, the leader of the PKK's intention to end the war did not help reach a peace agreement due to the transformation of the actors on the pro-Kurdish side from Öcalan only to a trilateral structure consisting of the HDP, PKK and Öcalan.

As a result, even though the structure of the bilateral talks in both conflicts provided an understanding of the major claims of the warring sides, minor reforms in the political structure aimed at building trust were necessary but not sufficient steps for an ongoing peace process. The interview data showed that the issues, actors and structures that caused the violent conflict were successfully transformed by incorporating the British and Irish governments and Northern Irish parties, as this provided inclusiveness and strengthened the conflict resolution processes. As neither factor existed in Turkey's peace process, the negotiations were limited to the efforts of the Turkish government and its pro-Kurdish opponents.

The findings of this book illustrate that the conflict resolution processes in Northern Ireland and Turkey have witnessed many political resolution attempts. Efforts by political elites to transform the underlying reasons for these conflicts were responded to differently by their adversaries, the opposing parties and wider Northern Irish and Turkish societies. This resulted in failure in the Turkish case, but facilitated the GFA in Northern Ireland. To understand the conflict resolution approaches, this book suggested a tripartite framework: backchannel initiatives to examine unofficial efforts, peace organisations to assess informal and semi-official peace efforts, and official negotiations to analyse official resolution attempts towards peace. These three approaches constitute a comprehensive understanding of the conflict resolution processes.

This book makes four major contributions to the existing conflict resolution literature. The first contribution relates to the process of conflict resolution efforts. These efforts are more comprehensive than official negotiations as they begin at the pre-negotiation stage by addressing backchannel initiatives. By investigating secret talks between the main armed protagonists in the Northern Irish and Turkey's Kurdish peace processes, this book revealed that conflict resolution attempts were in operation before the official negotiation efforts. In particular, backchannel talks provide a flexible environment in which to discuss the demands and claims of the governments and sub-state armed groups, which then form the basis of official negotiations. The book suggests that these characteristics of backchannel communications emerge at the pre-negotiation stage, leading to official negotiations, demonstrating conflict resolution as an ongoing process. Therefore, the book has demonstrated an understanding of this stage by integrating these efforts within a broader conflict resolution framework.

The second contribution of the book is in regard to the role of P/CROs, which previously had been analysed under middle-range approaches. However, this book states that P/CROs additionally contribute to peacemaking, rather than merely providing a link between war-torn societies and political elites. Therefore, an analysis of the role of peace organisations in making a political agreement is crucial. The book has revealed that these track-two initiatives promoted and encouraged both political elites and their adversaries in their peace efforts by unifying communities against the violence of the IRA and PKK, and the British and Turkish governments' armed response, which resulted in pressure on political elites to downplay the legal differences between ethnic groups. Peace groups are significant in reducing the level of violence, which is imperative for a political resolution. These groups in particular help reduce the gap between conflicting communities and thus, conflicting parties form a broader understanding at a national level to accept ethnic differences within the society. The PP successfully encouraged the Catholic and Protestant communities to demonstrate against violence through its popular marches, and this put pressure on political elites to focus on soft-line policies for overcoming identity disputes. In contrast, the BIA focused more on political conferences, working to included representatives of all political parties and other policy-makers. Although the contribution of peace groups was limited in Turkey, the WPC and LPP managed to unite the support of Turkish and Kurdish communities for a political resolution instead of an armed struggle through hundreds of public meetings, protests and conferences. The key point is that the link between these groups and the political elites helped them influence decisions by insisting on maintaining peace efforts and pushing for a change to political regulations.

The third contribution relates to the results that contradict the existing literature on conflict resolution. Despite a large consensus regarding the negative influence of a lack of trust for maintaining a peace process,[13] the interview data demonstrated that the UUP's mistrust in the British government resulted in the party joining negotiations and playing an active role towards the GFA. This surprising finding needs to be assessed with respect to other ethno-nationalist conflicts to determine whether it results in a contradictory outcome in other cases too. In addition, the existing literature assumes that it is possible for peace groups to establish dialogues with inappropriate or ineffective people due to inadequate information.[14] However, the peace groups in Northern Ireland and Turkey were able to reach the decision makers and put pressure on the governments to reform the constitution. The direct contact between the P/CROs and governments necessitates a more comprehensive investigation of these groups – not only at the grassroots level, but also at the elite level of conflict resolution. Similarly, one of the major assumptions related to backchannel initiatives is that there is no cost of entry into this sort of talks.[15] However, the analysis of secret talks demonstrated that even though both sides participated in many of the backchannels without any preconditions, the objectives of the two governments (to reduce the level of violence) and the aim of opposition movements (to tie the resolution efforts to ethnic identity problems) still came into effect. This was discovered in interviews with intermediaries in the Turkish case and the declassified secret papers in the Northern Irish case. For instance, PM Demirel and President Özal asked the PKK to declare a ceasefire through an intermediary before initiating direct talks.[16] Similarly, both the IRA and British government had preconditions during the indirect communications to come together in the Whitelaw talks.[17] Although the majority of these initiatives did not have a prerequisite, these situations from the two studied cases contradict the theoretical assumptions. Although it is difficult to argue that these contradictions require a modification of conflict resolution theory as a whole, it can be said that it is necessary to rethink these assumptions.

The last contribution of the book relates to the cases selected for examination. By assessing political resolution efforts of two comprehensive ethno-nationalist cases, this book presented a broader understanding than any single case study would (Chapter 2). As the book compared the Northern Irish case, as a successfully resolved ethno-nationalist conflict, with the Turkish case, which is an unsuccessful one, this is a unique piece of research that shows the implications of conflict resolution theory. Although there is existing literature on the negotiation process of the Northern Irish conflict, it has paid little attention to the influence of backchannel initiatives and peace organisations. Similarly, the existing literature has paid little attention to the peace process in Turkey. This research aimed to close this gap in our understanding by challenging the current literature. The book includes three different levels of conflict resolution approaches to achieving a peace agreement. First, it has illustrated the influence of the local level, namely the impact on conflicting communities through P/CROs, and revealed the demands of ethnic identities and claims for resolution. Second, Chapters 4 and 6 have demonstrated the resolution efforts at the national level through secret talks between the main armed protagonists and official negotiations between stakeholders. Last, Chapter 6 has revealed that despite the national borders of ethno-nationalist conflicts, political resolution attempts might be carried out at the international level through the involvement of international third parties. This book, therefore, can be extended to other conflicts which have ethnic and nationalist characteristics, and involve non-violent initiatives by political elites, opposition groups and peace groups at these three levels.

The Northern Irish and Kurdish cases provided a far-reaching analysis of conflict resolution processes by investigating the underlying reasons for their successes and failures. The investigation aimed to aid understanding of how political elites, leaders of sub-state armed groups, opposition parties and groups, and peace groups have shaped these peace processes. Because Turkey's conflict resolution process failed, the findings of this book can be applied to future peace efforts in Turkey. Lessons can be learned from both the failed Kurdish process and the Northern Irish resolution. The top-down approaches assessed in this book can be implemented in other ethno-nationalist conflicts, which embody non-violent, political resolution efforts. The Israeli–Palestinian and Bosnian conflicts both experienced conflict resolution processes aimed at ending ethno-nationalist conflicts, which helped inform conflict resolution theory. In addition, the P/CROs in both these peace processes need to be assessed with regard to their role in peacemaking. More broadly, this book suggests that these groups should focus more on political reforms and transforming issues that are the causes of identity problems in ethno-nationalist conflicts with similar characteristics. For example, as Meyer indicates, the South African peace process illustrated a top-down approach,[18] but the influence of peace groups during the conflict resolution process has garnered little attention.

The Northern Irish and Kurdish cases illustrate that the dialogue between governments and sub-state armed groups should be continuous and form the basis of official negotiations by considering a win-win approach. Despite the reaction of opposition parties and wider society against 'talking to terrorists', the secret nature of these discussions can facilitate success. It is vital for governments and terrorist groups to come together to discuss their objectives as they are the main armed protagonists and sub-state armed groups claim to represent the ethnic communities. As examined in Chapter 4, these initiatives can facilitate a gradual move towards official negotiations. In this context, the Israeli–Palestinian secret talks could be compared to the Northern Irish and Kurdish cases. This can add value to understanding secret talks in a broader perspective. Hence, the main stakeholders of an ethnic conflict should seriously consider the influence of backchannels as pre-negotiation efforts towards peace.

This book has revealed that both top-down and bottom-up initiatives should work in conjunction in order to reach political settlements. This cooperation can emerge during the negotiation process, which produces an engagement between political parties and elites, peace organisations and opposition groups. I, therefore, suggest that the negotiation process should be supported by a mutual understanding of the necessary political steps for resolution as opposed to a zero-sum approach. These steps could successfully be taken if both conflicting communities react against violence. In this context, these findings can be investigated in other cases, such as the ethnic conflict deployed by ETA, which reveals both top-down and bottom-up approaches in the Spanish conflict.[19] To summarise, the political wings of conflicting parties should be willing to resolve ethno-nationalist conflicts in a political way, and peace efforts should be assisted and promoted by peace groups and wider society.

The peacemaking initiatives in Northern Ireland and Turkey demonstrated the different characteristics of peace efforts, which necessitated a detailed investigation. While official mediations and negotiations are at the core of each peace process, the significance of backchannel communications and the role of independent third parties towards establishing a peace agreement had been largely overlooked in the literature focused on analysing peace events. This is because pre-negotiation activities are not usually assessed as part of peace processes, as discussed in Chapters 1 and 2. However, the contribution of secret talks and the initiatives of peace and conflict resolution organisations are vital in encouraging conflicting parties to engage in official negotiations. This contribution might help political elites by forming a basis for political resolution attempts through an understanding of the demands of the conflicting sides and by revealing the desires of conflicting communities and the effort to include these desires in political decisions.

A wider problem emerged in Syria following the Arab uprisings in 2011. Many different states (including the US, Russia, Turkey, Iran and Iraq) and non-state actors –including the radical religious terrorist group ISIS, the PKK's Syrian branch, the PYD and its armed wing YPG, and other opposition armed groups such as the FSA – were involved in the Syrian civil war. The support for the PYD against ISIS from the US and Russia created an environment which enabled the PYD to gain control of the majority of northern Syria following the elimination of ISIS.[20] While Turkey strongly condemned the US and Russia for their support of the PYD/YPG, the US President Donald Trump approved a plan to arm the YPG. Although this conflict did not affect Turkey's Kurdish peace process directly, Turkey expressed concern about the potential use of these supplied weapons against Turkey.[21] In fact, the Kurdish peace process had collapsed before this concern was raised by the government. However, the civil war in Syria negatively affected the potential for relaunching the peace process in Turkey. This caused pessimism in society regarding the future of the peace process. As a result of ISIS militants entering the country, the region experienced many devastating attacks. This created a more complicated situation and affected the perceptions of both conflicting parties; the war in Syria caused a difference in perceptions between the Turkish government and pro-Kurdish movement. The government blamed the PKK for being unwilling to disarm due to the PYD's active role in the Syrian civil war and suggested the PKK-PYD aimed to expand the territory under their control.[22] The pro-Kurdish movement accused the government of not taking any steps toward political reform to reduce ethnic discrimination.[23] This instability in the region negatively affected the future of Turkey's Kurdish peace process and made it more difficult to relaunch a 'democratic opening' project to achieve constitutional reforms and to initiate a new peace process for ending the violent conflict. Therefore, this war has affected the future of the peace process negatively and future research could assess this influence with regard to attempts at peacemaking containing not only Turkey, Syria and Iraq, but also global powers, such as the USA and Russia.

There are indicators that suggest a cause for optimism with regard to the future of ethno-nationalist conflicts. The Northern Ireland conflict was successfully resolved through an agreement between all conflicting parties. Although the political settlement was not intended to transform the underlying reasons of the conflict, it was a framework in which steps could be taken towards a 'positive peace'. It also gave reason for optimism in regard to the resolution of ethnic identity issues in deeply divided societies. Whilst grassroots initiatives were vital for reconciliation in the conflict, political initiatives dominated the process for bringing the violence to an end, which is a great precedent for similar cases. For example, the Colombian government established an agreement with the FARC, but this peace deal was rejected in a subsequent referendum (the no vote won by 50.2%).[24] Despite ongoing opposition towards the peace process, how the official negotiations were conducted in the Northern Ireland case and how they finally came to be accepted by a majority of people in the GFA referendum might be a topic for future research.

This book has examined the pre-negotiation and negotiation stages of the peacemaking process by comparing the initiatives of political parties and actors, and independent third parties who affected the nature of the two different peace processes. A potential future study might involve analysis of the contributions of NGOs, community groups and local leaders towards reconciliation in Northern Ireland and Turkey during the terms of violence, and could demonstrate their part in elite-driven peacemaking efforts during both the pre-negotiation and negotiation stages. In addition, future research could explore whether social and regional concerns are transformed through this process, whether the relationships between conflicting communities affect the progress, and whether grassroots leaders help reduce the tension by closing the gap between communities in conflict. The post-negotiation, post-conflict stage is also a significant area that could be assessed in future research. This could involve an investigation of the role of political agents, sub-state armed groups, peace groups and independent third parties in conflict resolution processes in the post-agreement era. The GFA could be reassessed in order to understand these actors' perceptions and attitudes towards a sustainable peace. Such a potential study could ascertain the outcome of peace agreements and whether the root causes of the conflict had been transformed, such as by the initiation of constitutional changes intended to diminish dominance of the unionist community and identity issues.

Notes

1. Dalai Lama, 'His Holiness the 14. Dalai Lama's Message'.
2. Interview with Çandar, 29–30 June 2015.
3. TNA-CJ/4/319, *From the Principal Sir John Hackett to O'Connell*.
4. Interview with Işık, 19 June 2015; NUI-POL/35/69, *The Gardiner Report*.
5. TNA-CJ/4/1456, *The IRA Truce*.
6. Pruitt, 'Escalation, Readiness for Negotiation'; Wanis-St John, 'Back Channel Diplomacy'.
7. Beriker-Atiyas, 'The Kurdish Conflict in Turkey', pp. 446–7.
8. Spencer, 'Negotiating Peace'.
9. TNA-CJ/4/1456, *The IRA Truce*; TNA-PREM/15/1009, *Note of a Meeting with Representatives of the Provisional IRA*.
10. TNA-CJ/4/1549/2, *N.N. Cowling's letter to Mr Wilson*.
11. TNA-CJ/4/4173, *Secretary of State's BIA Speech*.
12. Interview with Oğur, 25 June 2015.
13. Fisher, *The Social Psychology of Intergroup and International Conflict Resolution*'; Ikle and Leites, 'Political Negotiation'; Knox and Quirk, *Peace Building in Northern Ireland*.
14. Kaye, *Talking to the Enemy*, p. 25.

15. Pruitt, 'Negotiation with Terrorists'; Wanis-St John, 'Back Channel Diplomacy'.
16. Interview with Çandar, 29–30 June 2015.
17. Smith and Neumann, 'Motorman's Long Journey'.
18. Meyer, 'Organizational Identity, Political Contexts, and SMO Action'.
19. For more information on ending the violent conflict in Spain, see Whitfield (*Endgame for ETA*), Encarnacion ('Managing Ethnic Conflict in Spain') and the US Institute of Peace's report by Idoiaga ('The Basque Conflict').
20. Kadıoğlu, 'Challenges of International Negotiations in the Syrian Civil War'.
21. Bozarslan, 'Will Arming of YPG Help Open Kurdish Corridor in Syria?'.
22. Interview with Uçum, 2 July 2015.
23. Yüksekdağ, cited in Sözcü, 'Türkiye IŞİD'e 3 Yıldır Destek Veriyor'.
24. The Guardian, 'Colombia Referendum'.

APPENDIX: INDEX OF INTERVIEWS

- **Algan, Cengiz.** Chairperson of the LPP, journalist and civil society activist; İstanbul, 30 June 2015.
- **Arıboğan, Deniz Ülke.** Chairperson of the WPC's Marmara Region, professor at İstanbul Bilgi University; İstanbul, 8 September 2015.
- **Baluken, İdris.** Deputy and Parliamentary Group Leader of the HDP, member of the İmralı Committee; Ankara, 1 September 2015.
- **Belge, Murat.** Member of the WPC's Southeastern Region, professor at İstanbul Bilgi University and civil rights activist; İstanbul, 30 June 2015.
- **Burkay, Kemal.** Founder of pro-Kurdish Rights and Freedoms Party (*Hak ve Özgürlükler Partisi*); Ankara, 2 July 2015.
- **Çalışlar, Oral.** Member of the WPC's Black Sea Region, journalist and author; İstanbul, 7 July 2015.
- **Can, Celalattin.** Member of the WPC's Central Anatolia Region; İstanbul, 25 June 2015.
- **Çandar, Cengiz.** Intermediary between the Turkish government and PKK, chief advisor to President Turgut Özal (1991–3); İstanbul, 29–30 June 2015.
- **Coşkun, Vahap.** Member of the WPC's Central Anatolia Region, associate professor at Dicle University; İstanbul, 4 September 2015.
- **Dedeoğlu, Beril.** Vice Chairperson of the WPC's Central Anatolia Region, later appointed the Minister for the EU; İstanbul, 17 June 2015.

- **Demir, İmran.** Member of the Resolution Commission (*Toplumsal Barış Yollarının Araştırılması ve Çözüm Sürecinin Değerlendirilmesi Amacıyla Kurulan Meclis Araştırma Komisyonu*, known as *Çözüm Komisyonu*), assistant professor at Marmara University; Leeds, 15 September 2015.
- **Empey, Reginald.** Lord, former leader of the UUP and member of the House of Lords; London, 27 January 2015.
- **Ensaroğlu, Yılmaz.** Chairperson of the WPC's Southeastern Anatolia Region, the chief advisor to PM Ahmet Davutoğlu on the peace process; Ankara, 2 July 2015.
- **Erdem, Tarhan.** Chairperson of the WPC's Aegean Region, former Deputy of the CHP; İstanbul, 10 July 2015.
- **Ete, Hatem.** Chief advisor to PM Ahmet Davutoğlu, on behalf of the AKP government; Ankara, 03 July 2015.
- **Gibney, Jim.** Member of the Executive Committee of SF; Belfast, 20 January 2015.
- **Haşimi, Haşim.** Kurdish politician, former Deputy of the RP and FP; Ankara, 3 July 2015.
- **Hatemi, Kezban.** Vice Chairperson of the WPC's Southeastern Anatolia Region, lawyer; İstanbul, 7 September 2015.
- **Haughey, Dennis.** Founder member of the Social Democratic and Labour Party; Belfast, 19 January 2015.
- **Işık, İlhami.** Intermediary between the Turkish government and pro-Kurdish movement, columnist; İstanbul, 19 June 2015.
- **Karatepe, Şükrü.** Member of the WPC's Mediterranean Region, former Mayor of Kayseri; Ankara, 13 July 2015.
- **Korkut, Levent.** Secretary of the WPC's Marmara Region, Chairperson of the Association of Civil Society Development Centre; Ankara, 10 July 2015.
- **Mahçupyan, Etyen.** Member of the WPC's Southeastern Anatolia Region, the chief advisor to PM Ahmet Davutoğlu; İstanbul, 22 June 2015.
- **Mallon, Ben.** The Democratic Unionist Party Councillor for Lisburn and Castlereagh; Belfast, 19 January 2015.
- **Mason, Gary.** Reverend, Methodist Minister of Belfast Mission; Belfast, 20 January 2015.

- **Oğan, Ayhan.** Secretary of the WPC's Eastern Anatolia Region; İstanbul, 18 June 2015.
- **Oğur, Yıldıray.** Member of the WPC's Black Sea Region, columnist; İstanbul, 25 June 2015.
- **Oran, Baskın.** Member of the WPC's Aegean Region, former professor at Ankara University and civil rights activist; Ankara, 18 June 2015.
- **Sancar, Mithat.** Deputy of the HDP; Ankara, 8 July 2015.
- **Sayman, Yücel.** Member of the WPC's Marmara Region, professor at Medipol University; Ankara, 3 July 2015.
- **Tan, Altan.** Deputy of the HDP; Ankara, 24 June 2015.
- **Uçum, Mehmet.** Deputy of the AKP; Ankara, 2 July 2015.
- **Walsh, Seanna.** Member of SF, former member of the PIRA and the leader of the Blanket Protest; Belfast, 19 January 2015.
- **Yayla, Atilla.** Member of the LPP, professor at İstanbul Ticaret University; İstanbul, 7 July 2015.
- **Yüksekdağ, Figen.** Co-Leader of the HDP; Ankara, 13 July 2015.
- **[Name Withheld].** Head of a department at the Undersecretariat of Public Order and Security (*Kamu Düzeni ve Güvenliği Müsteşarlığı*); Ankara, 1 July 2015.

BIBLIOGRAPHY

Primary Documents

National Archives, Kew, London

CAB 128, 129, 134:
TNA-CAB/128/48/3. *Confidential Annex: Northern Ireland Secretary.* 15 June 1972.
TNA-CAB/128/71/17. *Conclusions of a Meeting of the Cabinet.* 19 November 1981.
TNA-CAB/128/81/34. *Cabinet Conclusion.* 28 November 1985.
TNA-CAB/128/81/37. *Conclusions of a Meeting of the Cabinet.* 19 November 1985.
TNA-CAB/128/83/36. *Conclusions of Meeting of the Cabinet.* 6 November 1986.
TNA-CAB/134/3921. *Memo on IRA ceasefire from Merlyn Rees to IRN (75), Cabinet Committee on Northern Ireland.* 18 February 1975.
CJ 4:
TNA-CJ/4/296. *Nick Stadlen's letter to Mr Howell: British–Irish Association Programme.* 31 January 1973.
TNA-CJ/4/319. *From the Principal Sir John Hackett to O'Connell.* 15 October 1973.
TNA-CJ/4/582. *F.S.L. Lyons letter to Roy Hattersley.* 31 July 1974.
TNA-CJ/4/839. *Force Levels and the Ceasefire: Note of a Meeting.* 2 May 1975.
TNA-CJ/4/860. *Church Leader's Meeting with the IRA.* 18 December 1974.
TNA-CJ/4/1456. *The IRA Truce 26 June–10 July 1972.* 10 July 1972.
TNA-CJ/4/1549/1. *Mr David Goodall's letter to Peter Foster.* 18 March 1977.
TNA-CJ/4/1549/1. *Northern Ireland Peace People Telgram No.236.* 7 April 1977.
TNA-CJ/4/1549/1. *Peace Leader Denies Helping Killers, see Irish Times.* 25 January 1977.

BIBLIOGRAPHY | 245

TNA-CJ/4/1549/2. *Community of the Peace People: Annex B to Northern Ireland Office's report on the Peace People Report No.110/381/04.* 5 December 1979.

TNA-CJ/4/1549/2. *J.E. Henderson's letter to Abbott: Relations with the Peace People: Betty Williams' Visit to West Germany.* 7 September 1977.

TNA-CJ/4/1549/2. *M.W.J. Buxton's letter to the Secretary of State: The Peace People and the Army.* 24 October 1977.

TNA-CJ/4/1549/2. *N.N. Cowling's letter to Mr Wilson: Evolution of Attitude towards the Security Forces in Annex: Assembly of the Peace People.* 10 November 1977.

TNA-CJ/4/1549/2. *Northern Ireland Office's Report: The Peace People.* 5 December 1977.

TNA-CJ/4/1947. *J.A. Marshall's letter to Lord Melchett Annex: British–Irish Conference.* 5 September 1977.

TNA-CJ/4/2228. *British–Irish Association Conference: HMG's View on the Way Ahead.* 22 June 1978.

TNA-CJ/4/2263. *Statement by the IRA Ending the Ceasefire on December 22nd 1974.* 16 January 1975.

TNA-CJ/4/2380. *Note for the Record: Assembly of the Peace People.* 9 October 1978.

TNA-CJ/4/2380. *Note of a Meeting between the Peace People and Mr Concannon.* 1 December 1978.

TNA-CJ/4/2380. *Peace Leader Ciaran McKeown, see the Irish Independent.* 30 January 1978.

TNA-CJ/4/2380. *Emergency Provision Legislation in Northern Ireland, J.A. Marshall's Note.* 21 November 1979.

TNA-CJ/4/2580. *British–Irish Association Conference: T.H. Gee's letter to Mr Lane.* 27 July 1979.

TNA-CJ/4/2580. *A.P. Wilson's letter to Secretary of State: After Dinner Speech to BIA.* 13 July 1979.

TNA-CJ/4/3706. *Community of the Peace People's Report by Peter McLachlan.* 1 June 1979.

TNA-CJ/4/3706. *Marshall's letter to A.P. Wilson.* 12 June 1979.

TNA-CJ/4/3706. *Mairead Corrigan's letter to Prime Minister Margaret Thatcher.* 19 March 1981.

TNA-CJ/4/4024. *Direct Rule not Acceptable, Says Peace Leader, see Irish News.* 5 July 1979.

TNA-CJ/4/4025. *J.H.G. Leahy's letter to Graham Greene Attachment: Women's Peace Movement in Northern Ireland.* 21 September 1976.

TNA-CJ/4/4025. *Ulster Woman Advocates Peace is Heckled by Dorchester Group.* 27 May 1977.

TNA-CJ/4/4169. *D. Chesterton's letter to Lord Gowrie: BIA Lambeth Conference.* 20 November 1981.

TNA-CJ/4/4169. *R.A. Harrington's letter to Mr Chesterton: British–Irish Association.* 30 November 1981.

TNA-CJ/4/4169. *Minister's Case 7849: British–Irish Association Written by B.A. Blackwell.* 23 August 1982.

TNA-CJ/4/4169. *N.C. Abbott's letter to Mr Merifield.* 27 October 1982.

TNA-CJ/4/4173. *B.A. Blackwell's letter to Mr Abbott and Secretary of State.* 23 August 1982.

TNA-CJ/4/4173. *C.L. Angel's letter to Miss Mulligan about Mrs Marigold Johnson.* 10 August 1982.

TNA-CJ/4/4173. *Secretary of State's BIA Speech.* 29 November 1982.

TNA-CJ/4/4174. *Hayes's letter to Mr Bell.* 1 December 1981.

TNA-CJ/4/4245. *Account of Meeting with Tom Caldwell MP and R O'Bradaigh, President of Sinn Fein.* 24 February 1972.

FCO 87:

TNA-FCO/87/1303. *The Irish Association: Kilkenny Conference, D.E. Tatham's letter to Mr Whiteway.* 4 October 1982.

PREM 15, 16, 19:

TNA-PREM/15/1009. *Note of a Meeting with Representatives of the Provisional IRA.* 21 June 1972.

TNA-PREM/15/1016. *Frank Steele, IRA and Peace: From UKREP Belfast to Dublin.* 28 November 1972.

TNA-PREM/15/1127. *Correspondence with Tom Caldwell MP on Northern Ireland Matters.* 25 February 1972.

TNA-PREM/16/158. *Principal Private Secretary.* [No Date] 1974.

TNA-PREM/19/509. *Anglo-Irish Summit: Draft Communique.* 5 November 1981.

TNA-PREM/19/509. *Anglo-Irish Summit: Steering Brief by Foreign and Commonwealth Office.* 29 October 1981.

TNA-PREM/19/814. *Note of a Meeting Held in the Northern Ireland Office.* 26 January 1982.

TNA-PREM/19/1068. *Irish General Election: Comments by Mr Prior Telegram Number 322.* 17 November 1982.

Hansard, Parliamentary Debates

HC Deb. *House of Commons Debates, vol. 838, cols. 1073–4.* 12 June 1972.

National University of Ireland Archive, Galway

NUI-POL/35/4/62. *Duddy Papers.* 1 June 1975.

NUI-POL/35/9/279. *Robert McLarnon's Message to Brendan Duddy.* 1 May 1993.

NUI-POL/35/68/1. *A Letter from the IRA to the British Prime Minister.* 24 January 1975.
NUI-POL/35/69. *The Gardiner Report.* 1 August 1975.
NUI-POL/35/166/2. *The Red Book.* 6 July 1981.
NUI-POL/35/166/3. *The Red Book.* 6 July 1981.
NUI-POL/35/167/3. *The Red Book.* 7 July 1981.
NUI-POL/35/266/1. *IRA Ceasefire Offer.* 14 May 1993.

Turkish Armed Forces Archives, Ankara

TSKA-EK/980/26. *Report about Implimentation of the State of Emergency Rule in Various Countries.* Türk Silahlı Kuvvetleri Arşivi. 1980.
TSKA-EK/984/34. *Report about the Village Guard System.* Türk Silahlı Kuvvetleri Arşivi. 1984.
TSKA-MGK/988/9. *Meeting of the National Security Council.* Türk Silahlı Kuvvetleri Arşivi. September 1988.
TSKA-MGK/989/4. *Meeting of the National Security Council.* Türk Silahlı Kuvvetleri Arşivi. September 1988.
TSKA-MGK/993/4. *Meeting of the National Security Council.* Türk Silahlı Kuvvetleri Arşivi. April 1993.

Parliamentary and International Official Reports

BDP. *Toplumsal Barış Yollarının Araştırılması ve Çözüm Sürecinin Değerlendirilmesi Komisyonu Raporu.* Ankara: BDP, 2013. Unpublished report, accessed on 10 July 2015.
EU. *European Charter of Local Self-Governments*, CETS No. 122. Brussels: The Council of Europe, 1988.
European Parliament. *The Impact and Consequences of Brexit for Northern Ireland*, Report No. PE 583 116. Brussels: European Parliament, 2017.
EUROPOL. *TE-SAT 2013: EU Terrorism Situation and Trend Report.* Van Deventer: European Police Office, 2013.
Mitchell, G., J. De Chastelain and H. Holkeri. *Report of the International Body on Arms Decommissioning.* Belfast: Northern Ireland Office, 1996.
New Ireland Forum. *Final Report.* Belfast: Stationery Office, Northern Ireland, 1984.
TBMM, *Temel Hak ve Hürriyetlerin Geliştirilmesi Amacıyla Çeşitli Kanunlarda Değişiklik Yapılmasına Dair Kanun,* 6529 C.F.R. 2014.
TBMM. *Terör ve Şiddet Olayları Kapsamında Yaşam Hakkı İhlallerini İnceleme Raporu.* Ankara: Türkiye Büyük Millet Meclisi, 2013.
TBMM, *Terörün Sona Erdirilmesi ve Toplumsal Bütünleşmenin Güçlendirilmesine Dair Kanun,* 6551 C.F.R. 2014.

TBMM. *Toplumsal Barış Yollarının Araştırılması ve Çözüm Sürecinin Değerlendirilmesi Amacıyla Kurulan Meclis Araştırma Komisyonu Raporu*. Ankara: Türkiye Büyük Millet Meclisi, 2013.

TBMM. *Toplumsal Barış Yollarının Araştırılması ve Çözüm Sürecinin Değerlendirilmesi Komisyonu Görüşme Tutanakları*. Ankara: Türkiye Büyük Millet Meclisi, 2013.

Secondary Sources

21YYTE. *Terörle Mücadelede Verdiğimiz Şehitler 1984-2013 [Martyrs of the Fight against Terrorism 1984-2013]*. Ankara: 21YYTE, 2013.

Aall, P. 'What do NGOs Bring to Peacemaking?' In C. Crocker, F. O. Hampson and P. Aall (eds), *Turbulent Peace: The Challenges of Managing International Conflict*, pp. 365–83. Washington: United States Institute of Peace Press, 2001.

Abramowitz, M. 'Dateline Ankara: Turkey after Ozal'. *Foreign Policy*, 91 (1993), pp. 164–81.

Abramowitz, M., and H. J. Barkey. 'Turkey's Transformers: The AKP Sees Big'. *Foreign Affairs*, 88:6 (2009), pp. 118–28.

Abu-Nimer, M. 'Conflict Resolution Approaches: Western and Middle Eastern Lessons and Possibilities'. *American Journal of Economics and Sociology*, 55 (1996), pp. 35–52.

Adams, G. *Free Ireland: Towards a Lasting Peace*. Niwot: Roberts Rineheart, 1994.

Agha, H., S. Feldman, A. Khalidi and Z. Schiff. *Track 2 Diplomacy: Lessons from the Middle East*. Cambridge, MA: MIT Press, 2003.

Akbulut, O. 'A Critical Analysis of Current Legal Developments on the Political Participation of Minorities in Turkey'. *International Journal on Minority and Group Rights*, 17:4 (2010), pp. 551–60.

Akşam. 'PKK İlk Kez Açıkladı . . . Oslo'da Neler Oldu?' [PKK Declared for the First Time . . . What Happened in Oslo?]. *Akşam*, 24 April 2013, http://www.aksam.com.tr/siyaset/pkk-ilk-kez-acikladiosloda-neler-oldu/haber-199057 (last accessed 17 March 2016).

Al Jazeera. 'Ortak Açıklamanın Tam Metni'. *Al Jazeera*, 28 February 2015, http://www.aljazeera.com.tr/haber/ortak-aciklamanin-tam-metni (last accessed 1 March 2015).

Aliboni, R., and D. Pioppi. 'The Öcalan Affair Revisited'. *Italian Journal of International Affairs*, 35:3 (2000), pp. 37–47.

Alonso, R. 'Pathways out of Terrorism in Northern Ireland and the Basque Country'. *Terrorism and Political Violence*, 16:4 (2004), pp. 695–713.

Alphan, C., and Y. Albayrak. *Erbakan'ın Gizli PKK Zirvesi: Zirvenin Kilit Adamı İsmail Nacar*. İstanbul: Ares, 2010.

ANF. 'Öcalan: Kürtlerin Kellesine Karşı ABD-Türkiye Anlaştı' [Öcalan: The USA and Turkey Made an Agreement to Slaughter Kurds]. *Sendika*, 20 May 2011, http://sendika59.org/2011/05/ocalan-kurtlerin-kellesine-karsilik-abd-turkiye-anlasti-anf/ (last accessed 23 May 2015).

Angelo, P. 'The Colombian Peace Process: Trial and Error'. *Survival*, 59:1 (2017), pp. 135–48.

Anglo-Irish Agreement. *Agreement between The Government of Great Britain and Northern Ireland and the Government of the Republic of Ireland*. London: Her Majesty's Stationery Office, 1985.

Annan, K. *We the Peoples: The Role of the United Nations in the 21st Century*. New York: United Nations, Department of Public Information, 2000.

Archick, K. *Northern Ireland: The Peace Process*. Washington: Library of Congress Congressional Research Service, 2014.

ARK. 'The 1998 Referendums'. *ARK*, 14 January 2001, http://www.ark.ac.uk/elections/fref98.htm (last accessed 24 January 2016).

ARK. 'Westminster By-elections, 23 January 1986'. *ARK*, 4 November 2001, http://www.ark.ac.uk/elections/fw86.htm (last accessed 20 January 2016).

Art, R. J., and L. Richardson. 'Introduction', in R. J. Art and L. Richardson (eds), *Democracy and Counterterrorism: Lessons from the Past*, pp. 1–24. Washington: United States Institute of Peace Press, 2007.

Arthur, P. *Government and Politics of Northern Ireland*. London: Longman, 1984.

Arthur, P. 'Negotiating the Northern Ireland Problem: Track One or Track Two Diplomacy?' *Government and Opposition*, 25:4 (1990), pp. 403–18.

Aslan, G. 'TC'nin PKK ile Görüşmeleri' [The Republic of Turkey's Talks with the PKK]. *Taraf*, 10 July 2010, http://www.taraf.com.tr/haber-tc-nin-pkk-ile-gorusmeleri-53564/ (last accessed 9 June 2014).

Assefa, H. *Mediation of Civil Wars*. London: Westview, 1987.

Ataman, M. 'Özal Leadership and Reconstructing of Turkish Ethnic Policy in the 1980s'. *Middle Eastern Studies*, 38:4 (2002), pp. 123–42.

Aughey, A. 'A State of Exception: The Concept of the Political in Northern Ireland'. *Irish Political Studies*, 12:1 (1997), pp. 1–12.

Austin, B. 'Introduction'. In A. Beatrix, M. Fischer and H.-J. Giessmann (eds), *Advancing Conflict Transformation: The Berghof Handbook II*, pp. 9–22. Opladen: Budrich, 2011.

Aydın, S., and Y. Taşkın. *1960'tan Günümüze Türkiye Tarihi*. İstanbul: İletişim, 2014.

Aydınlı, E., and N. A. Özcan. 'The Conflict Resolution and Counterterrorism Dilemma: Turkey Faces its Kurdish Question'. *Terrorism and Political Violence*, 23:3 (2011), pp. 438–57.

Azar, E. 'Protracted Social Conflicts and Second Track Diplomacy'. In J. Davies and E. Kaufman (eds), *Second Track/Citizens' Diplomacy: Concepts and Techniques for Conflict Transformation*, pp. 15–30. Oxford: Rowman & Littlefield, 2003.

Babbitt, E. 'The Evolution of International Conflict Resolution: From Cold War to Peacebuilding'. *Negotiation Journal*, 25:4 (2009), pp. 539–49.

Babbitt, E., and F. O. Hampson. 'Conflict Resolution as a Field of Inquiry: Practice Informing Theory'. *International Studies Review*, 13 (2011), pp. 46–57.

Bahar, H. İ. *Çözüm Süreci*. Ankara: Ankara Strateji Enstitüsü, 2013.

Bar-Siman-Tov, Y. 'The Arab-Israeli Conflict: Learning Conflict Resolution'. *Journal of Peace Research*, 31:1 (1994), pp. 75–92.

Bar-Siman-Tov, Y. *From Conflict Resolution to Reconciliation*. New York: Oxford University Press, 2004.

BarışaBak Platformu. 'Barışa Bak!'. *Vivahiba*, 4 November 2014, http://vivahiba.com/article/show/barisa-bak/ (last accessed 28 December 2015).

Barkey, H. J. 'The People's Democracy Party (HADEP): The Travails of a Legal Kurdish Party in Turkey'. *Journal of Muslim Minority Affairs*, 18:1 (1998), pp. 129–38.

Barkey, H. J. 'Turkey's Kurdish Dilemma'. *Survival*, 35:4 (1993), pp. 51–70.

Barkey, H. J., and G. E. Fuller. 'Turkey's Kurdish Question: Critical Turning Points and Missed Opportunities', *Middle East Journal*, 51:1 (1997), pp. 59–79.

Barlas, M. 'Osmanlı'da Oyun Bitmez: Derin Devlet'. *Sabah*, 29 January 2007, http://arsiv.sabah.com.tr/2007/01/29/yaz09-40-105.html (last accessed 27 November 2011).

Barrinha, A. 'The Political Importance of Labelling: Terrorism and Turkey's Discourse on the PKK'. *Critical Studies on Terrorism*, 4:2 (2011), pp. 163–80.

Barros, C. P. 'An Intervention Analysis of Terrorism: The Spanish ETA Case', *Defence and Peace Economics*, 14:6 (2003), pp. 401–12.

Bartoli, A. 'Mediating Peace in Mozambique: The Role of the Community of Sant'Egidio'. In C. A. Crocker, F. O. Hampson and P. Aall (eds), *Herding Cats: Multiparty Mediation in a Complex World*, pp. 245–74. Washington: United States Institute of Peace Press, 1999.

Başaran, E. 'Oslo, Çözüm Süreci ve Hepimizin Bilmesi Gerekenler' [Oslo, the Peace Process and All We Need to Know]. *Radikal*, 10 February 2016, http://www.radikal.com.tr/yazarlar/ezgi-basaran/oslo-cozum-sureci-ve-hepimizin-bilmesi-gerekenler-1507850/ (last accessed 3 March 2016).

Başbuğ, İ. *Terör Örgütlerinin Sonu*. İstanbul: Remzi, 2015.

Baser, B., and A. Özerdem. 'Conflict Transformation and Asymmetric Conflicts: A Critique of the Failed Turkish-Kurdish Peace Process'. *Terrorism and Political Violence*, online (2019), pp. 1–22.

Baser, B., and A. Özerdem. 'Turkey'. In A. Özerdem and R. MacGinty (eds), *Comparing Peace Processes*, pp. 319–35. Abingdon: Routledge, 2019.

Baser, B., and A. E. Öztürk. 'In Lieu of an Introduction: Is It Curtains for Turkish Democracy?' In B. Baser and A. E. Öztürk (eds), *Authoritarian Politics in Turkey: Elections, Resistance and the AKP*, pp. 1–20. London: I. B. Tauris, 2017.

Baser, B., S. Akgönül, and A. E. Öztürk. '"Academics for Peace" in Turkey: A Case of Criminalising Dissent and Critical Thought via Counterterrorism Policy'. *Critical Studies on Terrorism*, 10:2 (2017), pp. 274–96.

Baybars-Hawks, B. 'Will Peace Flourish in the End? The History of Suffering: Terrorism in Turkey'. *Mediterranean Journal of Social Sciences*, 4:10 (2013), pp. 278–82.

BBC. 'PKK'dan Açıklama: Gerillayı Durduruyoruz'. *BBC*, 5 September 2013, http://www.bbc.com/turkce/haberler/2013/09/130905_bayik_pkk_cekilme_durdu (last accessed 28 April 2014).

BBC. 'Yıldırım'dan ABD'ye Tepki: PKK DEAŞ'a Karşı Kullanılmamalı'. *BBC*, 10 May 2017, http://www.bbc.com/turkce/haberler-turkiye-39856911 (last accessed 15 May 2017).

Bell, J. B. 'The Escalation of Insurgency: The Provisional Irish Republican Army's Experience, 1969–1971', *The Review of Politics*, 35:3 (1973), pp. 398–411.

Bell, J. B. *The IRA, 1968–2000: Analysis of a Secret Army*. Oxford: Taylor & Francis, 2000.

Ben-Porat, G. 'Introduction: Implementing Peace Agreements'. In G. Ben-Porat (ed.), *The Failure of the Middle East Peace Process?*, pp. 1–18. New York: Springer, 2008.

Bendana, A. 'Conflict Resolution: Empowerment and Disempowerment'. *Peace & Change*, 21:1 (1996), pp. 69–70.

Bennis, W. G., K. D. Benne and R. Chin. *The Planning of Change*, vol. 4. New York: Holt, Rinehart & Winston, 1985.

Benson, J. K. 'The Interorganizational Network as a Political Economy', *Administrative Science Quarterly*, 20:2 (1975), pp. 229–49.

Bercovitch, J. 'International Mediation'. *Journal of Peace Research*, 28:1 (1991), pp. 3–6.

Bercovitch, J. 'International Mediation: A Study of the Incidence, Strategies and Conditions of Successful Outcomes'. *Cooperation and Conflict*, 21:3 (1986), pp. 155–68.

Bercovitch, J., and A. Houston. 'Influence of Mediator Characteristics and Behaviour on the Success of Mediation in International Relations'. *International Journal of Conflict Management*, 4:4 (1993), pp. 297–321.

Bercovitch, J., and J. Langley. 'The Nature of the Dispute and the Effectiveness of International Mediation'. *Journal of Conflict Resolution*, 37:4 (1993), pp. 670–91.

Bercovitch, J., V. Kremenyuk and I. W. Zartman (eds). *The SAGE Handbook of Conflict Resolution*. London: Sage, 2009.

Bercovitch, J., J. T. Anagnason and D. L. Wille. 'Some Conceptual Issues and Empirical Trends in the Study of Successful Mediation in International Relations'. *Journal of Peace Research*, 28:1 (1991), pp. 7–17.

Beriker, N. *Çatışmadan Uzlaşmaya: Kuramlar, Süreçler ve Uygulamalar*. İstanbul: Bilgi Üniversitesi Yayınları, 2009.

Beriker-Atiyas, N. 'The Kurdish Conflict in Turkey: Issues, Parties and Prospects'. *Security Dialogue*, 28:4 (1997), pp. 439–52.

Bew, P., and G. Gillespie. *The Northern Ireland Peace Process: 1993–1996*. London: Serif, 1996.

BIA. 'The British–Irish Association'. *The British–Irish Association*, 2015, http://www.britishirishassociation.org/aboutus.htm (last accessed 4 May 2015).

BiaNet. 'Barışa Bak Kampanyası 69 İmzayla Başladı'. *BiaNet*, 4 November 2014, https://www.bianet.org/bianet/siyaset/159691-barisa-bak-kampanyasi-69-imzayla-basladi (last accessed 27 December 2015).

BiaNet. 'İki Buçuk Yıldır Gündemdeki "KCK" nedir?' [What is the 'KCK' Which is in Question for Two and a Half Years?]. *BiaNet*, 28 June 2013, http://bianet.org/bianet/siyaset/131077-iki-bucuk-yildir-gundemdeki-kck-nedir (last accessed 28 October 2015).

Birand, M. A., and S. Yalçın. *The Özal: Bir Davanın Öyküsü [The Özal: The Story of an Objective]*. İstanbul: Doğan Kitap, 2001.

Bishop, P., and E. Mallie. *The Provisional IRA*. London: Corgi, 1988.

Blair, T. *A Journey: My Political Life*. London: Hutchinson, 2010.

Bloomfield, D. *Peacemaking Strategies in Northern Ireland: Building Complementarity in Conflict Management Theory*. London: Macmillan, 1998.

Blum, A. 'The Futures of Conflict: Exploring the Use of Comparative Scenarios in Track II Peacebuilding'. *International Studies Perspectives*, 6 (2005), pp. 342–58.

Boulding, K. E. *Conflict and Defense*. New York: Harper & Brothers, 1962.

Boulding, K. E. 'Future Directions in Conflict and Peace Studies'. *Journal of Conflict Resolution*, 22:2 (1978), pp. 342–54.

Boulding, K. E. 'Is Peace Researchable?' *The Background*, 6:4 (1963), pp. 70–7.

Boulding, K. E. 'Organization and Conflict'. *Journal of Conflict Resolution*, 1:2 (1957), pp. 122–34.

Boyle, K., and T. Hadden. 'The Peace Process in Northern Ireland'. *International Affairs*, 71:2 (1995), pp. 269–83.

Bozarslan, H. 'Turkey's Elections and the Kurds'. *Middle East Report*, 199 (1996), pp. 16–19.

Bozarslan, M. 'Will Arming of YPG Help Open Kurdish Corridor in Syria?' *Al-Monitor*, 15 May 2017, http://www.al-monitor.com/pulse/originals/2017/05/turkey-united-states-will-guns-open-kurdish-corridor.html (last accessed 16 May 2017).

Brewer, J. D., K. Bishop and G. I. Higgins. *Peacemaking among Protestants and Catholics in Northern Ireland*. Belfast: Queen's University of Belfast, 2001.

British and Irish Governments. 'Joint Communiqué'. *Centre for the Study of Conflict, University of Ulster*, 1995, http://cain.ulst.ac.uk/events/peace/docs/com281195.htm (last accessed 25 January 2016).

British and Irish Governments. 'Joint Declaration on Peace: Downing Street Declaration'. *Centre for the Study of Conflict, University of Ulster*, 1993, http://cain.ulst.ac.uk/events/peace/docs/dsd151293.htm (last accessed 20 January 2016).

British Government. 'Ground Rules for Substantive All-Party Government'. *University of Ulster CAIN Web Service*, 15 March 1996, http://cain.ulst.ac.uk/events/peace/docs/cp15396.htm (last accessed 24 January 2016).

Brooke, P. 'Peter Brooke's "No Selfish Strategic Interest" Speech'. *BBC*, 9 November 1990, http://news.bbc.co.uk/1/hi/northern_ireland/4072261.stm (last accessed 20 January 2016).

Brown, M. E. *Ethnic Conflict and International Security*. Princeton: Princeton University Press, 1993.

Brown, R. *Group Processes: Dynamics Within and Between Groups*. Oxford: Blackwell, 2000.

Buchanan, S. 'Transforming Conflict in Northern Ireland and the Border Counties'. *Irish Political Studies*, 23:3 (2008), pp. 387–409.

Burton, J. W. *Conflict & Communication*. London: Macmillan, 1969.

Burton, J. W. *Conflict: Human Needs Theory*. London: Springer, 1990.

Burton, J. W. *Conflict: Resolution and Provention*. London: Macmillan, 1990.

Burton, J. W. *Resolving Deep-Rooted Conflict: A Handbook*. Lanham: University Press of America, 1987.

Burton, J. W. *World Society*. London: Cambridge University Press, 1972.

Bush, R. A. B., and J. P. Folger. *The Promise of Mediation: Responding to Conflict Through Empowerment and Recognition*. San Francisco: Jossey-Bass, 1994.

Byrne, S. 'Conflict Regulation or Conflict Resolution: Third Party Intervention in Northern Ireland Conflict'. *Terrorism and Political Violence*, 7:2 (1995), pp. 1–24.

Byrne, S. 'Consociational and Civic Society Approaches to Peacebuilding in Northern Ireland'. *Journal of Peace Research*, 38:3 (2001), pp. 327–52.

Byrne, S. 'Toward Tractability: The 1993 South African Record of Understanding and the 1998 Northern Ireland Good Friday Agreement'. *Irish Studies in International Affairs*, 13 (2002), pp. 135–49.

Cagaptay, S. 'Can the PKK Renounce Violence?' *Middle East Quarterly* (2007), pp. 45–52.

Cairns, E., and J. Darby. 'The Conflict in Northern Ireland: Causes, Consequences, and Controls'. *American Psychologist*, 53:7 (1998), pp. 754–60.

Çalışlar, O. *Öcalan ve Burkay'la Kürt Sorunu.* İstanbul: Pencere Yayınları, 1993.

Çandar, C. *Dağdan İniş-PKK Nasıl Silah Bırakır? Kürt Sorununun Şiddetten Arındırılması.* İstanbul: TESEV, 2011.

Çandar, C. 'The Kurdish Question: The Reasons and Fortunes of the "Opening"'. *Insight Turkey,* 11:4 (2009), pp. 13–19.

Çandar, C. *Mezopotamya Ekspresi: Bir Tarih Yolculuğu [The Mesopotamia Express: A Journey in History].* İstanbul: İletişim, 2014.

Carayannis, T., V. Bojicic-Dzelilovic, N. Olin, A. Rigterink and M. Schomerus. *Practice Without Evidence: Interrogating Conflict Resolution Approaches and Assumptions.* London: Justice and Security Research Programme, 2014.

Carnevale, P. J., and D. G. Pruitt. 'Negotiation and Mediation', *Annual Review of Psychology,* 43 (1992), pp. 531–82.

Cederman, L.-E., H. Buhaug and J. K. Rod, 'Ethno-nationalist Dyads and Civil War: A GIS-Based Analysis'. *Journal of Conflict Resolution,* 53:4 (2009), pp. 496–525.

Celep, Ö. 'Can the Kurdish Left Contribute to Turkey's Democratization?' *Insight Turkey,* 16:3 (2014), pp. 165–80.

Çelik, A. B. 'Etnik Çatışmaların Çözümünde Siyaset Bilimi ve Uyuşmazlık Çözümü Yaklaşımları'. In N. Beriker (ed.), *Çatışmadan Uzlaşmaya: Kuramlar, Süreçler ve Uygulamalar,* pp. 163–88. İstanbul: Bilgi Üniversitesi Yayınları, 2009.

Cemal, H. *Kürtler.* İstanbul: Doğan Kitap, 2003.

Cemal, H. 'Murat Karayılan ile Kandil'de 5,5 Saat' [Five and a Half Hours with Murat Karayılan in Qandil]. *t24.com,* 24 March 2013, http://t24.com.tr/yazi/karayilan-geri-cekilme-sonbahara-sarkar-kalici-baris-aponun-ozgurlugunden-gecer/6390 (last accessed 4 April 2016).

Charters, D. A. '"Have a Go": British Army/MIE Agent-running Opearations in Northern Ireland, 1970–72'. *Intelligence and National Security,* 28:2 (2013), pp. 202–29.

Chertkoff, J., and M. Conley. 'Opening Offer and Frequency of Concessions as Bargaining Strategies'. *Journal of Personality and Social Psychology,* 7:2 (1967), pp. 181–5.

Chigas, D. 'Negotiating Intractable Conflicts: The Contribution of Unofficial Intermediaries'. In C. A. Crocker, F. O. Hampson and P. Aall (eds), *Grasping the Nettle: Analyzing Cases of Intractable Conflict,* pp. 123–60. Washington: United States Institute of Peace Press, 2005.

Çiçek, C. 'Elimination or Integration of Pro-Kurdish Politics: Limits of the AKP's Democratic Initiative'. *Turkish Studies,* 12:1 (2011), pp. 15–26.

Çıtak, M. C., and N. Alkan. 'Terörden Kaynaklı Çatışmaların Çözümü ve Akil İnsanlar Heyeti Uygulamaları'. *Bilge Strateji,* 7:12 (2015), pp. 79–99.

Cizre, Ü. 'Demythologyzing the National Security Concept: The Case of Turkey'. *The Middle East Journal*, 57:2(2003), pp. 213–29.

Cizre, Ü. 'The Emergence of the Government's Perspective on the Kurdish Issue'. *Insight Turkey*, 11:4 (2009), pp. 1–12.

CNNTürk. 'Geçmişten Bugüne PKK Ateşkesleri'. *CNNTürk*, 28 June 2010, http://www.cnnturk.com/2010/turkiye/06/28/gecmisten.bugune.pkk.ateskesleri/581570.0/ (last accessed 1 June 2016).

Cochrane, F. 'Irish-America, the End of the IRA's Armed Struggle and the Utility of "Soft Power"'. *Journal of Peace Research*, 44:2 (2007), pp. 215–31.

Cochrane, F. *Northern Ireland: The Reluctant Peace*. New Haven, CT: Yale University Press, 2013.

Cochrane, F. 'Peace and Conflict Resolution Organisations in Northern Ireland', In B. Gidron, S. Katz and Y. Hasenfeld (eds), *Mobilizing for Peace: Conflict Resolution in Northern Ireland, Israel/Palestine, and South Africa*, pp. 151–74. Oxford: Oxford University Press, 2002.

Cochrane, F. *Unionist Politics and the Politics of Unionism since the Anglo-Irish Agreement*. Cork: Cork University Press, 1997.

Cochrane, F. 'Unsung Heroes or Muddle-Headed Peaceniks? A Profile and Assessment of NGO Conflict Resolution Activity in the Northern Ireland "Peace Process"'. *Irish Studies in International Affairs*, 12 (2001), pp. 97–112.

Cochrane, F., and S. Dunn. 'CAIN: CSC Report: International Study of Peace/Conflict Resolution Organisations'. *Centre for the Study of Conflict, University of Ulster*, 23 September 1999, http://cain.ulst.ac.uk/csc/reports/cochrane99.htm (last accessed 23 December 2015).

Coleman, P. T. 'Conflict, Complexity, and Change: A Meta-Framework for Addressing Protracted, Intractable Conflicts – III'. *Journal of Peace Psychology*, 12:4 (2006), pp. 325–48.

Coleman, P. T. 'Paradigmatic Framing of Protracted, Intractable Conflict'. *Journal of Peace Psychology*, 10:3 (2004), pp. 197–235.

Coleman, P. T. 'Redefining Ripeness: A Social-Psychological Perspective'. *Peace and Conflict*, 3:1 (1997), pp. 81–103.

Collier, P., and A. Hoeffler. 'Greed and Grievance in Civil Wars', *Oxford Economic Papers*, 56:4 (2004), pp. 563–95.

Connolly, M., and J. Loughlin. 'Reflections on the Anglo-Irish Agreement'. *Government and Opposition*, 21:2 (1986), pp. 146–60.

Coogan, T. P. *The IRA*. New York: Palgrave Macmillan, 2002.

Cordell, K., and S. Wolff. *Ethnic Conflict*. Cambridge: Polity Press, 2010.

Cortazzi, H. *The Japanese Achievement*. London: Sidgwick & Jackson, 1990.
Coşkun, V. 'HDP Torn Between Violence and Politics', *Insight Turkey*, 17:4 (2015), pp. 47–55.
Craig, T. 'From Backdoors and Back Lanes to Backchannels: Reappraising British Talks with the Provisional IRA, 1970–1974', *Contemporary British History*, 26:1 (2012), pp. 97–117.
Crenshaw, M. *Explaining Terrorism: Causes, Processes, and Consequences*. Abingdon: Routledge, 2011.
Criss, N. B. 'Parameters of Turkish Foreign Policy under the AKP Governments'. *UNISCI Discussion Papers*, 23 (May 2010), pp. 9–22.
Crocker, C. A., F. O. Hampson and P. Aall. 'Introduction'. In C. A. Crocker, F. O. Hampson and P. Aall (eds), *Herding Cats: Multiparty Mediation in a Complex World*, pp. 3–18. Washington: United States Institute of Peace Press, 1999.
Cronin, A. K. *How Terrorism Ends: Understanding the Decline and Demise of Terrorist Campaigns*. Princeton: Princeton University Press, 2009.
Cronin, A. K. *When Should We Talk to Terrorists?* Washington: United States Institute of Peace Press, 2010.
Cunningham, D. E. 'Veto Players and Civil War Duration'. *American Journal of Political Science*, 50:4 (2006), pp. 875–92.
Curle, A. *Making Peace*. London: Tavistock, 1971.
Curle, A. 'New Challenges for Citizen Peacemaking', *Medicine and War*, 10:2 (1994), pp. 96–105.
Curran, D., J. K. Sebenius and M. Watkins. 'Two Paths to Peace: Contrasting George Mitchell in Northern Ireland with Richard Holbrooke in Bosnia-Herzegovina'. *Negotiation Journal*, 20:4 (2004), pp. 513–37.
Daily Sabah. 'Erdoğan Renounces Dolmabahçe Declaration, Says HDP Should Try its Best for PKK's Disarmament'. *Daily Sabah*, 17 July 2015, http://www.dailysabah.com/politics/2015/07/17/erdogan-renounces-dolmabahce-declaration-says-hdp-should-try-its-best-for-pkks-disarmament (last accessed 30 August 2015).
Dalai Lama. 'His Holiness the 14. Dalai Lama's Message on the Commemoration of the 1st Anniversary of September 11, 2001'. *tibet.net*, 1 September 2002, http://tibet.net/2002/09/his-holiness-the-dalai-lamas-message-on-the-commemoration-of-the-1st-anniversary-of-september-11-2001-2/ (last accessed 28 October 2016).
Darby, J. 'Northern Ireland: The Background to the Peace Process'. *Centre for the Study of Conflict, University of Ulster*, 23 September 2003, http://cain.ulst.ac.uk/events/peace/darby03.htm (last accessed 8 April 2016).

Darby, J., and R. MacGinty. *Contemporary Peacemaking: Conflict, Peace Processes, and Post-War Reconstruction*. London: Palgrave Macmillan, 2008.

Darby, J., and R. MacGinty. 'Northern Ireland: Long, Cold Peace'. In J. Darby and R. MacGinty (eds), *The Management of Peace Processes*, pp. 61–106. London: Macmillan, 2000.

Davidson, W. D., and J. V. Montville. 'Foreign Policy According to Freud'. *Foreign Policy*, 45 (1981), pp. 145–57.

De Breadun, D. *The Far Side of Revenge: Making Peace in Northern Ireland*. Cork: Collins, 2001.

De Tocqueville, A. *Democracy in America, Book Three* (Chapter XXII: Why Democratic Nations are Naturally Desirous of Peace, and Democratic Armies of War). New York: J. & H. G. Langley, 1840.

Dearden, L. 'Isis vs Islamic State vs Isil vs Daesh: What Do the Different Names Mean – and Why Does it Matter?', *Independent*, 23 September 2014, http://www.independent.co.uk/news/world/middle-east/isis-vs-islamic-state-vs-isil-vs-daesh-what-do-the-different-names-mean-9750629.html (last accessed 9 September 2019).

Deligöz, Ö. *KCK: Demokrasi Kılıfında Terör [KCK: Terrorism Under the Cover of Democracy]*. İstanbul: Timaş, 2012.

Demir, F. 'Debates over "Negotiations in Oslo" in Context of Finding Solutions to the Terrorism Problem and its Reflections on Turkish Media', *International Journal of Human Sciences*, 10:1 (2013), pp. 1314–31.

DHA. 'Eski MİT Müsteşarı Emre Taner: Yapamadık, Alamadık' [Former Undersecretary of MIT Emre Taner: We Could Not Make It and Take Him]. *DHA*, 9 November 2016, http://www.dha.com.tr/eski-mit-mustesari-emre-taner-yapamadik-alamadik_1376379.html (last accessed 9 November 2016).

Diamant, N. J. 'Conflict and Conflict Resolution in China: Beyond Mediation-Centered Approaches'. *Journal of Conflict Resolution*, 44:4 (2000), pp. 523–46.

Dixon, P. 'British Policy towards Northern Ireland 1969–2000', *British Journal of Politics and International Relations*, 3:3 (2001), pp. 340–68.

Dixon, P. *Northern Ireland: The Politics of War and Peace*, 2nd edn. London: Palgrave Macmillan, 2008.

Dochartaigh, N. O. 'The Role of an Intermediary in Back-channel Negotiation: Evidence from the Brendan Duddy Papers'. *Dynamics of Asymmetric Conflict*, 4:3 (2011), pp. 214–25.

Dochartaigh, N. O. 'Together in the Middle: Back-channel Negotiation in the Irish Peace Process'. *Journal of Peace Research*, 48:6 (2011), pp. 767–80.

Donat, Y. 'Anılar Denizi' [The Sea of Memories]. *Sabah*, 12 October 2011, http://www.sabah.com.tr/Yazarlar/donat/2011/10/12/anilar-denizi (last accessed 5 October 2014).

Donnelly-Cox, G., F. Donoghue and T. Hayes. 'Conceptualizing the Third Sector in Ireland, North and South', *Voluntas*, 12:3 (2001), pp. 195–204.

Doob, L. W., and W. J. Foltz. 'The Impact of a Workshop upon Grassroots Leaders in Belfast', *Journal of Conflict Resolution*, 18 (1974), pp. 237–56.

Doyle, M. W. 'Liberalism and World Politics'. *American Political Science Review*, 80:4 (1986), pp. 1151–69.

Druckman, D. 'Dimensions of International Negotiations: Structures, Processes, and Outcomes', *Group Decision and Negotiation*, 6 (1997), pp. 395–420.

Druckman, D., J. Martin, S. A. Nan and D. Yagcioglu. 'Dimensions of International Negotiation: A Test of Ikle's Typology'. *Group Decision and Negotiation*, 8 (1999), pp. 89–108.

Duffy, T. 'Peace Education in a Divided Society: Creating a Culture of Peace in Northern Ireland'. *Prospects*, 30:1 (2000), pp. 15–29.

Dunn, S., and J. Nolan-Haley. 'Conflict in Northern Ireland after the Good Friday Agreement'. *Fordham International Law Journal*, 22:4 (1998), pp. 1372–88.

Efegil, E. 'Turkey's New Approaches toward the PKK, Iraqi Kurds and the Kurdish Question'. *Insight Turkey*, 10:3 (2008), pp. 53–73.

Egeland, J. 'The Oslo Accord: Multi-party Facilitation through the Norwegian Channel'. In C. A. Crocker, F. O. Hampson and P. Aall (eds), *Herding Cats: Multi-party Mediation in a Complex World*, pp. 527–46. Washington: United States Institute of Peace Press, 1999.

EGM. 'Aranan Teröristler: Kırmızı Liste'. *T.C. Emniyet Genel Müdürlüğü*, 2016, http://www.teroraranan lar.pol.tr/detaylar/Sayfalar/kirmizi.aspx.

EGM. 'Aranan Teröristler: Mavi Liste'. *T.C. Emniyet Genel Müdürlüğü*, 2016, http://www.teroraranan lar.pol.tr/detaylar/Sayfalar/mavi.aspx.

Eisinger, P. K. 'The Conditions of Protest Behavior in American Cities', *American Political Science Review*, 67:1 (1973), pp. 11–28.

Ekici, N. *Ethnic Terrorism and the Case of the PKK: A Comparative Study*. Saarbrücken: VDM Publishing, 2010.

Encarnacion, O. G. 'Managing Ethnic Conflict in Spain'. *Orbis*, 47:1 (2004), pp. 89–105.

English, R. *Armed Struggle: The History of the IRA*. Oxford: Oxford University Press, 2003.

Ensaroğlu, Y. 'Turkey's Kurdish Question and the Peace Process'. *Insight Turkey*, 15:2 (2013), pp. 7–17.

Entessar, N. 'The Kurdish Mosaic of Discord'. *Third World Quarterly*, 11:4 (1989), pp. 83–100.

Erbaş, F. 'Farkında Bile Olmadan Karayılan'la Öpüşmüşüm'. *Akşam*, 15 March 2013, http://www.aksam.com.tr/siyaset/farkinda-bile-olmadan-karayilanla-opusmusum/haber-177405 (last accessed 14 January 2016).

Ergil, D. 'The Kurdish Question in Turkey', *Journal of Democracy*, 11:3 (2000), pp. 122–35.

Evans, J., and J. Tonge. 'Catholic, Irish and Nationalist: Evaluating the Importance of Ethno-national and Ethno-religious Variables in Determining Nationalist Political Allegiance in Northern Ireland'. *Nations and Nationalism*, 19:2 (2013), pp. 357–75.

Fairmichael, R. 'The Peace People Experience'. *Dawn Train*, 5 (1987).

Felstiner, W. L. F. 'Influences of Social Organization on Dispute Processing'. *Law and Society Review*, 9:1 (1974), pp. 63–94.

Field, A. 'The "New Terrorism": Revolution or Evolution?', *Political Studies Review*, 7 (2009), pp. 197–207.

Financial Times. 'Turkish Government and Kurds in Bid to Revitalise Peace Talks'. *Financial Times*, 28 February 2015, http://www.ft.com/cms/s/0/5d305c18-bf67-11e4-99f8-00144feab7de.html (last accesed 1 March 2015).

Fisher, R., and W. Ury. *Getting to Yes*. London: Business Books, 1996.

Fisher, R. J. 'Assessing the Contingency Model of Third-party Intervention in Successful Cases of Prenegotiation'. *Journal of Peace Research*, 44:3 (2007), pp. 311–29.

Fisher, R. J. 'Coordination between Track Two and Track One Diplomacy in Successful Cases of Prenegotiation'. *International Negotiation*, 11:1 (2006), pp. 65–89.

Fisher, R. J. 'Cyprus: The Failure of Mediation and the Escalation of an Identity-based Conflict to an Adversarial Impasse', *Journal of Peace Research*, 38:3 (2001), pp. 307–26.

Fisher, R. J. 'Developing the Field of Interactive Conflict Resolution: Issues in Training, Funding and Institutionalization'. *Political Psychology*, 14:1 (1993), pp. 123–38.

Fisher, R. J. *Interactive Conflict Resolution*. New York: Syracuse University Press, 1997.

Fisher, R. J. 'The Problem-Solving Workshop in Conflict Resolution'. In R. L. Merritt (ed.), *Communication in International Politics*, pp. 168–204. Urbana: University of Illinois Press, 1972.

Fisher, R. J. *The Social Psychology of Intergroup and International Conflict Resolution*. New York: Springer, 1990.

Fisher, R. J. 'Third Party Consultation as a Method of Intergroup Conflict Resolution', *Journal of Conflict Resolution*, 27:2 (1983), pp. 301–34.

Fisher, R. J., and L. Keashly. 'The Potential Complementarity of Mediation and Consultation within a Contingency Model of Third Party Intervention'. *Journal of Peace Research*, 28:1 (1991), pp. 29–42.

Fisher, R. J., and L. Keashly. 'Third Party Consultation as a Method of Intergroup and International Conflict Resolution', In R. J. Fisher (ed.), *The Social Psychology of Intergroup and International Conflict Resolution*, pp. 211–38. New York: Springer, 1990.

Fitzduff, M. *Beyond Violence: Conflict Resolution Process in Northern Ireland*. New York: United Nations University Press, 2002.

Fitzduff, M. 'Managing Community Relations and Conflict: Voluntary Organizations and Government and the Search for Peace'. In N. Acheson and A. Williamson (eds), *Voluntary Action and Social Policy in Northern Ireland*, pp. 63–81. Aldershot: Avebury, 1995.

Forest, J. J. F. 'Kidnapping by Terrorist Groups, 1970–2010: Is Ideological Orientation Relevant?'. *Crime & Delinquency*, 58:5 (2012), pp. 769–97.

Fortnight. 'Tom Caldwell's Initiative'. *Fortnight*, 36 (1972), pp. 5–6.

Gagnon, V. P. 'Ethnic Nationalism and International Conflict: The Case of Serbia', *International Security*, 19:3 (1994), pp. 130–66.

Galtung, J. 'Institutionalized Conflict Resolution: A Theoretical Paradigm', *Journal of Peace Research*, 2:4 (1965), pp. 348–97.

Galtung, J. *Peace by Peaceful Means: Peace and Conflict, Development and Civilization*. London: Sage, 1996.

Galtung, J. 'Twenty-Five Years of Peace Research: Ten Challenges and Some Responses'. *Journal of Peace Research*, 22:2 (1985), pp. 141–58.

Galtung, J. 'Violence, Peace, and Peace Research'. *Journal of Peace Research*, 6:3 (1969), pp. 167–91.

Galtung, J. 'What Does Professionalization Mean in Peace Research?' In L. Reychler, J. F. Deckard and K. H. Villanueva (eds), *Building Sustainable Futures: Enacting Peace and Development*, pp. 351–65. Bilbao: University of Deusto, 2009.

Galtung, J., and T. Duffy. 'Northern Ireland: Further Steps in the Dialogue'. *The Furrow*, 51:11 (2000), pp. 602–9.

Gardner, L. C., and T. Gittinger. *The Search for Peace in Vietnam, 1964–1968*. College Station: Texas A&M University Press, 2004.

Gartner, S. S., and J. Bercovitch. 'Overcoming Obstacles to Peace: The Contribution of Mediation to Short-Lived Conflict'. *International Studies Quarterly*, 50:4 (2006), pp. 819–40.

Gersick, C. J. G. 'Revolutionary Change Theories: A Multilevel Exploration of the Punctuated Equilibrium Paradigm'. *Academy of Management Review*, 16:1 (1991), pp. 10–36.

Gidron, B., and S. Katz. 'The International Study of Peace/Conflict Resolution Organizations: Preliminary Findings'. Paper presented at the *Third Conference of the International Society of Third Sector Research, Geneva, 7 September 1998*.

Gidron, B., S. N. Katz and Y. Hasenfeld. *Mobilizing for Peace: Conflict Resolution in Northern Ireland, Israel/Palestine, and South Africa*. Oxford: Oxford University Press, 2002.

Giugni, M., D. McAdam and C. Tilly. *How Social Movements Matter*, vol. 10. Minneapolis: University of Minnesota Press, 1999.

Goodman, M. S. *The Official History of the Joint Intelligence Committee*. Abingdon: Routledge, 2014.

Gormley-Heenan, C., and A. Aughey. 'Northern Ireland and Brexit: Three Effects on "the Border in the Mind"', *The British Journal of Politics and International Relations*, 19:3 (2017), pp. 497–511.

Greenhouse, C. J. 'Mediation: A Comparative Approach'. *Man*, 20:1 (1985), pp. 90–114.

The Guardian. 'Colombia Referendum: Voters Reject Peace Deal with FARC Guerrillas'. *The Guardian*, 3 October 2016, https://www.theguardian.com/world/2016/oct/02/colombia-referendum-rejects-peace-deal-with-farc (last accessed 7 November 2018).

The Guardian. 'Turkey will not Cooperate in US Support for Kurds in Syria, Says Erdogan'. *The Guardian*, 19 October 2014, https://www.theguardian.com/world/2014/oct/19/turkey-will-not-cooperate-us-support-kurds-erdogan (last accessed 27 December 2019).

Guelke, A. (1995). *The Age of Terrorism and International Political System*. London: I. B. Tauris.

Guelke, A. 'Negotiations and Peace Processes'. In J. Darby and R. MacGinty (eds), *Contemporary Peacemaking: Conflict, Violence, Peace Processes*, pp. 53–64. New York: Macmillan, 2003.

Güller, M. A. *Hükümet-PKK Görüşmeleri (1986–2011) [The Government-PKK Negotiations (1986–2011)]*. İstanbul: Kaynak Yayınları, 2012.

Gunter, M. M. 'The Continuing Kurdish Problem in Turkey after Ocalan's Capture'. *Third World Quarterly*, 21:5 (2000), pp. 849–69.

Gunter, M. M. *The Kurds and the Future of Turkey*. New York: Palgrave Macmillan, 1997.

Gunter, M. M. 'Reopening Turkey's Closed Kurdish Opening?' *Middle East Policy*, 20:2 (2013), pp. 88–98.

Gursel, K. 'Erdogan Asks "Wise People" to Make Case for Peace'. *Al-Monitor*, 15 April 2013, http://www.al-monitor.com/pulse/fr/originals/2013/04/erdogan-wise-people-commission-peace-process.html (last accessed 24 June 2016).

Gurses, M. *Anatomy of a Civil War*. Ann Arbor: University of Michigan Press, 2018.

Haas, R. N. *Conflicts Unending: The United States and Regional Disputes*. New Haven: Yale University Press, 1990.

HaberTürk. 'Barış ve Çözüm Sürecinde Geri Dönmek Mümkün Değil'. *HaberTürk*, 29 April 2013, https://www.haberturk.com/polemik/haber/839973-baris-ve-cozum-surecinde-geri-donmek-mumkun-degil (last accessed 12 August 2016).

Hadfield, B. 'The Anglo-Irish Agreement 1985 – Blue Print or Green Print?' *Northern Ireland Legal Quarterly*, 37:1 (1986), pp. 1–28.

Hafıza Merkezi. 'Çocuklar Aynı Çatının Altında Derneği'. *Hafıza Merkezi*, 15 November 2015, http://yeni.hafiza-merkezi.org/calisma/sivil-toplumun-kurt-sorununun-cozumune-etkin-katilimi-icin-kapasite-gelistirme/turkiyeden-stklar/cocuklar-ayni-catinin-altinda-dernegi-caca/ (last accessed 15 December 2015).

Hahn, J. *Situation in the South East of Turkey*, SPEECH/16/120. Speech given at European Commission, 2016.

Haines, J. *The Politics of Power*. London: Coronet Books, 1977.

Hakyemez, S. 'Turkey's Failed Peace Process with the Kurds: A Different Explanation'. *Middle East Brief*, 111 (2017), pp. 1–10.

Halpin, P. 'Sinn Fein Calls for Irish Unity Poll as Brexit Fallout Begins', *Reuters*, 24 June 2016, https://www.reuters.com/article/us-britain-eu-ireland/sinn-fein-calls-for-irish-unity-poll-as-brexit-fallout-begins-idUSKCN0ZA0NX (last accessed 5 January 2020).

Hammer, J. 'In Northern Ireland, Getting Past the Troubles'. *Smithsonian Magazine*, 1 March 2009, http://www.smithsonianmag.com/people-places/in-northern-ireland-getting-past-the-troubles-52862004/?no-ist (last accessed 16 July 2013).

Hancock, L. E. 'The Northern Irish Peace Process: From Top to Bottom', *International Studies Review*, 10 (2008), pp. 203–38.

Hancock, L. E. 'To Act or Wait: A Two-Stage View of Ripeness'. *International Studies Perspectives*, 2 (2001), pp. 195–205.

Hanley, B. '"I Ran Away"? The IRA and 1969'. *History Ireland*, 17;4 (2009), pp. 24–7.

Hartzell, C. A. 'Explaining the Stability of Negotiated Settlements to Intrastate Wars'. *Journal of Conflict Resolution*, 43:1 (1999), pp. 3–20.

Hasenfeld, Y. *Human Services as Complex Organizations*. London: Sage, 2010.

Hashim, A. *When Counterinsurgency Wins: Sri Lanka's Defeat of the Tamil Tigers*. Philadelphia: University of Pennsylvania Press, 2013.

Hauss, C. *International Conflict Resolution* (2nd ed.). London: Continuum, 2010.

Haverty, D. 'With Parliament Voting for Brexit, is Irish Unification Inevitable?', *Foreign Policy*, 9 January 2010, https://foreignpolicy.com/2020/01/09/irish-unification-brexit/ (last accessed 10 January 2020).

Hayes, R. E., S. R. Kaminski and S. M. Beres. 'Negotiating the Non-negotiable: Dealing with Absolutist Terrorists', *International Negotiation*, 8:3 (2003), pp. 451–67.

Hayward, K., and M. C. Murphy. 'The EU's Influence on the Peace Process and Agreement in Northern Ireland in Light of Brexit', *Ethnopolitics*, 17:3 (2018), pp. 276–91.

HDN. 'Chronology of Oslo Dialogues with PKK'. *Hürriyet Daily News*, 29 September 2012, http://www.hurriyetdailynews.com/chronology-of-oslo-dialogues-with-pkk.aspx?pageID=238&nID=31190&NewsCatID=338 (last accessed 3 March 2016).

HDN. 'CHP Reveals "Documents" of Collapsed PKK-Gov't Talks'. *Hürriyet Daily News*, 22 September 2015, http://www.hurriyetdailynews.com/chp-reveals-documents-of-collapsed-pkk-govt-talks-.aspx?pageID=238&nID=90207&NewsCatID=338 (last accessed 3 March 2016).

HDN. 'Kurdish Peace Call Made Amid Row on Security Bill'. *Hürriyet Daily News*, 28 February 2015, http://www.hurriyetdailynews.com/kurdish-peace-call-made-amid-row-on-security-bill.aspx?pageID=238&nID=78999&NewsCatID=338 (last accessed 28 February 2015).

HDP. 'History of Kurdish Political Parties in Turkey'. *HDP Europe*, 2015, http://en.hdpeurope.com/?page_id=537 (last accessed 1 July 2015).

Hennessey, T. *The First Northern Ireland Peace Process: Power-Sharing, Sunningdale and the IRA Ceasefires, 1972–76*. London: Palgrave Macmillan, 2015.

Heper, M. *The State and Kurds in Turkey: The Question of Assimilation*. London: Palgrave Macmillan, 2007.

Herbolzheimer, K., and E. Leslie. *Innovation in Mediation Support: The International Contact Group in Mindanao*. 2013, http://www.c-r.org/downloads/PracticePaper_MindanaoICG_ConciliationResources_0.pdf (last accessed 1 May 2014).

Hinnebusch, R., and Ö Tür. *Turkey-Syria Relations: Between Enmity and Amity*. Farnham: Ashgate, 2013.

Holsti, K. J. *Peace and War: Armed Conflicts and International Order 1648–1989*. Cambridge: Cambridge University Press, 1991.

Holsti, K. J. 'Resolving International Conflicts: A Taxonomy of Behaviour and Some Figures on Procedures'. *Journal of Conflict Resolution*, 10:3 (1966), pp. 272–96.

Holsti, K. J. *The State, War, and the State of War*. Cambridge: Cambridge University Press, 1996.

Hopmann, P. T. 'Two Paradigms of Negotiation: Bargaining and Problem Solving'. *Annals of the American Academy of Political and Social Science*, 542 (1995), pp. 24–47.

HRW. (2016). '"Turkey". World Report 2016: Events of 2015'. *Human Rights Watch*, 2016, https://www.hrw.org/world-report/2016/country-chapters/turkey (last accessed 2 January 2020).

Hughes, J., and C. Knox. 'For Better or Worse? Community Relations Initiatives in Northern Ireland'. *Peace & Change*, 22:3 (1997), pp. 330–55.

Hume, J., and G. Adams. 'Joint statement issued by Sinn Féin President Mr Gerry Adams MP and the Social Democratic and Labour Party Leader Mr John Hume MP'. *Sinn Féin*, 18 July 1997, http://www.sinnfein.ie/contents/15222 (last accessed 2 February 2016).

Hürriyet. '"Akil" Rapor Tamam', *Hürriyet*, 27 June 2013, http://www.hurriyet.com.tr/akil-rapor-tamam-23595419 (last accessed 30 August 2013).

Hürriyet. '6-7 Ekim'in Bilançosu 50 Ölü'. *Hürriyet*, 6 November 2014, http://www.hurriyet.com.tr/6-7-ekim-in-aci-bilancosu-50-olu-27525777 (last accessed 21 February 2015).

Hürriyet. 'İşte Öcalan'ın Mesajı'. *Hürriyet*, 21 March 2013, http://www.hurriyet.com.tr/iste-ocalanin-mesaji-22866213 (last accessed 1 May 2013).

Hürriyet. '33 Şehitli O Günden Beri Hiç Kahkaha Atamadım'. *Hürriyet*, 9 April 2012, http://www.hurriyet.com.tr/33-sehitli-o-gunden-beri-hic-kahkaha-atamadim-20303221 (last accessed 1 May 2014).

Hylton, R. 'Opportunities for Peacemaking'. *The Furrow*, 33:1 (1982), pp. 29–35.

Hylton, R. 'The Peace-making Role of Christians in Ireland and Britain'. *The Furrow*, 32:5 (1981), pp. 333–5.

ICC. 'Turkey: The PKK and a Kurdish Settlement', *International Crisis Group*, 11 September 2012, http://www.crisisgroup.org/~/media/Files/europe/turkey-cyprus/turkey/219-turkey-the-pkk-and-a-kurdish-settlement.pdf (last accessed 24 January 2014).

Idoiaga, G. E. *The Basque Conflict: New Ideas and Prospects for Peace*. Washington: United States Institute of Peace Press, 2006, pp. 1–12.

Ikle, F. C. *How Nations Negotiate*. New York: Harper, 1964.

Ikle, F. C., and N. Leites. 'Political Negotiation as a Process of Modifying Utilities'. *Journal of Conflict Resolution*, 6:1 (1962), pp. 19–28.

İmset, İ. G. *The PKK: A Report on Separatist Violence in Turkey (1973–1992)*. Ankara: Turkish Daily News, 1992.

Ingraham, J. 'The Irish Peace Process', *University of Ulster CAIN Web Service*, 1998, http://cain.ulst.ac.uk/events/peace/talks.htm.

IRA. 'Irish Republican Army Statement Ending the Ceasefire'. *University of Ulster CAIN Web Service*, 9 February 1996, http://cain.ulst.ac.uk/events/peace/docs/ira9296.htm (last accessed 1 February 2016).

IRA. 'Irish Republican Army (IRA) Ceasefire Statement'. *University of Ulster CAIN Web Service*, 19 July 1997, http://cain.ulst.ac.uk/events/peace/docs/ira19797.htm (last accessed 10 February 2016).

Jackson, R. 'Constructivism and Conflict Resolution', In J. Bercovitch, V. Kremenyuk and I. W. Zartman (eds), *The Sage Handbook of Conflict Resolution*, pp. 172–90. London: Sage, 2009.

Jackson, R. 'Successful Negotiation in International Violent Conflict'. *Journal of Peace Research*, 37:3 (2000), pp. 323–43.

Jacoby, T., & A. Özerdem. *Peace in Turkey 2023: The Question of Human Security and Conflict Transformation*. Lanham: Lexington Books, 2013.

Jenkins, G. *Context and Circumstance: The Turkish Military and Politics*. Oxford: Taylor and Francis, 2001.

Jeong, H.-W. *Peace and Conflict Studies an Introduction*. Farnham: Ashgate, 2000.

Kadıoğlu, İ. A. 'Challenges of International Negotiations in the Syrian Civil War', *Turkish Journal of Middle Eastern Studies*, 7:1 (2020).

Kadıoğlu, İ. A. (2016, 15/02). 'The End of Turkey's Kurdish "Peace Process"?' University of Nottingham, 15 February 2016, http://nottspolitics.org/2016/02/15/theendofturkeyskurdishpeaceprocess/ (last accessed 16 February 2016).

Kadıoğlu, İ. A. 'Great Effort, Little Help? Peace and Conflict Resolution Organisations in Northern Ireland and Turkey'. *Conflict, Security & Development*, 18:3 (2018), pp. 207–32.

Kadıoğlu, İ. A. 'Not Our War: Iraq, Iran and Syria's Approaches towards the PKK', *The Rest: Journal of Politics and Development*, 9:1 (2019), pp. 44–57.

Kadıoğlu, İ. A. 'The Oslo Talks: Revealing the Turkish Government's Secret Negotiations with the PKK'. *Studies in Conflict & Terrorism*, 42:10 (2019), pp. 915–33.

Kadıoğlu, İ. A. 'The Proxy Warfare in Syria', *Political Reflection*, 4:4 (2018), pp. 10–15.

Kadıoğlu, İ. A. 'Yaşamın Sınırını Geçmek: Avrupa Birliği Suriyeli Sığınmacılar İçin Güvenli Bir Liman Mı?' [Crossing the Border of Life: Is the European Union a Safe Haven for Syrian Refugees?]. In E. Özensel, G. Bozbaş, F. Kaleci and N. Salur (eds), *Ortadoğu'da Göç Hareketleri ve Değişen Dinamikler [Migration Movements in the Middle East and Changing Dynamics]*, pp. 48–78. Konya: Aybil, 2018.

Kaliber, A., and N. Tocci. 'Civil Society and the Transformation of Turkey's Kurdish Question'. *Security Dialogue*, 41:2 (2010), pp. 191–215.

Kanlı, Y. 'The Turkish Deep State'. *Hürriyet Daily News*, 29 January 2007, http://www.hurriyetdailynews.com/the-turkish-deep-state.aspx?pageID=438&n=the-turkish-deep-state-2007-01-29 (last accessed 18 December 2011).

Kapmaz, C. *Öcalan'ın İmralı Günleri [İmralı Days of Öcalan]*. İstanbul: İthaki, 2011.

Karayılan, M. *Bir Savaşın Anatomisi: Kürdistan'da Askeri Çizgi*. İstanbul: Gün Matbaacılık, 2014.

Karayılan, M. 'Karayılan: Son Kararımız . . .' *Rudaw*, 14 July 2015, http://rudaw.net/turkish/middleeast/turkey/140720152 (last accessed 31 July 2015).

Kaufman, E. 'Sharing the Experience of Citizens' Diplomacy with Partners in Conflict'. In J. Davies and E. Kaufman (eds), *Second Track/Citizens' Diplomacy: Concepts and Techniques for Conflict Transformation*, pp. 183–223. Oxford: Rowman & Littlefield, 2003.

Kaye, D. D. *Talking to the Enemy: Track Two Diplomacy in the Middle East and South Asia*. Santa Monica: RAND, 2007.

Kaye, D. D. 'Track Two Diplomacy and Regional Security in the Middle East'. *International Negotiation*, 6:1 (2001), pp. 49–77.

KDGM. *Demokratikleşme Paketi*. Ankara: T. C. Başbakanlık Kamu Düzeni ve Güvenliği Müsteşarlığı, 2013.

Kelman, H. C. 'Creating the Conditions for Israeli-Palestinian Negotiations'. *Journal of Conflict Resolution*, 26:1 (1982), pp. 39–75.

Kelman, H. C. 'Group Processes in the Resolution of International Conflicts: Experiences from the Israeli-Palestinian Case'. *American Psychologist*, 52 (1997), pp. 212–20.

Kelman, H. C. 'Informal Mediation by the Scholar/Practitioner'. In J. Bercovitch and J. Z. Rubin (eds), *Mediation in International Relations*, pp. 64–96. New York: St. Martin's Press, 1992.

Kelman, H. C. 'Interactive Problem-Solving: A Social-Pyschological Approach to Conflict Resolution'. In J. W. Burton and F. Dukes (eds), *Conflict: Readings in Management and Resolution*, pp. 199–215. London: Macmillan, 1990.

Kelman, H. C. 'Interactive Problem Solving: An Approach to Conflict Resolution and Its Application in the Middle East'. *Political Science and Politics*, 31:2 (1998), pp. 190–8.

Kelman, H. C. 'The Interactive Problem-Solving Approach'. In C. A. Crocker, F. O. Hampson and P. Aall (eds), *Managing Global Chaos: Sources of and Responses to International Conflict*, pp. 500–20. Washington: Institute of Peace Press, 1996.

Kelman, H. C. 'Interactive Problem Solving as a Tool for Second Track Diplomacy'. In J. Davies and E. Kaufman (eds), *Second Track/Citizens' Diplomacy: Concepts and Techniques for Conflict Transformation*, pp. 82–105. Oxford: Rowman & Littlefield, 2003.

Kelman, H. C. 'Interactive Problem Solving: Changing Political Culture in the Pursuit of Conflict Resolution'. *Peace and Conflict*, 16 (2010), pp. 389–413.

Kelman, H. C. 'The Political Psychology of the Israeli-Palestinian Conflict: How Can We Overcome the Barriers to a Negotiated Solution?' *Political Psychology*, 8:3 (1987), pp. 347–63.

Kelman, H. C. 'Reconciliation as Identity Change: A Social-Psychological Perspective'. In Y. Bar-Siman-Tov (ed.), *From Conflict Resolution to Reconciliation*, pp. 111–24. New York: Oxford University Press, 2004.

Kelman, H. C. 'Social-psychological Dimensions of International Conflict'. In J. L. Rasmussen and I. W. Zartman (eds), *Peacemaking in International Conflict: Methods and Techniques*, pp. 191–237. Washington: United States Institute of Peace Press, 1997.

Kennedy-Pipe, C., and A. Mumford. 'Is Torture Ever Justified? Torture, Rights and Rules from Northern Ireland to Iraq'. In A. F. Lang and A. R. Beattie (eds), *War, Torture and Terrorism*, pp. 54–68. Abingdon: Routledge, 2009.

Keohane, R. O. *Neorealism and Its Critics*. New York: Columbia University Press, 1986.

Keyman, F. 'Çözüm Süreci, Müzakere, Güven ve Demokrasi'. In M. Aktaş (ed.), *Çatışma Çözümleri ve Barış*, pp. 15–28. İstanbul: İletişim, 2014.

Kili, S. 'Kemalism in Contemporary Turkey'. *International Political Science Review*, 1:3 (1980), pp. 381–404.

Kirişci, K., and G. M. Winrow. *The Kurdish Question and Turkey: An Example of a Trans-State Ethnic Conflict*. London: Frank Cass, 1997.

Kızılkaya, M. *Barışa Katlanmak: Bir Akilin 83 Günü*. İstanbul: Alfa Yayınları, 2015.

Kleiboer, M. 'Ripeness of Conflict: A Fruitful Notion'. *Journal of Peace Research*, 31 (1994), pp. 109–16.

Knox, C. 'See No Evil, Hear No Evil'. *British Journal of Criminology*, 42:1 (2002), pp. 164–85.

Knox, C., and J. Hughes. 'Crossing the Divide: Community Relations in Northern Ireland'. *Journal of Peace Research*, 33:1 (1996), pp. 83–98.

Knox, C., and P. Quirk. *Peace Building in Northern Ireland, Israel and South Africa: Transition, Transformation and Reconciliation*. London: Palgrave Macmillan, 2000.

Koch, K. F. *War and Peace in Jalemo*. Cambridge, MA: Harvard University Press, 1974.

Kochan, T. A., and T. Jick. 'The Public Sector Mediation Process'. *Journal of Conflict Resolution*, 22:2 (1978), pp. 209–40.

Kraslow, D., and S. H. Loory. *The Secret Search for Peace in Vietnam*, vol. 152. New York: Random House, 1968.

Kremenyuk, V. A. *International Negotiation: Analysis, Approaches, Issues*. San Francisco: Jossey-Bass, 2002.

Kressel, K., and D. G. Pruitt. *Mediation Research*. San Francisco: Jossey-Bass, 1989.

Kriesberg, L. *Constructive Conflicts: From Escalation to Resolution*. Lanham: Rowman & Littlefield, 1998.

Kriesberg, L. 'Coordinating Intermediary Peace Efforts'. *Negotiation Journal*, 12:4 (1996), pp. 341–52.

Kriesberg, L. 'The Evolution of Conflict Resolution', In J. Bercovitch, V. Kremenyuk and I. W. Zartman (eds), *The Sage Handbook of Conflict Resolution*, pp. 15–32. London: Sage, 2008.

Kriesberg, L. *International Conflict Resolution: The US-USSR and Middle East Cases*. New Haven: Yale University Press, 1992.

Kriesberg, L. 'The State of the Art in Conflict Transformation'. In A. Beatrix, M. Fischer and H.-J. Giessmann (eds), *Advancing Conflict Transformation: The Berghof Handbook II*, pp. 49–74. Opladen: Barbara Budrich Publishers, 2011.

Kriesberg, L. 'Timing and the Initiation of De-Escalation Moves'. *Negotiation Journal*, 3:4 (1987), pp. 375–84.

Kuenne, R. L. 'Conflict Management in Mature Rivalry'. *Journal of Conflict Resolution*, 33:3 (1989), pp. 554–66.

Laqueur, W. *No End to War, Terrorism in the Twenty-First Century*. London: Continuum International Publishing, 2004.

Lavery, B. 'I.R.A. Apologizes for Civilian Deaths in Its 30-Year Campaign'. *New York Times*, 17 July 2002, http://www.nytimes.com/2002/07/17/world/ira-apologizes-for-civilian-deaths-in-its-30-year-campaign.html (last accessed 16 July 2013).

Lebow, R. N. 'Generating Learning and Conflict Management'. *International Journal*, 40:4 (1985), pp. 555–85.

Lederach, J. P. *Building Peace: Sustainable Reconciliation in Divided Societies*. Washington: United States Institute of Peace Press, 1997.

Lederach, J. P. *Preparing for Peace: Conflict Transformation across Cultures*. Syracuse: Syracuse University Press, 1995.

Licklider, R. 'The Consequences of Negotiated Settlements in Civil Wars, 1945–1993'. *The American Political Science Review*, 89:3 (1995), pp. 681–90.

Lieberfeld, D. 'Evaluating the Contributions of Track-two Diplomacy to Conflict Termination in South Africa, 1984–90'. *Journal of Peace Research*, 39:3 (2002), pp. 355–72.

Little, D. *Peacemakers in Action: Profiles of Religion in Conflict Resolution*. Cambridge: Cambridge University Press, 2006.

Love, M. T. *Peace Building through Reconciliation in Northen Ireland*. Aldershot: Avebury, 1995.

Lynch, T. J. 'The Gerry Adams Visa in Anglo-American Relations'. *Irish Studies in International Affairs*, 14:1 (2003), pp. 33–44.

McAdam, D., J. D. McCarthy and M. N. Zald. *Comparative Perspectives on Social Movements*. New York: Cambridge University Press, 1996.

McDaid, S. *Template for Peace, Northern Ireland, 1972–75*. Manchester: Manchester University Press, 2013.

McDonald, J. W. 'Further Exploration of Track Two Diplomacy'. In L. Kriesberg and S. Thorson (eds), *Timing the De-escalation of International Conflicts*, pp. 201–20. Syracuse: Syracuse University Press, 1991.

McDonald, J. W., and D. B. Bendahmane. *Conflict Resolution: Track Two Diplomacy*. Washington: Foreign Service Institute, US Department of State, 1987.

McDowall, D. *Modern History of the Kurds*. London: I. B. Tauris, 2004.

McGarry, J., and B. O'Leary. *Explaining Northern Ireland*. Oxford: Blackwell, 1995.

McGarry, J., and B. O'Leary. *The Politics of Ethnic Conflict Regulation*. London: Routledge, 2013.

McGarry, J., and B. O'Leary. 'Power Shared After the Deaths of Thousands'. In R. Taylor (ed.), *Consociational Theory*, pp. 15–84. Abingdon: Routledge, 2009.

MacGinty, R. '"Biting the Bullet": Decommissioning in the Transition from War to Peace in Northern Ireland'. *Irish Studies in International Affairs*, 10 (1999), pp. 237–47.

McGlynn, C., U. Niens, E. Cairns and M. Hewstone. 'Moving out of Conflict: The Contribution of Integrated Schools in Northern Ireland to Identity, Attitudes, Forgiveness and Reconciliation'. *Journal of Peace Education*, 1:2 (2004), pp. 147–63.

McGuire, M. *To Take Arms: A Year in The Provisional IRA*. London: Macmillan, 1973.

McKeown, C., and P. McLachlan. *Strategy for Peace*. Belfast: Peace People, 1977.

McKittrick, D., S. Kelters, B. Feeney, C. Thornton and D. McVey. *Lost Lives: The Stories of the Men, Women and Children Who Died as a Result of the Northern Ireland Troubles*. Edinburgh: Mainstream Publishing, 2007.

McKool, K. 'Valuable Lesson in British Duplicity'. *An Phoblacht*, 6 August 1987.

McVeigh, R., and B. Rolston. 'From Good Friday to Good Relations: Sectarianism, Racism and the Northern Ireland State'. *Institute of Race Relations*, 48:4 (2007), pp. 1–23.

Major, J. *John Major: The Autobiography*. New York: HarperCollins, 2000.

Mallie, E., and D. McKittrick. *The Fight for Peace: The Secret Story Behind the Irish Peace Process*. London: Reed International, 1997.

Mango, A. *Turkey and the War on Terror: For Forty Years We Fought Alone*. Abingdon: Routledge, 2005.

Mapendere, J. 'Track One and a Half Diplomacy and the Complementarity of Tracks'. *Culture of Peace Online Journal*, 2:1 (2005), pp. 66–81.

Marcus, A. *Kan ve İnanç*. İstanbul: İletişim, 2015.

Mayer, B. 'The Dynamics of Power in Mediation and Negotiation'. *Mediation Quarterly*, 16 (1987), pp. 75–86.

Megahey, A. *The Irish Protestant Churches in the Twentieth Century*. New York: Macmillan, 2000.

Melaugh, M. 'Sutton Index of Deaths'. *Centre for the Study of Conflict, University of Ulster*, 2002, http://cain.ulst.ac.uk/sutton/chron/index.html (last accessed 17 September 2015).

Meyer, M. 'Organizational Identity, Political Contexts, and SMO Action: Explaining the Tactical Choices Made by Peace Organizations in Israel, Northern Ireland, and South Africa'. *Social Movement Studies*, 3:2 (2004), pp. 167–97.

Milliyet. 'Bakan Atalay "Kürt Açılımını" Açıkladı'. *Milliyet*, 31 August 2009, http://www.milliyet.com.tr/bakan-atalay--font-color-red-kurt-acilimini--font--acikladi/siyaset/siyasetdetay/31.08.2009/1133933/default.htm (last accessed 15 May 2015).

Milliyet. 'Son On Yıldaki Şehit Sayımız'. *Milliyet* Blog, 22 June 2012, http://blog.milliyet.com.tr/son-on-yildaki-sehit-sayimiz/Blog/?BlogNo=368048 (last accessed 8 April 2014).

Mitchell, G. *Making Peace*. London: William Heinemann, 1999.

Modelski, G. 'International Settlement of Internal War'. In J. N. Rosenau (ed.), *International Aspects of Civil Strife*, pp. 122–53. Princeton: Princeton University Press, 1964.

Moloney, E. *A Secret History of the IRA*. London: Penguin Books, 2002.

Montalvo, J. G., and M. Reynal-Qerol. 'Ethnic Polarization, Potential Conflict, and Civil Wars', *American Economic Review*, 95:3 (2005), pp. 796–816.

Montville, J. V. 'The Arrow and the Olive Branch: A Case for Track-Two Diplomacy'. In J. W. McDonald and D. B. Bendahmane (eds), *Conflict Resolution: Track-Two Diplomacy*, pp. 161–75. Washington: Foreign Service Institute, US Department of State, 1987.

Montville, J. V. 'Track Two Diplomacy: The Work of Healing History'. *Whitehead Journal of Diplomacy and International Relations*, 7 (2006), pp. 15–25.

Moore, J. 'Paramilitary Prisoners and the Peace Process in Northern Ireland'. In A. O'Day (ed.), *Political Violence in Northern Ireland: Conflict and Conflict Resolution*, pp. 81–94. Westport: Praeger, 1997.

Morgenthau, H. J. 'Six Principles of Political Realism'. In H. J. Morgenthau (ed.), *From Politics Among Nations: The Struggle for Power and Peace*, pp. 34–8. New York: Alfred A. Knopf, 1973.

Morrison, D. 'By Ballot and Bullet'. *An Problacht/Republican News*, 5 November 1981.

Muircheartaigh, J. O. 'The Death of Ruairí O Bradaigh and the Feakle Peace talks of 1974'. *Clare People*, 12 June 2013, http://www.clarepeople.com/2013/06/11/the-death-of-ruairi-o-bradaigh-and-the-feakle-peace-talks-of-1974/ (last accessed 30 July 2015).

Mumford, A. *The Counter-insurgency Myth: The British Experience of Irregular Warfare*. Abingdon: Routledge, 2012.

Mumford, A. 'Covert Peacemaking: Clandestine Negotiations and Backchannels with the Provisional IRA during the Early "Troubles", 1972–1976'. *The Journal of Imperial and Commonwealth History*, 39:4 (2011), pp. 633–48.

Murray, G., and J. Tonge. *Sinn Fein and the SDLP: From Alienation to Participation*. London: C. Hurst, 2005.

Nagle, J., and M.-A. C. Clancy. 'Constructing a Shared Public Identity in Ethno-Nationally Divided Societies: Comparing Consociational and Transformationist Perspectives'. *Nations and Nationalism*, 18:1 (2012), pp. 78–97.

Nan, S. A. 'Complementarity and Coordination of Conflict Resolution Efforts in the Conflicts over Abkhazia, South Ossetia, and Transnistria'. PhD Dissertation, George Mason University, 1999.

Nan, S. A. 'Track One-and-a-Half Diplomacy: Contributions to Georgia-South Ossetian Peacemaking', In R. J. Fisher (ed.), *Paving the Way*, pp. 161–73. Lanham: Lexington Books, 2005.

Nan, S. A. 'Track One and a Half Diplomacy: Searching for Political Agreement in the Caucasus'. In M. Fitzduff and C. Church (eds), *NGOs at the Table: Strategies for Influencing Policies in Areas of Conflict*, pp. 57–76. Oxford: Rowman & Littlefield, 2004.

Nan, S. A. *Track I Diplomacy*. 2003, http://www.beyondintractability.org/essay/track1-diplomacy (last accessed 1 November 2011).

Nan, S. A., and A. Strimling. 'Coordination in Conflict Prevention, Conflict Resolution and Peacebuilding', *International Negotiation*, 11 (2006), pp. 1–6.

Nardin, T. 'Theories of Conflict Management'. *Peace Research Reviews*, 4:2 (1971), pp. 1–93.

Neumann, P. R. 'Negotiating with Terrorists'. *Foreign Affairs*, 86:1 (2007), pp. 128–38.

Northern Ireland Office. *Statement by the Independent Chairmen of the Northern Ireland Talks*. Belfast: Northern Ireland Office, 1996.

NTV. 'İşte Demokratikleşme Paketi'. *NTV*, 30 September 2013, http://www.ntv. com.tr/turkiye/iste-demokratiklesme-paketi,E5m3xY2fFEeYMJ7ZCLopSA (last accessed 1 November 2013).

NTV. 'Ömer Çelik: Kılıçdaroğlu'nun Belgeleri Açıklamasını Bekliyoruz'. *NTV*, 22 October 2015, http://www.ntv.com.tr/turkiye/omer-celik-kilicdaroglunun-belgeleri-aciklamasini-bekliyoruz,JfnFVsX-5kmraMZ6CXGF2g (last accessed 1 May 2016).

NYT. 'Kurdish Rebel Group to Withdraw from Turkey'. *New York Times*, 25 April 2013, http://www.nytimes.com/2013/04/26/world/europe/kurdish-rebel-group-to-withdraw-from-turkey.html (last accessed 2 May 2013).

NYT. 'Trump to Arm Syrian Kurds, Even as Turkey Strongly Objects'. *New York Times*, 9 May 2017, https://www.nytimes.com/2017/05/09/us/politics/trump-kurds-syria-army.html?mcubz=0&_r=2 (last accessed 16 May 2017).

O'Donnell, D. *The Peace People of Northern Ireland*. Victoria: Widescope, 1977.

O'Dowd, L., and C. McCall. 'Escaping the Cage of Ethno-National Conflict in Northern Ireland? The Importance of Transnational Networks', *Ethnopolitics*, 7:1 (2008), pp. 81–99.

O'Duffy, B. 'British and Irish Conflict Regulation from Sunningdale to Belfast. Part II: Playing for a Draw 1985–1999'. *Nations and Nationalism*, 6:3 (2000), pp. 399–435.

O'Hagan, S. 'The Real Maze Men Speak'. *The Guardian*, 19 October 2008, http://www.theguardian.com/film/2008/oct/19/northernireland (last accessed 26 February 2016).

O'Kane, E. 'Anglo-Irish Relations and the Northern Ireland Peace Process: From Exclusion to Inclusion'. *Contemporary British History*, 18:1 (2004), pp. 78–99.

O'Kane, E. 'When Can Conflicts be Resolved? A Critique of Ripeness'. *Civil Wars*, 8:3–4 (2006), pp. 268–84.

Öcalan, A. 'Demokratik Anayasal Çözüm Gelişmezse Halkın Direnme Hakkı Vardır!' [If a Democratic and Constitutional Resolution Is Not Applied, Public Has a Right to Resist!]. *PKK*, 18 July 2011, http://www.pkkonline.com/tr/index.php?sys=article&artID=932 (last accessed 20 June 2015).

Öcalan, A. *Demokratik Kurtuluş ve Özgür yaşamı İnşa (İmralı Notları)*. Neuss: Mezopotamya Yayınları, 2015.

Öcalan, A. 'Öcalan's Newroz Message'. *BiaNet*, 21 March 2013, http://bianet.org/bianet/diger/163204-ocalan-s-newroz-message (last accessed 22 March 2013).

Öcalan, A. 'Önümüzde İki Yol Var: Demokratik Anayasal Çözüm ile Devrimci Halk Savaşı'. *PKK*, 27 June 2011, http://www.pkkonline.com/tr/index. php?sys=article&artID=890 (last accessed 30 February 2015).

Öcalan, A. *Özgür İnsan Savunması [Defense of an Independent Person]*. İstanbul: Çetin Yayınları, 2003.

Öcalan, A. *PKK IV. Kongresi'ne Sunulan Politik Rapor*. İstanbul: Zagros Yayınları, 1993.

Official Gazette. *Anayasa Mahkemesi'nin 11.12.2009 Tarih E. 2007/1, K. 2009/4 Sayılı Kararı*. Resmi Gazete, 14 December 2009.

Oğur, Y. 'Asker Üç Yıl Boyunca PKK ile Görüştü'. *Taraf*, 14 April 1996, http://arsiv.taraf.com.tr/yazilar/yildiray-ogur/asker-uc-yil-boyunca-pkk-ile-gorustu/11993/ (last accessed 29 May 2015).

Olszanska, J., R. Olszanki and J. Wozniak. 'Do Peaceful Conflict Management Methods Pose Problems in Posttotalitarian Poland?' *Mediation Quarterly*, 10 (1993), pp. 291–302.

Oran, B. *'Ben Ege'de Akilken . . .': Kürt Barışında Batı Cephesi*. İstanbul: İletişim, 2014.

Ott, M. C. 'Mediation as a Method of Conflict Resolution: Two Cases'. *International Organization*, 26:4 (1972), pp. 595–618.

Özcan, A. K. *'Araf'taki Çözüm Süreci*. Ankara: Savaş, 2014.

Özcan, N. A. *PKK (Kürdistan İşçi Partisi) Tarihi, İdeolojisi, Yöntemi*. Ankara: ASAM, 1999.

Ozcelik, S. 'Theories, Practices, and Research in Conflict Resolution and Low-Intensity Conflicts: The Kurdish Conflict in Turkey'. *Journal of Conflict Studies*, 26:2 (2006), pp. 133–53.

Özdağ, Ü. *PKK ile Pazarlık: Öcalan ile Anayasa Yapmak*. Ankara: Kripto, 2014.

Özerdem, A. 'Insurgency, Militias and DDR as Part of Security Sector Reconstruction in Iraq: How Not to Do It'. *Disasters*, 34 (2010), pp. S40–S59.

Özerdem, A. 'Türkiye'ye Barış Gelir Mi?' *Panorama Khas*, 10 (2013), pp. 26–8.

Özerdem, A., and T. Jacoby. 'Conflict-Induced Internal Displacement'. In Z. F. Kabasakal-Arat (ed.), *Human Rights in Turkey*, pp. 159–69. Philadelphia: University of Pennsylvania Press, 2007.

Özerdem, A., and F. Özerdem. 'Introduction'. In A. Özerdem and F. Özerdem (eds), *Human Security in Turkey: Challenges for the 21st Century*, pp. 1–10. London: Routledge, 2013.

Özgür Haber. 'İşte AKP ve PKK Arasındaki Yapılan Anlaşmaların Ses Kayıtları' [The Voice Records of the Agreement between AKP and PKK]. *YouTube*, 19 September 2012, https://www.youtube.com/watch?v=qOy0LQAksjo (last accessed 28 February 2013).

Özgürel, A. 'İşte Avni Özgürel'in Karayılan Röportajı' [Avni Özgürel's Karayılan Interview]. *Demokrat Haber*, 13 June 2012, http://www.demokrathaber.net/roportajlar/iste-avni-ozgurelin-karayilan-roportaji-h9428.html (last accessed 8 February 2014).

Özhan, T. *Normalleşme Sancısı: Açılımdan Çözüm Süreci'ne Kürt Meselesi*. Ankara: Özgür, 2015.

Ozkahraman, C. 'Failure of Peace Talks between Turkey and the PKK: Victim of Traditional Turkish Policy or of Geopolitical Shifts in the Middle East?' *Contemporary Review of the Middle East*, 4:1 (2017), pp. 1–17.

Özkan, M. 'Shaping Peace Processes: A Comparison between Turkey and Colombia'. *Turkish Policy*, 16:4 (2018), pp. 87–99.

Parlar-Dal, E. 'Impact of the Transnationalization of the Syrian Civil War on Turkey: Conflict Spillover Cases of ISIS and PYD-YPG/PKK', *Cambridge Review of International Affairs*, 29:4 (2017), pp. 1396–420.

Pearson, F. S. 'Dimensions of Conflict Resolution in Ethnopolitical Disputes', *Journal of Peace Research*, 38:3 (2001), pp. 275–87.

Perinçek, D. *Abdullah Öcalan'la Görüşmeler*. İstanbul: Kaynak Yayınları, 2014.

Pfeffer, J., and G. R. Salancik. *The External Control of Organizations*. Stanford: Stanford University Press, 2003.

Pillar, P. R. 'Ending Limited War: The Psychological Dynamics of the Termination Process'. In B. Glad (ed.), *Psychological Dimensions of War*, pp. 252–63. London: Sage, 1990.

Polley, R. B. 'Intervention and Cultural Context: Mediation in the U.S. and Norway'. *Journal of Management*, 14 (1988), pp. 617–29.

Post, J. M. *The Mind of the Terrorist: The Psychology of Terrorism from the IRA to al-Qaeda*. New York: Palgrave Macmillan, 2007.

Potapchuk, W. R. 'Building Sustainable Community Politics: Synergizing Participatory, Institutional, and Representative Democracy'. *National Civic Review*, 85:3 (1996), pp. 54–9.

Powell, J. *Great Hatred, Little Room: Making Peace in Northern Ireland*. London: The Bodley Head, 2008.

Powell, J. 'How to Talk to Terrorists'. *The Guardian*, 7 October 2014, https://www.theguardian.com/world/2014/oct/07/-sp-how-to-talk-to-terrorists-isis-al-qaida (last accessed 8 November 2014).

Prei, D. 'Empathy in Conflict Management'. *International Journal*, 40:4 (1985), pp. 586–98.

Princen, T. *Intermediaries in International Conflict*. Princeton: Princeton University Press, 1992.

Pruitt, D. G. 'Back-channel Communication in the Settlement of Conflict'. *International Negotiation*, 13:1 (2008), pp. 37–54.

Pruitt, D. G. 'Escalation, Readiness for Negotiation, and Third-party Functions'. In I. W. Zartman and G. O. Faure (eds), *Escalation and Negotiation in International Conflict*, pp. 251–70. Cambridge: Cambridge University Press, 2005.

Pruitt, D. G. 'Indirect Communication and the Search for Agreement in Negotiation'. *Journal of Applied Social Psychology*, 1:3 (1971), pp. 205–39.

Pruitt, D. G. 'Negotiation Between Organizations: A Branching Chain Model'. *Negotiation Journal*, 10:3 (1994), pp. 217–30.

Pruitt, D. G. 'Negotiation with Terrorists', *International Negotiation*, 11:2 (2006), pp. 374–94.

Pruitt, D. G. 'Readiness Theory and the Northern Ireland Conflict'. *American Behavioral Scientist*, 50:11 (2007), pp. 1520–41.

Pruitt, D. G. 'Ripeness Theory and the Oslo Talks'. *International Negotiation*, 2 (1997), pp. 237–50.

Pruitt, D. G. 'Strategy in Negotiation'. In V. Kremenyuk (ed.), *International Negotiation: Analysis, Approaches, Issues*. San Francisco: Jossey-Bass, 1991.

Pruitt, D. G., and J. Z. Rubin. *Social Conflict: Escalation, Stalemate and Settlement*, vol. 1. New York: McGraw-Hill, 1986.

Radikal. 'CHP'den Ömer Çelik'e Yanıt: Protokol AKP-PKK Mutabakat etnidir'. *Radikal*, 22 October 2015, http://www.radikal.com.tr/politika/chpden-omer-celike-yanit-protokol-akp-pkk-mutabakat-metnidir-1457434/ (last accessed 23 October 2015).

Radikal. '"Kürt Meselesine İslami Çözüm" Çalıştayı'. *Radikal*, 7 March 2013, http://www.radikal.com.tr/diyarbakir-haber/kurt-meselesine-islami-cozum-calistayi-1308384/ (last accessed 15 November 2015).

Ramsbotham, O., T. Woodhouse and H. Miall. *Contemporary Conflict Resolution*, 3rd edn. Cambridge: Polity, 2011.

Rea, D. 'The Political Dimension of Northern Ireland'. *International Journal of Social Economics*, 23:12 (1996), pp. 30–57.

Read, B. L., and E. Michelson. 'Mediating the Mediation Debate: Conflict Resolution and the Local State in China'. *Journal of Conflict Resolution*, 52:5 (2008), pp. 737–64.

Renwick, D. 'FARC, ELN: Colombia's Left-Wing Guerrillas'. *Council on Foreign Relations*, 1 December 2014, https://www.files.ethz.ch/isn/186229/FARC,%20ELN_%20Colombia's%20Left-Wing%20Guerrillas.pdf.

Richmond, O. P. 'Ethno-nationalism, Sovereignty and Negotiating Positions in the Cyprus Conflict: Obstacles to a Settlement'. *Middle Eastern Studies*, 35:3 (1999), pp. 42–63.

Richmond, O. P. 'Rethinking Conflict Resolution: The Linkage Problematic Between "Track I" and "Track II"'. *Journal of Conflict Studies*, 21:2 (2001).

Richter-Devroe, S. 'Gender, Culture, and Conflict Resolution in Palestine', *Journal of Middle East Women's Studies*, 4:2 (2008), pp. 30–59.

Romano, D. *The Kurdish Nationalist Movement: Opportunity, Mobilization and Identity*. Cambridge: Cambridge University Press, 2006.

Romano, D., and M. Gurses. 'Introduction'. In D. Romano and M. Gurses (eds), *Conflict, Democratization, and the Kurds in the Middle East: Turkey, Iran, Iraq, and Syria*, pp. 1–16. New York: Palgrave Macmillan, 2014.

Rothman, J. *Resolving Identity-Based Conflict: In Nations, Organizations, and Communities*. San Francisco: Jossey-Bass, 1997.

Rouhana, N. N. 'Key Issues in Reconciliation: Challenging Traditional Assumptions on Conflict Resolution and Power Dynamics'. In D. Bar-Tal (ed.), *Intergroup Conflicts and Their Resolution: A Social Psychological Perspective*, pp. 291–314. New York: Psychology Press, 2011.

Rousseau, J. J. *The Social Contract or Principles of Political Right, Book I, Chapter III. The Right of the Strongest*. Ohio: Allen and Unwin, 1895.

Rowan, B. *Behind the Lines: The Story of the IRA and Loyalist Ceasefires*. Belfast: Blackstaff Press, 1995.

Ruane, J., and J. Todd. *The Dynamics of Conflict in Northern Ireland: Power, Conflict and Emancipation*. Cambridge: Cambridge University Press, 1996.

Rubin, J. Z. *Dynamics of Third Party Intervention: Kissinger in the Middle East*. New York: Praeger, 1981.

Sabah. 'Barış Treni Yola Çıktı'. *Sabah*, 11 March 2015, http://www.sabah.com.tr/gundem/2015/03/11/baris-treni-yola-cikti (last accessed 10 December 2015).

Saeed, S. *Kurdish Politics in Turkey: From the PKK to the KCK*. Abingdon: Routledge, 2017.

Sanchez-Cuenca, I. 'The Dynamics of Nationalist Terrorism: ETA and the IRA', *Terrorism and Political Violence*, 19:3 (2007), pp. 289–306.

Sanders, A. *Inside the IRA: Dissident Republicans and the War for Legitimacy*. Edinburgh: Edinburgh University Press, 2012.

Sanson, A., and D. Bretherton. 'Conflict Resolution: Theoretical and Practical Issues'. In D. J. Christie, R. V. Wagner and D. D. N. Winter (eds), *Peace, Conflict, and Violence: Peace Pychology for the 21st Century*, pp. 193–209. Upper Saddle River: Prentice-Hall, 2007.

Sapio, A., and A. Zamperini. 'Peace Psychology, Theory and Practice'. In C. Webel and J. Galtung (eds), *Handbook of Peace and Conflict Studies*, pp. 265–78. Abingdon: Routledge, 2007.

Saunders, H. H. 'Prenegotiation and Circum-Negotiation: Arenas of the Peace Process', In C. A. Crocker, F. O. Hampson and P. Aall (eds), *Managing Global Chaos*, pp. 419–32. Washington: United States Institute of Peace Press, 1996.

Savir, U. *The Process: 1100 Days that Changed the Middle East*. New York: Random House, 1998.

Saybaşılı, K. *DYP-SHP Koalisyonu'nun Üç Yılı*. İstanbul: Bağlam Yayıncılık, 1995.

Schiff, A. '"Quasi Track-One" Diplomacy: An Analysis of the Geneva Process in the Israeli–Palestinian Conflict'. *International Studies Perspectives*, 11:2 (2010), pp. 93–111.

Schultz, B. 'Conflict Resolution Training Programs: Implications for Theory and Research'. *Negotiation Journal*, 5:3 (1989), pp. 301–9.

Sebenius, J. K., and E. B. Kogan. 'Henry Kissinger's Negotiation Campaign to End the Vietnam War', Harvard Business School, Working Paper 17-053, 2016.

Selvi, A. 'Çözüm Süreci Stres Altında' [Peace Process Is Under Pressure]. *Yeni Şafak*, 3 November 2014, http://www.yenisafak.com/yazarlar/abdulkadirselvi/cozum-sureci-stres-testinde-56757 (last accessed 2 May 2016).

Sendika. 'Öcalan'la Görüşme Notu: Kolektif Haklar Tanınmazsa Savaş 50 Yıl Sürer'. *Sendika*, 25 December 2009, http://www.sendika.org/2009/12/ocalanla-gorusme-notu-kolektif-haklar-taninmazsa-savas-50-yil-surer-anf/ (last accessed 15 May 2015).

Simon, S., and D. Benjamin. 'The Terror', *Survival*, 43:4 (2001), pp. 5–18.

Sinn Féin. *Freedom Struggle by the Provisional IRA*. Dublin: Irish Republican Publicity Bureau, 1973.

Slim, R., and H. Saunders. 'The Inter-Tajik Dialogue: From Civil War towards Civil Society', In C. Barnes and K. Abdullaev (eds), *Politics of Compromise: The Tajikistan Peace Process*, pp. 44–7. London: Conciliation Resources, 2001.

Smith, M. L. R. *Fighting for Ireland?: The Military Strategy of the Irish Republican Movement*. London: Routledge, 1997.

Smith, M. L. R., and P. R. Neumann. 'Motorman's Long Journey: Changing the Strategic Setting in Northern Ireland', *Contemporary British History*, 19:4 (2005), pp. 413–35.

Snow, D. A., and R. D. Benford. 'Ideology, Frame Resonance, and Participant Mobilization'. *International Social Movement Research*, 1:1 (1988), pp. 197–217.

Sohn, D.-W., and J. A. Wall. 'Community Mediation in South-Korea: A City-Village Comparison'. *Journal of Conflict Resolution*, 37:3 (1993), pp. 536–43.

Somer, M., and E. G. Liaras. 'Turkey's New Kurdish Opening: Religious versus Secular Values', *Middle East Policy*, 17:2 (2010), pp. 152–65.

Söylemez, H. 'Oslo'daki o Kadın Konuştu: İradenin Yürütücü Gücü Kandil'dir' [The Woman in Oslo Said: Qandil Is Our Executive Power]. *Aksiyon*, 14 January 2013, http://www.aksiyon.com.tr/dosyalar/oslo-daki-o-kadin-konustu-iradenin-yurutucu-gucu-kandil-dir_534522 (last accessed 17 March 2016).

Sözcü. 'Türkiye IŞİD'e 3 yıldır destek veriyor'. *Sözcü*, 9 August 2015, http://www.sozcu.com.tr/2015/gundem/turkiye-iside-3-yildir-destek-veriyor-905016/ (last accessed 28 February 2017).

Sözen, A., and K. Özersay. 'The Annan Plan: State Succession or Continuity'. *Middle Eastern Studies*, 43:1 (2007), pp. 125–41.

Spector, B. I. 'Negotiating with Villains Revisited'. *International Negotiation*, 8:3 (2003), pp. 613–21.

Spencer, G. 'Negotiating Peace: Politics, Television News and the Northern Ireland Peace Process'. *Irish Studies Review*, 8:2 (2000), pp. 217–31.

Spencer, G. 'The Northern Ireland Peace Process'. In G. Spencer (ed.), *The Media and Peace*, pp. 123–41. Basingstoke: Palgrave Macmillan, 2005.

Starkey, B., M. A. Boyer, and J. Wilkenfeld. *Negotiating a Complex World: An Introduction to International Negotiation*. Oxford: Rowman & Littlefield, 2005.

START. *Global Terrorism Database, National Consortium for the Study of Terrorism and Responses to Terrorism*. 2013, http://www.start.umd.edu/gtd/ (access date 10 June 2014).

Stavenhagen, R. *Ethnic Conflicts and the Nation-State*. London: Macmillan, 1996.

Stedman, S. J. *Peacemaking in Civil War: International Mediation in Zimbabwe, 1974–1980*. Boulder: L. Rienner, 1991.

Stedman, S. J. 'Spoiler Problems in the Peace Process'. *International Security*, 22:2 (1997), pp. 5–53.

Stein, J. G. 'A Common Aversion to War: Regime Creation by Egypt and Israel as a Strategy of Conflict Management'. In G. Ben-Dor and D. B. Dewitt (eds), *Conflict Management in the Middle East*, pp. 59–77. Lanham: Lexington Books, 1987.

Stephenson, M. J., and L. Zanotti. *Peacebuilding through Community-based NGOs: Paradoxes and Possibilities*. Boulder: Kumarian Press, 2012.

Stern, P. C., and D. Druckman. *International Conflict Resolution after the Cold War*. Washington: National Academies Press, 2000.

Stevenson, J. 'Does Brexit Threaten Peace in Northern Ireland?', *Survival*, 59:3 (2017), 111–28.

T24. 'Beşir Atalay'dan Öcalan'a Övgü, BDP'ye Sert Eleştiri'. *T24*, 13 October 2013, http://t24.com.tr/haber/besir-atalaydan-ocalana-ovgu-bdpye-sert-elestiri/241823 (last accessed 24 December 2013).

Tan, A. *Kürt Sorunu: Ya Tam Kardeşlik Ya Hep Beraber Kölelik [The Kurdish Question: Either Full Fraternity, Or Slavery Altogether]*. İstanbul: Timaş, 2015.

Tannam, E. 'Explaining the Good Friday Agreement: A Learning Process', *Government and Opposition*, 36:4 (2001), pp. 493–518.

Taraf. 'PKK-MİT Görüşmeleri Tam Metin' [The Full Transcript of the PKK-MİT Negotiations]. *Taraf*, 14 September 2011, http://arsiv.taraf.com.tr/haber-pkk-mit-gizli-gorusmeleri-tam-metin-78057/ (last accessed 5 January 2012).

Taylor, P. *Brits: The War against the IRA*. London: Bloomsbury, 2002.
Taylor, P. *Provos: The IRA and Sinn Fein*. London: Bloomsbury, 1998.
Taylor, R. 'South Africa: The Role of Peace and Conflict Resolution Organizations in the Struggle against Apartheid'. In B. Gidron, S. N. Katz and Y. Hasenfeld (eds), *Mobilizing for Peace: Conflict Resolution in Northern Ireland, Israel/Palestine, and South Africa*, pp. 69–93. Oxford: Oxford University Press, 2002.
Tayyar, Ş. 'Apo'ya 'Acil' Kodlu Mesaj'. *Star*, 15 October 2008, http://www.star.com.tr/gazete/yazar/samil-tayyar/apo-ya-acil-kodlu-mesaj-136307.htm (last accessed 5 February 2010).
Thatcher, M. *The Downing Street Years*. London: HarperCollins, 1993.
Thatcher, M. *Interview with Prime Minister Margaret Thatcher/Interviewer: D. M. Belfast Telegraph*, 13 December 1985. Thatcher Archive.
Thatcher, M. *Speech at Stormont Castle Lunch* [Press release]. 1981.
TNA. *The National Archive of London: Meetings and Papers*. 2015, http://www.nationalarchives.gov.uk/cabinetpapers/cabinet-gov/meetings-papers.htm (last accessed 1 June 2019).
Tocci, N. 'Turkey's Kurdish Gamble'. *Italian Journal of International Affairs*, 48:3 (2013), pp. 67–77.
Touval, S., and I. W. Zartman. *International Mediation in Theory and Practice*. Boulder: Westview, 1985.
Uğur, A. H. *Abdullah Öcalan'ı Nasıl Sorguladım: İşte Gerçekler [How Did I Interrogate Abdullah Öcalan: The Truths]*. İstanbul: Kaynak Yayınları, 2014.
UPOS (Undersecreateriat Public Order and Security). *Demokratikleşme Paketi [Democratisation Package]*. 2013, http://www.kdgm.gov.tr/snetix/solutions/KDGM/resources/uploads/files/kitabcik.pdf (last accessed 39 September 2013).
Ural, İ. *Bir Emniyet Müdürünün Kaleminden Oslo Görüşmeleri [The Oslo Negotiations from the Perspective of a Chief of Police]*. İstanbul: İleri Yayınları, 2014.
US Department of State. '1999 Country Reports on Human Rights Practices'. *US Department of State*, 2000, http://www.state.gov/www/global/human_rights/1999_hrp_report/ turkey.html (last accessed 20 May 2019).
van Bruinessen, M. *Ağa, Şeyh, Devlet*. İstanbul: İletişim, 2013.
van Bruinessen, M. 'Shifting National and Ethnic Identities: The Kurds in Turkey and the European Diaspora'. *Journal of Muslim Minority Affairs*, 18:1 (1998), pp. 39–52.
van de Voorde, C. 'Sri Lankan Terrorism: Assessing and Responding to the Threat of the Liberation Tigers of Tamil Eelam', *Police Practice and Research*, 6:2 (2005), pp. 181–99.

van der Merwe, H. *The South African Truth and Reconciliation Commission and Community Resolution*. 1998, http://www.csvr.org.za/index.php/publications/1735-the-south-african-truth-and-reconciliation-commission-and-community-resolution.html (last accessed 25 January 2020).

Vatan. 'Akil İnsanlar Heyeti'ne Amasya'da Protesto'. *Vatan*, 30 April 2013, http://www.gazetevatan.com/akil-insanlar-heyetine-amasya-da-protesto-27628-galeri-haber-fotogaleri/?Sayfa=1 (last accessed 11 May 2013).

Vayrynen, R. 'To Settle or to Transform? Perspectives on the Resolution of National and International Conflicts'. In R. Vayrynen (ed.), *New Directions in Conflict Theory: Conflict Resolution and Conflict Transformation*, pp. 1–25. London: Sage, 1991.

Walker, P., and J. Elgot. 'Sinn Féin: Vote on Irish Reunification Must Follow No-Deal Brexit', *The Guardian*, 31 July 2019, https://www.theguardian.com/uk-news/2019/jul/31/sinn-fein-border-poll-ireland-unity-must-follow-no-deal-brexit (last accessed 3 January 2020).

Wall, J. A. 'Mediation: A Current Review'. *Journal of Conflict Resolution*, 37:1 (1993), pp. 160–94.

Wall, J. A. 'Mediation: An Analysis, Review and Proposed Research'. *Journal of Conflict Resolution*, 25:1 (1981), pp. 157–80.

Wall, J. A., J. B. Stark and R. L. Standifer. 'Mediation: A Current Review and Theory Development'. *Journal of Conflict Resolution*, 45:3 (2001), pp. 370–91.

Wallensteen, P. *Understanding Conflict Resolution*, 2nd edn. London: Sage, 2007.

Walton, R. E. *Interpersonal Peacemaking: Confrontations and Third Party Consultation*. Boston, MA: Addison-Wesley, 1969.

Waltz, K. N. *Man, the State and War*. New York: Columbia University Press, 2001.

Wanis-St John, A. 'Back Channel Diplomacy – Implications for Practice and Theory'. *IACM 17th Annual Conference Paper*, 10 October 2004, https://ssrn.com/abstract=602042 (last accessed 30 August 2014).

Wanis-St John, A. 'Back-Channel Negotiation: International Bargaining in the Shadows'. *Negotiation Journal*, 22:2 (2006), pp. 119–44.

Warren, E. L. 'Mediation and Fact Finding'. In A. W. Kornhauser, R. Dubin and A. M. Ross (eds), *Industrial Conflict*. New York: McGraw-Hill, 1954.

Waslekar, S. *Track-two Diplomacy in South Asia*. Urbana-Champaign: Arms Control, Disarmament, and International Security, University of Illionis, 1995.

Watts, N. F. 'Allies and Enemies: Pro-Kurdish Parties in Turkish Politics, 1990–94', *International Journal of Middle East Studies*, 31:4 (1999), pp. 631–56.

Welsh, D. 'Domestic Politics and Ethnic Conflict'. In M. E. Brown (ed.), *Ethnic Conflict and International Security*, pp. 43–60. Princeton: Princeton University Press, 1993.

White, P. J. *Primitive Rebels or Revolutionary Modernizers?: The Kurdish National Movement in Turkey*. London: Zed, 2000.

White, R. W. 'From Peaceful Protest to Guerrilla War: Micromobilization of the Provisional Irish Republican Army'. *American Journal of Sociology*, 97:6 (1989), pp. 1227–302.

Whitelaw, W. *The Whitelaw Memoirs*. London: Aurum Press, 1989.

Whitfield, T. *Endgame for ETA: Elusive Peace in the Basque Country*. Oxford: Oxford University Press, 2014.

Whiting, M. *Sinn Féin and the IRA: From Revolution to Moderation*. Edinburgh: Edinburgh University Press, 2018.

Wilson, R. 'Time for Magnanimity'. *Fortnight*, 309 (1992), p. 5.

Wirsing, R. *India, Pakistan, and the Kashmir Dispute: On Regional Conflict and Its Resolution*. London: Macmillan, 1998.

Wolff, S. 'Conflict Management in Northern Ireland'. *International Journal on Multicultural Societies*, 4:1 (2002), pp. 41–73.

Woolpert, S., C. D. Slaton and E. W. Schwerin. *Transformational Politics: Theory, Study and Practice*. New York: State University of New York Press, 1998.

WPCAG. *Akil İnsanlar Heyeti Ege Bölgesi Raporu (Wise People Committee Aegean Region's Report)*. 2013. http://barisicinakademisyenler.net/ (last accessed 5 May 2015).

WPCBSG. *Akil İnsanlar Heyeti Karadeniz Bölgesi Raporu (Wise People Committee Black Sea Region's Report)*. 2013. http://www.yeniturkiye.org/wp-content/uploads/2015/09/AKIL-INSANLAR-KARADENIZ-GRUBU-RAPORU-28.06.2013.pdf (last accessed 5 May 2015).

WPCCAG. *Akil İnsanlar Heyeti İç Anadolu Bölgesi Raporu (Wise People Committee Central Anatolia Region's Report)*. 2013. http://barisicinakademisyenler.net/ (last accessed 5 May 2015).

WPCEAG. *Akil İnsanlar Heyeti Doğu Anadolu Bölgesi Raporu (Wise People Committee Eastern Anatolia Region's Report)*. 2013. http://barisicinakademisyenler.net/ (last accessed 5 May 2015).

WPCMG. *Akil İnsanlar Heyeti Marmara Bölgesi Raporu (Wise People Committee Marmara Region's Report)*. 2013. http://barisicinakademisyenler.net/ (last accessed 5 May 2015).

WPCMRG. *Akil İnsanlar Heyeti Akdeniz Bölgesi Raporu (Wise People Committee Mediterranean Region's Report)*. 2013. http://barisicinakademisyenler.net/ (last accessed 5 May 2015).

WPCSG. *Akil İnsanlar Heyeti Güneydoğu Bölgesi Raporu (Wise People Committee Southeastern Anatolia Region's Report)*. 2013. http://bianet.org/system/uploads/1/files/attachments/000/000/885/original/Do%C4%9Fu_Anadolu_Akil_Raporu.pdf?1372324271 (last accessed 5 May 2015).

Yavuz, M. H., and N. A. Özcan. 'The Kurdish Question and Turkey's Justice and Development Party'. *Middle East Policy*, 13:1 (2006), pp. 102–19.

Yayman, H. *Türkiye'nin Kürt Sorunu Hafızası*. Ankara: SETA, 2011.

Yeğen, M. *Devlet Söyleminde Kürt Sorunu [The Kurdish Question in the State Discourse]*. İstanbul: İletişim, 2015.

Yeğen, M. 'The Kurdish Peace Process in Turkey: Genesis, Evolution and Prospects', *Global Turkey in Europe III* (Working Paper 11), (2015). pp. 1–15.

Yeni Çağ. 'Bir Yılda 532 Şehit Verdik'. *Yeni Çağ*, 6 June 2016, http://www.yenicaggazetesi.com.tr/bir-yilda-532-sehit-verdik-138996h.htm (last accessed 27 October 2016).

Yeni Çağ. 'Özal'dan Sonra Hoca da Apo'yla Temas Kurmuş'. *Yeni Çağ*, 23 October 2009, http://www.yenicaggazetesi.com.tr/ozaldan-sonra-hoca-da-apoyla-temas-kurmus-25162h.htm (last accessed 9 October 2014).

Zartman, I. *Ripe for Resolution: Conflict and Intervention in Africa*. New York: Oxford University Press, 1989.

Zartman, I. W. *Elusive Peace: Negotiating an End to Civil Wars*. Washington: Brookings Institution Press, 1995.

Zartman, I. W. 'Ripeness: The Hurting Stalemate and Beyond'. In P. C. Stern and D. Druckman (eds), *International Conflict Resolution after the Cold War*, pp. 225–50. Washington: National Academy Press, 2000.

Zartman, I. W. 'The Timing of Peace Initiatives: Hurting Stalemates and Ripe Moments'. In J. Darby and R. MacGinty (eds), *Contemporary Peacemaking: Conflict, Violence and Peace Processes*, pp. 19–29. London: Palgrave Macmillan, 2003.

Zartman, I. W., and M. R. Berman. *The Practical Negotiator*. New Haven: Yale University Press, 1982.

Zartman, I. W., and S. Touval. 'International Mediation: Conflict Resolution and Power Politics'. *Journal of Social Issues*, 41:2 (1985), pp. 27–45.

INDEX

Adams, G., 82, 83, 84, 105, 119, 120, 187, 188, 189, 190, 193, 210, 211, 213, 215, 216, 220, 230, 232
African National Congress (ANC), 43
amnesty, 94, 121, 131, 135, 159, 160, 163, 174, 206
Anglo-Irish Agreement (AIA), 37, 54, 82, 101, 156, 186, 187, 188, 209,
Anglo-Irish Intergovernmental Council (AIIC), 184, 185
Atalay, B., 96, 108, 200, 211, 217, 220
autonomy, 14, 16, 17, 29, 72, 99, 200, 203, 214
Aydar, Z., 92, 131, 134, 207,

backchannel, 2, 3, 5, 6, 7, 17, 18, 20, 36, 38, 39, 40–7, 61, 73, 75, 77, 78, 81, 98, 110–19, 122, 124, 125, 127, 128, 129, 130–9, 158, 187, 222, 224–6, 232–7
Balüken, İ., 199, 200, 201, 217, 218

Basque Country and Freedom (ETA), 13, 237, 240
Blair, T., 86, 183, 193, 194, 216
Brexit, 8, 9, 20, 21
British–Irish Association (BIA), 51, 80, 102, 151–7, 171–8, 182, 227, 228, 233, 239
Bloody Sunday, 77, 78

Caldwell, T., 77, 79, 112, 113, 119, 137, 138, 142, 226,
Çandar, C., 66, 96, 100, 108, 125, 126, 127, 128, 144
ceasefire, 28, 34, 38, 39, 42, 45, 74, 76, 78, 79, 80, 83–6, 89, 92, 94, 98, 99, 100, 101, 111, 113–16, 118, 119, 120, 123–9, 130–1, 137–9, 140, 142, 148, 163, 189, 19, 192–4, 200, 215, 216, 219, 224, 225, 230, 234
Çiller, T., 46, 88, 91, 92, 127, 128
Clinton, B., 8, 84, 86, 189, 190, 196, 211, 213, 232

283

Community Relations Commission
  (CRC), 75, 151,
Conservative Party, 8,
Constitutional Court, 90, 97, 108,
  217
Cooper, F., 80, 114, 123, 142
Copenhagen Criteria, 94, 99
counter-insurgency, 1, 89, 142
counter-terrorism, 1, 11, 18, 75, 88,
  92, 127, 128, 167, 173, 206,
  209,
Cyprus, 2, 13, 20, 22, 50, 51, 55

de-escalate, 44, 60, 93, 125, 133,
  136, 138, 141, 158, 174, 175,
  227, 231
Demirel, S., 45, 88, 91, 125, 144,
  234
Democratic Opening, 37, 46, 96, 98,
  197, 198, 210, 238
Democratic Union Party (PYD), 9, 10,
  95, 214, 237, 238
Democratic Unionist Party (DUP),
  86, 161, 186, 187, 194, 195, 212,
  215, 229, 231
direct rule, 77, 80, 154, 155, 161,
  179
disarmament, demobilisation and
  reintegration (DDR), 34, 64,
  200
Dolmabahçe Declaration, 54, 98, 101,
  197, 202, 203, 210–12, 218, 220
Downing Street Declaration (DSD),
  82, 83, 188, 189, 191, 209,
  213, 232
Duddy, B., 4, 79, 81, 100, 114, 115,
  116, 116–18, 124, 137, 138, 139,
  142, 143, 148, 224, 226

Erbakan, N., 88, 92, 129, 131, 133,
  139, 140, 145, 146, 223, 225
Erbaş, F., 92, 131, 146
Erdoğan, R. T., 21, 88, 96, 98, 134,
  136, 146, 162, 166, 181, 197,
  203, 212, 214, 218, 220

Feakle talks, 80, 105, 122, 123, 139,
  140, 225
Fidan, H., 134, 135, 136, 140, 147,
  148, 207
Fitzgerald, G., 80, 153, 173
Free Syrian Army (FSA), 9, 237

Good Friday Agreement (GFA), 54,
  74, 77, 80, 84, 86, 87, 101, 142,
  183, 195, 196, 212, 213, 215,
  232, 234, 238, 239

H-Block, 159, 160, 174, 175
Habur, 97, 98, 99, 136, 137, 141, 147,
  225
Hackett, J., 113, 114, 137, 142, 223,
  239
Haşimi, S. H., 128, 129, 137, 145,
  148, 223
Heath, E., 77, 78
Hume, J., 82, 120, 155, 187, 188,
  189, 193, 210, 211, 213, 216,
  230, 232
hunger strike, 11, 15, 81, 82, 98, 100,
  117, 185
hurting stalemate, 60, 121, 123, 128,
  132, 133, 140, 189, 210

İmralı, 93, 98, 107, 108, 129, 139,
  141, 197, 199, 200, 201, 210,
  211, 212, 217, 230

Independent International Commission on Decommissioning (IICD), 193, 216
intermediary, 3–5, 17, 18, 31, 32, 40–4, 47, 66, 73, 77, 79, 89, 91, 92, 100, 101, 111–15, 118, 119, 123–9, 130, 131, 137, 138, 139, 141, 142, 144, 145, 174, 223, 224, 225, 234
internment, 76, 159, 174, 229
Iraq War, 95, 130, 131
Irish National Liberation Army (INLA), 11, 179
Irish Republican Army (IRA), 2–11, 14, 15, 17, 18, 20, 34, 38, 42, 44, 45, 55, 56, 58, 61, 66, 69, 72, 73, 74, 75, 76, 77–86, 89, 100, 103–8, 110–24, 137–44, 148, 158, 159, 160, 161, 171, 179, 180, 185, 189, 192–5, 209, 211, 215, 216, 221, 224, 227, 230, 233, 234, 237–9.
Islamic State of Iraq and Syria (ISIS), 9, 21, 237
Israeli-Palestinian, 2, 12, 30, 43, 49, 50, 51, 63, 68, 236
Işık, İ., 4, 129, 130, 137, 138, 139, 145, 148, 224, 239

Johnson, B., 8, 216
Joint Intelligence Committee (JIC), 75, 104
Justice and Development Party (AKP), 11, 22, 88, 130, 132, 135, 136, 140, 166, 170, 176, 180, 181, 197, 198, 204, 205, 212, 219

Kılıçdaroğlu, K., 136
Kurdistan Communities Union (KCK), 95, 108, 135, 200
Kurdish Freedom and Democracy Congress (KADEK), 93, 130
Kurdistan People's Congress (Kongra-Gel), 93, 96, 130
Kurdistan Workers' Party (PKK), 2–6, 9–11, 14, 15, 17, 18, 22, 23, 34, 37, 38, 42, 44, 46, 56, 57, 58, 59, 61, 63, 70, 72, 73, 87–103, 106–11, 124–41, 145–8, 163–6, 169, 198–203, 205–11, 213, 214, 216, 218–21, 223–5, 227, 230–4, 237, 238

Labour Party, 8, 78, 82, 86, 90, 119, 143, 180, 193, 214, 216
Look at Peace Platform (LPP), 146, 147, 161–3, 169–72, 174–7, 227, 228, 234
Loyalist, 8, 9, 14, 79, 83, 84, 179, 189, 191, 194, 227

MacStiofain, S., 112, 120
McGuinness, M., 8, 20, 120, 121, 143
McKee, B., 115, 123, 124, 138, 144
Mahçupyan, E., 132, 146, 169, 171, 181, 182, 207, 219
Major, J., 83, 84, 118, 188, 190, 191, 192, 215
Mayhew, P., 118, 157, 178, 188
Middle East, 9, 68, 214
Mitchell, G., 39, 55, 59, 69, 71, 85, 86, 101, 102, 105, 191, 193, 194, 195, 196, 212, 213, 215, 216, 220, 231

Nacar, İ., 92, 107, 129, 131, 223
National Security Council (MGK), 127, 131, 144, 145
Nationalist Movement Party (MHP), 98, 109, 166, 170, 204, 212, 231
negative peace, 7, 56
New Ireland Forum (NIF), 81, 82
non-governmental organisations (NGOs), 6, 22, 33, 36, 40, 47, 48, 65, 67, 164, 173, 238
Northern Ireland Office (NIO), 120, 123, 154, 158–60, 174, 227

O'Bradaigh, R., 76, 112, 114, 123, 142, 224
O'Connell, D., 76, 113, 114
Oatley, M., 79, 114, 124, 134, 138, 142
Öcalan, A., 87, 89, 92–4, 96, 98, 106, 107, 108, 125–31, 134, 135, 138, 139, 144–7, 163, 170, 198–203, 208, 210, 211, 213, 214, 216–18, 220, 223, 224, 230, 231, 232
Operation Motorman, 77, 113
Özal, T., 45, 70, 88, 89, 91, 106, 107, 125–7, 138, 144, 146, 223, 234

paramilitary, 10, 15, 83–5, 104, 179, 189, 191, 192, 214
peace and conflict resolution organisations (P/CROs), 3, 4, 6, 7, 17, 18, 19, 36, 37, 47–9, 51–3, 61, 100, 102, 149–51, 153, 161–3, 167, 171, 172, 174, 176, 177, 222, 223, 227–9, 233–6

Peace and Democracy Party (BDP), 98, 108, 168, 197, 199, 204–6, 217, 219
Peace People (PP), 102, 152, 154, 158–62, 171, 172, 174–7, 227, 228, 233
Peace Train Organisation (PTO), 169, 175
Peoples' Democratic Party (HDP), 15, 20, 23, 99, 103, 108, 110, 134, 137, 141, 147, 168, 170, 171, 197, 199, 200, 202, 203, 205, 211, 213, 217, 220, 230, 231, 232
People's Protection Unit (YPG), 9, 10, 95, 214, 237
Powell, J., 105, 142, 183, 214, 220
pre-negotiation, 2, 3, 7, 17–19, 24, 25, 31, 32, 35–7, 40–2, 49, 51, 53, 59–61, 78, 79, 83, 110, 111, 221, 222, 224, 233, 236–9
Prior, J., 151, 156, 173
Protestant community, 14, 22, 75–7, 80, 101, 122, 123, 140, 144, 150, 156, 158, 159, 161, 172, 185, 226, 233

reconciliation, 6, 19, 23, 26, 27, 30, 35, 62, 64, 68, 151, 161, 238, 239
Rees, M., 80, 115, 116, 119, 121, 122, 139, 142, 153, 173
republican movement, 4, 5, 8, 14, 15, 34, 44, 45, 73, 74, 80, 81, 83, 102, 103, 110, 111, 112, 113, 114, 118, 121, 123, 140, 185, 188, 189, 192, 226

Republican People's Party (CHP), 98, 109, 132, 136, 146, 170, 180, 204, 212, 231
Resolution Commission, 96, 141, 197, 204, 206
Revolutionary Armed Forces of Colombia (FARC), 13, 38, 45, 66, 205, 238
ripeness, 53, 60, 71, 142–4, 146, 210, 215, 238

Sands, B., 81, 82, 161
Sinn Féin (SF), 4, 44, 76, 79, 81–3, 85, 86, 103, 110–12, 118, 122, 123, 161, 179, 186–90, 193–5, 211, 213, 214, 215, 224, 230–2
Social Democratic and Labour Party (SDLP), 23, 82, 111, 118, 120, 186, 187, 215, 216
spoiler, 19, 45, 55, 69, 117, 124, 127, 128, 131, 132, 137, 139, 140, 144, 173, 186, 187, 196, 202, 210, 214, 225, 229
Sunningdale Agreement, 79, 101, 114
Steele, F., 77, 79, 114, 119, 134, 138, 141
Syrian civil war, 8, 9, 21, 214

Talabani, J., 89, 92, 100, 125–8, 137, 138
Taner, E., 93, 134, 207, 219
terrorism, 1, 11, 16, 18, 22, 23, 72, 75, 88, 89, 90, 92, 103, 104, 109, 127, 128, 147, 158, 160, 167, 168, 173, 195, 206, 209, 217, 220, 221
Thatcher, M., 81, 82, 117, 142, 160, 179, 184–6, 209, 214, 220

track-one, 19, 31, 38, 42, 51, 54, 61, 149, 192, 203, 222
track one-and-a-half, 40, 42, 61, 222
track-two, 12, 19, 22, 33, 42, 47, 51–4, 61, 65, 69, 149, 152, 153, 156–8, 160, 164, 173, 222, 233
triumphalism, 185
Troubles, 2, 18, 73, 75–8, 96, 100, 113
Turkish Military Forces (TSK), 5, 90–2, 106, 107, 125, 128, 130–2, 139–40, 144, 145

Ulster Unionist Party (UUP), 80, 86, 155, 186, 187, 191, 192, 194, 212, 215, 229, 231, 234

veto player, 7, 57, 70, 211, 214, 220, 229, 230, 231
Vuralhan, E., 92, 127, 128

Whitelaw, W., 45, 78, 79, 112–14, 119–21, 139, 140, 143, 223, 225, 226, 234
Wilson, H., 78, 80, 105, 112, 114, 118, 119, 122, 138, 139, 178, 179, 182, 226, 227, 239
win–win approach, 57, 204, 236
Wise People Committee (WPC), 98, 102, 144, 146, 161, 162–8, 171–4, 176, 177, 179, 180, 181, 182, 203, 216, 227, 228, 234

Yüksekdağ, F., 147, 202, 205, 218, 219, 240

zero-sum game, 16, 89

EU representative:
Easy Access System Europe
Mustamäe tee 50, 10621 Tallinn, Estonia
Gpsr.requests@easproject.com